# Stability and Strife

England 1714–1760

## W. A. Speck

Edward Arnold

First published 1977
by Edward Arnold (Publishers) Ltd
25 Hill Street, London W1X 8LL

*British Library Cataloguing in Publication Data*

Speck, William Arthur
    Stability and strife. — (The history of England; 6).
    1. Great Britain — Politics and government — 1714–1760    2.
    Great Britain — History — George I–III, 1714–1760
    I. Title   II. Series
    942.07′2          DA498

ISBN 0 7131 5974 X
        0 7131 5975 8  Pbk

Printed in Great Britain by
Richard Clay (The Chaucer Press) Ltd,
Bungay, Suffolk

# The New History of England

General Editors
A. G. Dickens and Norman Gash

## 6

# The New History of England

1   J. R. Lander          Government and Community
                          England 1461–1509

2   G. R. Elton           Reform and Reformation*
                          England 1509–1558

3   Patrick Collinson     The Queen and the Realm
                          England 1558–1603

4   Derek Hirst           Authority and Conflict
                          England 1603–1658

5   J. R. Jones           Country and Court*
                          England 1658–1714

6   W. A. Speck           Stability and Strife*
                          England 1714–1760

7   Ian Christie          Wars and Revolutions
                          Britain 1760–1815

8   Norman Gash           Aristocracy and People
                          Britain 1815–1865

9   H. J. Hanham          Industry and Ascendancy†
                          Britain 1865–1914

10  Max Beloff            Wars and Welfare†
                          Britain 1914–1952

*Publication 1977 or 1978
†Provisional title

# Contents

Preface     vii
Introduction     1

I STABILITY

1   The Constitution     11
2   Social Structure     31
3   Social Change     62
4   The Established Church and its Rivals     91
5   The Economy of Early Hanoverian Britain     120
6   The Making of the English Ruling Class     143

II STRIFE

7   The Establishment of the Hanoverian Dynasty     169
8   Stanhope's Ministry     185
9   The Robinocracy     203
10   The Opposition to Walpole     219
11   The Rule of the Pelhams     239
12   Newcastle and Pitt     258

Notes     275
Bibliography     288
Appendix: English Social Structure, 1690–1760     297
Index     299

# Maps

1   England and Wales, showing the parliamentary boroughs   18
2   England and Wales, showing principal routes and products  122

NOTE ON DATES

Until 1752 England followed the Julian or Old Style calendar which differed from the Gregorian or New Style used in most of Europe in two ways: it was eleven days behind the New Style, and started the year on 25 March (see below, pp. 254–5). Dates before 1752 are uniformly Old Style, save that the year is taken to have begun on 1 January.

# Preface

When I began to write this book my main foothold in the eighteenth century was planted in the years 1701 to 1715. Before stepping out I made it firmer with a study of the general election of 1715, which appeared as an article in the *English Historical Review*. The editors of that journal kindly allowed me to use some of the material from that contribution in the account of the election given in chapter seven. While venturing through unfamiliar territory after 1715 I followed those guides who seemed to me most reliable. Although I have indicated my major debts in the suggestions for further reading, I am acutely aware that their work is inadequately acknowledged, and can only hope that I make up for the deficiency by admitting here how I would have been hopelessly lost without their guidance.

Occasionally I have followed trails into the thickets of original sources. Thanks to the generosity of the Huntington Library, which awarded me a visiting fellowship in the summer of 1974, and of the University of Newcastle upon Tyne, which financed my flight to Los Angeles, and several trips to London and Oxford, I was able to consult many pamphlets of the period, and to dip into some of its manuscript collections.

Several people rescued me from precipices. I wish to thank David Aldridge, Gary Bennett, John Cannon, Joyce Ellis, Geoffrey Holmes, Jeanne Howard and John Walsh for reading chapters in typescript and making critical comments which saved me from many errors. I am also grateful to the General Editor, Professor Norman Gash, who read the whole text and made many valuable suggestions. Sheila's help was invaluable. If I have nevertheless gone astray then I have only myself to blame.

*Newcastle upon Tyne*                                               W.A.S.
June 1977

IN
MEMORY OF
MY
FATHER

# Introduction

Although this is primarily a political history of the period 1714 to 1760, it is concerned with politics in a far wider sphere than the workings of central government. Proceedings in cabinet, ministerial changes, parliamentary debates, the stuff of national politics, are mainly dealt with in the second part of the book. They are given depth and meaning, however, by being placed in a constitutional, social, economic and religious context in the first part.

Of course, even the narrowest approach to national politics cannot ignore altogether their social dimensions. Historians who described the political debates at Westminster in terms of a struggle between national parties, the tories and the whigs, made assumptions about the nature of those parties and their role in society. Thus they analysed the issues which divided the parties in constitutional and religious terms, and saw the ebb and flow of their support in parliament as the result of their popular appeal. Even historians who denied that politicians were divided along party lines, played down the role of issues and refuted the notion that the strength of groups at Westminster in any way reflected public opinion, nevertheless placed the national political system firmly in a social context. The 'connections' delineated by Sir Lewis Namier and his followers as the real political groupings of the period were based on the familial and electoral interests of leading politicians, so that tracing genealogical and political relationships in the localities became something of a namierite industry.

Broadening the spectrum from Westminster to the nation enables the student of the period to reconcile these divergent interpretations, to some extent at least. On the accession of George I, as this book seeks to show, the country was divided into two political parties, the tories and the whigs, both in parliament and in the constituencies. By the accession of George III this division had been largely obliterated, though it still remained like a palimpsest behind the new political order. How British politics moved from the rage of party of Queen Anne's last months to the stable oligarchy of George II's final years is the major theme of this volume, and an explanation is attempted primarily in the first part which deals with various aspects of the problem.

It is one thing to list these aspects, and quite another to weigh them. Some would stress that political events provide the main dynamic force of history, and that significant changes are reflected in the constitutional developments which have taken place over time. Others would argue that shifts in social structure provide the great seismological movements in history, while yet others would insist that economic change is fundamental. The fact that the chapters in the first part follow more or less that sequence is not meant to assert or even to imply that social and economic changes are consequent upon constitutional adjustments. On the contrary, no special weight is meant to be allotted to any one trend, for whether one is more significant than another 'in the final analysis' awaits just that, the final analysis.

Rather, the arrangement of the first part was chosen because it seemed that it would have made most sense to contemporaries. If we were able to go back and ask educated men of the time what made English society different from others in Europe or elsewhere in the world, most of them would answer 'the constitution'. They argued that mixed or constitutional monarchy made England a more liberal country than the absolutist regimes on the continent, and that this in turn produced social and economic benefits. Population growth, regarded as vitally important at a time when strength was measured by a country's total numbers, was allegedly the by-product of liberty, while populations under absolute regimes were thought to decline. Landed property was more secure under mixed monarchy than under an arbitrary monarch. Similarly trade flourished with freedom, and was stifled by absolutism. *A Tract of the National Interest* argued in 1757 that 'riches, trade and commerce are nowhere to be found but in the regions of freedom, where the lives and properties of the subjects are secured by wholesome laws. Nowhere else, in no other soil can they grow or subsist: oppression and slavery being weeds the most obnoxious and ever deemed the greatest enemies to industry, art and science.'

Referring to 'the constitution', Englishmen of the time would generally have added 'in church and state'. This was tending to become a mere formula, but it had not quite atrophied into one. The notion that protestantism in general and the Church of England in particular were inextricably bound up with liberty was also axiomatic to their thinking. Absolutism, so they claimed, was inimical to egalitarian protestant attitudes and was usually to be found in alliance with catholicism. There was not only a theoretical association between the absolutism of popes and monarchs but a historical example in the reign of James II. James's catholicism and his desire for absolute power were regarded as manifestations of a coherent ideology. The legend was symbolized by the association of popery with wooden shoes. Catholicism plus absolutism produced slavery and poverty. Again, the idea that social and economic consequences flowed from constitutional considerations, and not the reverse, was stressed by these symbols.

Of course, one could argue that they put the cart before the horse, and that the constitution stemmed from the Glorious Revolution, which in turn was the product of earlier social and economic upheavals. Certainly no attempt is made here to argue that the social, economic or even religious trends of the period were consequential upon the Revolution Settlement. On the contrary, many could be traced back long before 1688, while those which sprang up after 1688 had their own impetus. At the same time political and constitutional developments did have a bearing on social and economic trends. To give one spectacular example, however autonomous economics might be, there can be no denying that 1707 is an important date in Scottish economic history. The union also affected the English economy. When Daniel Defoe published his *Tour through the whole island of Great Britain* in the 1720s he claimed that there was already a British economy over and above the local economies of England and Scotland. The chapter on the economy investigates this claim.

The final chapter of the first part attempts to pull the threads of the others together to illustrate a development basic to English history at the time, a trend here called 'the making of the English ruling class'. In 1714 England was ruled by two rival elites, which manifested themselves in the tory and whig parties. By 1760 these elites had become fused into a ruling class which was to preserve itself in power through the revolutionary period ahead. In the concluding words of Macaulay's essay on William Pitt:

> The situation which Pitt occupied at the close of the reign of George the Second was the most enviable ever occupied by any public man in English history. He had conciliated the King; he domineered over the House of Commons; he was adored by the people; he was admired by all Europe. He was the first Englishman of his time; and he had made England the first country in the world. . . . The nation was drunk with joy and pride. The parliament was as quiet as it had been under Pelham. The old party distinctions were almost effaced; nor was their place yet supplied by distinctions of a still more important kind. A new generation of country squires and rectors had arisen who knew not the Stuarts. The dissenters were tolerated; the catholics not cruelly persecuted. The church was drowsy and indulgent. The great civil and religious conflict which began at the Reformation seemed to have terminated in universal repose. Whigs and tories, churchmen and

puritans, spoke with equal reverence of the constitution, and with equal
enthusiasm of the talents and services of the minister.

The establishment of stability did not produce completely tranquil
politics under the first two Georges. Although the high drama of the
party conflict of Anne's reign was over, there was still plenty of action
on the political stage. The rage of party was superseded by the strife
of faction.

This strife is the subject of the second part of the volume, which
focuses on the factions at Westminster and the activities of their
leaders. To some extent this is due to the fact that there was a
narrowing of the political arena after 1714. The circumvention of the
electorate, both by the Septennial Act and by the growth of oligarchy
in the constituencies, which was itself a product of the restriction of
politics to a narrow ruling class, led to a concentration of politicians'
energies on the centre. Activities in parliament and at court
inevitably became more prominent once the great party issues had
been exhausted, and men became politicians more to advance
themselves than a cause.

Yet the strife of faction did not degenerate totally into a struggle
between the 'ins' and the 'outs', nor was it purely confined to peers
and MPs. As implied by the expression, 'the Country', used to describe
the opposition in this period, a much broader section of society was
engaged in politics than the few hundred families which monopol-
ized seats in parliament. A description of Country attitudes is
presented in the chapter on the opposition to Walpole, but a
definition here might serve a useful purpose as they pervade the
whole period.

Before defining 'the Country' some definition of its opposite, 'the
Court' is required. By 'the Court', contemporaries did not just mean
the royal establishments at Kensington, St James's and Windsor or
the thousand or so people who waited upon the monarchs in them.
Insofar as it included those in royal service, to these should be added
all government officials, who were then regarded as 'the king's
servants' just as much as his household staff. The treasury, the offices
of the two secretaries of state, the admiralty and navy boards, the
paymaster's office and the ordnance, the main administrative bodies
at the centre, were comprehended in the term 'the Court'; and so was
the fiscal system, involving customs and excise officers throughout the
length and breadth of the land. In short, anybody in the pay of the
government was held to be part of 'the Court'. Between 1688 and
1714 the numbers of officials had increased as government agencies
expanded to service the military machine brought into being during
the wars with France. This increase was in itself a cause of concern to
Country politicians.

They did not just oppose the administration as such, although the attitude that 'that government is best which governs least' can be detected in some of their writings; rather, it was the methods of recruiting the personnel of 'the king's servants' which worried them. The use of the crown's patronage to give places to members of parliament or to build up a Court interest in parliamentary constituencies, was held by them to be a sinister, corrupt influence in the constitution. Systematically deployed, they argued, it could be used to erode the independence of both the Commons and the electorate, thereby reducing the 'popular' element in the constitution to a fig leaf covering the absolute power of the executive.

Another development which made Country supporters anxious, and which was linked to the expansion of the bureaucracy, was the growth of the standing army. They insisted that this was a threat to constitutional liberties even more sinister than that posed by patronage, since an army could be used to crush liberty, and had indeed been so used—in classical antiquity, in the English civil wars and in contemporary Europe. It became an essential part of the Country parliamentary campaign, therefore, to reduce the number of placemen in the Commons, to eliminate the government's influence over elections and to keep the armed forces small. These campaigns united both tories and whigs into a Country party against the Court in William III's reign and again under the first two Georges.

The Country campaign was not confined to parliament, for corruption was seen not just as a political but as a social evil. Corrupt politicians were presiding over a corrupt society. The rot at the top was spreading down, infecting the manners of professional and business men, and demoralizing the lower orders. The nation's standards had fallen so low that a parliamentary solution was not enough: nothing short of a national revival could avert the wrath to come. Here the Country mentality merged with a whole range of attitudes which diagnosed corruption as the reigning disease of the times and prescribed moral reformation as the cure. The gamut of these attitudes can best be measured by the extent of the attacks made upon the theatre, for reformers of all kinds regarded stage productions as a prime agent of corruption and theatres as very seminaries of vice. Among the most outspoken in their criticisms of the stage were the nonjurors Jeremy Collier and William Law; their attitudes were reinforced by nonconformists like Daniel Defoe and by those combinations of low-church anglicans and dissenters, the societies for reformation of manners.

These societies must be seen in the context of the Country programme, for they argued that the nation's morals could only be reformed by a concerted policy on the part of the government to appoint virtuous magistrates, who would implement the legislation against such vices as drunkenness, swearing, whoring and Sunday trading. Sir Richard Cocks was a rare example of the kind of magistrate they wished to see on the bench and in his own person embodied the Country mentality. As a whig member of parliament for Gloucestershire in William's reign, he fought stoutly against placemen and soldiers; as chairman of the county quarter-sessions in George I's reign he delivered charges to the grand jury which emphasized, as much as any sermon preached to the societies for reformation of manners, how vital it was for the state to punish vice. The concern to suppress vice also informed Country tory thought, though it tended to be expressed more in demands that convocation and the church courts should be reinvigorated in order to combat breaches of the moral code.

In their obsession with moral offenders, Country supporters both tory and whig harked back nostalgically to a mythical golden age when manners had been effectively controlled by the squire and the parson in small villages. They lamented the growth of populous parishes, and above all the great increase in the population of London which had caused the old, personal agencies of social control to break down. There was a large element of Country fear of the city in the efforts of moral reformers to revive the controls against immorality.

The rage of party kept Country tories and whigs apart in Anne's reign. For instance, Country tory energies were channelled into the charity school movement, which was regarded as Jacobite shortly after George I's accession, while Country whigs supported the societies for reformation of manners, which tories denounced as 'mongrel institutions' because their ranks included both anglicans and dissenters. After Anne's death, however, when party passions cooled, they found that they had much in common, especially in their religious view of reality. Increasing secularization under George I brought about a closing of the ranks of Christians, who felt themselves under attack. Whatever their differences, high- and low-church anglicans and dissenters at least agreed that God had ordered the universe and that his providence regulated human affairs, rewarding the just and punishing the wicked. During Walpole's ministry it appeared to many of them that the providential ordering of the world had been suspended, indeed that Satan reigned over a land where wickedness was rewarded and virtue punished. The merging of Country elements into a united campaign was in many ways a reaction to the rise of secular politics. Ministers like Stanhope, Sunderland and Walpole were a new breed of politicians who did not appeal to divine sanction to justify their policies. Unlike their predecessors, from Danby to Oxford, they were unabashedly secular, justifying their system on the ground that it worked. There was more than a generation gap between these men and their Country opponents: there was a massive cultural gulf. Although many Country politicians, of whom Bolingbroke is the most outstanding, were remarkably secular in their own outlook, their supporters lived in a world where good and evil were realities and locked in endless conflict. The Court whigs under the first two Hanoverians, by contrast, spoke a very different language. It is hard to imagine any minister before 1714 boasting, as Walpole did, that he was 'no saint, no spartan, no reformer'. Between that attitude and the Country mentality there could be no common ground, let alone agreement. The strife of faction was the more strident because the battle cries of each side were almost unintelligible to the other.

Since there are several interpretations of party politics in this period, it seems appropriate to sum up here, albeit briefly and at the risk of oversimplification, that which is put forward in the following pages. Under Anne, politics primarily took the form of a struggle for power between the tory and whig parties. Each party had a Court and Country wing, Court tories and whigs being those who were prepared to take office under the crown, while Country politicians preferred to sit on the backbenches and occasionally might even combine to oppose the government, whatever its party complexion. After 1714, however, the tory party lost its Court wing, becoming essentially an opposition or Country party. The tories no longer had the strength to be effective rivals for power, and under the first two Georges ministries were made up overwhelmingly of Court whigs. Country whigs, on the other hand, went into opposition soon after Anne's death, to be joined from time to time by Court politicians who were temporarily out of power. Together they allied with the tories in attempts to form a Country party to oppose the Court. These attempts were frustrated by the survival of old rivalries among Country tories and whigs, distinctions which Court whigs worked on assiduously to keep their opponents divided. Thus they unfairly accused the tories of Jacobitism, attributing to the whole party a loyalty to the Pretender only held by a minority, to deter Country whigs from allying with them. Despite such impediments, by 1760 Court and Country had effectively replaced tory and whig.

# I Stability

# 1 The Constitution

George I's title to the English throne was parliamentary rather than hereditary. Over fifty people had a more direct claim to the crown by descent from the main Stuart line, besides James Francis Edward, the son of James II, styled James III by his supporters and 'the Pretender' by his opponents. Other claimants had been passed over by the Act of Settlement in 1701 because they were catholics, while the Electors of Hanover were protestant. Moreover, although the Hanoverians were lutheran, the act stipulated that they had to be anglicans when they inherited the throne; nor were they to be allowed to marry catholics. Safeguarding the protestant succession was regarded as the primary purpose of the act.

Indeed, the requirement of constitutional safeguards for the anglican establishment was so axiomatic that contemporaries referred not just to 'the constitution' but to 'the constitution in church and state'. They held that the Church of England was such an integral part of the settlement, so essential to the maintenance of the crown, that it must be protected from its rivals whether protestant or catholic. Thus the Corporation Act of 1661, enacted to defend the church from dissenters, and the Test Act of 1673, passed to protect it from papists, remained on the statute book. Only once, in 1736, was there a determined effort to get them repealed. The Corporation Act stipulated that members of borough corporations should have received communion in the Church of England within six months before obtaining an office. Since many posts in boroughs were subject to yearly elections this meant in practice at least annual attendance at an anglican communion service. The Test Act likewise laid down that anybody appointed to an office under the crown should receive communion within three months after his appointment. These acts were intended to deprive dissenters of full participation in the state, and did keep catholics and most nonconformists out of office both locally and nationally.

However, some protestant dissenters broke the spirit of this legislation by sticking strictly to its letter, by attending anglican communion services once a year to qualify for office, the rest of the time frequenting their own conventicles. To stamp out the practice of occasional conformity, as it was called, an act had been passed under Anne in 1711 penalizing those who attended dissenting services after appointment to offices in corporations or under the crown. This act was not repealed until 1719. Thereafter dissenters were protected from prosecutions for occasional conformity by indemnity acts, which eventually were passed annually. The principle of an anglican monopoly of power, however, was upheld in theory until the early nineteenth century. The Hanoverians swore in the coronation oath that they would, to the utmost of their power, 'maintain the laws of God, the true profession of the gospel and the protestant reformed religion established by law'. They also undertook to 'preserve unto the bishops and clergy of this realm, and to the churches there committed to their charge, all such rights and privileges as by law do or shall appertain unto them'.

The Act of Settlement was subtitled 'an act for the further limitation of the crown and the better preserving the liberties of the subject'. It thereby emphasized that it was not just a measure for limiting the descent of the crown to the house of Hanover but also limited the monarchy itself. This was in line with the prevalent notion that the type of polity to which George I succeeded by virtue of the act was a limited or mixed monarchy as distinct from an absolute kingship. There were specific restrictions on the power of the crown in a number of statutes passed between the Revolution of 1688 and George's accession. The Bill of Rights of 1689 had taken away the suspending and dispensing powers, declared extra-parliamentary taxation illegal and made the maintenance of a standing army in peacetime dependent on the approval of parliament. The Triennial Act of 1694 had impaired the prerogative of summoning and dissolving parliament at pleasure by requiring a general election to be held every three years. Finally the Act of Settlement had added greatly to the list of restrictions and, since it did not become operative until Anne died, George I was the first monarch to be limited by it. Although some of the more irksome constraints had been repealed in Anne's reign, George nevertheless could not reward his German supporters with ministerial posts or places in the privy council, while his prerogative of formulating foreign policy was circumscribed by the provision that he could not declare war in defence of Hanover without permission of parliament. According to one clause which was repealed shortly after he came to the throne, he could not even visit his electorate without parliamentary approval. More seriously, the independence of the judiciary was assured by the provision that the tenure of judges was not dependent on the will of the crown but was permanent, subject only to good behaviour. At the highest level this affected the composition of the three common law courts at Westminster, King's Bench, Common Pleas and Exchequer. Chancery was not involved, since the post of lord chancellor remained primarily a political rather than a judicial appointment.

Although their jurisdictions overlapped, by and large King's Bench was the highest court in the land below the house of lords for actions between crown and subject, Common Pleas for actions between parties, and Exchequer for cases involving abuses in the revenue system. Each court had four judges, a lord chief justice and three justices in King's Bench and Common Pleas, a lord chief baron and three barons in Exchequer. Together they comprised 'the twelve men in scarlet' whose collective opinion could be consulted on issues of constitutional significance. In 1758, for instance, the House of Lords referred to them a bill for amending the law on Habeas Corpus, before rejecting it. Under Charles II and James II there had been a deliberate policy of appointing them at pleasure in order to produce a compliant judicial bench. Judges who refused to go along with the king's wishes were systematically purged and replaced with more obliging colleagues. After the Revolution the demand that the crown should be deprived of the power to remove judges for political purposes found expression in the Act of Settlement. When it became operative on George I's accession, judges could only be appointed on good behaviour, save that 'upon the address of both houses of parliament it may be lawful to remove them.'

The letter of the law, however, limited the monarchy only in some particulars. It was the spirit of the Revolution Settlement, or at least the way the constitution developed between 1689 and 1714, that really restricted the monarch by obliging him to work with parliament. For instance, there was nothing on the statute book to oblige the king to summon parliament every year. The Mutiny Act is often cited as a factor making annual sessions necessary, because it was usually passed for a year at a time and was essential for military discipline; but in fact it lapsed between 1697 and 1701 even though the houses assembled every year. Annual sessions became essential not from any theoretical consideration but from a quite practical necessity. They were required to vote taxation—initially after the Revolution to pay for the wars against Louis XIV which required unprecedented revenues, and eventually to service the national debt which really became a fixture during the reign of William III. This led to the abandonment of the old notion that the crown should live of its own, though some tories, perhaps ironically, revived it for the last time on George I's accession. In reality the crown was so dependent upon parliamentary supply that from William's reign on a special sum was voted, known as the civil list, apart from the other revenues. In 1689 a sum of £700,000 was set aside for William and Mary, £400,000 from the royal estates and £300,000 from the excise. George I incurred debts of £1,000,000 over his entitlement, which were paid off by parliament. George II was guaranteed a sum of £800,000 a year by the Commons in 1727.

This heavy dependence on parliament eroded royal prerogatives of making peace and declaring war and of choosing ministers, which in theory had survived the Revolution. Appropriation of supplies for specific naval and military objects became normal, while the convention arose of laying treaties of peace and even of alliance before parliament for its approval. The choice of ministers became restricted to politicians who could command sufficient parliamentary support to get the king's business through both houses.

By 1714, therefore, the king in parliament had finally triumphed over the prerogative. Yet this did not mean that the crown was subservient to parliament either in theory or even in practice—far from it. When contemporaries thought of the king and of parliament they did not regard them as a single agency but as three separate though interdependent entities—king, lords and commons. The king represented the monarchial element in the state, the lords the aristocratic and the commons the popular or even democratic. It was agreed that this gave England the best of all possible polities for, in the popular Classical theory, a pure monarchy tended to degenerate into tyranny, a pure aristocracy into oligarchy and a pure democracy into anarchy. The mixture tended to prevent this degeneration, since each element acted as a check or balance on the other two, so that the lords and commons prevented monarchy from acting tyranically, the king and commons prevented the lords from becoming oligarchic, and the king and lords checked the commons' tendency towards anarchy. In theory a polity thus constituted could last forever.

When Englishmen spoke of the balanced constitution they had in mind this older view of an equilibrium of king, lords and commons, rather than the somewhat novel idea of a threefold division into executive, judicial and legislative branches. Locke had made these distinctions in his *Two Treatises of Government*, but he did not assert or even imply, like Montesquieu, that they were or could be separate and equal powers. On the contrary, he maintained the primacy of the legislative branch by which he meant the king, lords and commons. Yet the notion that these were separate was just as questionable. After all, the crown had the right to make peers, and Queen Anne used this blatantly in 1712, creating twelve peers at a stroke to give her ministers a majority in the upper house. Although the constitutional propriety of her action was doubted even by some of her own supporters, few questioned its legality. Stanhope's attempt to restrict the prerogative of making peers, the peerage bill of 1719, was defeated in the Commons, so that the first two Georges had the power to ennoble whom they pleased, though they exercised it very sparingly. Nor did they resort to the veto of bills, Anne being the last monarch to use it in 1708.

The monarch's influence over the Commons caused more constitutional controversy under the early Hanoverians than the right to make peers, even though the lower house was less amenable to Court control. There were fewer than two hundred hereditary English peers, and only 16 elected Scottish peers, while there were 513 MPs for England and Wales, and 45 for Scotland, making a total of 558. The crown's influence stemmed directly from its policy of rewarding members of parliament with pensions and places in the administration, the exercise of which had been a lively political issue at least since the Exclusion Crisis of Charles II's reign. Under William III the objectors to the king's use of patronage to build up parliamentary support had managed to restrict it in certain circumstances. By 1700 no customs or excise officer could sit in the Commons, and in 1701 a clause was added to the Act of Settlement which, had it come into effect, would have completely removed the right to appoint members to places. It said quite simply that 'no person who has an office or place of profit under the king, or receives a pension from the crown, shall be capable of serving as a member of the House of Commons.' If this momentous clause had come into operation it would have prevented the development of the cabinet system, and almost certainly have arrested the growth of the Commons as the more important of the two houses.

Fortunately for the crown, it was decided that it could only come into effect along with the rest of the act on the death of Anne. During her reign the opportunity was taken to repeal it, and a less sweeping measure was enacted in the Regency Act of 1706. This drew a distinction between offices in existence at the time of its being passed and any posts which were to be created in future. Members of parliament could not be appointed to any 'new' offices, nor to certain specified 'old' offices, including most of those involved in supplying the armed forces. Any who were promoted had to vacate their seats and could not seek re-election. Those appointed to 'old' offices not specifically listed as disqualifying their occupants from seats in the Commons had similarly to be removed from the house, but could seek re-election. The theory was that the member's constituents should endorse the fact that their member had become a placeman, to express their approval of his becoming the king's servant as well as their own.

The notion that re-election somehow ensured popular endorsement of a member's promotion to an office under the crown seems
distinctly odd in view of the unrepresentative nature of the electoral
system at that time. No regard was paid to the principle of 'one man,
one vote' and many of the constituencies were extremely small. At
first sight, it appears absurd that a by-election in such a system should
square with the constitutional theory allowing the popular element
to express its approval or disapproval of the king's choice of a
member to fill a particular post. Yet on a closer investigation some
modern assumptions, that only the propertied classes could vote and
that the typical constituency in the unreformed electoral system was
a rotten borough, can be shown to be grossly misleading. The system
was much more representative, at least at the outset of the
Hanoverian era, than it is generally considered.

There is no way of knowing for certain the actual size of the
electorate in the early eighteenth century. In 1701 Defoe guessed that
there were about 200,000 voters, a figure confirmed by modern
research as about right for William's reign, but too small for Anne's
since the electorate was still growing rapidly. A calculation based
largely on turn-out figures put it at 250,700 by 1715, but this was a
serious underestimate as the highest turn-out was under eighty per
cent.[1] There must in fact have been at least 300,000 people eligible to
vote when George I came to the throne. Even this was only 5·5 per
cent of the total population, which seems derisory until we recall that
on the eve of the first Reform Act only 2·6 per cent of the people of
England and Wales had the right to vote, while even after 1832 the
franchise encompassed only 4·7 per cent. Thus at George I's
accession England was more 'democratic' than it was to be again
until well into Victoria's reign. Assuming that slightly less than a
quarter of the population consisted of adult males, a lower proportion than in the nineteenth century, then between one in five
and one in four of men over twenty-one were enfranchised in 1714.
This took the right to vote considerably lower down the social
scale than the level of the wealthy property owners. John Dennis
assumed in 1725 that 'if we include in the working poor those who
every day labour to maintain themselves and their families, we
comprehend ... perhaps, above a third of the electors of our
representatives.'[2]

Manhood was not the criterion for having the right to vote. Instead
there were a number of different qualifications which varied
according to the type of constituency. In the fifty-two counties of
England and Wales, the franchise had been restricted since the
fifteenth century to those in possession of freeholds to the annual value
of forty shillings. For the 217 boroughs there was a multiplicity of

franchises. Burgages, or pieces of property, conferred the right to vote on their proprietors or tenants in some forty-one, such as Appleby in Westmorland, Cockermouth in Cumberland, Northallerton in Yorkshire and Old Sarum in Wiltshire. Only the members of the corporations were allowed to vote in nineteen, for example Buckingham, Bury St Edmunds and Truro. There were a hundred, including Bristol, Liverpool and Norwich, where the freemen voted. In the remaining fifty-five apart from the universities of Cambridge and Oxford, the franchise rested on some kind of residential qualification. At Preston any adult male residents, even if they were only staying the night, could apparently vote. In most boroughs, however, various restrictions were imposed. The least restrictive was the provision that inhabitants should be householders. This obtained in Callington, Cornwall, where a contemporary observed that the right to vote was enjoyed by 'every man who is a householder and has lived here a year'.[3] Then came the boroughs where men had to be self-sufficient and not in receipt of alms or charity—in the quaint contemporary expression, 'potwallopers' or men able to boil their own pot. Thus in Tregoney the right to vote was declared in 1695 to be 'in all the householders who boil the pot, or, in other words, provide for themselves'.[4] According to Defoe, in Taunton the 'pot walloners' (sic) included lodgers.[5] Finally there were boroughs where the householders had actually to be paying church and poor rates, local taxes known as scot and lot. The four parliamentary boroughs of Berkshire, Abingdon, Reading, Wallingford and Windsor, were all of this type.

If the electorate was not qualified by universal manhood suffrage, neither was it distributed into equal electoral districts—another requirement for a modern democratic system. Although, when first introduced, the forty-shilling freehold franchise in the counties had been intended to restrict the right to vote to fairly substantial landowners, subsequent inflation had eroded the qualification, until by the eighteenth century it extended well down the social scale. In 1715 there were about 180,000 forty-shilling freeholders, which took the right to vote below Gregory King's 66,000 'gentlemen and freeholders of the better sort' into the ranks of his 140,000 'freeholders of the lesser sort'.[6] The result was that, apart from Rutland and about half the Welsh counties where the voters numbered several hundreds, most county electorates consisted of thousands of freeholders and Yorkshire, the biggest, had over 10,000. Only twenty-three boroughs could count their voters in thousands, including London with 8,200, Westminster with about 6,500 and Southwark with around 4,200. A third of the boroughs, however, had over five hundred voters. The remaining boroughs, with fewer than five hundred voters, were

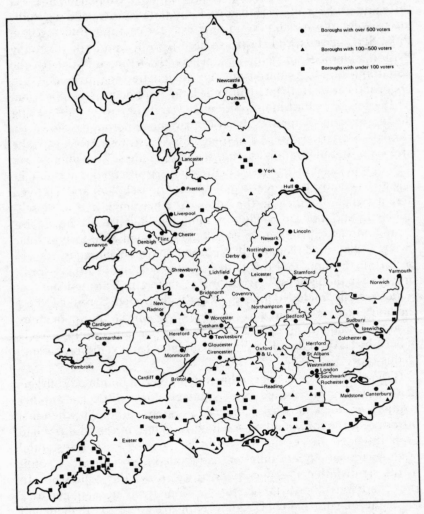

Map 1   England and Wales, showing the parliamentary boroughs.

roughly evenly split between those with over and those with under one hundred.

It was the existence of tiny boroughs which in practice helped the government defeat the Regency Act's intention of ensuring that MPs appointed to places had their promotions endorsed by the popular element in the constitution. For the smaller the electorate, the easier it was to employ patronage, influence and even downright bribery to secure the return of a candidate. This is what made Cornwall so attractive to men intent on buying their way into parliament, since sixteen of the Cornish boroughs had under a hundred electors. To 'cornwallize' became a popular term for scattering guineas in order to secure an election. The Court cultivated patrons of Cornish seats to secure a safe retreat for placemen, who tended to represent, if that is the right word, the smaller constituencies. Henry Pelham was quite exceptional in representing the county of Sussex while occupying the post of first lord of the treasury. Most of his colleagues on the treasury bench sat for tiny boroughs impervious to the vagaries of public opinion. So it happened that, between 1715 and 1761, 509 members vacated their seats upon appointment to office, but only eight were actually defeated when they subsequently sought re-election.[7]

Yet curiously the campaign against placemen, which became almost a hardy annual under the first two Georges, did not take the logical step of going on to demand electoral reform but confined itself to their reduction, if not elimination from parliament. To be sure there were critics of the unrepresentative nature of some constituencies. Defoe complained that Queenborough, 'a miserable, dirty, decayed, poor, pitiful fishing town', should send two members to parliament, 'as many as the borough of Southwark, or the city of Westminster'.[8] John Macky, too, was contemptuous of the rotten boroughs he encountered in his travels, saying of Hindon, Stockbridge and Wilton that 'if all the houses were to be sold by auction, they would not bring £4,000.'[9] Even John Wesley observed that Old Sarum 'in spite of common sense, without house or inhabitant, still sends two members to the parliament.'[10] Very occasionally a voice would be raised for amending this state of affairs. *A proposal for altering the method and manner of electing members of the House of Commons* advocated in 1747 that all boroughs should be disfranchised and their seats given to the counties; it even recommended a secret ballot. But this was a very lone voice indeed and there was never a parliamentary attempt to reform the electoral system in these years.

On the contrary, there seems to have been an almost universal agreement that the constitution was the most excellent that could have been devised. Referring to the balance of power between the crown, aristocracy and commons, Joseph Addison wrote in 1719 'it is the usual boast of Englishmen, that our government is fixed upon this triple basis, which has been allowed even in speculation, and that by persons who could have no eye to our constitution, a form the most accommodated to the happiness of a community, and the most likely to stand secure in its own strength.'[11] Sir Daniel Dolins echoed the theme of many chairmen of quarter-sessions when he expatiated to the grand jury of Middlesex in 1726 on 'the excellence of our constitution and frame of government; of the wisdom, justice and goodness of our laws . . . legally settled, secure enjoyment and free use of life, property and estate, with all our other invaluable blessings, rights and privileges, civil and religious'.[12] Roger Acherley anticipated Blackstone's encomiums in his study of *The Britannic Constitution*, published in 1727, where he claimed that 'tis the Britannic constitution that gives this kingdom a lustre, above other nations; for it is *imperium legum*; it equally advances the greatness and power of the crown, at the same time as it secure Britons their private property, freedom and liberty, by such walls of defence as are not to be found in any other parts of the universe.' On the eve of the accession of George III, Robert Wallace observed that 'by the Revolution the constitution has been rendered more perfect. That admirable and singular mixture of a hereditary limited monarchy and splendid aristocracy, without the power of oppressing, and of an equal democracy without its unsteadiness and confusion, shines with superior lustre.'[13]

Even opposition writers could speak the same language. John Trenchard in one of *Cato's Letters* actually compared the monarchy of England with the government of heaven.[14] Bolingbroke, in his *Dissertation on Parties*, agreed that 'it is by this mixture of monarchial, aristocratical and democratical power, blended together into one system, and by these three estates balancing one another, that our free constitution of government hath been preserved so long inviolate.'[15] They accepted, therefore, that the Revolution Settlement had established a perfect polity. They disagreed with the Court writers, however, in insisting that certain abuses had crept in since 1688 which should be eliminated to restore the pristine purity. Swift satirized the archetypal complacent Englishman, convinced that his country and its constitution were the best in the world, in the person of Lemuel Gulliver. Gulliver gives the king of Brobdingnag a typically whiggish eulogy of the British constitution, but the monarch's probing questions imply that under Walpole the reality had fallen far short of the ideal. Country writers were particularly concerned to demonstrate that the constitutional equilibrium had become unbalanced with the growth of the executive since the

Revolution. In order to restore the balance they advocated three measures on every possible parliamentary occasion—the repeal of the Septennial Act, the reduction of the standing army and the elimination of placemen from the Commons.

The Septennial Act was the biggest change to the constitutional machinery made under the first two Georges. It repealed the Triennial Act of 1694, whereby general elections had been obligatory every three years and altered the interval to seven. Furthermore William and Anne had twice preferred not to let parliament run its full term, in 1701 and 1710, so that in fact elections were held on average every two years between 1695 and 1715. George I and George II, on the other hand, allowed parliament to run its course, except in 1747 when only six years had elapsed since the previous general election. Between 1716 and 1761, therefore, elections were held on average every six and a half years. Opposition politicians protested at this evasion of the electorate, both when the measure was passed and repeatedly after 1716. At the time one argument used was that the Triennial Act was fundamental law, since it stipulated that forever after 1694 elections must occur at least once every three years. This was constitutional nonsense, however, since no parliament could bind its successor not to alter or repeal a statute. A more telling argument was that the voice of the people had been muted, and that since power came from the populace a basic principle of the constitution had been violated. This notion of popular sovereignty had powerful backing in the contract theory propounded by Locke. But in the years 1714 to 1760, the concept of parliamentary sovereignty was upheld even by politicians who paid lip-service to Locke's view that men could resist rulers who broke the contract.

Locke's influence on the constitutional thought of the period, once taken to be fundamental, has tended to be discounted of late. It is true that his reputation with contemporaries rested primarily on his *Essay concerning human understanding* and not on his *Treatises of Government* which were published anonymously. But even if the *Treatises* were not extensively read, they were widely popularized by apologists for the whig ascendancy such as Addison, Defoe and perhaps above all Benjamin Hoadly. To these writers Locke's demolition of divine, indefeasible hereditary right was more significant than his defence of the right to resist. Indeed, they tended to play down the radical origins of government which they found in Locke, in favour of his more conservative stress on the role of the state in the protection of life, liberty and above all property. Locke himself wrote that 'the great and chief end . . . of men's uniting into commonwealths and putting themselves under government is the preservation of their property', though he took care to define property as 'lives, liberties and estates'.[16] This definition was somewhat lost sight of during the eighteenth century, so that when Lord Camden judged in the case of Entick *versus* Carrington in 1765 that 'the great end for which men entered into society, was to secure their property', he was echoing Locke without the refinement.

In their attacks on soldiers and placemen the Country writers drew on an older tradition, owing more to Machiavelli, Hobbes and Harrington than to Locke. As far as their notions of the balanced constitution were concerned, they picked up from Harrington's *Oceana* the concept of the 'Gothic constitution' and adapted it for their own purposes, for which they have been called 'neo-Harringtonians'. These included such 'commonwealthmen' as the third earl of Shaftesbury, John Trenchard and Thomas Gordon, to whom some would add Bolingbroke. Harrington had talked of a 'Gothic balance' of king, lords and commons which the 'neo-Harringtonians' identified with the 'ancient constitution' of England. Where in *Oceana* it was argued that Henry VII had dissolved the 'Gothic constitution' by alienating land, and therefore power, to the Commons, they insisted that despite many vicissitudes it had survived until after the civil wars and that, though it had been threatened by Charles II and above all by James II, it had been restored in 1688. Under Walpole, however, it was at risk of being subverted by soldiers and placemen. The danger arose through the threat to the independence of the Lords and above all of the Commons by the use of the crown's powers, either directly by building up an armed force capable of challenging the authority of the two houses, or indirectly by employing patronage to corrupt members of parliament. In order to reverse this process and revert to the purity of the ancient constitution, the ability of corrupt and unscrupulous ministers to employ the powers of the crown for these ends must be curtailed. The standing army, the main tool of monarchs bent on absolutism on the continent, must be reduced to a manageable size, one which did not endanger the constitution, while placemen should be eliminated from parliament. Not least, frequent elections should be held to preserve the independence of the House of Commons.

In contrast, the Court apologists argued that there was in fact no ancient, balanced constitution. They insisted that before 1688 the English polity had been one of almost unlimited monarchy, and that the happy equilibrium of king, lords and commons which guaranteed the preservation of Englishmen's lives, liberties and properties was the consequence of the Glorious Revolution. Walpole and his followers thus ironically took up the much more scholarly historiography of Stuart apologists such as Robert Brady, while their opponents had to rely on the appeal of a largely mythical past which had characterized the historic justification of the opposition to the Stuarts from the accession of James I to the Revolution of 1688. Walpole went even further in insisting that the use of influence, far from being detrimental, was absolutely necessary to preserve the balance, since king, lords and commons were not independent but interdependent powers.

The main link between the crown and the two houses was in fact the cabinet. This was a relatively new body in 1714 and had a dubious constitutional status. In 1701 the framers of the Act of Settlement had expressed their suspicion of it when they inserted a clause in the act insisting that 'all matters and things relating to the well governing of this kingdom, which are properly cognizable in the privy council ... shall be transacted there.' The privy council, however, was an unwieldy body of some eighty members under Anne, and although George I reduced it to about thirty, it was too big for day-to-day policy making. It still met to declare war or ratify a peace treaty and to advise upon the dissolution of parliament, and of course it played a vital role in the drama surrounding Queen Anne's death bed; but apart from these great formal ceremonies of state it was rarely summoned. Instead the king's business was transacted in much smaller bodies, which survived because the privy council clause in the Act of Settlement was repealed under Anne. In her reign invitations to attend cabinet meetings were extended to ministers more on account of their political than their administrative importance. Thus Sir Edward Seymour attended, though he was only comptroller of the household, while the earl of Kent did not, despite being lord privy seal. Appointment to certain posts, however, was a sign of political prestige, and their occupants normally sat in cabinet under Anne. These included the lord treasurer, the two secretaries of state, the commander in chief, the lord admiral, the lord chancellor and the lord president. They usually met once a week in the presence of the Queen, and about twice a week without Anne, when they were known as the lords of the committee. It was at such a meeting and not, as is often alleged, in the privy council, that Guiscard was being examined when he made his attempt to assassinate Harley in 1711. More routine meetings of the lords of the committee worked out policies, though these had to be agreed by the full cabinet council.

While a great deal is known about the workings of the cabinet under Anne, its operation under George I is shrouded in mystery and even legend. It is said that the King stopped attending the cabinet council because he could not speak English, or alternatively because he did not wish the Prince of Wales to attend and thereby become privy to the deliberations of ministers at a time when he was consorting with the opposition. Yet it is not even clear that George I did stay away from cabinet meetings; indeed, there is some evidence that the system of Anne's reign survived until about 1720.

The situation becomes clearer again under Walpole. It seems that by the 1720s the cabinet council, like the privy council before it, had already become a dignified rather than an efficient part of the constitution. At all events Walpole distinguished between it and a smaller body known as the inner or efficient cabinet. This usually consisted of the prime minister himself, as first lord of the treasury, the two secretaries, the lord chancellor and the lord president, who were known as 'the lords of confidence'. Like William III, though unlike Anne, the first two Georges were often abroad. In the absence of George I lords justices were appointed, who were in fact the titular cabinet council under another name. Even so, formal business remained in the hands of a smaller number, though tension frequently developed between the secretary who accompanied the king and the ministers back home. This was less of a problem in the first decade of George II's reign, when the cabinet was more united and Queen Caroline was virtually left in charge in her husband's absence. But after Caroline's death and Walpole's fall the old tensions revived, and the conflict between the Pelhams and Carteret was in many ways a revival of the strife between the treasury and the secretary's office which had marked George I's early years.

The friction between absentee secretaries and their ministerial colleagues in England arose over foreign policy, the formulation of which was the overwhelming consideration of eighteenth-century cabinets. At a time when security was regarded as the main, if not the only, function of government, it is not surprising that the vast majority of cabinet discussions concerned relations with foreign powers. It was not until relatively recently that they have been obliged to discuss education, housing, health, welfare, roads and the myriad preoccupations of modern governments. Surprisingly, though, they rarely discussed finance, even the ways and means of implementing foreign policy. Parliamentary management was the concern of informal bodies, such as the regular meetings with junior ministers and even backbench supporters, which Walpole arranged to concert government tactics in the Commons in order to pilot important legislation, particularly that involving finance, through the house.

Nevertheless the problems of getting parliament to approve the financial implications of foreign policy frequently underlay the tensions between ministers. Because foreign policy loomed large in cabinet discussions the secretaries of state, and especially the senior secretary, could exert a powerful influence over their deliberations. Each secretary was in charge of relations with different parts of Europe, as well as with home affairs: one handled British relations with northern Europe, the other those with southern Europe. Depending upon the prevailing interests of Britain, or rather of the British crown, one office would have more important relations to handle than the other, and thereby its incumbent would become senior to the other secretary. Under Anne, involvement in the War of the Spanish Succession had made the southern secretaryship the more important. Under George I the affairs of the Electorate of Hanover made the secretary for the north the more influential. How much influence the post could yield was questionable. When Robert Harley became secretary of state for the south in 1704 Defoe told him that the post could make its occupant prime minister. This was not so, however, for in the end foreign commitments had to be paid for, and this gave ascendancy to the chief financial minister in the cabinet. Under Anne this was the lord treasurer. The first two Georges dispensed with her practice of appointing a single man to this post, and under them the treasury was always in the control of a board, of which the first lord was the most important. In the eighteenth century the first lord of the treasury emerged as prime minister, though not without struggles with secretaries of state.

The cabinet would decide upon a line of action, but the execution of it would devolve on junior ministers who were not usually members of it. For instance, the cabinet might agree to raise money and troops for a continental expedition. The chancellor of the exchequer would be involved in administering the supply of money, the secretary at war in raising men, the paymaster general with paying them, the master of the ordnance with equipping them, the admiralty board with despatching them, and so on. The cabinet might call in these junior ministers for advice and briefing, but they would not be instrumental in taking decisions, only in executing them. They could, nevertheless, find themselves defending those policies in the House of Commons, especially if, as was normal in these years, all the members of the cabinet sat in the House of Lords except the prime minister.

What was unusual was not that most members of the cabinet were peers, but that the prime minister remained in the Commons. Walpole set this important precedent when he succeeded Sunderland, and to some extent it justifies his claim to be the first prime minister, since predecessors to whom that title had been given were all peers. It is misleading, however, to suggest that just because he and his successors were called prime ministers they therefore had the same powers as a modern premier. Today a prime minister forms an

administration by appointing ministers of his own choice, whom he
can dismiss for disloyalty to himself. Under the first two Georges all
ministerial appointments were decided by the crown, including that
of prime minister. The king might even choose men who had not got
the confidence of the Commons, though when George II did this in
1746, appointing Granville as prime minister on the resignation of
the Pelhams, business was virtually paralysed. Nor did the crown
necessarily appoint as ministers nominees of their prime ministers.
Both Walpole and the Pelhams had to endure as fellows in the cabinet
men with whom, far from being friendly, they were scarcely on
speaking terms. If this became intolerable they might succeed in
obtaining their removal. Walpole had Carteret transferred from the
post of secretary of state in 1724 to that of lord lieutenant of Ireland,
and from the lord lieutenancy also in 1729, while the Pelhams
obtained the dismissal of Carteret, then Lord Granville, again in
1744. However, it was rare that they could positively recommend the
appointment of men whom the king disliked. The Pelhams insisted
on the promotion of Lord Chesterfield in 1744, but they had to draw
the line at Pitt.

The difficulties experienced by both the King, who wanted to keep
Granville, and the Pelhams, who wanted rid of him, have often been
used to illustrate the workings of the system of ministerial appointment under the early Hanoverians. At the time, the Prince of Wales
exploited these conflicts to argue that George II was 'in toils', forced
to yield to the demands of the Pelhams. Whig historians of the
nineteenth century saw them as precedents to illustrate their thesis
that the Commons had gained the power not only to approve or
disapprove of appointments but to veto those they disliked. Sir Lewis
Namier and his followers, on the other hand, drew the very different
conclusion that they bring out sharply the residual powers of the
crown, and demonstrate that without the king's backing no ministry
could be stable for long. The incidents were, however, unusual and
even untypical in that they took place against the background of
deep involvement in a major war. Such times always limited the
crown's freedom of manoeuvre. In 1708 Anne had to capitulate to
the whig junto, giving high office to two of them, because she could
not do without whig support in parliament for the war effort. In 1757
likewise George II had to give power to Pitt. But when the crown was
no longer fully committed to hostilities and was preparing to
withdraw from a war, then it to a large extent recovered the
initiative. Thus in 1710 Anne could dispense with the Junto and
bring in the tories because she was about to pull England out of the
War of the Spanish Succession; and in 1761 George III felt able to
manage without Pitt because he was prepared to negotiate peace

with France. In peacetime the monarch's ability to choose ministers was nowhere near so restricted as in wartime. George II could with impunity have dismissed Walpole on his accession in 1727. In the final analysis only the prime minister's patently superior ability to Spencer Compton saved him from dismissal. He certainly was not forced on a reluctant sovereign by the necessity of having huge revenues voted in parliament to pay for a major war.

The crown, therefore, retained real as well as theoretical power, despite having to work through parliament. Indeed, in many ways the central executive was stronger under the early Hanoverians than it had been under the later Stuarts. Certainly it was financially much stronger. Parliamentary backing for foreign policy enabled post-Revolution regimes to raise money beyond the wildest dreams of Charles II and James II, without ever running the risk of repeating the Stop of the Exchequer of 1672, when Charles had defaulted on his creditors. The growth of the executive after the Revolution at first created a monster which wreaked havoc in politics and threatened to smash the workings of the constitutional machinery. But when it was tamed by Walpole it became a powerful agency of government, making the British crown the strongest and most stable monarchy in Europe.

While the power of the central government was enormously strengthened by the Glorious Revolution, paradoxically in local government George I exerted less influence than had the Stuarts. To some extent this, too, was the result of the Revolution. In 1688 the localities of England served notice on the crown that as far as their own affairs were concerned they wanted to be left alone. The result was that under the early Hanoverians the provinces virtually governed themselves. As Sidney and Beatrice Webb put it:[17]

> The century and a half lying between the dismissal of the Stuarts and the Reform Parliament constitutes, for the historian of the internal administration of England and Wales, a distinct period of extraordinary significance. For the first, and perhaps for the last, time in English history, the national government abstained from intervention in local affairs, practically leaving all the various kinds of local governing bodies to carry out their several administrations as they chose, without central supervision or central control.

The main units of local government were the county and the parish. In the counties the machinery of government revolved around the lord lieutenant and the commission of the peace. By the eighteenth century the lot of the sheriffs was onerous but relatively unimportant, except in election years when they acted as returning officers for the counties. Because the post involved considerable expense, for instance in entertaining the visiting assizes every year, most of those eligible sought desperately to avoid appointment, and members of

parliament and ministers were besieged with begging letters from the
principal gentry of the counties pleading to be excused the duty. By
contrast the posts of lord lieutenant and justice of the peace, though
also unpaid, were highly prized. Since Tudor times each county had
a lord lieutenant who was the head of the county militia. Originally
conceived as a contribution to national defence, the militia was
largely superseded in its military function by the rise of the standing
army in the late seventeenth century, and its role as a fighting force
became a joke, until invasion scares led to its reorganization at the
outset of the Seven Years' War. An act of 1757 put it on a new footing,
establishing a national force of 32,000 to be raised by quotas in each
county from all men between the ages of eighteen and fifty. In theory
the old militia had been much bigger than this, calculated nationally
to number about 90,000 men. In practice, however, inefficiencies in
mustering the militia had meant that it was much smaller. Efficient
musters were now to be enforced by means of a census of those eligible
in each county, lists of those recorded being forwarded to the lord
lieutenant who was to choose the men to fill his county's quota by
ballot. Those chosen were to serve for seven years.

Until the reforms of 1757 the militia played little part in the
machinery of local government. Although considered a law-
enforcing agency, it rarely acted as a police force except when there
were scares about Jacobite activity, and then it might be mustered to
apprehend and disarm those suspected of disaffection, usually the
papists and nonjurors in the county. Otherwise it played a social
rather than an administrative role. Deputy lieutenancies in the
militia were coveted as status symbols by the leading and aspirant
gentry of a county.

This class also filled the commissions of the peace, though
metropolitan areas of Middlesex, where there were frequent complaints against the humble origins of 'trading justices', were an
exception. Justices of the peace exercised a bewildering and growing
variety of functions. The Reverend Richard Burn, himself a JP,
published a popular guide to their work in 1755 listing their various
jurisdictions under more than two hundred headings, two of which,
'excise and customs' and 'the poor', occupied over two hundred
pages apiece. These unpaid officials were the general drudges of local
government in the eighteenth century. A single justice could practise
summary jurisdiction on the basis of informations against offenders
allegedly breaking the laws on vagrancy, drunkenness, profaneness
and Sunday trading, hearing those charged and sentencing them to a
small fine or even to public chastisement. In conjunction with one
other magistrate they could execute justice in a 'petty' sessions over
such offenders as unlicensed alehouse keepers, unmarried mothers,

runaway servants and apprentices. Three justices could even sentence a person to seven years' transportation for rickburning. Groups of neighbouring justices could supervise affairs in a particular part of a county. Yet more serious offences were heard in quarter-sessions, when the active magistrates on the commission met to hear cases presented by a grand jury of the county and determined by a petty jury of twelve. Besides acting as judges they also administered the laws covering a whole gamut of activities, such as repairing highways, licensing alehouses and implementing the poor laws. They even assumed a legislative role, making their own laws to keep the peace, for instance by regulating fairs and other methods of buying or selling. They also appointed the constables of hundreds who were responsible for law and order in the county at large. In theory they were also responsible for appointing petty constables, overseers of the poor and surveyors of highways; but this was often left to parish vestries, since the duty of maintaining law and order, looking after the poor, and repairing the roads fell on each parish.

The parishes, therefore, in addition to the church wardens they were obliged to select, usually appointed the appropriate officers. The parish vestry could also assess the incidence of local taxation required for the proper execution of parochial duties, normally a rate in the pound on an assessment of property values. The typical vestry consisted only of those property-owners in the parish who were liable to pay these rates. Sometimes a very small number formed a self-perpetuating 'close' vestry, and this type was quite widespread in some areas, especially County Durham and Northumberland. Elsewhere, however, the vestry might be attended by the inhabitants at large, and such 'open' vestries could be remarkably democratic. Whitechapel is an example of a London parish where by 1734 the vestry was regularly attended by a 'great multitude of persons'.

All residents were obliged by law to serve in parish offices for a year without remuneration, although gentlemen and substantial tradesmen usually paid to be exempted from the burden of unpaid drudgery. Often the obligation was shared by more humble parishioners in rotation. This involved the poor and even the illiterate in the workings of local government, and ensured a surprising degree of popular participation in the constitutional machinery.

Although the churchwardens of a remote parish might seem a long way down from the crown, care must be taken not to isolate local government completely from national affairs in this period. After all, the sheriffs and lord lieutenants were crown appointees, while justices of the peace were selected by the lord chancellor. This was by no means an entirely formal mechanism, for in the early eighteenth century at least they were part of the political spoils system. As the political see-saw brought now the tories to the top and now the whigs, so the changes at the centre could affect the remotest counties: lords lieutenant and justices of the peace who had been active for the declining party were removed and replaced by supporters of the rising party. In turn new lords lieutenant would similarly purge and remodel the deputy lieutenancies, while the new justices would regulate the parochial machinery below them. So the localities were not left entirely undisturbed in the years of political upheaval at the outset of the century. Only with the coming of stability under Walpole did the regime begin to consider itself safe enough to relax its vigilance of local affairs until, by 1744, ironically on the eve of the Jacobite rebellion, even tories were once more admitted to the commissions of the peace.

Ultimate justice in the localities, however, lay with the assize judges. On their regular circuits of the counties they tried the most serious offences, which were beyond the jurisdiction of the commissions of the peace. This brought the King's justice down from Westminster to the provinces. It has become a historical truism that the student of national politics ignores at his peril local and regional history. It is equally true that provincial affairs cannot be considered in total isolation from those of the nation. The constitutional machinery was such that the advent of the Hanoverians was felt throughout the land.

# 2 Social Structure

The model of social structure most familiar today is probably that of the three-layered cake, with a thin top layer, a thicker filling, and a very thick base, representing respectively the upper, middle and lower classes. Such a simple view of a three-class society is, of course, totally inadequate to account for the complexities of modern society. The general analyses used by the census office and advertising agencies employ five categories. The registrar-general refers to the following broad classes—professional and proprietorial; intermediate; skilled manual and white collar workers; semi-skilled workers; and unskilled workers. Similarly the British Market Research Bureau divides the population into five groups, A to E—the well-to-do; the middle class; the lower middle class; the working class; and the poor. Even these divisions into five classes require further subdivision and refinement before social structure can be meaningfully discussed.

Yet the idea of a threefold division is not only stubbornly persistent but has a long history. Not that the word class itself has been long in the popular vocabulary, for it seems to have come into common usage to describe a broad horizontal stratum of society only with the advent of industry. Before then some such word as 'rank', 'degree' or 'station' was more generally used, in itself an important clue to the differences between society then and now. When the word 'class' was employed it indicated more the notion of 'type' or 'species' than a social layer. Nevertheless, even in the eighteenth century men found it convenient to divide their society into three broad categories. Daniel Defoe, for instance, distinguished between 'the gentry, 'the tradesmen' and the 'mere labouring people'.[1] Gregory King, the leading demographer of his day, wrote that he divided people 'into classes', and described them as 'the poorest sort ... the middle sort ... the better sort'.[2] David Hume wrote of 'the middle station of life', and distinguished those in it from 'the great' and 'the poor'.[3] Thomas Parnell, in his *Night-Piece on Death*, observed that a glance at a graveyard revealed a threefold hierarchy.

Those Graves, with bending Osier bound,
That nameless heave the crumbled Ground,
Quick to the glancing Thought disclose,
Where *Toil* and *Poverty* repose.

The flat smooth Stones that bear a Name,
The Chissels slender help to Fame,
(Which e'er our Sett of Friends decay
Their frequent Steps may wear away)
A *middle* Race of Mortals own,
Men, half ambitious, all unknown.

The Marble Tombs that rise on high,
Whose Dead in vaulted Arches lye,
Whose Pillars swell with sculptur'd Stones,
Arms, Angels, Epitaphs and Bones,
These (all the poor Remains of State)
Adorn the *Rich*, or praise the *Great*.

Since contemporaries seem to have thought of three broad social divisions their use here seems justified, though we must go beyond the general descriptions to ascertain exactly whom Defoe and King had in mind by 'the gentry' and 'the better sort', 'the tradesmen' and 'the middle sort', 'the mere labouring people' and 'the poorest sort'. Defoe himself defined 'the gentry' as 'such who live on estates, and without the mechanism of employment, including the men of letters, such as clergy, lawyers and physicians'. By 'tradesmen' he meant 'such as merchants, shopkeepers of all sorts, and employers of others, either in trade or manufactures, farmers of land, publick houses, such as vintners, innkeepers, ale-house-keepers, coffee houses, brewers etc.'. Finally 'the mere labouring people' were those 'who depend upon their hands, such as weavers, butchers, carpenters, shoemakers, labourers with all kinds of manufacturers and husbandmen, etc., including apprentices, servants of all sorts, with vagabonds, loiterers and unaccountable people'.[4]

Defoe's descriptions were a bit muddled and haphazard, and King provided a much more sophisticated analysis of English society in the late seventeenth century.[5] This consisted of a table of twenty-six 'ranks, degrees, titles and qualifications' ranging from the lords spiritual and temporal at the top, to 'vagrants: as gypsies, thieves, beggars, etc.' at the bottom. King clearly ranked people by status rather than by wealth, for he assessed the yearly incomes per family of the various ranks, and these do not reduce rank by rank from top to bottom. For instance, the sixth, seventh and eighth ranks are of 'gentlemen, persons in greater offices and places, and persons in lesser offices and places', while the ninth rank is of 'eminent merchants and traders by sea'. King estimated that the yearly income per family of the gentlemen was £280, that of the persons in greater and lesser offices £240 and £120 respectively, while the families of eminent merchants and traders were in receipt of a yearly income of £400. Again he put clergymen above freeholders, although he calculated that the families of the inferior clergy were in receipt of only £50 per annum, which was less than his estimated yearly income for the families of freeholders.

King's table provides a useful scale of categories for a discussion of social structure under the early Hanoverians. Before we tumble down its rungs, however, a word of caution is necessary about its validity as a model of English society in the early eighteenth century. The 'scheme of the income and expenses of the several families of England . . . for the year 1688' has so often been reproduced and used as though it were such a model that its usefulness for this purpose seems to have been established by frequent reference to it. Yet King himself did not intend his table to provide such a model, but drew it up for fiscal purposes.[6] Moreover, although he compiled it in 1696, he deliberately backdated it to 1688, and his statistical estimates were so cautious that they were almost all too conservative even for the earlier date. Given the demographic, social and economic changes that occurred between 1688 and 1714, his quantitative data must be considerably revised, generally upwards, to adjust his table satisfactorily to conditions at the accession of George I. Consequently his figures have been largely ignored here, and only his social categories employed; even these have occasionally been expanded or subdivided to reflect the fact that English social structure under the early Hanoverians was not exactly what it had been under the later Stuarts.

The social rather than economic distinctions provided by Gregory King enable us to place his twenty-six ranks, degrees and qualifications into three 'classes' which contemporaries might have recognized. His first six categories, from temporal lords down to the rank of gentlemen, should be put into a class of their own, which we might call the landed gentry. Although the lords were socially apart from the baronets, knights, esquires and gentlemen, their numbers were too small for them to be seriously considered as a separate class, while economically they were virtually indistinguishable since they were nearly all landlords. It is true that landownership was not the sole or even the most important economic function for all this group. There were also administrators, professionals and businessmen, like Thomas Coke esquire, vice-chamberlain of the royal household, Sir Gilbert Heathcote, one time governor of the Bank of England, Sir Peter King, an eminent lawyer, and Sir Samuel Garth, the physician-poet whom George I knighted with the duke of Marlborough's sword. Others invested surplus capital in non-landed securities such as government annuities, Bank, East India and South

Sea Company stock, town houses, shipbuilding, and turnpike trusts. Nevertheless, the bulk of them were landed proprietors, and what held them all together, and distinguished them from the mass of the population below them, as we shall see, was their gentility.

King's next twelve classifications, from 'persons in greater offices and places' down to 'shopkeepers and tradesmen' could have formed his 'middle sort'. Admittedly this is a very elastic class, including at the top eminent clergymen from whom the bishops were recruited, substantial merchants involved in overseas trade, rich factors engaged as domestic middlemen, and barristers, and at the bottom the inferior clergy, many of whom were desperately poor, tenant farmers and even Grub Street writers. Any concept of 'the middle sort' is bound to be wide, although it is perhaps better to call them the middle classes rather than the middle class.

Again the lower classes, as we might call them, include a great variety of people whom King ranged in eight ranks, from 'artisans and handicrafts' to 'vagrants'. Moreover, in common with most contemporaries, he included domestic servants with families, so that one of the most significant occupations of all, domestic service, is left out of his table. Within the category of domestic servant there was a vast discrepancy, from the land steward, who should be placed in the middle classes along with other professional men, down to the postillion, who was often a small boy from a very poor family. The valets, butlers, cooks, chambermaids and gardeners formed a hierarchy all their own in the eighteenth century, though most of them were included by Defoe as 'servants of all sorts' within his category of 'the mere labouring people'.[7]

So great is the range within the lowest band that the one horizontal division indicated by King in his table cuts right through the middle of it. This is his line distinguishing those who were increasing the wealth of the kingdom from those who were decreasing it, which he places immediately below military officers. At first sight this seems an unaccountable distinction, especially since bishops appear above the line, and labouring people below it. King's figures for yearly income and expense, however, show that he was not thinking in terms of a labour theory of value. What informed his distinction was that those above the line had surplus income over expenditure, while those below it spent more than they earned in a year. It seems incredible that he put over half the population in the second category, but investigations into the living standards of the period have tended to confirm that he was not far out. Something near to half the population was indeed regularly or occasionally dependent upon charity, either parochial or private, to keep above the subsistence level in early Hanoverian England. According to King, they included common seamen, labouring people and outservants, cottagers and paupers, common soldiers and vagrants. Contemporaries grouped them together into the amorphous mass 'the poor'. They should be borne in mind as a separate category within the lower classes, to distinguish them from the artisans whom King placed above the line.

Gregory King's twenty-six 'ranks, degrees, titles and qualifications' can therefore be divided into three groups, enabling us to see some of the social and occupational distinctions which he and his contemporaries had in mind when they thought of society in terms of 'classes'. Thus the top six ranks can be regarded as the upper classes, the next twelve as the middle classes, and the last eight as the lower classes. The rest of this chapter climbs down the twenty-six rungs of King's ladder in order to add further refinement to these divisions.

Top of the table, in both status and wealth, were the temporal lords. In 1714 there were 171, a number which increased only slightly under the first two Georges. Taking the period as a whole there were on average about 180 peers in England and Wales. These were the dukes, marquesses, earls, viscounts and barons who could sit in the House of Lords by virtue of hereditary right. In addition there were about forty Scottish or Irish peers mainly resident in England. Dukes were supposed to have more substantial means than marquesses and earls, and marquesses and earls more than viscounts and barons. In 1701 a proposal was made in the House of Lords that £4,000 per annum should be the minimum income for a viscount, and £3,000 for a baron. Some peers were worth a very great deal more than this. In 1715 the duke of Newcastle was in receipt of about £32,000 a year. The dukes of Beaufort and Bedford were almost as wealthy. Lord Foley was alleged to have left assets worth £28,000 a year in 1766 plus £500,000 in the funds. Such noblemen ranked in wealth with the princes of the German Empire, and indeed the first duke of Marlborough actually was a prince of that empire, his palace at Blenheim rivalling the noblest private houses in Europe. Other stately homes were almost as palatial, such as Chatsworth, rightly called the Palace of the Peak, Castle Howard, built for the earl of Carlisle by Vanbrugh, and Cannons, the Edgware home of the duke of Chandos. The inhabitants of these houses were among the richest subjects of the early Hanoverians. Other peers were much less wealthy, and were economically indistinguishable from some of the baronets, knights, esquires and gentlemen whom King places in the ranks immediately below the lords spiritual. The earl of Lincoln, for example, had only a pension to live on.

Nevertheless they shared the dignity and privileges of peers. In one respect they were more privileged than the European aristocracy, for noble descent in England went only to the eldest son and this kept the English peerage relatively much smaller than its continental counterparts. On the other hand, apart from the right to sit in the House of Lords and to be tried by their peers, they had few privileges which distinguished them legally from the non-noble elements in society. They were not, for example, immune from taxation. Yet the differences between the English aristocracy and the continental nobility can be exaggerated. It is often maintained, for instance, that the marriages of their daughters and the careers of their younger sons allied them with other sections of society and prevented them from becoming a separate caste. In disposing of their daughters, however, noblemen sought marriage alliances with other noble families. The earl of Nottingham made sure that all except one of his seven girls married peers, and she married a baronet. Moreover, while younger sons went into the professions, very few went into trade. If anything, the English aristocracy was more of a closed circle in the eighteenth century than at any other time in history.

Among the lords spiritual, the two archbishops and twenty-four bishops of the Church of England, there were also great differences in income. Around 1760 the archbishop of Canterbury was in receipt of about £7,000 per annum, while the archbishop of York received £4,500. Two bishoprics, Durham and Winchester, were worth more than York, yielding some £6,000 and £5,000 respectively. Most obtained between £1,000 and £3,000, though some were poorer. Bristol, for instance, had an annual income of only £450. Incumbents of the poorer sees, however, almost invariably had their revenues augmented from livings held *in commendam*.

Below the peers were the baronets, knights, esquires and gentlemen. Baronetcies and knighthoods were titles bestowed by the crown, the first being hereditary, the second only for life. Esquire and gentlemen, on the other hand, were titles acquired by general acceptance. Traditionally they were restricted to those with the right to wear a sword, though this was rapidly being assumed at this time. The *Craftsman* lamented that the title, esquire, was being usurped by anybody with 'a spendthrift disposition and a paltry piece of cold iron'.[8] An act of Charles II's reign had permitted esquires to kill game, but by 1753 this was a meaningless distinction. As one critic of the act put it in that year, 'I would gladly know what the true and determinate meaning of the word esquire is; I do not believe the law has determined its true sense, and for my part, I have no idea what it is, though I give that title (if it is one) to many of my acquaintance; but do not know by what right they claim it.'[9] Quite what constituted gentility was even vaguer. One test was the ability to display a coat of arms, though it was not particularly difficult to purchase a patent from the College of Heralds, or even to assume arms, especially since the practice of holding heraldic visitations to inspect the claims of armigerous families had ceased in the seventeenth century. When John Warburton published a map of London and Middlesex in 1749, illustrated with the arms of over five hundred subscribers, the Lord Marshal was informed that the greater part of the arms was either fictitious or did not belong to those who claimed them.[10] Guy Miège did not exaggerate, therefore, when he wrote in 1715 that 'the title of gentleman is commonly given in England to all that distinguish themselves from the common sort of people, by a good garb, genteel air, or good education, wealth or learning.'[11]

We can, however, distinguish the landed gentry from the increasing number of gentlemen without estates, 'pseudo gentry' and pretenders to gentility. Most country gentlemen derived their income from rents paid by tenant farmers on their estates, though this need not be the sole source of revenue, even from land. Exploitation of mineral resources, in Cumberland, Durham and Northumberland especially, was an extension of landowning activities which could be very lucrative indeed. Coal-owners like Sir James Lowther of Whitehaven and George Bowes of Durham were among the richest men in the kingdom, wealthier than most peers. Investments in the funds or the holding of office also realized a return for some. There were enormous discrepancies of wealth and income among the landed gentry. Nor did these necessarily reflect the social gradations from baronet to gentleman. George Pitt esquire of Strathfieldsaye in Hampshire was reputedly in receipt of rents worth between £10,000 and £12,000 a year, while Thomas Coke of Holkham, Norfolk was worth £10,000 per annum. On the other hand, in 1713 Sir Roger Bradshaigh, a baronet, was so financially embarrassed that his return as member of parliament for Wigan was actually challenged on the grounds that he was not possessed of real estate to the annual value of £300, required by the Property Qualifications Act of 1711.

Because economically they were all part of the same class whatever their gradations of status, the most useful analysis of King's first six ranks is in terms of landed wealth. This was recognized in Joseph Massie's similar calculation for the years 1759–60. Instead of distinguishing substantial landowners by their titles, he divided them into twelve categories according to their annual incomes and expenditure, ranging from £20,000 to £200. Within the upper class of landowners as a whole one can distinguish three broad strata— those with large estates, those with medium holdings, and those in possession of land not much more extensive than that owned by 'freeholders of the better sort'. Some historians prefer to use the size of

rent rolls to distinguish between the three types, and it has been
suggested that in the early eighteenth century estates bringing in over
£2,000 per annum were large, those realizing between £800 and
£2,000 were medium, and those worth less than £800 were small.
Attractive though this analysis seems it is too crude to apply to the
whole country, for then as now the value of property varied in
different areas, similarly sized estates generally being more re-
munerative in the southeast than in the north and west. This was
recognized in the proverbial expression:[12]

> A knight of Cales
> A gentleman of Wales
> And a laird of the North Countree
> A yeoman of Kent
> With his yearly rent
> Will buy them out all three.

In Cumberland and Westmorland any landowner worth over £100
per annum would have probably been considered to have belonged
to the gentry, while according to Guy Miège there were 'yeomen, in
Kent especially, that have £1,000 and some more per annum'.[13]

Life at the top of the landed class, in the episcopal palaces and
stately homes, was marked by a level of conspicuous consumption
which set the really substantial landowner apart from the rest of the
population, including even the bulk of the gentry. The very building
and maintenance of the fabric of their houses demanded a considerable outlay of money, and this was the period when the classic
Palladian palaces of Lord Burlington and William Kent were being
built. The earl of Leicester's house at Holkham, built between 1732
and 1765, cost £90,000. Such structures as Stowe, Viscount
Cobham's seat, and Seaton Delaval Hall, built for the Delavals by
Vanbrugh, marked their owners out from the less substantial gentry
around them. Kent also led the way in the fashion for landscape
gardening which further embellished the larger houses, such as the
duke of Newcastle's at Claremont. These gardens alone could involve
considerable expense. The duke of Chandos employed no fewer than
nineteen gardeners at Cannons. Within doors he had an army of
ninety-three household servants, a large retinue even by aristocratic
standards, though many other noblemen employed scores of domestics. There were over thirty to wait on the duke of Newcastle at
Claremont in 1734, while the duke of Bedford had forty in his
Bloomsbury house.

These magnates vied with each other in elegance and taste,
ransacking Europe for art treasures and patronizing native artists
and men of letters. Few could rival the princely Chandos, who kept a
private orchestra at Cannons, and commissioned Handel to write the

music and Pope and Gay to write the librettos of operas. It seems odd
in view of this that Chandos should have been regarded as the model
for Pope's Timon, the archetype of the aristocrat who was joining in
the craze for building and embellishment without the taste of
Bathurst or Burlington, Pope's more celebrated patrons. 'Timon's
villa' could just as easily have been Blenheim or Houghton or any
number of houses built by the whig aristocrats whom Pope despised:

> Lo, what huge heaps of littleness around!
> The whole, a labour'd Quarry above ground.

The great landowners assiduously attended the winter season in
London and the summer season in Bath. They sent their sons to
Oxford and Cambridge after privately educating them at home, and
completed the education of the eldest with the grand tour which was
at the height of its fashion in the 1730s and 1740s. While the eldest son
would inherit the estate, daughters and younger sons had to be
provided for, the first with marriage dowries, the second by the
purchase of commissions in the army, or the payment of premiums for
apprenticeships in respectable professions. Both could be expensive.
It cost the earl of Nottingham £32,000 to endow his daughters.
Around 1750 a premium to a reputable London lawyer to take on a
younger son as a clerk could cost over £600.

Owners of middle-sized estates could not hope to compete with
such an expensive way of life. Nevertheless they tried to ape the
aristocracy, even if they had to limit their aspirations to rather more
modest aims. Adding a wing to the ancestral hall rather than
constructing a new one was the most they could contribute to the
building mania of the period. Their retinues of servants were small in
comparison with the impressive arrays employed by those above
them, seven being apparently the norm. Instead of frequenting the
London and Bath seasons they would attend the assemblies which
were springing up in county towns and other provincial centres
throughout the period. They might send their sons to university. For
example, a quarter of the gentry families of Cumberland and
Westmorland educated their sons at Oxford or Cambridge, most of
them going to The Queen's College, Oxford. Few would go on the
grand tour. The middling gentry would try their best to marry their
daughters into landed families, though when they did so they would
find themselves in competition with professional and even business
men. Those who could not match pound for pound with these
competitors would have to be content with clergymen, physicians
and even tradesmen as sons-in-law. Rather than demean themselves
and their families, the daughters in some impoverished gentry
households preferred to remain spinsters. It was said of Preston in

1750 that 'this town subsists ... by many families of middling fortunes who live in it, and it is remarkable for old maids, because these families will not ally with tradesmen, and have not sufficient fortunes for gentlemen.'[14]

The lesser gentry lived even more modestly. Their smaller households required fewer servants, five being considered the optimum establishment. They rarely if ever travelled outside their own counties. It is at this level that we find the kind of country gentlemen whom Macaulay considered to be typical of the whole class, the untravelled, ill-educated boor who appears in the pages of his celebrated third chapter with the following characteristics.

> His chief serious employment was the care of his property. He examined samples of grain, handled pigs, and, on market days, made bargains over a tankard with drovers and hop merchants. His chief pleasures were commonly derived from field sports and from an unrefined sensuality. ... His table was loaded with coarse plenty; and guests were cordially welcomed to it. ... The coarse jollity of the afternoon was often prolonged till the revellers were laid under the table. ... His opinions respecting religion, government, foreign countries and former times ... were the opinions of a child.

If such backwoods gentry really existed they were far from being typical of the country gentlemen as a whole. Macaulay was seriously misled by the biased sources, mainly literary, which he used to build up his description of them. He drew on Burnet's observations of the Wiltshire gentry in his *History of my own time*, on such stereotype booby squires as Sir Tunbelly Clumsy in Vanbrugh's *Relapse* and Sir Harry Gubbin in Steele's *The Tender Husband*, Sir Roger de Coverley in the *Spectator*, and above all the caricature of 'Foxhunter' in Addison's *Freeholder*, which he greatly admired and regarded as the prototype of Fielding's Squire Western.[15] The distortion in all these sources was as much political as social, for Burnet, Vanbrugh, Steele and Addison were all whigs, and thus unwittingly reinforced Macaulay's own distaste for a class of which he spoke truly when he observed that they were commonly tories. Since Macaulay wrote, more trustworthy evidence about the life styles of the gentry has become available in the personal papers of hundreds of gentry families. These inform us at first hand how they lived, and show that the bulk of the gentry were in fact literate, educated and reasonably civilized.

Insofar as class-consciousness is a prerequisite for the notion of class as a horizontal stratum or layer of society, then the landed gentry formed the one recognizable social class in England at this time. They were very conscious of being distinct from the mass of the population below them, and prided themselves on the privileges of gentle birth.

Gentility, however, was not confined to the landed gentry. There were a growing number of rentiers, now called 'pseudo gentry', who lived on their investments in a wide range of securities as relatively rich men of leisure in London and several provincial towns. Then again Defoe included among the gentry 'men of letters, such as clergy, lawyers and physicians'. One of the signs of upward mobility in the period was the increasing assumption of the title 'gentleman', by farmers, and by professional and business men. 'Gentlemen farmers' and 'gentlemen clothiers' made their appearance in the west country. The lawyers organized themselves into the Society of Gentlemen Practisers in the Courts of Law and Equity, while the leading clothiers in Leeds called themselves gentlemen merchants. Defoe insisted that the appellation 'gentlemen-tradesmen' was not an absurdity. In 1746 Lillo's *The London Merchant* was put on at Southwark at the 'desire of the united body of gentlemen salesmen'. The *Gentleman's Magazine*, launched in 1731, sought to cater for this aspirant clientele. All those who styled themselves gentlemen, and were accepted as such, might be included among the upper classes in this period. But land conveyed such unique status upon its owners that the landed gentry ought properly to be considered as a class above professional and business men, however widely their pretensions were accepted.

The two rungs immediately below 'gentlemen' on King's ladder were occupied by persons in greater and lesser offices and places, of whom he calculated there were 10,000 in 1690. By 1714 there would have been more, for the administration expanded between the Revolution and the accession of George I. Joseph Massie estimated that there were 16,000 civil officers in 1760. The expansion between 1690 and 1714 occurred mainly in the newer departments of state. The court, for instance, decreased under William and Anne and employed about 1,000 people under George I, while the treasury did not grow significantly after 1695. Substantial expansion occurred in the post office, the excise, the customs, the ordnance, and the salt and leather offices. The staff of the inland and foreign offices of the postal service grew from 82 to 233. By the middle of the eighteenth century the penny post and country offices employed about 500, while at the end of the century the post office also had some 850 sailors on its pay roll. According to Daniel Defoe the excise accounted for nearly 4,000 officers by 1724, though as usual he exaggerated and there were in fact probably just over half that number. By 1718 the customs employed 560 full time officers in London alone as well as some 1,000 part time, not to mention the host of officials in other ports. Between them the ordnance, salt and leather offices had about 1,300 officers in 1714.

The salaries of these civil servants varied considerably. For example, the range in the ordnance ran from £1,500 received by the master to the £40 paid to the clerks. However, a difficulty about using official salaries to estimate the income of civil servants in this period is that they were only part of their total revenues. Fees and perquisites could still form a substantial portion of their incomes. The salaries of the secretary and solicitor of the post office, for instance, were the same at £200; but the income of the first was around £1,000, while that of the second was about £550. There was a tendency, very noticeable in the ordnance, to eliminate the dependence upon perquisites and to augment official salaries by way of compensation, but this process still had a long way to go in 1714. Subsistence and travel allowances, even accommodation, were also made available to government officials and could significantly improve their real earnings.

Even so there can be no doubt that King was right to calculate the average incomes of 'eminent merchants and traders by sea', who appear below the persons in lesser offices, as being more than that of the greater officials. There were some fabulously wealthy merchants, in London especially. 'In this famous city' according to *The Exact Dealer's Daily Companion* in 1721, 'is a great number of merchants, who for wealth, for stately houses within the city in winter, and without in summer, for rich furniture plentiful tables, honourable living; for great estates in money and land, excel some princes in some of our neighbour nations.' He presumably had in mind men like Sir Theodore Janssen whose wealth by his own estimation amounted to £300,000, or Sir Peter Delmé, whose investments in the Bank, East India and South Sea Companies amounted to over £400,000 in 1724. Among the wealthiest were financiers like Sir Gilbert Heathcote, and a number of Jews of whom the most celebrated in the period was Sampson Gideon. These merchant princes preferred town houses in the City, Janssen being unusual as a resident of the newly built Hanover Square from 1720 to 1723. Thus Aldergate, Cannon, Fenchurch and Threadneedle Streets were more typical addresses for wealthy merchants. But they did have their country retreats too, which travellers noticed on the approaches to London in Essex and Surrey. In Stratford, Essex, John Macky observed in 1714 'above two hundred little country houses for the conveniency of the citizens in summer, where their wives and children generally keep, and their husbands come down on Saturdays and return on Mondays'.[16] On the other side of town, from Richmond to London, Defoe observed 'citizens's country houses, whither they retire from the hurries of business, and from getting money, to draw their breath in a clean air'.[17]

The leading merchants of other major ports, Bristol, Liverpool, Glasgow, Newcastle and Hull, lived in similar style. In Bristol John Macky noted 'behind the key is a very noble square, as large as that of Soho in London . . . and most of the eminent merchants who keep their coaches reside there.'[18] In Glasgow the tobacco merchants formed the dominant group, led at the end of the century by men like William Cunningham and Alexander Speirs, whose town houses in the city cost respectively £10,000 and £3,000 to construct. They also acquired country houses within easy reach of Glasgow, and commuted between them and their town residences. A similar pattern is discernible in Hull, with the development of elegant new streets in the town during the century, and the move of the richer merchants to country retreats within easy reach. Leeds too was dominated by its 'gentlemen merchants', such as the Denisons and the Milneses. The Denisons had a house in Kirkgate, while others built in New Town, Boar Lane, Meadow Lane and Hunslet Lane, to the south of the main business district, between 1660 and 1760. They also acquired small estates in the immediate countryside. These men lived in a grand manner and, as their historian observes, 'The only point that separates the Denisons and the average north-country squire is that whereas the latter was unlikely to afford even a half-length Gainsborough portrait, much less a Nollekens memorial, William and Robert Denison could proudly sit to two of the leading painters of their day and plan their park with the north's most fashionable architect.'[19]

King did not have a separate category of industrialist but, when Joseph Massie drew up his similar table in 1760, he added 'master manufacturer' to the list of occupations. Although this took into account industrial developments which had taken place since 1688, there were still few entrepreneurs who could match fortunes with the eminent merchants. Massie himself estimated that his leading master manufacturers had average incomes of only £200 per annum, which put them on a par with King's lesser merchants. Most industry was still undertaken on a small scale, with the household workshop as the basic unit of production. Mining, one of the few heavy industries, was largely in the hands of landed proprietors rather than industrial entrepreneurs, since exploitation of the country's mineral resources was regarded as an extension of their agricultural interests. Thus the Northumberland coal trade was dominated by Northumbrian landowners like the Blacketts of Wallington and the Ridleys of Blagdon, that of Cumberland by the Lowthers of Whitehaven, and that of Durham by the Liddells and Wortley Montagus. George Bowes, who represented County Durham in parliament from 1727 to 1760, was another coal-owning landlord, who left an estimated £600,000. The extractive industries raised a few families that might be considered along with the eminent merchants, such as the Darbys of Coalbrook-dale and the Crowleys of Winlaton who made fortunes as iron-masters.

Below these merchant princes and industrial entrepreneurs there were the lesser merchants noted by King. These were the increasingly essential middlemen of English commerce. As the population became more urbanized, above all in London but also in ports such as Bristol and Liverpool and the newer manufacturing towns of Birmingham, Manchester and Leeds, so the distribution of goods between producer and consumer became more complex. The result was a significant increase in the numbers of wholesale suppliers between 1688 and 1760. Exact figures are unascertainable, but a comparison between the tables of Gregory King and Joseph Massie gives a rough indication. Some idea of the change can be seen from the very categories employed by the two early social analysts. Where King drew a distinction between eminent merchants with an average yearly income of £400 and lesser merchants in receipt of £198 per annum, Massie divided his merchants into three income groups. Massie's equivalent of King's 2,000 eminent merchants would appear to have been his 3,000 merchants with annual incomes of £400 or more. By the same computation his categories which cover King's 8,000 lesser merchants were the 10,000 merchants in receipt of £200. Thus between 1688 and 1760 the merchant community increased from about 10,000 to about 13,000 if we accept these figures. Even if there was a massive discrepancy between King, Massie and reality, there is still reason to believe that the proportion of middlemen to the total population increased significantly between the Glorious Revolution and the accession of George III. Their main function was to distribute goods from the producer to the markets in the cities and towns. Most of them would be involved in supplying London, for the capital had twelve cattle markets, of which the greatest was Smithfield, three fish markets, including Billingsgate, three fruit and vegetable markets, Covent Garden being one, two corn markets, four meal markets, six hay markets, two leather markets, two coal markets and two cloth markets. It was precisely this kind of London merchant Isaac Ware had in mind when he designed houses for 'the middle road of people' in 1756 and included rooms for three or four servants. Then there were between 750 and 800 much smaller markets in towns and villages scattered all over England. Some wholesale merchants, especially those involved in supplying London, might specialize in one commodity, such as coal or livestock or corn, but most seem to have diversified their activities and to have been quite ready to deal in almost any bulk merchandise.

The next rung of King's ladder is occupied by persons in the law, whom he estimated at 10,000, while Massie calculated that they numbered 12,000 in 1760. Although these figures presumably include all professional lawyers below the level of judges, from the king's sergeants at law to the humblest country attorney, they do appear high. In 1729 it was estimated that there were 4,829 attorneys of the courts of Common Pleas, King's Bench and Chancery, but this is an unreliable estimate. As late as 1800 there were only 5,300 solicitors in the whole country. However many there were, contemporaries were convinced, especially at the outset of the period, that there were too many and that this encouraged pettifogging.

King put the average salary of a lawyer at £154, while Massie curiously gave the lower calculation of £100. Again these averages conceal great discrepancies. The professional hierarchy of barristers and solicitors was already established, although solicitors were generally still called attorneys. Barristers, of course, earned far greater fees than attorneys. But London attorneys in large practices grossed over £1,000 a year, and could employ several clerks. Even some country attorneys could do well from their practices, as did Joseph Banks of Sheffield who rose to be a substantial landowner in Lincolnshire. These could afford town houses in London and the provinces which ranked with the best. At the other end of the scale it was a common complaint about mid-century that broken tradesmen, bailiffs, farmers, even sailors, set themselves up as attorneys.

Many attorneys acted as stewards to country estates, a position for which their legal training admirably suited them. Even though it was objected that a land steward's duties necessitated full time employment, some attorneys undertook to supervise the affairs of several estates. Joseph Banks was steward to the dukes of Norfolk, Leeds, and Newcastle, while Edward Lawrence, the author of *The Duty of a Steward to his Lord*, who deprecated this part-time activity of attorneys, claimed in 1727 that he had 'known instances where a country attorney has been steward to seven or eight noblemen'.[20] Conversely land stewards became attorneys, as for instance Daniel Eaton, steward to Lord Cardigan's estate. Estate agents in the eighteenth century can therefore be considered along with the legal profession, although King does not mention them and presumably subsumes them in the numbers per household along with other servants. Yet they were quite distinct from the rest of the servant body, at least on the larger estates. The duke of Bedford's steward had his salary raised from £300 to £700 in 1732, while Sir Henry Liddell appointed a steward at £400 a year in 1729. These were exceptional and indeed prodigious sums. 'On smaller estates, a salary of £50 with a house and a small farm on the estate, was the more usual thing.' Thomas Sisson, steward to William Cotesworth of Gateshead, 'was paid £40 a year, plus diet and horse allowance'. Some stewards, instead of being on a fixed salary, were paid on a commission basis. The duke of Chandos offered a sliding scale in 1741, based on the amount of rent collected half yearly: 'for the first £200 you shall receive 18*d* in the pound, for the next £100, 2*s* in the pound ... whatever you shall collect above that sum, 2*s* 6*d*.' The steward could hope to gross over £100 per annum if he collected every penny of the rents on time.[21]

Why Gregory King put clergymen below civil servants, merchants and lawyers is not altogether clear. Joseph Massie originally dealt with them immediately after the gentry in his table, which possibly reflects an improvement in the status of clergymen during the seventy years between 1690 and 1760. Certainly a career in the church became more attractive to the younger sons of the gentry and even of the nobility than it had seemed in the late seventeenth century. As Warburton put it in 1752, 'our grandees have at last found their way back into the church.'[22] This was true only of the Church of England, for dissenting clergymen still came from humble backgrounds during the eighteenth century. Both King and Massie distinguished between eminent and lesser clergymen. Within the established church at least this was very necessary, for the inferior clergy below the bishops formed a hierarchy stretching from the deans and chapters of cathedrals to the curacies of remote country parishes. Some of the prebends' stalls in the anglican church were rated on a par with the poorer bishoprics. Prebends could expect annual incomes of £450 at Windsor, £400 at Oxford, £350 at Canterbury and £300 at Westminster. A few parishes were worth more, Sedgefield in County Durham being alleged to bring in £1,200 a year. At the same time over half the 10,000 livings were worth less than £50 a year, while twelve per cent of them brought in less than £20 and some of them as little as £5. It was to augment the stipends of poor clergymen that ecclesiastical taxes were earmarked in 1704 for the fund known as Queen Anne's Bounty.

Macaulay drew a distinction between the urban and rural clergy which is almost as celebrated as his depiction of the country gentlemen. The first, he argued, included 'divines qualified by parts, by eloquence, by wide knowledge of literature, of science and of life, to defend their church victoriously against heretics and sceptics'. The second, by contrast, 'consisted chiefly of persons not at all wealthier, and not much more refined, than small farmers or upper servants'.[23] His admiration of the first has tended to be overlooked in criticisms of his denigration of the second. His vivid picture of the rural clergymen toiling on the glebe, feeding swine and loading dung-carts, lucky to be able to afford ten or twelve dog-eared volumes, has been condemned as a caricature which, like his portrait of the country gentlemen, relied too much on literary sources. Certainly he leaned heavily on such 'evidence' as Fielding's Parson Adams, whose curacy, worth only £23 per annum, had to maintain himself, his wife and six children, and Parson Trulliber, who kept a hog farm and a dairy to supplement his income. Yet the more prosaic records of Queen Anne's Bounty tell a similar story. Nevertheless, as the period progressed, the condition of the inferior clergy slowly improved, partly as a result of the Bounty, but mainly owing to an increase in land values. By the end of the eighteenth century the majority of the church's livings were worth £250 and more. Even the poor parsons of the Lake District benefited from this improvement; Robert Walker, for instance, perpetual curate of Seathwaite in Cumberland, augmented his income from £5 at the start of his incumbency to over £17 when he died.

Few of the thousand or so dissenting clergymen would have been as poor as this but nor were any as wealthy as bishops. Their stipends depended on the size, affluence and dedication of their congregations, some of which were very large and very wealthy. The presbyterian conventicle in Taunton was supposedly the biggest with a congregation of 2,000, while that in Sheffield had nearly 1,200. Perhaps the richest dissenters were in London, where in 1730 the presbyterians collected £2,000, £280 of which came from Salter's Hall alone, the independents £1,700 and the baptists £500. The large rich congregations of the capital and other urban centres could afford to pay their preachers £100 and more a year, and provide them with houses while elsewhere £30 to £50 appears to have been more normal. When the Particular Baptist Fund was founded in 1717, £25 was regarded as a minimum, though over a hundred of their ministers worth less than that applied immediately for relief. In 1752 the methodists allowed £12 per annum to their preachers, and in 1757 their wives were allotted four shillings per week. Many baptist and methodist preachers, however, followed trades in addition to their ministry, and were therefore not dependent simply on their stipends.

Immediately after the clergy, King dealt with freeholders; by these he meant landowners not of the status of gentlemen, for of course the estates of the aristocracy and gentry were freeholds, while church livings and even some offices in the state were regarded as such. The better freeholders tended to be called yeomen, though this was a term of social rather than of economic significance, sometimes used of leaseholders and even of tradesmen. Neither King nor Massie uses it, and some modern historians prefer the expression 'owner-occupier'. To be called a yeoman was to aspire to social status of a sort, even though it was less exalted than gentleman. Indeed some yeomen slipped over the boundary if they could. James Fretwell of Pontefract, for instance, described himself as a yeoman in his will but appears as a gentleman on his tombstone. Some of the better freeholders were economically indistinguishable from the lesser gentry anyway. Bonham Hayes, a Kentish yeoman, kept 'three farms totalling 400 acres, £350 in money, and some houses and wharves at Gravesend'. In 1710 a Sussex yeoman could afford to lend out as much as £800 at interest, while in 1724 a Norfolk yeoman died worth £625, of which £517 was out on loan.[24]

The lesser freeholders could be styled peasants, although the term itself was rarely used in eighteenth-century England. In Wigston Magna, Leicestershire, there was a peasant economy which survived from the early middle ages until well into the eighteenth century. As late as 1765 there were nearly a hundred landowners in the village, of whom seventy had holdings of less than 24 acres. At this level it appears that there was less incentive to retain holdings intact by primogeniture. Thus the small holdings in Wigston had been subdivided between collateral branches of the same families, while in Kent and Sussex too 'it seems to have been quite common . . . to share the family property fairly equally, although giving preference to the elder children.'[25]

The distinction between King's freeholders and farmers was legal rather than economic. Freeholders were owner-occupiers while farmers were tenants, even though both managed farms for their livelihoods and many freeholders rented property in addition to their patrimony. Although King placed farmers below lesser freeholders there were some tenants who financially were on a par with the better sort of freeholders. Massie recognized this in 1760 when he divided farmers into four income groups ranging from £150 to £40 a year. Substantial tenants inhabited the robust farmhouses which remain as a familiar feature in the English countryside. Most of them were improvements on earlier dwellings, for there was little new building between 1725 and 1760; sturdier materials, more rooms, more comfortable accommodation reflected the prosperity of the wealthy farmer. At the other end of the scale were the wattle-and-daub cottages of the small farmer who was not far removed from the mere husbandman below him. Inventories of the contents of farmhouses also reflect diverse living standards among those who occupied them, whether freeholder or tenant. Some inventories record goods worth hundreds of pounds, including luxuries such as clocks and silverware, while the small farmer's possessions might only be worth £15 or £20.

'Persons in liberal arts and sciences', King's next group, are not immediately recognizable in the same way as merchants, clergymen and farmers. To some extent this is due to a change in terminology since the eighteenth century, when 'liberal' in this sense indicated an activity above the necessary labour of the lower orders, which even gentlemen might engage in for leisure and someone between a mechanic and a gentleman could undertake for a livelihood. Strictly there were only seven liberal arts: grammar, rhetoric, logic, arithmetic, music, geometry and astronomy, the traditional subjects of the university curriculum. However, from the sheer numbers involved—15,000 in 1690, 18,000 in 1760—it seems clear that the category was not restricted by either King or Massie to the professors of these subjects. Certainly it would include teachers, from university dons at Oxford and Cambridge to charity school masters, though many of these would be clergymen and therefore presumably subsumed under that heading. It would also extend to artists, musicians and writers as professors of liberal arts, and include physicians as 'persons in science'.

Because of the nature of liberal arts and sciences there was a great overlap between the amateur and the professional. Gentlemen of leisure turned their hands to painting, music and writing. Even architecture was not yet a distinct profession, and an amateur like Sir John Vanbrugh, better known earlier as a playwright, could become an eminent architect, although he had not designed a house before he built the impressive pile of Castle Howard for the earl of Carlisle. Men like Lords Bolingbroke, Burlington and Chesterfield achieved fame in the worlds of architecture and letters but cannot be regarded solely or primarily as professors of liberal arts. Even writers like Addison and Swift derived their main income from politics and the church. There were, however, painters, musicians, poets, playwrights, essayists and novelists who lived almost entirely by their talents in this period, for example, Defoe, Handel, Hogarth, Pope and Richardson. It was indeed the first age where the profession of writing could sustain a livelihood for a great many people. With the advent of the mass market for ephemeral literature there came into being a host of writers to cater for it, a development disdained by Pope, Swift and the wits with the contemptuous label 'Grub Street'. Booksellers became publishers to act as middlemen for the new market, establishing the reputation of a Jacob Tonson or the notoriety of an Edmund Curll as the leading lights of a business which would have been impossible a generation earlier.

There were fewer amateur physicians, for 'the eighteenth century was a period of decline for the English medical amateur.'[26] It may seem strange that medicine should be considered inferior to law as a profession, but this was certainly its image in the eighteenth century.

Comparing the two in 1799 a writer observed :[27]

> So many gentlemen of great figure and independent fortune embrace the
> profession of law, that it is natural to infer that greater liberality exists in its
> government. . . . Physicians in this country are almost universally taken from the
> middle ranks of men. They cannot therefore be expected to conduct themselves, as
> a body, in the same liberal manner as the members of the profession which
> contains a number of persons of high birth and large hereditary fortunes.

What makes this remark even more pointed is that the physicians
were regarded as the gentlemen of the medical profession, a cut
above the apothecaries and surgeons. The social prestige of physicians was jealously guarded by the Royal College, which would
admit only graduates of Oxford, Cambridge and Trinity College,
Dublin as fellows and enrolled graduates of other universities as
licentiates. Compared to the progress in medical teaching elsewhere,
particularly Edinburgh and Leyden, medicine was moribund at the
English universities; but this was not the point. The sons of
gentlemen went to Oxford and Cambridge, foreign universities
attracted the middle ranks of men. At the beginning of the period
apothecaries were regarded as mere dispensers of drugs, and the
physicians strenuously opposed their attempts to diagnose and
prescribe as well as to dispense. In retaliation they themselves set up
dispensaries, a move which was equally vigorously resisted by the
apothecaries. Gradually, however, and grudgingly, physicians accepted the necessity of apothecaries acting as doctors to people who
could not afford their fees, and accorded them recognition as medical
practitioners to the extent of having intending physicians apprentice
themselves to apothecaries.

King's equation of shopkeepers and tradesmen would apparently
not have been recognized in Scotland and Ireland where, according
to Defoe, 'when you speak of a tradesman you are understood to
mean a mechanic, such as a smith, a carpenter, a shoemaker, and the
like.' But in England, he went on to observe, 'and especially in
London and the south part of Britain . . . shopkeepers, whether
wholesale dealers or retailers of goods, are called tradesmen . . . such
are . . . our grocers, mercers, linen and woollen drapers . . .
tobacconists, haberdashers, whether of hats or small wares, glovers,
hosiers, milliners, booksellers, stationers, and all other shopkeepers
who do not actually work upon, make or manufacture the goods they
sell.' He considered that it was impossible to calculate their number,
'we may as well count the stars.'[28] King, however, estimated that
there were 50,000 of them, while Massie calculated 162,500. This is
the single biggest discrepancy between the two calculations, and
while it cannot be taken at its face value for King himself admitted
that his estimate was too low, it probably does reflect the most

striking shift in social structure between 1690 and 1760. This increase was so remarkable that in 1776 Adam Smith was to anticipate Napoleon in describing England as 'a nation of shopkeepers'.

A butcher in Eastcheap is such a long way below an East India Company director that it would be stretching even the elastic concept of the middle classes too far to go lower. Before descending King's ladder further, therefore, it is appropriate to pause here to consider what characteristics, if any, his 'middle sort' had in common.

Today we would distinguish between the professional and business elements among the middle class. Such a distinction was blurred in the eighteenth century by the practice among most professional men of serving as apprentices just like any tradesman. Lawyers were apprenticed as clerks to attorneys and, as we have seen, intending physicians were often the apprentices of apothecaries. By an act of 1729 five years' apprenticeship became statutory for the clerks of attorneys. At the start of the century the system of apprenticeship was very lax, attorneys being accused of having more regard for the premiums which they received than for the education of their clerks. Certainly these could be handsome, of the order of £250 and more for London attorneys. Few attorneys in the capital charged less than £100, though country attorneys were not as demanding. The return on this outlay varied. Some clerks complained that they were used as little more than drudges by their masters, and even by their masters' wives. The wife of the attorney to whom Philip Yorke was articled 'frequently annoyed him with household errands'.[29] Others were more fortunate, and received formal instruction like any modern clerk. Formal training for the medical profession was greatly improved during the century, especially with the rise of the teaching hospitals like the London Hospital and Guy's, which permitted surgeons to have as many as four apprentices.

Although the distinction was blurred, contemporaries did consider some professions to be apart from trade, and particularly the church, the law, medicine and the armed forces. As Partridge informed Tom Jones in Fielding's novel 'a surgeon is a profession, not a trade.' Massie in fact appears to have been aware of these as professions when he grouped them together in his original classification. King did not actually employ a separate category for the armed services, for although he has rungs on his ladder for naval and military officers, these are so low down the table of ranks, their numbers are so high and their salaries so small, that he must have been referring to junior officers and not to the officer class as a whole. The senior officers in the armed forces cannot have numbered as many as 4,000 in the army, out of a total force of only 35,000, or 5,000 in the navy, which are the figures provided by King. Moreover they were paid a great deal more than the £80 which he indicates as being the salary of naval officers, and the £60 he gives as the annual pay of army officers. Admirals received up to £1,325, senior army officers up to £1,000. Senior officers therefore, must have been assumed to be gentlemen, and some indeed were noblemen. Entry into the upper reaches of the army was regulated by a recognized system of purchasing commissions, which would have been far beyond the means of men of only £60 a year. The earl of Westmorland's regiment reportedly cost him £8,000 yet when he was cashiered in 1733 he received no compensation for it. In fact King's salaries were for junior officers, who were paid between £73 and £91 in the navy, while ensigns in foot regiments, who were at the very bottom of the officer class in the army, received £55 a year in the late seventeenth century.

In the first half of the eighteenth century the professions did not have a good image. Priests were portrayed as casuists, lawyers as pettifoggers and doctors as ignorant quacks; only soldiers appear to have escaped the general censure. Individual representatives of the professions on the stage conformed to these stereotypes. Fielding's Puzzletext in *The Grub Street Opera* is a typical clergyman whose very name is a clue to his character, Steele's lawyers in *The Funeral* and *The Tender Husband* extol the chicanery of tautology as a means of duping clients, while Seringe, the doctor in Vanbrugh's *The Relapse*, typifies the quack medical man. Significantly, only soldiers appear on the stage as individuals rather than stereotypes, Plume and Kite in Farquhar's *The Recruiting Officer* having more personality than most other professional men put together. The typecasting carries over from drama to the early novels. Few of the professional men in Fielding and Richardson, Parsons Adams and Harrison apart, appear in a good light. Fielding especially castigated doctors and lawyers; the most vicious criticisms appear in *Amelia* but Amelia's husband, by contrast, was a soldier.

These denunciations of individuals merged into a general onslaught on the professions. The very first edition of the *Craftsman* announced as its manifesto an intention 'to lay open the frauds, abuses and secret iniquities of all professions, not excepting those of my own [law]; which is at present notoriously adulterated with pernicious mixtures of craft, and several scandalous prostitutions. The same malignant contagion has infected the other learned faculties and polite professions.' In *The Beggar's Opera* one of Gay's songs includes the words

> All professions berogue one another
> The priest calls the lawyer a cheat
> The lawyer beknaves the divine.

Fielding summed up the generally hostile attitude in *Pasquin*:

> Religion, law, and physic were designed
> By heaven the greatest blessing on mankind;
> But priests, and lawyers, and physicians made
> These general goods to each a private trade,
> With each they rob, with each they fill their purses,
> And turn our benefits into curses.

By the end of the century the professions had acquired that aura of respectability which became their principal characteristic under the Victorians. To be a clergyman, a lawyer or a doctor was no longer generally regarded as to be on the make at the expense of the credulity of others. On the contrary, it conferred dignity upon a man, making him respectable if not genteel. To some extent the professions were themselves responsible for improving their image by being more rigorous in admitting entrants and more ruthless about expelling the unethical. The Society of Gentlemen Practisers began to perform the same function for London attorneys as the Royal College of Physicians for medical practitioners. The status of surgeons was improved in 1745 when they finally separated from the barbers, though it was not until 1800 that they had their own royal college.

On the other hand, there appears to have been an ambiguous attitude to men engaged in farming or trade. At times they were depicted as the embodiments of respectability, fair dealing, hard work and the backbone of the nation. Yeomen in particular were signalled out as 'the best and most valuable set of men in the nation'.[30] The respect in which merchants were held can to some extent be judged by the popularity of Lillo's *The London Merchant* when it appeared in 1746, with the title part significantly named 'Thorowgood'. By some the 'middling people of England' were held to be 'good natured and stouthearted'.[31]

Yet at other times they could be accused of sharp practice, foul play and even idleness. Farmers and merchants were regarded as exploiters of market conditions, especially during seasons of dearth. Then they were bitterly attacked, not only by the hungry poor but by the gentry above them, as forestallers, engrossers and regrators. Thus in 1758 a writer of *A Short Essay on the Corn Trade* could comment on 'the general opinion, that the present dearness of corn arises principally from the avarice of the farmers and iniquity of the factors, merchants, bakers and dealers in corn.'[32] It also became a common charge that tradesmen neglected their businesses, that shops which used to open at five in the morning and close at nine at night opened at 7a.m. and closed at 8p.m. This idleness was attributed to a desire for gentility among tradesmen generally.

There was at least some truth in the accusation that businessmen aspired to become gentlemen. As Sealand asserted, in Steele's *The Conscious Lovers*, 'we merchants are a species of gentry that have grown into the world this last century and are as honourable.' Moll Flanders looked for a tradesman as a husband 'that was something of a gentleman too; that when my husband had a mind to carry me to the court, or to the play, he might become a sword, and look as like a gentleman as another man', and she eventually found 'this amphibious creature, this land water thing, called a gentleman-tradesmen' in the person of a draper. Such social pretensions so incensed one moralist that he urged that it should be an offence to appear in public 'with a dress peculiar to a gentleman, unless he really was such by birth or fortune'; but he was fighting a losing battle.[33] In Bath, Scarborough and other spas during the season, gentlemen took to appearing 'in all places naked', that is, without their swords, 'from a polite declaration that in places of public resort, all distinctions ought to be lost in a general complaisance'.[34]

One of the more significant signs that 'the middling sort' aspired to become gentlemen is that there was little if anything of a distinctly middle-class culture or morality. The early novel, for instance, so often taken as a bourgeois art form, displays surprisingly genteel values. After many vicissitudes their heroines must end happily married to country gentlemen if not to peers, while their heroes must finish up as landed gentry in charge of broad acres, which they have either been fraudulently denied or have earned through their superior merits. These are scarcely bourgeois aspirations. They reflect a society in which the dominant values are still overwhelmingly those of its landed proprietors.


The gap between shopkeepers and tradesmen on the one hand, and artisans and craftsmen on the other, though very narrow, can be used to demarcate the boundary between the middle and lower classes. Defoe distinguished between shopkeepers, who sold goods made elsewhere, and handicraftsmen who 'make the goods they sell, though they do not keep shops to sell them ... such as smiths, shoemakers, founders, joiners, carpenters, carvers, turners and the like'.[35] Such craftsmen were not part of a working class in the modern sense, and certainly did not form a marxist proletariat. They manufactured goods in small workshops in which master craftsmen trained apprentices and employed journeymen, or day workers. This fact makes it hard to sustain the marxist distinction between a bourgeoisie owning the means of production and a proletariat selling their labour on the market. The master craftsman might be classified as bourgeois, since he owned a workshop in which he exercised his trade and employed other artisans; but at the same time he was a skilled workman, and some of his journeymen might set themselves up as masters in time. When the household workshop was a principal unit of production, social concepts applicable to the Industrial Revolution are irrelevant. The working class was hardly in the making before 1760.

Even though England was not industrialized, the multiplicity of trades was striking. Over 350 were listed alphabetically, from anchor smith to woollen draper, in the *London Tradesman* of 1747. Income from these varied considerably. The masters, of course, got what they could from the sale of their products, and of some, like the builders, it was said that 'they live handsomely.' The wages of journeymen were more or less fixed, which enables some comparisons between trades to be made. Thus bricklayers earned at best twenty-one shillings a week, while bodice-makers earned at worst seven. To some extent this was due to the fact that bodice-makers tended to be women, though there does not appear to have been marked discrimination in wages between the sexes. Quilters, for instance, who were nearly all women, could earn twelve shillings a week, while bellows-makers earned only ten. In the end it is impossible to draw up a sliding scale of occupations because some, like watermen, received tips, others, like blacksmiths, obtained small beer in addition to their earnings, while others, such as bakers, were given accommodation as well as wages. Board was a significant item. It was estimated in 1754 that a workman's lodgings in London would cost him one shilling a week, and his victuals a further five shillings.[36] Outside London the cost of living was lower than this, but then so were the wages.

Artisans and craftsmen appear on King's table above naval and military officers, which again makes his treatment of the armed forces distinctly odd. These three categories appear just above his line separating those increasing the wealth of the nation from those decreasing it, and it is interesting to note that he considered artisans and craftsmen to be nearer the line than officers: he calculated that a craftsman's family spent only ten shillings per head less than it earned during a year, while the gap between expenditure and income was £2 per head in a naval officer's family and £1 in an army officer's.

The common seamen, who come immediately below the line, included not just those in the royal navy but those whom Defoe regarded as sailors, among whom were 'all persons employed on the sea, or about the works relating to navigation, such as shipwrights, watermen, bargemen, keelmen and all sorts of fishermen'.[37] Defoe estimated that these were about four per cent of the population, which on King's calculation would work out at 55,000 men, not far off his own figure of 50,000, or Massie's of 60,000. This merchant navy was vital not only for the importation and exportation of goods from overseas, but also for the coasting trade which carried merchandise all round the British Isles, connecting principally such great ports as Newcastle upon Tyne, Hull, London, Southampton, Bristol, Liverpool, Whitehaven and Glasgow. It was engaged in fishing, both from these cities and from a host of towns and villages scattered all around the island. Seamen and fishermen also frequented remote coasts and harbours in pursuit of the profitable, if illegal, trade in smuggled goods.

Labouring people and outservants, who occupy the next place on King's table, formed a vast army which he computed at 364,000. This amorphous mass must be broken down, at least into country and town labourers, as Massie did when he distinguished husbandmen from the rest. Although most had not been apprenticed to any trade, it would be a mistake to regard them as totally unskilled. On the contrary, the skills acquired by husbandmen could be prodigious. They were expected to work among livestock and crops. The care of cattle, sheep and pigs in itself required expert knowledge, while the cultivation of crops, from ploughing to threshing, involved a myriad of techniques which mechanization has since simplified or eliminated. For all this the husbandman could expect about six shillings a week, although agricultural labourers could negotiate better wages at peak times of the year like haymaking, harvesting and fruit-picking. Many farmers also provided accommodation for their workers, often in the farmhouse itself. Village labourers can hardly be distinguished from husbandmen, since so many farm workers were employed in domestic industries like spinning and hand loom weaving, especially in the intervals between labour intensive operations when there was underemployment in the countryside. Even in London there was a resident labour force which went out into the fields daily to work on the dairy farms in Islington, again blurring the distinction between urban and rural occupations.

Nevertheless, there was a difference between employment in town and country. Even in small towns 'the majority of townsmen did not work the land directly'.[38] Thus in Petworth, Sussex in about 1700, only five per cent of the tradesmen also had a significant means of livelihood from the land. Towns with hundreds rather than thousands of inhabitants would have few tradesmen not engaged in the basic service industries. Those with over 2,000 inhabitants, however, could generate local manufacturing industries, such as brewing, tool-making and shipbuilding. Urban centres with populations in excess of 5,000 had quite varied economies, while London had a highly sophisticated business structure. Almost every trade employed labourers as well as journeymen, while there were heavy jobs for unskilled workers such as carters, coal-heavers, porters and sawyers. Women, too, found employment as milk sellers, fish hawkers and rag pickers, while even children could take up labouring jobs such as chimney sweeping. Labourers could earn between one and five shillings a day, though most probably came nearer the bottom than the top of this range. King's association of outservants with labourers is indicative of the variety of services necessary to sustain an urban and especially a metropolitan population. The shops of all sorts employed a host of assistants. Many households hired servants to come in daily for domestic service.

Domestic service, indeed, was far and away the biggest employer of labour. Although neither King nor Massie attempted to enumerate servants who lived in with their families it is possible to calculate their numbers. In forty London parishes in 1694 there were 28,507 people, of whom 5,805 were servants, or approximately twenty per cent of the population. It seems likely, however, that the ratio of servants was higher in the capital than elsewhere. The proportion of them in one hundred villages was about thirteen per cent which, projected on a national scale, would account for something like 715,000 people on King's table. By 1760 there would certainly be a higher absolute figure, and perhaps also a higher relative figure, for domestic service appears to have been a growth industry in the early eighteenth century. In 1747 a tract complained that 'there are in London and Westminster and the towns within ten miles round, take every way, above an hundred thousand more maid servants and footmen at this time in place than used to be in the same compass of ground above thirty years ago.'[39] This was a highly exaggerated account, but the inference that there had been a great increase in the number of servants in the metropolitan area since the accession of George I is probably sound.

Servants themselves were arranged in a distinct hierarchy. First came the upper servants, starting with the clerks of the stables and kitchens and descending via the cook, the confectioner, the baker, the bailiff, the valet, the butler and the gardener to the groom of the chamber. Then there were the lower servants who appeared in public and wore their master's livery. The highest of these was the coachman and the lowest the page. Female domestics also had different ranks, ranging from the lady's maid to the scullery maid. All these servants had different wages, but these were only part of their incomes. In addition they had board, lodgings, even clothes, while the custom of extracting tips, known as vails, from their master's guests could augment their wages substantially. So great were the rewards expected that people became reluctant to accept invitations to stay at large households because of the expense involved. After

1760 there was a concerted effort to abolish vails, and to increase the wages of servants to make up for the loss.

Cottagers and paupers were the single biggest category on King's table, numbering 400,000. Quite what provision Massie made for them in 1760 is obscure, since he has no separate entry for paupers and accounts for only 40,000 cottagers, whom he includes with ale-sellers. There is no reason to suppose that there had been a spectacular decline in the numbers of the poor since 1688. On the contrary, it seemed to contemporaries that the poor were not only always with them, but were on the increase. There would be few parishes where the office of overseer of the poor was purely nominal. Almost every parish would have its share of impoverished orphans and the old, sick or insane who could not look after themselves. In addition seasonal underemployment in agricultural districts, a sudden increase in the price of food following a poor harvest, or cyclical depressions in manufacturing towns could throw able-bodied men onto the poor rate. This baffled contemporaries, who tended to attribute it to idleness, although a more sympathetic observer in 1720 could ask 'whether there is not four or five hundred thousand poor men, women and children in England that want work?', and suggest as a remedy that they should be employed in the fishing industry.[40]

Common soldiers could find themselves on the parish in quite another way, as the unwelcome guests of innkeepers upon whom they were billeted by the government in preference to building barracks. This was done not so much to avoid expense as to disguise the actual size of the army, since soldiers were unpopular and every effort was made by the opposition in parliament to keep their numbers down. The size of the army therefore fluctuated between 8,000 and 17,000 in peacetime, rising to between 35,000 and 74,000 in wartime. The lowest paid soldiers were supposed to receive 3s 6d per week, but deductions for keep often reduced this to a mere sixpence, and anyway most of them were in arrears. They were therefore frequently reduced to a miserable condition, which probably accounts for King's placing them lower in his table even than paupers. Many of them, either unemployable or facing unemployment in post-war depressions, turned to crime when they were demobilized.

It is surprising that King's class of vagrants should be so small, a mere 30,000, in view of the concern among contemporaries that vagrancy was on the increase and the belief entertained by many historians that there was an enormous criminal underworld, especially in London. Yet he was clearly referring to all sorts of rogues and vagabonds in this category, since he defines them as 'gypsies, thieves, beggars, etc.'. Gypsies played a role in such early novels as

*Moll Flanders*, *Joseph Andrews* and *Tom Jones*, while in 1753 the notorious Elizabeth Canning perjured herself by claiming that she had been robbed and confined by gypsies for 28 days. The trial aroused a great deal of popular anger against gypsies. It was in fact a capital offence under sixteenth-century statutes for gypsies to reside in England, until an act of George III's reign, a rare example of the death penalty being removed rather than imposed in the eighteenth century. The laws against other kinds of vagrants, on the other hand, were stiffened by an act of 1744, which defined three types of offenders—idle and disorderly persons; rogues and vagabonds; and incorrigible rogues. The first type were described as people who deserted their families, drunkards who did not provide for their families, people who refused work, and beggars. The second included fencers, strolling players, minstrels, fortune tellers, gamblers, un-licensed pedlars and pretended scholars. The third consisted of offenders who had escaped after apprehension or who had committed a second offence.

The notion that there was a permanent criminal underworld seemed to receive alarming confirmation in the early 1720s with the activities of the Waltham Blacks and Jonathan Wild. In 1723 the Waltham Black Act was thought necessary because 'several ill-designing and disorderly persons have of late associated themselves under the name of Blacks, and entered into confederacies to support and assist one another in stealing and destroying of deer, robbing of warrens and fishponds, cutting down plantations of trees, and other illegal practices and have, in great numbers . . . unlawfully hunted in forests belonging to his majesty, and in the parks of divers of his majesty's subjects.'[41] At his trial in 1725 Jonathan Wild was accused of being 'a confederate with great numbers of highwaymen, pick-pockets, housebreakers, shoplifters and other thieves' with whom 'he had form'd a kind of corporation of thieves'. It was further alleged that he had 'divided the town and country into so many districts, and appointed distinct gangs for each' and 'had under his care and direction several warehouses for receiving and concealing stolen goods, and also a ship for carrying off jewels, watches, and other valuable goods, to Holland'.[42] The belief that crime was being organized on a large scale fired the imaginations of contemporaries and found lasting expression in Gay's *The Beggar's Opera* and Fielding's *The Life of Mr Jonathan Wild the Great*. It also informs the modern comparisons of Wild to Al Capone.

The reality, however, appears to have been very different. On investigation the 'confederacies' and 'gangs' of 'great numbers' shrink into small groups of truly professional criminals and even undergo a metamorphosis into ordinary citizens. There were at most

ten gangs operating in London during Wild's lifetime, with a total
membership of around 150.[43] E. P. Thompson's analysis of the Blacks
has shown that far from being professional criminals they had
respectable occupations: 'a few gentry sympathizers, more substantial farmers, more again of yeomen and tradesmen or craftsmen,
and a few of the poor foresters' in Berkshire; farmers, tradesmen,
labourers and servants in Hampshire. 'Only one of those brought to
trial in either county was accused of a previous criminal record.'[44]

Studies of those convicted of participating in London riots, such as
the demonstrations against the Gin Act of 1736, and of those hanged
at Tyburn, also cast doubt on the existence of an underworld of
professional criminals in this period. Rioting crowds usually turn out
to have been composed principally of journeymen and apprentices.
Those who ended their days on 'Albion's Fatal Tree' also had
identifiable occupations. According to Peter Linebaugh, 'of the
eighteen criminals hanged in 1740, two were gentlemen's servants,
two were agricultural labourers, one was an apprentice butcher, one
a weaver, a plumber, a waterman, a prostitute, a journeyman
butcher, a sailor, a labourer, a bargeman, an apprentice glazier, a
chimney sweep, and a former English teacher in the West Indies
since come to London as a clerk in a merchant trading house.'[45] He
concludes of those hanged at Tyburn during the century, 'they were,
as far as we can tell, of a piece with the London labouring poor as a
whole, heterogeneous and defying a simple classification between the
criminal class and the working class.'[46] Another indication that
crime was a spare-time activity of people otherwise employed, rather
than a full-time career, is the fact that indictments in rural areas
fluctuated according to the price of bread, while in London they were
geared more to involvement in war, demobilization at the end of
hostilities in 1713, 1748 and 1763 being followed by an upsurge in the
metropolitan crime rate.

If it is difficult to characterize the professional and business men of
eighteenth-century England, it is impossible to generalize about
individuals as disparate as the skilled artisan and the landless
cottager. They had not yet acquired a collective consciousness as the
working class. Nor did they produce a body of literature to describe
their attitudes, so that we know little more about their outlook on life
than what was said of them by their superiors. These were scarcely
complimentary, characterizing the labouring classes as 'idle,
extravagant, thankless and impudent'.[47] Impudence or insubordination was regarded as the prime characteristic of domestic
servants, and informs a whole range of literature about them from
Swift's *Directions to Servants* to Townley's *High Life Below Stairs*.
Idleness was held to be the chief vice of journeymen, apprentices and

labourers and the prime cause of pauperism. 'The poor in the manufacturing counties', wrote one observer, 'will never work any more time in general, than is necessary just to live and support their weekly debauches.'[48] In a sermon of 1745 Josiah Tucker claimed that 'the lower class of people' were characterized by 'brutality and insolence, . . . debauchery and extravagance, . . . idleness, irreligion, cursing, and swearing, and contempt of all rule and authority'.[49] Hogarth depicted a popular view of apprentices in his *Industry and Idleness*. Although the industrious apprentice rose to marry his master's daughter, and became lord mayor of London, the drunken, gaming, whoring idle apprentice whom he subsequently sentenced to the gallows, was regarded as being much more typical.

Idleness appears to have been considered a characteristic of urban rather than of rural working men. Husbandmen were regarded as hardworking and healthy, indulging in manly sports and harmless pastimes, while journeymen, apprentices and labourers in towns were depicted as idle and unhealthy, inclined to gamble and frequent cockfights, and addicted to strong drink and whores. In part this was merely a contemporary manifestation of the age-old dichotomy between the country and the city, the pastoral myth becoming ever more powerful as manufacturing centres grew. At another level, however, it represents a real concern to discipline the worker to the demands of urban working routines. Where rural employment fluctuated to the rhythm of the seasons, with cycles of inevitable idleness alternating with bouts of frenzied activity, urban employment was governed by the artificial measure of the clock. Inuring town labourers to the discipline of daily work, let alone of hourly rates, was an increasing problem in the eighteenth century. One obstacle to a disciplined workforce was the prevalence of holidays which had survived the Reformation and regularly punctuated the seasonal routine of the countryside. In towns these were a hindrance to trade which employers wished to reduce. The authorities were prepared to lend a hand. Saunders Welch congratulated the constables of London in 1754 for suppressing fairs, 'whereby eighty days in the year, dedicated to idleness and vice, are happily restored to industry'.[50] But the abolition of official holidays did little to eliminate the unofficial rest days, the 'Saint Mondays' of the working man. It was not until the coming of factories and railways that norms of time and wages could be established at national level, and with them national campaigns to reduce the time and increase the wages which did as much as anything to rouse the working-class consciousness. Until then there could be no working class as such, and those on the bottom rungs of King's table are best termed the lower orders in the social structure under the early Hanoverians.

# 3 Social Change

Describing the social structure of England in the early eighteenth century inevitably presents a static picture of society. To some extent this is reasonable since, in comparison with the demographic, geographical and above all economic dislocations which were to transform English society after 1760, social structure was stable under the first two Georges. Indeed, socially England had changed relatively little since the twelfth century. However, it would be a grotesque distortion to suggest that there was little or no social change between the death of Queen Anne and the accession of George III. On the contrary, many of the changes which occurred after 1760, even the growth of population, were foreshadowed in the previous half century.

On the death of George II there were about six and a half million people in England and Wales, perhaps a million more than there had been at the time of the Glorious Revolution. In the first half of the eighteenth century, therefore, the population was increasing, but it was a modest increase in comparison with that which was to occur towards the end of the century. By the time of the first census in 1801 there were over nine millions living in England and Wales. Clearly, there was no steady rise from 1700 to 1800. What apparently happened was that the overall population expanded quite rapidly between 1690 and 1720, stagnated from 1720 to 1740, and then began to grow again around 1740, until by 1760 the rate of growth was rapidly accelerating.[1]

The reasons for the rise in the population are mysterious. It was, as far as can be seen, a natural growth, and not the result of immigration, since probably as many people left the country as arrived. A natural increase in numbers is due either to higher birth rates or lower death rates, and the rise after 1740 has been attributed to both.

Those who favour a rise in the birth rate as the more significant motor of demographic change attribute it to a lowering of the age of marriage, and to an increase in the married section of society. The mean age of marriage in the seventeenth and early eighteenth centuries was twenty-four for brides and twenty-six for grooms. The evidence for the late eighteenth century, in England at least, is contradictory. Most so far examined does not indicate any significant change in the age structure of marriages, but there is some which suggests that the mean age of brides was lowered. If this were a general phenomenon, as it appears to have been in Ireland at the same time, then it could have materially lengthened the average span of years in which women could conceive, and consequently the number of births per marriage.

Economic considerations were primarily responsible for the deferment of marriage in this period, since couples were expected to be able to maintain themselves and set up their own independent households. The notion that the extended family was the norm in pre-industrial England, still stubbornly entertained by some sociologists, has been exploded as a myth by demographic historians. From the earliest recorded times the nuclear family of husband, wife and children has been far and away the most common unit in western Europe. To maintain this as an economically viable unit meant putting off marriage until sufficient resources had been accumulated. There are signs that better economic opportunities in the period after 1730 encouraged earlier marriages and thus a rise in the birth rate. In this respect it is interesting that fertility was higher in industrial towns and villages than in agricultural parishes.[2]

There might even have been a decrease in the proportion of the nubile but unmarried element in society in the years before 1760. Several commentators in the early eighteenth century expressed concern that marriage was going out of fashion, especially in London. Some blamed it on the availability of whores, others on the expense of supporting a wife and children in the city, and yet others on the vast and increasing number of domestic servants in the capital, who traditionally were not allowed to marry. Later in the century economic deterrents to marriage were less formidable, while it is possible that there was a relaxation of the rules against servants marrying, which would increase the married portion of the population quite considerably. Not that the rise in the birth rate was entirely due to an increase in the number of children born in wedlock, for there seems to have been a rise in the incidence of bastardy during the century. Ludlow's rate of illegitimate births doubled between 1590–1640 and 1748–1755. It seems unlikely that this reflects an actual increase in the rate of illegitimate conceptions, so much as a more relaxed attitude to extramarital conceptions on the part of the authorities. In the seventeenth century mothers of bastards were frequently whipped and ducked, to avoid which women would resort to forced weddings and even infanticide. Although the disciplinary weapons of public humiliation were still available in the eighteenth century, they tended to become rusty, perhaps especially in the anonymity of the growing towns and above all in London.

However attractive the case for an increase in the birth rate might be, as far as England is concerned it can only be judged doubtful. At a time when the birth rate was high it would have taken a spectacular increase to improve it. In the age group twenty-four to forty-nine celibacy among women was low, as low as five per cent in some areas. Between these ages most married women had as many children as it was biologically possible for them to bear, although there is some evidence of family limitation. Since a general decrease in the mean age of marriage of brides cannot yet be shown to have occurred, it seems unlikely that there was enough spare capacity among women of childbearing age to generate a significant increase in overall population.[3]

Consequently, a drop in the death rate rather than a rise in the birth rate seems the more plausible explanation of population increase. The death rate throughout the eighteenth century was horrendous by modern standards. From 1700 to 1749 infant mortality among the aristocracy in the first twelve months after birth was between 165 and 170 per thousand, while among the humbler people who inhabited Colyton in Devon it fell between 162 and 203. Babies in the care of parishes, especially in London, perished at an even more alarming rate. When parliament investigated the problem in St Martin in the Fields in 1715 it was found that about 900 of the 1,200 children born in that parish every year and left in the care of the parochial authorities died shortly after birth. Later in the century these rates eased significantly. Between 1750 and 1774 infant mortality among aristocrats dropped to 102 per thousand, and in Colyton it fell to between 122 and 153. After 1760 the mortality among children abandoned in London was reduced to one in four, possibly a result of the opening of the Foundling Hospital in 1745.

Other hospitals were established under the first two Georges, so that where in 1700 there had been only four general hospitals in England and Wales, two in London, one in Bath and another in Rochester, by 1760 there were at least twenty. Five had made their appearance in London between 1720 and 1745—the Westminster in 1720, Guy's in 1724, St George's in 1733, the London in 1740 and the Middlesex in 1745. Provincial hospitals were founded in Winchester in 1736, Bristol in 1737, York in 1740, Exeter in 1741 and Northampton in 1742. How far these institutions made a positive contribution to public health is a debatable point. Some claimed remarkable cures, Exeter even boasting that it had restored to health two men who had been admitted in their coffins. Historians have been misled by such evidence into seeing hospitals as partly responsible for the declining death rate in the eighteenth century, but this is dubious. Not only did they affect a very limited number of people, but even those admitted were probably in greater danger of contracting a fatal illness within hospital than outside. Certainly there were higher institutional than domicilary death rates until the twentieth century.

Nevertheless, chances of avoiding or surviving serious disease did improve during the period, though not necessarily because of advances in medical science. Some diseases were on the wane, for instance the bubonic plague, which was not known in England after 1667. Influenza, smallpox and typhus continued to ravage the population in the opening years of the eighteenth century and might even have contributed to a net reduction in numbers between 1720 and 1730. After about 1740, however, epidemics waned and some diseases became less deadly. Quite why this was so is not known. The incidence of some diseases was no doubt autonomous, and can only be understood in terms of bacterial biology. For instance, it seems to be agreed that the plague disappeared because the brown rat eliminated the black rat and with it the fleas which carried the disease.[4] But there were some limited medical advances in the treatment of disease. Quinine and bark were effectively used to combat malaria, or ague as it was called. More spectacular was the use of inoculation against smallpox, which was introduced into England around 1720. This was practised on a very wide scale after mid-century, indeed to such an extent that some historians have argued that this alone was enough to account for the increase in population after 1750.

Environmental improvements might have helped the elimination of disease. Better nutrition thanks to a more abundant food supply possibly produced a healthier population, though attempts to prove the reverse by establishing a connection between high food prices and mortality rates have on the whole proved abortive. Moreover, better nutrition would scarcely have affected the mortality rates of the aristocracy, since they were well fed throughout the period, their high protein diets giving rise to a heavy incidence of gout. Yet their chances of surviving their first twelve months also improved significantly during the period. London, despite the dreadful mortality rates of its overcrowded streets, probably became a healthier place to live in as the century progressed and better building materials and more sanitary conditions became more widespread. Then again the Gin Act of 1751, which effectively forced victuallers to be licensed where earlier measures had failed, sharply reduced the amount of gin drinking in the capital and with it a hideous source of demographic control, the elimination of which alone brought down mortality rates.

Even so the death rate in London, and in other towns, remained so high that their populations were not reproducing themselves. The growth in the number of London's inhabitants, therefore, from 575,000 in 1700 to 675,000 in 1750, was due to a remarkably high rate of internal migration. In 1781, 3240 adults were examined in the Westminster General Dispensary, of whom only 824 had been born in London. Of the rest, 1,874 came from England and Wales, 280 from Ireland, 209 from Scotland and 53 from abroad. It seems, not surprisingly, that men were more inclined to migrate than women, for of the Irish 162 were men, as were the same number of Scots, and 40 of the foreigners were male. There is no way of knowing how representative a sample of patients examined at the Dispensary would be, but by any test the proportion of London's population which had migrated there must have been great. In 1757 George Burrington thought it 'very probable that two thirds of the grown persons at any time in London come from distant parts', while 'not above one in twenty of shop and alehousekeepers and labourers living in the bills of mortality were either born or served their apprenticeships in town.'[5] According to a modern estimate as many as one in six of the total population of England and Wales spent some part of their lives in the capital.

This rate of geographical mobility might seem incredible in a country whose inhabitants lived mainly in scattered village communities. London was a giant: no other town in Britain and few in Europe approached it in size. In 1700 only about seven towns in England could count their populations in tens of thousands— Colchester, Exeter, Newcastle upon Tyne, Yarmouth and York, with between 10,000 and 15,000 inhabitants; Bristol with around 20,000; and Norwich with about 30,000. Below these were about twenty-five towns with a population of between 5,000 and 10,000, which included such growing commercial and industrial centres as Birmingham, Hull, Leeds, Liverpool and Manchester. Then there were over forty towns with a population of between 2,000 and 5,000. However, the total number of people living in the eighty or so towns with over 2,000 inhabitants was less than the population of London. Over three quarters of all Englishmen lived in the countryside.

There was some urban expansion between 1700 and 1760. Indeed some towns grew quite rapidly, so that by mid-century there were at least fourteen towns with over 10,000 inhabitants, Birmingham, Coventry, Leeds, Liverpool, Manchester, Nottingham and Sheffield being added to those which were that size in 1700. A visitor to Birmingham in 1755 called it 'another London in miniature'.[6] John Dyer in his poem *The Fleece* observed in 1757:

> Th'increasing walls of busy Manchester
> Sheffield and Birmingham whose redd'ning fields
> Rise and enlarge their suburbs.

Liverpool prospered from the expansion of trade, especially with Ireland and North America, which also added between five and ten thousand people to the population of Bristol and helped Whitehaven to increase from about 4,000 in 1713 to 9,063 in 1762. The others grew because of the expansion of industry, which also stimulated growth in other towns, such as Leicester, whose population increased from 6,000 in 1713 to 8,000 by 1730. The expansion of industrial centres in this period begins to indicate the pattern of the modern map of urban England. Yet it was only a start. By 1750 the population of town dwellers was still not more than a quarter of the whole and most Englishmen lived in villages with at very most a few hundred inhabitants.

However, the view of villages in the pre-industrial age as stable communities in which the same families lived and died generation after generation is another myth like that of the extended family which, though still preserved by some sociologists, has not survived the researches of social historians. Their investigations have shown that, far from being fixed and stable, villages in early modern England had surprisingly fluid populations. Cardington in Bedfordshire offers a striking example. In 1782 there were 109 families living there, of whom only seven had parents who were both born in it, fifty-one had both parents from another parish, while two thirds of the men and nearly three quarters of the women had been born elsewhere. So far from it being the rule that people lived and died in the community into which they were born, it appears to have been the exception. Sixty-four per cent of the boys and fifty-seven per cent of the girls left Cardington before they were fifteen. For most of them this meant only a move into a nearby parish for employment or marriage. But for over a quarter it meant that they migrated out of Bedfordshire, mostly to London.

Although such a high rate of geographic mobility might at first sight appear surprising for this period, on reflection the notion that pre-industrial communities were more stable than modern societies is not, to say the least, self-evident. The system of primogeniture among most of the propertied classes almost dictated that younger sons would have to seek their fortune outside the community into which they had been born. Farmers and clergymen were famous for sending their children into the service of the gentry, which meant a move away from home. Indeed, the system of apprenticeship and domestic service took the sons and daughters of the middle and even of the lower classes away. Moreover, husbandmen and domestic servants, the main labour force of the period, could find it infinitely more easy to move around in search of work than industrial workers whose skills are only relevant in limited regions. As Defoe observed, there was a substantial number of migrant agricultural labourers in Hornsey, Essex, where 'if they did not hire our north and west country people, who in the season travel for harvest work, all the inhabitants could not mow half their grass.'[7] The notion of servants as old family retainers who served one household all their lives was also at odds with the facts. Sir Roger de Coverley's loyal retinue in his ancestral hall would strike readers of the *Spectator*, probably intentionally, as quaintly archaic and paternalistic. John Macdonald, who rose from being a postillion to become a gentleman's gentleman, was much more typical in moving from master to master.[8] The turnover of servants in London was so prodigious that the first employment exchanges, known as registry offices, were set up to deal with it.

At one time it was held that the people who migrated to towns had been forced off the land by the enclosure movement. Among contemporaries who held this view was Oliver Goldsmith, who insisted that he had seen his *Deserted Village* within a day's walk of London and not in his native Ireland, as his critics would have it. Another was the author of *A Proposal for a free and unexpensive election of parliament men* which appeared in 1753. Despite its title this was really an argument that enclosures were depopulating the countryside, especially in Northamptonshire which, it claimed, had 'at least fourscore thousand inhabitants less or fewer than otherwise there would have been had the same ground been kept in constant tillage and the inhabitants had been employed in open fields as formerly'. Modern economic historians of the 'pessimistic' school have argued similarly if rather more cautiously. Where enclosure encroached on the common or waste or converted the use of agricultural land from tillage to pasture, there was indeed some disruption of the population. However, unlike the enclosure movement of the sixteenth century, most enclosed land was used for arable in this period. Since traditional methods of arable farming, which were labour intensive, persisted until the coming of machinery, the demand for labour cannot have fallen in agricultural districts. On the contrary, there appears to have been an increase in the numbers of people employed on the land and, while in some areas older communities disappeared, in others they expanded and there were even new villages settled.

Those who went to towns, therefore, were not the unwilling

victims of improving capitalist landlords depicted in some of the more lurid studies of the period. It appears that, far from swelling the army of town labourers because they had been evicted from the countryside and had nowhere else to go, they migrated to towns because they were attracted by the higher wages paid there. Furthermore, workers in industry moved from town to town in pursuit of higher wages. One writer observed in 1752, 'We daily see manufacturers leaving the places where wages are low and removing to others where they can get more money.' At that time the highest wages were in London and the lowest in the west country, while northern workers were slowly gaining ground on those in the west and closing the gap between themselves and workers in London. In time this process was to lead to a redistribution of population—more heavily concentrated in the midlands and the north and relatively less dense in the south away from London.

The main legal deterrent to migration were the acts against vagrancy, the strictest of which was the Act of Settlement of 1662. This laid down that those likely to become a charge on the poor rate could be moved back from parish to parish until they returned to one where they had a settlement. People could claim a settlement if they had been born in a parish or had lived in one forty days. Such legislation led Adam Smith to conclude that 'it is often more difficult for a poor man to pass the artificial boundaries of a parish than an arm of the sea or a ridge of high mountains.'[9] But its effectiveness seems to have been minimal, and Henry Fielding was so convinced of this that he proposed a much more stringent system whereby magistrates would be empowered to issue passes to 'all labourers or servants or persons of low degree' for journeys over six miles from their habitations. The punishment for travelling without a valid pass was whipping and hard labour. He lamented that such a scheme would be opposed as 'derogatory of their liberty' and he was right. Even the statutory restrictions on migration which existed were not enforced because they were held to be too repressive. The law could not stop geographical any more than social mobility.[10]

Movement up and down the rungs of the social ladder is if anything harder to plot than the degree to which people moved about the country. Since far more is known about the landed gentry than any other class, attention has concentrated on whether it was easier, harder or presented much the same difficulty to rise into, or for that matter drop out of, the landowning elite in this period than it had been in earlier centuries. Among the middle classes there is some evidence for entry into various trades and professions in the form of stamp duties paid for apprenticeships. Below that level the evidence is piecemeal, being mainly biographical or literary in character, so that in general next to nothing is really known about the possibilities of climbing from the bottom of society to the level of an artisan. The administration of the poor law, however, tells us something about those who finished up at the bottom.

It was on the whole harder to enter the charmed circle of the aristocracy. Although the attempt to freeze the number of noble families by the peerage bill of 1719 failed when the measure was defeated in the Commons, its spirit was more or less respected by the first two Georges. Very few men were ennobled between 1714 and 1760, barely enough to keep pace with extinctions. This helped to preserve the nobility as a separate estate of the realm and even strengthened its prestige almost as a caste in early Hanoverian England.

Mobility within the landed class as a whole presents a pattern of such rich diversity that confident generalizations are now at a discount. This was not the situation a few years ago. Indeed the historians of changes in landownership between 1690 and 1760 could then look down smugly on their colleagues working in the period 1540 to 1640, for it seemed that while the storm over whether the gentry were rising or falling in the century before the civil war was creating a blizzard of confusion, the pattern for the century following the Revolution was crystal clear. They saw in the eighteenth century the consolidation of the large estates, an increase in the size and number of tenant farms, and a corresponding decline in the ranks of the lesser gentry and freeholders. The land market, it was claimed, was dominated by the large landowners, with relatively less activity in it on the part of non-landed elements, especially merchants, compared to the previous century.

Plausible explanations of these phenomena were confidently supplied. Legal changes during the seventeenth century, such as the strict settlement and the equity of redemption, made it harder to break up big landownings and easier to obtain long-term loans on the security of landed property. Money from mortgages could even be used to purchase property and thereby increase holdings. This helped the larger landowners, who were also able to augment their incomes from non-landed sources, such as government office, marriage and investments in the stock market. Such insurances against a depression in the landed economy were not available to smaller landowners, who had only income from rents to maintain them. After 1690 these revenues were hard hit. Rents at best remained static, at worst declined. Arrears of rent had to be written off in bad years, such as 1695–8 and 1708–10, when harvest failures made tenants unable to pay. Although rents rose between 1720 and

1730, they stagnated again between 1730 and 1750, when bumper harvests lowered prices and caused an agricultural depression. Once more landowners had to relieve their tenants of the burden, and the smaller landowners were less able to do this. Finally the land tax, fixed at four shillings in the pound for most of the period 1692–1713, meant a twenty per cent tax on rental income, the heaviest rate of direct taxation before the twentieth century.

These adverse conditions forced many smaller landowners into selling. Virtually the only willing buyers were the aristocracy and substantial gentry, since others traditionally active on the land market, such as lawyers and merchants, were attracted by the much higher return on their investments offered by the newly established market in government securities. Of non-landed buyers, only government officials and those at the top of the legal profession were active in the land market. Hard evidence to sustain these generalizations was adduced from the pattern of landownership in Bedfordshire, Northamptonshire and a few other counties, principally Kent and Sussex.

Then, just as the 'storm over the gentry' blew itself out, with the participants as much as the topic exhausted, the peace of the economic historians of Augustan England was disturbed by dissentient views. First, the plausibility of the explanations was challenged. For one thing, the strict settlement was by no means universal: at most only half the estates of England were subject to trustees for contingent remainders, who saw that the property survived intact for at least three generations so that a son's depredations could not impair the estate for a grandson. Again, the notion that mortgages could be used to finance the purchase of more land would not have occurred to many landowners, since the interest payable to the scrivener would be more than the return on the investment, a sure recipe for financial suicide. Government office might have made some landowners immensely wealthy, but it could, by its nature, be a source of wealth only to a few. Before 1720 it was a very precarious form of income, given the rapid political changes of the reigns of William and Anne, while after 1720 only the great whig families profited from office. Even these could find it a mixed blessing. Although Walpole undoubtedly waxed rich as prime minister, the duke of Newcastle found the expenses of keeping up his political interest more than his income from his high positions and nearly bankrupted himself. Marriage could be a prudent investment, but it depended on the offspring produced and on the longevity of the couple concerned. A brood of daughters could cause the asset of a wife's portion to become the debit of providing theirs. A long-lived widow entitled to a handsome jointure could become a financial liability on the estate. Such vagaries of demographic chance could not be anticipated in the most well-drawn marriage agreement. As for investment in the stock market, any confidence in the higher yield of paper securities was quickly destroyed by the bursting of the South Sea Bubble in 1720, when many large landowners lost heavily. It has been argued that the Bubble was 'a peculiarly dangerous trap for landowners, as more sophisticated speculators moved to convert their gains into first class long-term loans, secured on landed property'.[11] The land tax was by no means uniform in its incidence. It might have been levied at the full rate in the south east, an area heavily drawn upon to support the general thesis; but away from London, the home counties and East Anglia the real rate fell, so that in Westmorland and Cumberland four shillings in the pound realized about nine or ten pence. Finally, although land might have been less attractive as an economic investment than the stock market in the years 1690 to 1720, men bought estates in this as in any other period not only for a profitable return on capital but also for the social status it conferred, and this powerful sociological factor operated on professional and business men to sustain their interest in the land market throughout the period.

Not only were general doubts cast upon the plausibility of the explanations offered for the thesis that land drifted to the larger landowners in this period, but a number of local studies revealed a different pattern from that extrapolated mainly from the south and east. Thus Professor Hughes pointed out in 1938 that in the north east 'many ancient families, the Blenkinsops of Bellister, the Radcliffes of Redheugh, the Riddells of Shipcote, to mention only a few, mortgaged and later sold piecemeal their ancestral lands.'[12] Much of the land sold passed not to the bigger landowners in the area but to men who had made their money from coal and trade. More recent studies of Lincolnshire and Staffordshire also cast doubts upon the universality of the pattern established for the south east. In Lincolnshire there was a lively land market in the eighteenth century in which lesser landowners, local professional and business men, and London merchants all played a part along with the larger landlords. On the Leveson-Gower estates in Staffordshire there was indeed an increase in the size of farms, but this was not accompanied by the decline of the small landowner. On the contrary, there was a significant increase in the number of smallholdings. Finally a study of Cumbria has demonstrated rather paradoxically that while in the north west the pattern of landownership conforms by and large to that established for the southeast, hardly any of the explanations adduced in support of the general thesis holds good for Cumberland and Westmorland. The strict settlement was relatively rare, mort-

gages could break as well as make families, few Cumbrian landowners enjoyed government office, the land tax was the lowest in the
country between 1690 and 1712, and rents rose steadily between
1720 and 1740.[13]

This regional diversity makes it impossible to discuss English
landownership in general during this period. To a large extent the
social history of England in any period is the sum of its local histories,
and this is very true of landed society in the eighteenth century.
Whether a family rose or fell probably depended more on the
vagaries of individual family history than on any general social or
economic trends anyway. A spendthrift heir could run down the
family patrimony at a prodigal rate, as Frank Delaval of Seaton
Delaval proved when he spent a fortune on riotous parties in
Northumberland and loose living in London. The Delavals were only
saved from total disaster by the death of Frank and the succession of
his brother, a much more businesslike man, who not only wrote off
Frank's debts but built up the family's interests until he was
established as one of the wealthiest men in the northeast.

However, a few generalizations might be hazarded to conclude
this discussion of landed society. In comparison with the upheavals of
the seventeenth and nineteenth centuries it does appear that times
were more stable for the landed estate. Relatively few large
landowners sold in these years. Some of those who did so, like the earl
of Leicester, parted with outlying properties in order to concentrate
on building up the main estate. Certainly, the trend seems to have
been towards consolidation of holdings. Enclosures facilitated the
creation of large farms, though this did not necessarily mean the
breakup of smallholdings. There was a tendency for lawyers and
merchants to buy small estates in the vicinity of towns where they
continued to carry on their businesses, using the country house as a
leisure retreat. This trend is observable around London, Leeds, Hull,
Glasgow and Whitehaven. It was extended during the period as
communications improved, so that by mid-century it could be
observed of London that 'the improvement of the roads near this
metropolis, and the increasing conveniencies of conveyances to all
the villages around it . . . [enabled] great numbers who have business
to transact in London to come there for this purpose during a few
hours only of the day, and to retire into the country in the evening,
which is become a general practice.'[14] The commuting businessman
had arrived.

Land, indeed, was only one form of investment for many
businessmen, though an increasingly popular one after 1720 when
the bursting of the Bubble shattered confidence in the funds and led
investors to diversify their holdings. The surplus resources of the cloth

merchants of Leeds 'were allocated to various ventures. One year
government stock might appear the most attractive investment, three
years later a few closes of land in Leeds might seem the soundest
speculation.'[15] Hull merchants invested in the funds, in turnpikes, in
town property and in land. Land was often bought as a short-term as
well as a long-term investment. The attraction of becoming country
gentlemen does not appear to have held out an immediate appeal for
these men. The Leeds merchants remained essentially businessmen
with landed property until the end of the century, when they did sell
their business interests and retire to estates in the West Riding. Hull
merchants held out a little longer, few moving 'from staith to estate in
the eighteenth century', though they followed the same route into the
East Riding and Lincolnshire countryside during the nineteenth
century.[16] The Glasgow tobacco lords, by contrast, though they
invested heavily in land around the city, stayed in trade and did not
become country gentlemen. It seems as though the drive to move
from trade into the ownership of a country estate was to some extent
less compulsive during the eighteenth century than it had been
earlier, perhaps because merchants were enjoying more social esteem
than in previous centuries.

Entry into the business and professional worlds was usually by way
of an apprenticeship, a system which reflects a measure of both
downward and upward mobility—downward because the younger
sons of landed gentlemen were provided for in this way, upward
because apprentices were by no means confined to the sons of
gentlemen and merchants. There were, however, differential premiums, which made it easier for the gentry and middle classes to
apprentice their sons to some trades and professions than it was for
fathers of lower birth. Apprenticeship fees for the houses of Leeds
cloth merchants varied from £40 to £450. Few below the rank of
gentleman could have afforded the £250 which Sir Arthur Kaye paid
to William Cookson for his son Robert in 1715. In Hull, on the other
hand, there seems to have been a decline in gentry recruitment into
the merchant houses during the century, and mercantile apprentices
came increasingly from business families and even lower, including
the sons of clerks and master mariners. London houses on the whole
charged more than the Leeds and Hull firms. Samuel Whitbread
paid £300 to be apprenticed to a brewer, while the premium for a
banker in 1755 was £600. On the other hand some country
tradesmen charged a good deal less. Jedediah Strutt started out as a
wheelwright's apprentice for a premium of only £10. Premiums for
the profession also varied, between apothecaries and attorneys for
example, the lawyers charging more, and between London, other
towns and the country. Clerks to attorneys, who were apprenticed for

a minimum of five years, paid anything from £20 to a country attorney to £525 to a London lawyer. While the higher fees were beyond the reach of any but the gentry, the smaller premiums were within the means of quite humble men.

The system of apprenticeship, therefore, acted as a bridge between the upper and lower classes. It was possible for a self-made man to rise very high through business. William Cotesworth, who started out as an impoverished apprentice to a tallow chandler ended as a substantial landowner in the northeast with the title of esquire. His trading interests extended from Tyneside to Cumberland, down the east coast of England and across the North Sea. There were few commodities he was not prepared to handle. He also became a leading figure in the coal trade of the northeast, and the biggest manufacturer of salt in the region. Josiah Wedgwood started from nothing and died worth £500,000. Robert Darling started out as a boy looking after cows, was apprenticed to a lapidary, became a very wealthy London merchant, received a knighthood, entered parliament and died with extensive property. Banking brought fortunes to a few families, such as the Childs and the Hoares. But such achievements were relatively rare. The author of a study of the merchant community of Hull was led to conclude that 'rags to riches in one generation is little more than a comforting myth.'[17]

Business could be very hazardous in this period too, and contemporaries were much struck by the rapidity with which people could move down as well as up the ladder in trade, especially in London. 'Here are continually such ups and downs or various turns of fortune', wrote one, 'that the winds and waves are not more uncertain than the circumstances of the merchants and tradesmen of the City of London.'[18] The vicissitudes of fortune, buoying people up one day and breaking them the next, forms one of the major themes in the novels of the period, from *Robinson Crusoe* to *Roderick Random*. Crusoe and Random had their counterparts in real life. Defoe himself knew what it was to go bankrupt, and was known as a 'broken hosier'. Bankruptcies were common items in the newspapers—160 were reported in *The Gentleman's Magazine* in 1731. Defoe lamented 'that there are so many bankrupts and broken tradesmen now among us, more than ever were known before.'[19] Banking broke as well as made men, about a third of the London banks going under at the time of the South Sea Bubble. As on the land, whether individuals fared well or ill would depend upon accidents of personality to a large extent. However, there were more impersonal forces at work, forces which some were inclined to call providence, making trade more hazardous than farming. Business cycles are discernible in some industries, and the adverse effects of wars in others. Silk manufacture seems to have been exceptionally prone to changes in demand. Even a death at court, plunging polite society into mourning, could have an immediate and disastrous effect on Spitalfields. Yet on the whole, increasing affluence probably weighted the scales more towards prospering and advancing than towards failure and descending in trade as the period progressed.

The professions may have offered a safer and more stable career, not leading to dazzling riches but not running the same risk of bankruptcy either. There were some stories of great advancement through the professions. John Radcliffe, the son of the governor of a house of correction and called base born by his enemies, graduated MD at Oxford and rose to be perhaps the richest doctor in the century at the time of his death in 1714, when he left a fortune to endow the Radcliffe Infirmary, Camera and Observatory. Dudley Ryder, son of a linen draper in Cheapside, climbed via the law to become attorney general and eventually Baron Ryder of Harrowby. Thomas Clarke, the son of a carpenter, became master of the rolls. Sir Cloudesley Shovel went from being a cabin boy to become an admiral. Such men would have found it harder to ascend the hierarchy of the army or the church, where promotion was still much more dependent upon birth or patronage than upon merit. They were anyway exceptional. The professions generally offered the sons of tradesmen the prospect of moving a rung or two up the social ladder and did not escalate many from the lower to the upper class.

Mobility below the business and professional classes is an unknown factor. A handful of characters emerged from total obscurity to a comfortable place in society. Few men can have risen as far as Stephen Duck, who from being a thresher in a barn at four shillings and sixpence a week became a state pensioner of £30 a year, with house provided. Another Wiltshire man who rose to comfort by way of his writings was Thomas Chubb, son of a Salisbury maltster, whose tracts on deism earned him an annual salary from Sir Joseph Jekyll. Domestic service was a means whereby many moved from poverty to a respected occupation, though John Macdonald was perhaps exceptional in progressing from being an abandoned child to a gentleman's gentleman. Prostitution brought a few from abject poverty to the highest circles in the land, as Sally Salisbury demonstrated when she rose from being the daughter of a bankrupt bricklayer turned common soldier to be the mistress of several peers of the realm. But if we are to believe moralizing tracts of the times, the oldest profession was a route which much more frequently degraded the daughters of tradesmen and even gentlemen, until they became outcasts and derelicts of society, ending their days on the streets if not the gallows.

Rather more is known about those who tumbled to the bottom of the ladder, or rather their reception on arrival, because of the administration of the poor law. Precisely how many fell on the parish system is unknown, though contemporaries were certain that the numbers were rising. They tended to express concern by estimating the amount of money raised by the poor rate rather than the numbers who benefited from it. In 1695 it was estimated at £665,302. During the 1750s there were various guesses, ranging from £1,000,000 to £3,500,000. The fact was that nobody really knew, though the House of Commons probably got somewhere near the truth when it calculated the yield at £1,720,316 in 1776. This reflected an absolute rise in the number of recipients of poor relief, and almost certainly a relative one too, given that the increase in the amount was far greater than the growth of the population, while as far as can be ascertained there was no rise in the amount spent *per capita*. On the contrary, contemporaries adopted a variety of means to reduce this, which made for some interesting changes in the treatment of the problem of poverty during the period.

A popular device was the workhouse. In 1697 Bristol obtained a private act whereby its parishes were incorporated in order to provide a common workhouse, and this precedent was followed soon after by ten other provincial towns. These developments led in 1723 to the passing of a general act empowering parishes to acquire workhouses and to contract out their duty of providing for the poor. As a result of this legislation, about 110 workhouses came into being, fifty of them in London, as well as an entrepreneur who undertook to manage the new schemes, one Matthew Marryot. Marryot appears as the manager of workhouses in Buckinghamshire, St Giles, Greenwich, Luton and Peterborough. His appeal to these and to other parishes which adopted his measures was quite simply that he brought down the poor rate. Spectacular examples of this feat were reported to popularize his methods. St Albans reduced its rates from 6s in the pound in 1720 to 2s 6d by 1724, and its disbursements over the same period from £506 to £200. These rates seem to have been very high. At Olney in Buckinghamshire, where Marryot was directly in charge, he brought them down from 3s 9d to 1s 9d. At Rumford in Essex the impact of a workhouse was to bring the rate down from 1s 6d to 1s.[20]

Marryot and his supporters made no bones about the reasons for these results. For instance, the Maidstone workhouse report, which is fairly representative, claimed that:[21]

> The advantage of a workhouse does not only consist in this, that the poor are maintained at less than half the expense which their weekly pay amounted to, but that very great numbers of lazy people, rather than submit to the confinement and labour of the workhouse, are content to throw off the mask, and maintain themselves by their own industry.

This reaction is not surprising in view of the regimen imposed on the poor in these establishments. St Giles's workhouse, an institution run by Marryot, published its rules and orders in 1726. Inmates had to be in bed by nine in summer and eight in winter. The beds were in dormitories, separated according to age and sex. Boys and girls slept three in a bed, adults two in a bed. They were obliged to attend church on Sunday, on pain of missing supper for the first offence, and six months' confinement in the house for the second.[22] Such conditions were deliberately intended to be a deterrent, as the Rumford workhouse readily admitted:[23]

> The advantage of the workhouse to the parish does not arise from what the poor people can do towards their subsistence, but from the apprehensions the poor have of it. These prompt them to exert, and do their utmost to keep themselves off the parish, and render them exceedingly averse to submit to come into the house, till extreme necessity compels them. Pride, though it does ill become poor folks, won't suffer some to wear the badges; others cannot brook confinement and a third sort deem the workhouse to be a mere stable of slavery, and so numbers are kept out.

As F. M. Eden observed at the end of the century, 'the way in which these workhouses, on their first establishment, effected a reduction in parochial expenditure, was by deterring the poor from making applications for relief.'[24] Thus at Beverley, where there had been 116 on outdoor relief before the construction of a workhouse, there were only twenty-six resident within it in the year 1727–8. Not only were numbers drastically reduced, but the amount spent on each recipient of poor relief was also curtailed. At Hampstead, for instance, amounts paid directly to the poor varied from 2s 6d to 3s 6d a week; after a workhouse was built the maintenance of each resident worked out at 2s per week.

These schemes reflect a hardening of attitudes towards the poor. The act of 1723 fits in with a whole range of other measures adopted in the 1720s which demonstrate a more ruthless approach to social problems on the part of the ruling class. Charity was at the very interface between the propertied classes and the dispossessed in early modern England. Under the Tudors and early Stuarts a paternalistic attitude had prevailed, institutionalizing public charity with the poor laws and conspicuously bestowing private charities. Under the later Stuarts, and especially under the early Hanoverians, a less philanthropic attitude was adopted. The administration of the poor law was tightened up, with the excuse that it had kept the poor idle but in the interests of reducing the amount spent on poor relief. The springs of private charity also began to run out. Indiscriminate alms-giving was deplored by such writers as Defoe and Addison as a misplaced paternalism which aggravated rather than relieved poverty. Even discriminating charity was circumscribed. The pro-portion of bequests outside the family left in wills shrank significantly between 1650 and 1750. The Charitable Corporation, set up to lend small sums of money to the poor at ten per cent interest, collapsed in 1732 owing to the fraudulent practices of its administrators, one of whom was alleged to have said 'damn the poor.' Frauds in charities of this kind, according to the chaplain of the new Winchester hospital, were 'grown so general that the very foundations of charity have been almost dried up.'[25]

There are a few signs that the poor did not just acquiesce in the hardening of attitudes towards them. Throughout the period there was a struggle for control of certain parish vestries, and with it the power to choose the churchwardens and overseers of the poor rate. In rural areas the local gentry were in control of the vestries. In populous parishes, however, the grip of the propertied classes on the parochial machinery was often challenged from below. It was alleged in 1742 that in many London parishes 'the lower sort of people' had 'acquired the whole power of electing and perpetuating themselves in office'. In other heavily populated parishes a struggle raged, but where the victory went to the lower sort 'in the stead of substantial householders, according to the real intention of the law, you have a continual succession of mean people in office.' These shifted the incidence of the poor rate from habitations to land, since for the purposes of assessment land was rated at a higher valuation than buildings. Consequently a rate of, say, four shillings in the pound fell four times as heavily on land as on shops, tenements and other premises. Some churchwardens were accused of overlooking pay-ments from meaner habitations to keep up an interest against the next election of parish officers. Thus many parishes were a battleground where annual conflict broke out between those who had an interest in keeping the poor rate down and those who sought to keep it up.[26]

This was not a class war, for as yet there was no coherent and conscious working class, and therefore there could be no national campaign with regular pitched battles. There were, however, sporadic struggles throughout the period—here a riot, there a strike.

Riots were occasioned by a variety of stimuli, political, religious, social and economic. Between the Sacheverell riots of 1710 and the 'Wilkes and liberty' riots of the 1760s there were no large-scale political upheavals; but there were demonstrations by Jacobite crowds in various centres, especially in the opening years of George I's reign. Riots on the king's coronation day in Bedford, Birmingham, Chippenham, Norwich and Reading, violent scenes at the polls in Brentford, Bristol, Cambridge, Hertford, Leicester and Taunton in the general election of 1715, and constant disturbances in Oxford, led to the passing of the Riot Act in 1715. Thereafter those in a crowd of twelve or more could be found guilty of a capital offence if they did not disperse within one hour of being commanded to do so by the authorities. The framers of the Riot Act assumed that political demonstrations were the work of a few active ringleaders, who stirred up a mob which otherwise would not have acted spontaneously. This was a typical reaction to crowd activity at the time, which was alleged to be the result of discontented upper-class elements inducing the lower orders by bribes or threats to demonstrate. Thus a mythical 'Captain Tom' was purported to be the leader of political mobs throughout the period, where in fact no real 'Captain Tom' was ever identified, much less apprehended. Despite the beliefs of those above them, and of some historians, the 'lower orders' were quite capable of mounting spontaneous demonstrations about any and every conceivable grievance. Between 1715 and 1760 popular demonstrations against the government were relatively rare, though riotous crowds assembled in London after the bursting of the South Sea Bubble, and there were turbulent protests against the attempt to regulate the trade in spiritous liquors with the Gin Act of 1736. Rather more serious riots were occasioned by the Militia Act of 1757. These were provoked by the requirement that parish constables should draw up lists of men eligible for service in the newly constituted militia, and the main targets of the protesters were the constables and their lists. Between 1757 and 1761 there were serious riots on this score in at least fourteen counties. Although religious feeling did not inspire riots on the scale of the Sacheverell or Gordon Riots of 1710 and 1780, there were attacks on dissenting chapels and catholics throughout the period. The gin riots of 1736 coincided with violent demonstrations against Irish workmen. Thereafter the methodists became a prime target for mobs.

In comparison with political and religious demonstrations, little is known of social protests such as riots against enclosures or turnpikes. There is, however, reason to believe that these increased as the period progressed and the enclosure movement and turnpike mania both gathered force. Some of the most serious demonstrations against a turnpike occurred in Leeds and Wakefield in 1753, while the largest anti-enclosure riot took place at Shaw Hill, Wiltshire, in 1758.

Riots induced by increases in the price of bread, on the other hand, have attracted a great deal of attention. They were especially severe in the years 1727, 1740 and 1756–7. In 1727 tin miners plundered granaries in Falmouth. In 1740 hungry crowds protested against the high prices of bread in many scattered places and especially in Northumberland, Durham, Yorkshire and Wales. In 1756–7 the protests were if anything even more widespread, being reported as far apart as Berwick upon Tweed and Taunton. These were not just gut reactions, but the expression of a traditional 'moral economy' which sought to fix the price of bread in times of dearth below the 'natural' level that uncontrolled market forces would allow it to reach.

Although attempts to control prices were more characteristic of the labouring poor in the eighteenth century than the pursuit of higher wages, there were also strikes over wage rates in this period. The keelmen of Newcastle upon Tyne, for example, struck in 1719, 1744 and 1750. On the first occasion the authorities intervened with a regiment of soldiers and a warship. There were also riots in Wiltshire in 1738 by textile workers protesting at reductions in their wages; this ended with three being executed at Salisbury, though their example did not deter sporadic outbreaks of discontent from west country weavers for many years after 1738.

More constructive steps were taken to safeguard or improve the standard of living of workers in several industries at this time. It is during this period that friendly societies and even primitive trade unions make their appearance. The shoemakers of Newcastle upon Tyne formed a friendly society in 1719, and there was a general friendly society there in 1731. The wool-combers of Tiverton had a common stock for their old and sick colleagues. At St Albans a confraternity paid 3*d* a week each, which enabled them 'to maintain their members disabled for work through accidents, sickness or old age, and allow them seven shillings a week'.[27] Attempts to improve wages by such combinations, however, were firmly resisted. When 7,000 journeymen tailors assembled in London in 1721 to demand higher pay and shorter hours, an act was passed declaring such associations illegal.

Economic trends rather than industrial organization helped the labouring classes, along with most others, to experience a better standard of living after 1730. The agricultural depression which set in for the next twenty years or so brought food prices down, and this left a surplus over income for all but the destitute. Even the lowest could afford to indulge in gin, and what has been called an orgy of spirit drinking, vividly depicted by Hogarth, broke out in London in these years. A foreign visitor expressed his disgust with 'the lowest class of English', whom he found 'very brutish and barbarous, much of the nature of their bull dogs . . . much addicted to drunkenness, it being common to see them, both men and women, wallowing in the

streets and dying drunk'.[28] By 1757 the worst was over, and George
Burrington could claim that 'we do not see the hundredth part of
poor wretches drunk in the streets . . . as before.'[29] The surest sign of
increasing affluence at a higher level is the spate of moralizing tracts
expressing horror at the rise of luxury. 'Butlers, valets and grooms of
chambers', complained one in 1747, 'are become such fine gentlemen
that there is not one in eight without his gold watch and velvet
breeches.' As for shopkeepers, they were to be 'seen with their long
wigs and swords, velvet breeches and hunting caps, rather than with
their own hair bands and aprons as was formerly the figure they
made'.[30] Another tract was incensed because 'a tradesman of the
meanest rank' owned 'nothing less than gilt china ware, silver plate
and choice of foreign wines'.[31] Among the professional classes coaches
had become a status symbol, and where formerly they had been
rarely seen they now caused traffic jams in London streets.

Another manifestation of increasing affluence was the growth of
services which catered for leisure, or idleness as the moralists called it.
Entertainment became an industry in the eighteenth century, its
growth spearheaded by the spread of popular literature. The first
daily newspaper was born in London in 1702, and the first daily
magazine, the *Spectator*, made its debut in 1711. By 1760 there were
four daily London papers, and six which appeared three times a
week. Between 1714 and 1760 the numbers of provincial papers rose
from under ten to over thirty-five. It is debatable when the novel
arrived, but it established itself in the 1740s with the success of
Fielding and Richardson. Such literature found a readership among
merchants, tradesmen and craftsmen. Indeed it went further down
the social scale, though how far is a question involving the spread of
literacy and the economics of purchasing published matter in this
period.

The two main indications of the spread of literacy are the provision
of schools and the ability to sign marriage registers. There was no
educational system as such, but a number of different institutions
providing haphazard opportunities for children, largely dependent
on sex since most were for boys, and rank. The public schools of Eton,
Harrow, Westminster and Winchester catered for those who could
afford them, which included substantial farmers, lawyers and
merchants as well as the aristocracy and gentry. Sons of the more
affluent middle classes might well have been more in evidence than
those of peers or country gentlemen, since the landed classes sought to
have at least their heirs educated by private tutors. Grammar
schools, many in existence since the sixteenth century, catered for the
less substantial gentry and middle classes, and even well-to-do

tradesmen. Middle-class dissenters sent their sons to denominational academies. Below this level educational provision varied. Some parishes provided free instruction for poor children, especially if they had been orphaned or abandoned, while a number of charity schools were established with the particular aim of educating even the poorest children. In addition to these institutions there were at every level of society private schools, many very small, which charged fees ranging from several pounds at country boarding schools and at academies like Dr Newcombe's at Hackney to 6*d* or even 2*d* a week at dame schools. To what extent educational provision expanded in the period is questionable. Some historians argue that there was a charity school movement in the first half of the eighteenth century which established hundreds of schools throughout the country and made an enormous impact on popular education. But the evidence for this is very dubious, since many of the schools attributed to the so-called movement had in fact been in existence before it began. On the other hand, there is little doubt that private schools of all kinds proliferated during the course of the century, as advertisements for them in provincial newspapers testify.

How far educational provision raised literacy levels is another question, which can only be tentatively answered with the help of marriage registers. Lord Hardwicke's marriage act of 1753 was primarily designed to stop clandestine unions, to prevent which it insisted on due consent, publication and registration before a couple could be legally recognized as married. Making an entry in a marriage register thereby became obligatory, even if it was only a mark and not a signature, and since about ninety per cent of the adult population got married at least once during the course of their lives, this act provides historians with abundant evidence as to the ability of partners to sign the register. Of course this bare ability does not in itself indicate literacy in the sense of being able to read and write, but since most schools taught reading before they taught writing, it can be assumed that signatures mean that those signing could at least read. This evidence presents great methodological difficulties, and its exploitation has only recently begun, so that conclusions based upon it must be cautious and provisional. Nevertheless certain generalizations seem acceptable. Illiteracy was by no means uniform but varied enormously in its distribution, both geographically and socially. The rate of illiteracy could vary from parish to parish, but by and large around 1760 it was higher in country than in urban areas, and certainly lowest of all in London. It also varied from rung to rung down the social ladder. There was virtually no illiteracy among the gentry and professions, including government officials; among tradesmen and craftsmen it varied between five and forty per cent, while husbandmen, servants and labourers were the most illiterate sections of the population, between forty-five and sixty per cent being unable to sign marriage registers examined for the years 1754–84. Since substantially more women were illiterate than men, then female servants were probably among the least literate people in eighteenth-century England, which makes the highly articulate correspondence of Richardson's *Pamela* a most unlikely feat in reality.

The reading public generally could have extended as far down the social scale as journeymen and apprentices, and in London probably even further, since the capital appears to have been peculiarly literate. Thus children in the parish school in Islington had their ability to read recorded, and it seems that some three quarters of them could satisfy this requirement, with no significant differences between boys and girls.

As far as we can tell the potential readership for literature of all kinds was not only absolutely but relatively much greater in the years 1714 to 1760 than it had been a century before, especially in London. Certainly many contemporaries were concerned about the spread of literacy to the lower orders. Advocates of charity schools welcomed it as a means of inculcating social order and inuring poor children to their lot in life. Critics of the movement, such as Bernard Mandeville, were anxious that it would produce the very reverse, and make children born to be hewers of wood and drawers of water discontented with their lot.

How far the educated could put literacy to any use, however, depended upon the extent to which they had either the money or the time to spend on reading. Some literary works were beyond the means of all but the wealthy. Pope's *Iliad*, for example, cost six guineas a set. Those who subscribed to this and other works by Pope came almost exclusively from the upper classes. Pope and Swift expressed their awareness of, and preference for, an exclusive readership when they addressed themselves in their works to the 'gentle reader'. Novels, however, sold for between 2s 3d and 5s, and although this was beyond the means of labourers it was within the reach of tradesmen and craftsmen. Even those who could not afford to buy such productions might have consulted them in coffee houses or, more doubtfully, in the circulating libraries which spread outwards from London to several provincial towns and even large villages after 1740. They could also contribute to part books, the individual parts of which cost little, but which accumulated into a reasonably bulky work. 'More than three hundred new and reprinted works were so issued before 1750, on almost every conceivable subject.'[32] Below such improving works there was a vast range of ephemeral, popular literature—newspapers, ballads, chapbooks, broadsides and pamphlets. By 1760, therefore, a mass audience for news, popular fiction, improving works and Grub Street products had come into existence, the bulk of which lived in London, though it included inhabitants of provincial towns and villages as well.

There were other industries designed to exploit the fact that people had time and money on their hands. Moralists were offended that the newspapers were 'filled with advertisements of races, cock matches, plays, musick gardens, balls, assemblies, operas, concerts, masquerades, breakfasting houses, ridottos and fire works'.[33] Horse racing, previously arranged privately between gentlemen, became an organized sport in this period, with regular fixtures like the Derby being established. Theatres, the particular *bêtes noires* of the moralists, those 'seminaries of vice and infidelity' as they liked to call them, spread out from London to provincial towns in the eighteenth century. Assemblies were a peculiar institution of the period. Citizens of London, and other towns, subscribed to the building of assembly rooms, where music, dancing and lectures could be enjoyed. The most famous, Vauxhall, and Ranelagh Gardens rebuilt in 1749 at a cost of £16,000, were in London but they had their equivalents elsewhere. The social life of Bath revolved around the two assembly rooms presided over by Beau Nash. Defoe observed in York that 'the keeping up assemblies among the younger gentry was first set up here' though he added characteristically that he disapproved of it 'as a plan laid for the ruin of the nation's morals'.[34]

Not all writers inveighed against luxury. On the contrary, Mandeville argued in *The Fable of the Bees* that stimulating consumer demand for luxuries was an essential ingredient of economic growth. His was something of a lone voice at the time and he shocked his contemporaries. Before the end of the period, however, other writers, including David Hume, were to advocate the beneficial effects on the economy of conspicuous consumption. Indeed some went further than Mandeville, for he thought in terms of an economy where growth stimulated by demand could only occur from the consumption patterns of an affluent elite, while the mass of the labouring poor were producers rather than consumers and must remain so. He did not conceive of a static economy, arguing that growth based on demand for luxuries could generate wealth:

> To such a Height, the very Poor
> Lived better than the Rich before.

Nevertheless he did not foresee mass consumption, and deplored charity schools because they would interfere with production. Later writers, however, were prepared to consider a significant increase in the standard of living of the workers, and even to argue the case for a high-wage economy. Defoe, paradoxically, had extolled high wages in England as being a significant cause of prosperity and the higher quality of English manufactures. After 1750 an increasing number of economic thinkers were to postulate the advantages of high wages, not only for increased productivity but even for the creation of mass consumer demand, until Adam Smith was to advocate that 'the high price of labour ... is the very thing in which public opulence consists.'

Those who were concerned at the rise of luxury were also convinced that increased affluence had generated an increase in crime. Fielding in 1751 attributed the 'late increase in robbers' partly to the growth of wealth. William Hawkins, editing the sixth edition of *Pleas of the Crown* in 1786, noted that since the first edition had been published in 1715 'the increase of commerce, opulence and luxury' had 'introduced a variety of temptations to fraud and rapine, which the legislature had been forced to repel, by a multiplicity of occasional statutes, creating new offences and inflicting additional punishments'.[35] Certainly the number of capital offences was increased, from about fifty in 1690 to over two hundred by 1820, partly in response to the fear that crime against property was mounting. Whether it was in fact rising is now impossible to tell. Judging by indictments, the crime rate in rural Surrey and Sussex seems to have actually declined in the century 1660 to 1760. In the metropolitan areas of Surrey, on the other hand, there seems to have been a slight increase in the rate in the first half of the eighteenth century, which confirms that contemporaries were right in thinking that the incidence of crime was higher in London than in the provinces, but scarcely supports their view that they were experiencing a massive and almost uncontrollable crime wave.

They were also assured by moralists that vice was increasing during the period. Defoe wrote that vice was the 'reigning distemper' of the nation. Societies for reformation of manners, which sprang up in London and several provincial towns between 1690 and 1738, insisted that England was sinking under a deluge of sin, particularly of drunkenness and whoring. To others gambling was the prevalent vice of the age. 'The evil is now above ten times greater than when the last law was made' in Anne's reign, complained a pamphleteer of 1722, 'thousands of families since that time have been ruined by gaming only, and ... it daily increases.'[36] The clergy rarely lost an opportunity to inveigh against vice, arguing that the special dispensation which providence had granted England, as witnessed in the Glorious Revolution of 1688, would be removed and the fate of Sodom and Gomorrah visited upon the land if Englishmen did not mend their wicked ways. The South Sea Bubble in 1720, the outbreak of the plague in France in 1721, the Jacobite plot of 1722, the bad harvests of 1727, 1740 and 1756, the War of the Austrian Succession, the 'Forty-Five', the cattle plague, the earthquakes which shook London in 1750 and destroyed Lisbon in 1756, were all used to drive home this lesson. Such a cosmology lay behind the activities of the societies for reformation of manners which attempted to force people to be virtuous by prosecuting them for such vicious acts as cursing and swearing, drinking and whoring, and sabbath breaking.

To what extent vice was on the increase cannot be measured. It is possible that the tendency of churchwardens to stop presenting people before church courts for breaches of the moral code relaxed the agencies of social control, especially in urban areas. The societies seem to have been trying to replace the ecclesiastical machinery with secular sanctions by informing magistrates of breaches of moral laws, but by 1739 at the latest they had given up the unequal task. Unfortunately for the societies, the magistrates were extremely reluctant to prosecute. The lay authorities did not share either the cosmology or the moral philosophy of the reformers.

The decline of religion, and the acceptance of Newtonian concepts of the universe among the educated laity, led the magistracy less to refute the ideas of the societies than to ignore them as irrelevant. Ideas of providential intervention in mundane affairs gradually declined during the period yet it must be stressed that the decline was very gradual. The English Bill of Rights of 1689 considered 'how it hath pleased Almighty God, in his marvellous providence, and merciful goodness to this nation, to provide and preserve their said majesties royal persons most happily to reign over us', and the American Declaration of Independence of 1776 placed 'a firm reliance on the protection of divine providence'; but the framers of those documents were not merely enunciating pious platitudes. On the contrary, a deep conviction that providence not only intervened in history but had a manifest destiny for English-speaking peoples was axiomatic in all but the most sceptical circles throughout the period. At the same time God became a more remote 'first cause' in the eighteenth century than he had been in the seventeenth. The 'God of battles' whose vessel Cromwell claimed to be was much more immediate and real to Englishmen who fought at Marston Moor and Naseby than the 'invisible hand' regulating the economy in Adam Smith's *Wealth of Nations*.

The acceptance of Newtonian principles in science removed the need for the constant daily intervention of providence in men's affairs, as God became the supreme engineer who governed the machinery of a universe which, once set in motion, operated by its own sufficient laws. The notion of a moral universe, where natural events became acts of God intended to warn men by afflicting providences, became less and less convincing to the educated laity. The transition did not occur overnight. Men could still be sufficiently sensitive on the subject for Swift to feel obliged to alter a passage in *A Tale of a Tub* when he came to publish the fifth edition in 1710. Earlier editions had described how Jack, the calvinist, had blamed 'providence' for a bruising encounter with a post, whereas in 1710 Swift transferred the blame to 'fate'. Just how ingrained the notion of providential action could still be as late as 1724, even among the educated laity, can be seen from the diary of Francis Barrell, a substantial gentleman of Kent who served on the commission of the peace in that county and was MP for Rochester. It is full of dire warnings drawn from such 'afflicting providences' as a fall from a horse or a sore throat.

Perhaps only the undue significance attached by the devotees of the regular intervention of providence to the London earthquakes of 1750 finally tipped the scales in favour of sceptics who drew a distinction between natural disasters and acts of God. In 1750 London was shaken by earthquakes on 8 February and again on 8 March. This twin phenomenon gave rise to a number of clerical interpretations of warnings from on high; the most influential was Sherlock's *A Letter from the Lord Bishop of London to the clergy and people of London and Westminster on occasion of the late earthquakes*, which reputedly sold 105,000 copies and became a best selling publication of the eighteenth century. Sherlock drew attention to the immorality of the town, exemplified in Cleland's recently published *Fanny Hill*, and warned of the wrath to come if Londoners did not heed the message of the earthquakes. A dissenting minister was even bolder, and rashly predicted a third and devastating quake for 5 or 8 April. Although these warnings led to a substantial exodus from the capital before 5 April, they also provoked a number of ripostes refuting the idea that such natural occurrences were the work of providence. When the third earthquake failed to materialize the sceptics seemed vindicated and, as those who fled returned sheepishly to town, they were greeted with a satiric *Full and True Account of the dreadful and melancholy earthquake which happened . . . on . . . the fifth instant*; this purported to give a list of those who perished beginning, 'the very first man that was sunk by this earthquake was the B[ishop] of L[ondon]. It seems he might have escaped, but his zeal was so great in distributing copies of his letter.' Although it cannot have sold as well as the bishop's *Letter*, it became much more representative of educated opinion amongst the laity at that time.

The educated elite might have agreed with the reformers that man was responsible for his own moral condition, but whether they thought that he was predisposed towards benevolent or antisocial acts depended on whether they followed Locke or Hobbes, and not, like the reforming societies, upon their reading of the Bible. Those who subscribed to the view of human nature put forward by Locke, and developed by the third earl of Shaftesbury, were convinced that when men were governed by reason they behaved altruistically, and that when they performed antisocially they were acting irrationally. The law should be used to deter those few who could not see reason from the consequences of their irrationality. Those views are often considered to have been prevalent among the enlightened upper classes in eighteenth-century England, but there is evidence that many members of the ruling class, especially those who upheld the Country tradition, were sceptical about the theory of benevolence and more inclined to Hobbesian views. Hobbes would have agreed that if men considered their behaviour in the light of reason then they would be social animals, but he was much more pessimistic about the faculty of men to consider their actions rationally and more inclined to argue that by nature they were inclined to follow their personal interests, conceived very selfishly and narrowly. The role of the law, therefore, was to deter the majority of men from acting on their antisocial instincts by making the consequences more painful than the pleasure they anticipated from such actions. Such diverse writers within the Country tradition as Thomas Gordon and John Trenchard in *Cato's Letters* and Swift in *Gulliver's Travels* expressed the more gloomy Hobbesian view of human nature, and not the optimistic Lockeian view. *Cato's Letters* spoke of 'the violent bent of human nature to evil' and agreed with Hobbes that the state of nature was a state of war.[37] Swift contrasted Lockeian man and Hobbesian man with the Houyhnhnms and the Yahoos, and saw men as more inclined to the latter than the former.

As usual, Mandeville was untypical. He took a thoroughly Hobbesian view of human nature, and overtly scorned the benevolent theories of the third earl of Shaftesbury. At the same time he thought that some at least of man's natural instincts, even the most selfish, could be directed to social ends, and that indeed the prudent politician would be better advised to exploit men's pride rather than his reason. Mandeville drew a sharper contrast than most writers of the time in distinguishing between crimes and sins. Crimes were antisocial, and should be treated with the full rigour of the law. Indeed he did not think that the existing law was rigorous enough and sought to make the death penalty more of a deterrent than it was. At the same time, sins were not necessarily antisocial but could be quite the contrary. Even the seven deadly sins could be put to public use, which was the basis of his famous paradox that private vices could, by the dexterous management of a skilful politician, become public benefits. He even advocated state brothels, which flew right in the face of the societies for reformation of manners. Mandeville was at odds with his time, too, in his view that vice was as much the product of environmental conditions as of human nature. When advocating public brothels, he observed how in Amsterdam they performed a social function by absorbing the frustrations of sailors who had been to sea on long voyages; he was even ready to see that gin-drinking was an anodyne for those living in the hopeless squalor of London.

Few contemporary writers were prepared to follow Mandeville so far. On the contrary, the philosophical basis of the novel, the literary genre most characteristic of the period, was that men were morally autonomous and could choose between good and evil, however rich or however poor they were. Defoe was adamant on the subject of tradesmen. 'There must be some failure in the tradesman, it can be no where else; either he is less sober and less frugal, less cautious of what he does, who he trusts, how he lives, and how he behaves, than tradesmen use to be; or he is less industrious, less diligent, and takes less care and pains in his business, or something is the matter.'[38] Hogarth's prints, especially *Industry and Idleness* and *The Harlot's Progress*, were paradigms of the prevalent view that men chose to live a life of crime or vice. Yet more and more were prepared to admit that, having chosen, environmental factors made it increasingly difficult to reverse the choice. The criminal could be impeached by his associates, the harlot could be handed over to the authorities by her bawd, anybody who got into debt was at the mercy of his creditor. To rescue such people from their plight it was necessary not merely to exhort them to virtue, but to intervene in their predicament to get them out of the clutches of those whose power they were in. This was the attitude informing such men as Jonas Hanway and Saunders Welch when they collected subscriptions to set up the Marine Society to give boys a chance to escape from crime, and the Magdalen Hospital for penitent prostitutes, to rescue whores from the tyranny of bawds. These institutions, established towards the very end of our period, are typical of a new approach to social problems which recognized society as well as the offender as a culprit. They were the forerunners of that philanthropic movement which eventually was to transform attitudes towards the lower classes in England.

# 4 The Established Church and its Rivals

Under the terms of the Act of Settlement George I was required to be an anglican. He was thus the first king of England whose religion was dictated by statute and after his arrival in his new realm he was obliged, despite the fact that he was a lutheran in Hanover, to be crowned by the archbishop of Canterbury according to the rites of the Church of England. Nothing could symbolize more completely the ascendancy of the established church than the solemn ceremony in Westminster Abbey at his coronation. Lady Cowper, who 'saw all the ceremony', wrote that she 'never was so affected with joy in all my life. It brought tears several times into my eyes; and I hope I shall never forget the blessing of seeing our holy religion thus preserved.'[1] After a century of vicissitudes, during which it had been submerged in a sea of sects by the aftermath of the civil wars and undermined by catholicism under James II, the Church of England seemed to have survived the challenge of its rivals relatively unscathed.

Yet a substantial number of anglican clergymen, maybe a majority, responded sympathetically to the rallying cry 'the church in danger' in the parliamentary elections held only a few weeks after George was crowned. The cry was raised by the high-church clergy, who comprised a handful of the twenty-six bishops but the bulk of the inferior clergymen. Led by Bishop Atterbury of Rochester and Henry Sacheverell, rector of St Andrew's, Holborn, these clergymen had been preaching that the church was in danger for the best part of twenty-five years. They harked back nostalgically to the good old days of King Charles II, when the established church had enjoyed exclusive privileges in the state, guaranteed by the Act of Uniformity, the Test and Corporation Acts, and the Licensing Act—safeguards which the Revolution had removed.

The Act of Uniformity had imposed subscription to all the Thirty-nine Articles on the anglican clergy and had led to the secession from the church of nearly 2,000 nonconformists who could not accept them all. To the high-churchmen this had restored the purity of anglicanism. It had also granted to the Church of England a monopoly of worship, a privilege strengthened by stringent measures against dissenters, as nonconformists were called. The Test and Corporation Acts had guaranteed to anglican communicants a monopoly of power, both locally and nationally. Finally the Licensing Act had given the establishment control of published opinions: religious works could only receive an *imprimatur* from a bishop. After the Revolution of 1688 all three monopolies had been eroded. Exclusive anglican worship had been undermined by the Toleration Act, which allowed dissenters to hold services in their own conventicles, provided they were trinitarian protestants. The practice known as occasional conformity, whereby dissenters took communion in the Church of England merely to comply with the letter of the Test and Corporation Acts, and the rest of the time worshipped in their own conventicles, broke the spirit of those laws and with it the monopoly of political power. Then in 1695 the Licensing Act had lapsed, and with its end had appeared a deluge of literature, anti-anglican and anticlerical, which would never have got past the former ecclesiastical censors. It was primarily these developments which led Atterbury and his brethren to suggest that the church was in danger. To stem the advance of dissent and irreligion they had demanded the recall of convocation, which had not met since 1689, and the introduction of legislation to prevent the abuse of occasional conformity. In 1701 William III met their demands for a meeting of convocation, but when the body of divines assembled divisions immediately became clear. Not all wanted to re-establish the privileges of the church by proscription and persecution of its rivals. Those who opposed these remedies for the plight of post-Revolution anglicanism formed a majority of the bishops, but a minority of the inferior clergy. The consequent disputes in convocation had given the two sides the labels of the high- and low-church parties.

The high-church clergy had hoped for great things from Queen Anne, who on her accession openly expressed sympathy for their views and their plight. Their tory friends in parliament had introduced bills to outlaw the practice of occasional conformity in all three sessions of her first parliament, but each time they had failed to get them through the House of Lords, where a majority of whigs, conspicuous among whom were the low-church bishops, managed to prevent the passage of the bills. Thus the whigs were regarded by the high-church clergy as their chief opponents, more dangerous than their friends the dissenters. When the whigs were in the ascendant, the church could automatically be said to be in danger. This seemed proven during the years 1705 to 1710 when the whigs gradually took over the government. During that period no occasional conformity bills came into parliament, while from 1708 to 1710 convocation was kept permanently prorogued. Then in 1710 the whig ministry impeached Henry Sacheverell for preaching a sermon which boldly articulated the fears of all high-church clergymen about the dangers to which their church and their beliefs had been subjected since 1688. During the last four years of Queen Anne's reign the dreaded whigs had been kept at bay, and an occasional conformity bill had at last become law in 1711. At the height of the high-church reaction in 1714, the Schism Act had been passed to make the separate education of dissenters illegal. Ominously for the high-church cause Queen Anne died on the very day that the act was to come into force.

The death of the queen also brought to power the whigs, and this time permanently. The triumph of whiggery in the state meant the ascendancy of the low-church party in the church, and spelled an end to the hopes and expectations of the opposite party for containing the alleged threat from dissent and for preferment in the church.

Certainly, preferment went to low churchmen under the early Hanoverians. Shortly after his arrival in England in 1714 George I was advised by Lord Cowper 'to use the utmost caution not to prefer any of those ecclesiastics whose known principles lead them to scruple the validity of a limitation of the right to the crown by act of parliament'.[2] George took his advice, and during the first years of the new regime ecclesiastical promotions were carefully directed through channels which were blocked to high churchmen. Under Walpole a close alliance was forged between the prime minister and Bishop Gibson of London to ensure that only well-wishers to the ministry sat on the bishops' benches in the House of Lords. According to Norman Sykes 'the alliance of Gibson and Walpole settled itself to the exploitation of the land of promise and to the establishment of a virtual whig monopoly of episcopal preferment. Apart from the intrusion of Sherlock upon the bench in 1727 as bishop of Bangor, at the insistence of Queen Caroline, and his translation to Sarum in 1734, no tory divine broke through the fence of prohibition raised up by Gibson against their kind.'[3] When Walpole quarrelled with Gibson in 1736, he handed over ecclesiastical patronage to the duke of Newcastle, who dispensed it almost without a break for thirty years. Frustrated in their hopes of preferment from the regime, the high-church clergy tried to vent their exasperation through political propaganda and debates in convocation, but here again they were thwarted. In December 1714 George issued a proclamation prohibiting the clergy from preaching political sermons. In 1717 the high churchmen lost their national sounding board when convocation was suppressed. Apart from a brief resurrection in 1741 it did not assemble again to do synodical business until the nineteenth century.

Convocation was silenced after the lower house had censured Benjamin Hoadly, bishop of Bangor, for the erastian views he had expressed in two works, *A Preservative against the Principles and Practices of the Nonjurors both in Church and State*, which he published in 1716, and a sermon which he preached before the king on 31 March 1717. In the *Preservative* Hoadly defended the secular power's right to deprive those nine bishops and four hundred or so clergymen who had refused to take the oaths to William and Mary after the Revolution of 1688, and whose successors, known as nonjurors, maintained their separation from the Church of England. The original nonjurors had tolerated communion with the established church, but the second generation threatened to excommunicate from their own body, which they claimed was the one true church, those of their number who continued to attend the state church. Their more intransigent attitude under George I provoked a crisis of conscience among some high-church anglicans who had tried to have it both ways under Anne. It is ironic in view of their intransigence that by 1721 the nonjurors themselves were divided into three distinct parties, none of whom would communicate with the others. At the time, however, it seemed to threaten a major schism, with many high churchmen seceding from the established church.

Hoadly entered the great pamphlet debate precipitated by the threat with an assertion of the supremacy of the state over the church, which in itself trod on high-church as well as nonjuring susceptibilities. Not only high churchmen were offended when he went on to ridicule the nonjurors' claim that they were the one true church, by denouncing the notion of the apostolic succession which they had used in defence of their claim, and by reassuring laymen that their threats of excommunication were of no consequence since no church could exert sanctions on the laity. Even a moderate low-churchman like Edmund Gibson, whose *Codex Juris Ecclesiastici*, published as recently as 1713, systematized ecclesiastical law and who privately believed that the canons of the church were binding on laymen, took offence. Indeed the Bangorian controversy, as it came to be called, to some extent produced a closing of the ranks in the church. Against the extreme views of the bishop of Bangor there emerged a moderate churchmanship determined to preserve the rights and privileges of the Church of England in the new age ushered in by Anne's death. This phenomenon partly explains why low-church bishops who had formerly opposed the Occasional Conformity and Schism Acts were not prepared to vote for their repeal, and why Stanhope cautiously waited until 1719 before he felt the time to be ripe to remove them from the statute book.

Hoadly set out to clarify his views on the power of churches over

their members in the sermon preached before George I on the text
'Jesus answered, my kingdom is not of this world.' In it he equated
the notion of Christ's kingdom with that of his church and came to
the conclusion that Jesus 'had left behind him no visible, humane
authority: no vicegerents, who can be said properly to supply his
place; no interpreters, upon whom his subjects are absolutely to
depend; no judges over the consciences or religion of his people'. It
followed from this that churches had no absolute authority over their
members whatsoever.

The *Preservative* raised a storm, but the sermon produced a
hurricane. At bottom what was at issue were two completely different
concepts of the Church of England. To Hoadly the church was a
voluntary association of sincere believers, and as such was no better
or worse than other congregations of Christians, while to his
opponents it was the one true church. Where to the bishop its form of
government was the most convenient, they argued that episcopacy
was sanctioned by divine right and upheld by the apostolic
succession. In a way what he had done was to apply Locke's theories
about the state, which he had done more than anyone else to
popularize, to the church. Even men who had accepted Locke's
secular theories of civil government were not ready to repudiate the
divine right of the Church of England. The notion that men
contracted with a ruler for mutual convenience might be acceptable
as far as the state was concerned, but not where the church was
involved. This raised the whole question of the relationship between
church and state and whether the church was superior, independent
or subordinate to the state. His theory precipitated an avalanche of
refutation, by no means all of it from nonjurors or high churchmen.
Moreover the debate went on long after the Bangorian controversy
had subsided, perhaps the most important contribution to it being
William Warburton's *The Alliance between Church and State*, published
in 1736, which argued that both were in fact sovereign bodies allied
for mutual protection.

The immediate issues at stake in 1717, however, were settled in a
way which demonstrated the validity of Hoadly's view of the
relationship. When in May a committee of the lower house of
convocation drew up a report 'concerning several dangerous positions and doctrines contained in the bishop of Bangor's preservative
and his sermon', the session was prorogued by the king to November.
Successive prorogations ensured that Hoadly never had to appear
before it.

The Bangorian controversy was provoked in part by the re-
alization of the high-church clergy that their kingdom at least was
not to be of this world. Hoadly himself was the archetype of the low-

church clergymen who inherited the earth on Anne's death. In 1715
he was made bishop of Bangor, and only once set foot in that see
before his translation from it to Hereford in 1721, which he never
visited at all before climbing the ladder of preferment again in 1723,
this time to Salisbury, finally making Winchester in 1734.

Hoadly indeed became the whipping boy of historians who
castigated the eighteenth-century church for failing in its spiritual
duty and for identifying too much with the secular outlook of the
whig oligarchy. He was the prime example of the place-seeking
prelates of Hanoverian England, whom R. H. Tawney accused of
being 'servile appendages of a semi-pagan aristocracy'. In the
nineteenth and early twentieth centuries these bishops did not, on the
whole, get a good press. Owing their translations from one see to
another more to active service on the whig side in parliamentary
elections and voting for the government in the House of Lords than to
exemplary piety or to theological scholarship; publishing
pamphlets in defence of the ministry rather than treatises in defence
of the faith; spending all their time in London in attendance at
debates in the upper house or at ministerial levees rather than in their
dioceses taking care of souls, ordaining priests or confirming
laymen—no wonder they did not seem an exemplary episcopate.
Bishops who did not visit their bishoprics could ordain those who
were prepared to travel up to London to see them, but they could
hardly confirm *in absentia*. More scandalous in this respect, if possible,
than Hoadly was Lancelot Blackburne, archbishop of York from
1724 to 1743 who, in the whole of that time, did not conduct any
confirmations. It might not be true, as Horace Walpole swore, that
he kept a kind of harem, but in the words of Basil Williams he 'was a
great roistering ex-naval chaplain, who shocked even one of his vicars
by calling for pipes and liquor in the vestry' after a church service.[4]
However, it is a mistake to judge the eighteenth-century episcopate by these notorious examples. Alongside Hoadly were such
hardworking and conscientious prelates as Burnet of Salisbury,
Nicolson of Carlisle and Wake of Lincoln and Canterbury. Men like
these did not forget their spiritual duties even if politics made heavy
demands on their time. Not all bishops made ordinands visit them in
London to be ordained. On the contrary, of the 388 clergymen
ordained in Devon and Cornwall between 1689 and 1792 only
twenty-six had to travel to the capital for the laying-on of hands. Nor
was confirmation everywhere neglected. In 1718 Archbishop Wake
expressed the belief that 'confirmations had never been so regular
throughout the kingdom as within the last thirty years; nor the
episcopal visitations and that by the bishops in person, so constant.'[5]

Whatever the shortcomings of the episcopate in the eighteenth century they were no more glaring than those of their Caroline counterparts. No sudden deterioration of clerical morality set in around the turn of the century, for every charge that can be levied against the church after 1700 can be sustained in the period after 1660. Thus when Nicolson became bishop of Carlisle in 1702 he found that confirmations had not been administered in his diocese since 1684. He himself confirmed 5,449 during his first visitation.

The key difference between the Hanoverian and earlier or later eras is that the votes of the bishops became crucial in the House of Lords as far as the government was concerned; they were therefore under much greater pressure to attend than their predecessors or successors. Parliament had met only occasionally between 1660 and 1688, and between 1689 and 1715 the votes of the bishops tended to be more independent of the Court than they became under Walpole. Thus in 1711, in a key division for the ministry in the upper house, no fewer than fourteen of the seventeen bishops present voted against the government. This was because over the years the bulk of the episcopate had been promoted under whig auspices and the ministry was dominated by the tories in 1711. The predilection of most bishops to vote whig and their opposition in this particular division so galled Bolingbroke that he swore that, if the whigs were to bring in a bill to unbishop them, they would support it. After 1714, of course, all ministries were whig, and with the exception of a handful of high-church bishops inherited by George I from his predecessor, the Court could generally rely on the votes of the bishops, especially those preferred by Gibson and Walpole. These were often crucial. In 1733 a division in the House of Lords on a motion to enquire into the disposition of the forfeited estates of the South Sea Company directors was lost when the votes tied at seventy-five, a tie being regarded as a defeat in the upper house. Of the twenty-six bishops no fewer than twenty-four voted for the Court either in person or by proxy. For most of the eighteenth century a block of nearly twenty-six votes in the Lords was too important for the Court to spare, and bishops were consequently obliged to spend the parliamentary session in London. Later, when the upper house became relatively less important, the votes of bishops ceased to be so vital and they were relieved of this duty. Thus the eighteenth century was a peculiar period in which, in addition to their spiritual tasks, the bishops had to undertake arduous political duties at Westminster. In the circumstances they performed both functions remarkably well. As Norman Sykes concluded, 'in respect of the episcopate the eighteenth-century church may claim a greater proportion of credit than of censure.'[6]

The bishops were not the only churchmen to be censured in this

period, for accusations of time-serving, materialism and disregard for
their pastoral duties were levelled at all ranks of clergymen at the
time, and have been echoed since. Archdeacon Edward Cobden
wished to be made a canon, but in 1752 resigned in disgust from his
post of king's chaplain because in his opinion less worthy men were
being preferred before him, simply through being prepared to please
the Court. He instanced the cases of men who had been promoted in
the church for supporting Court candidates in parliamentary
elections, and suggested that ecclesiastical preferment should be
taken out of the hands of politicians and given to such 'as shall
execute it with justice and integrity'. This he believed would 'open
wide the fountains of science, give a new turn to the heads of our
rising divines, who, instead of frequenting the levees of the great, and
pursuing parliamentary politics, would make their application to
solid and rational studies, and endeavour to signalize themselves in
learning, virtue and piety.'[7] Cobden's complaints can be dismissed as
mere envy, though he must have had some integrity, since a king's
chaplain who was prepared to toe the Court line was usually
guaranteed rapid preferment. The men who generally rose most
quickly were the chaplains whom the Georges had accompany them
on their journeys to Hanover. Being a chaplain of a prominent
politician was almost as good. Francis Hare, to give a spectacular
example, had the good fortune to be both the duke of Marlborough's
chaplain and tutor to Sir Robert Walpole, which helped him up the
rungs in the ladder of preferment from the deanery of Worcester to
the bishopric of Chichester, via the deanery of St Paul's and the
bishopric of St Asaph. Ever since the Church of England was
established, it had paid to have friends at court in order to obtain
preferment; but there is something in Cobden's claim that in the
eighteenth century the church became too closely associated with the
whig oligarchy.

The clergy were also accused of hedonism and neglecting their
cures. A foreign visitor observed 'the air of health and prosperity of
the greatest part of them; and it is pleasant to see how fat and fair
these parsons are. They are charged with being somewhat lazy, and
their usual plumpness makes it suspected that there's some truth in it.
It is common to see them in coffee houses, and even in taverns, with
pipes in their mouths.'[8] One of their own brethren, John Brown, was
even more severe in his *Estimate of the Manners and Principles of the
Times*: 'It is grown a fashionable thing, among these gentlemen, to
despise the duties of their parish; to wander about, as the various
seasons invite, to every scene of false gaiety; to frequent and shine in
all public places, their own pulpits excepted.'[9]

Side by side with these polemics we get more favourable views of the clergy; Fielding's Parson Adams is perhaps the most famous, though his Dr Harrison in *Amelia* is almost equally worthy. 'All his parishioners, whom he treats as his children, regard him as their common father. Once in a week he constantly visits every house in the parish, examines, commands and rebukes, as he finds occasion.' Goldsmith's Dr Primrose, *The Vicar of Wakefield*, is rather more worldly, but despite his faults has admirable qualities.

Which stereotype most faithfully reflects the reality is now impossible to determine. Surviving diaries, such as that of Cole of Bletchley and the more celebrated Parson Woodforde depict ministers who, while enjoying worldly comforts, did not by any means neglect their spiritual calling. Moreover, the mass of the inferior clergy could not afford an extravagant standard of living. One complained bitterly that 'an ordinary bricklayer or carpenter . . . that earns constantly but his two shillings a day' was better off than a country curate or a city preacher.[10] William Jones agreed, claiming that 'a journeyman in almost any trade or business, even a bricklayer's labourer, or the turner of a razor-grinder's wheel, all circumstances considered, is generally better paid than a stipendiary curate.'[11] For many clergymen the only way to make ends meet was by holding livings in plurality, with the inevitable non-residence which that entailed and for which they were much criticized. They can scarcely be blamed if they sought to better their material condition by preferment, even if in order to obtain it they had to merit the approval of whig patrons.

Perhaps the best way to do this was to preach sermons in tune with the prevailing latitudinarian attitude in the church. Latitudinarianism was the awkward name given to views developed by divines in the late seventeenth and early eighteenth centuries in their attempts to define an anglican position against such critics as puritans, catholics and deists. Though the controversies they engaged in ranged far and wide over theology, philosophy and history, fundamentally what they disputed was the nature of authority. During the seventeenth century the age-old disputes about the relationship of reason and revelation took on a new twist which was profoundly to affect the polemical stance of the Church of England in the eighteenth century. The puritans insisted on the sole authority of the Bible as the repository of all truths necessary for salvation. This asserted the absolute precedence of revelation over reason. To the puritan, man since the fall of Adam, if left to his own devices, was literally beyond redemption. By nature he was inclined to sin, and what little reason God had left him, far from leading him into the paths of righteousness, only rationalized his waywardness and led him further and further into error. Truth had to be revealed in order to rescue mankind from the fate to which unaided reason alone condemned him. This pessimistic view of human nature was not shared by all anglicans. On the contrary, many held that God had endowed men with sufficient reason to ascertain certain eternal truths, such as the existence of God, the immortality of the soul and the certainty of a judgment after death. There were, they agreed, certain mysteries which unaided reason alone could not ascertain, such as the doctrine of the trinity. Therefore a judicious balance of reason and revelation was necessary in order to work out doctrines sufficient for salvation. This was a position shared by the catholics, but there was a significant distinction between them and the anglicans over the nature of revelation. While both agreed that the Bible was the source of revealed truth, catholics insisted that it should be interpreted in the light of the church's traditional teaching. Anglicans accepted the definitions of doctrine by the early fathers of the church, but took exception to those traditions appealed to by catholics to maintain that such mysteries as transubstantiation were among the truths which God had revealed to men.

The latitudinarians worked out their position on these issues in the spirit of seventeenth-century inductive science and philosophy, refusing to accept dogmatic statements merely because they had been uttered by an 'authority' such as Aristotle or St Augustine. In doing so they emphasized the faculty of reason to refute the claims of the puritans, on the one hand, to personal revelation and of the catholics, on the other, to corporate revelation. They thus sharpened weapons which were to be employed against their own position by the deists. Samuel Clarke, for instance, in his *Scripture Doctrine of the Trinity* published in 1712 came so close to deism that his opponents regarded him as being one himself. Deists argued that reason alone should be the arbiter of religious belief, and that such 'revelations' as the doctrine of the trinity and the biblical account of miracles were a positive hindrance to belief because they were incompatible with reason.

In the early eighteenth century the Church of England turned from defending itself against puritan dissenters and catholics to taking up the challenge from the deists and freethinkers. Dissent and catholicism no longer appeared to be formidable opponents, while the rise of deism and even atheism seemed to be threatening to destroy anglicanism itself. The danger from dissent which high churchmen dreaded under a whig ascendancy never materialized. So far from making further inroads into anglicanism under the early Hanoverians, the dissenters found it hard to keep up their numbers. In 1715 the total number of adult baptists, independents and presbyterians was probably about 300,000. These formed the bulk of the dissenters, the quakers, who were the largest of the lesser denominations, numbering no more than 50,000. By 1760 the three main groups of dissenters at best reached the same total, and might have dwindled to 250,000. Moreover the later years of George II's reign witnessed the start of a recovery of the dissenting interest from a recession which set in after Anne's death. One crude measure of this is the number of licenses issued to new congregations under the terms of the Toleration Act. In the years 1701 to 1710 the number issued totalled 1,260, while between 1751 and 1760 it came to only 757, which nevertheless represented an increase on the 448 issued between 1731 and 1740. This information, of course, tells us nothing about the overall number of meeting houses, since it does not record the many which ceased to function. It seems, however, that the number of congregations, like the number of worshippers, at best remained static and at worst declined between the accession of George I and that of George III.

Dissenters themselves were convinced that their strength was waning even more disastrously. This impression probably stemmed from a change in the social composition of their congregations. In the early days of nonconformity after the restoration of Charles II several peers and innumerable gentry were identifiable as dissenters. By 1715 there were few noble dissenting families left, though they still drew quite substantially on the support of the gentry. Indeed in some counties the gentlemen were almost as numerous as the tradesmen in dissenting congregations, and in Lincolnshire there were apparently more. Although in absolute terms tradesmen outnumbered the gentlemen, relatively the proportion of gentry families which still attended meeting houses made them the most significant social element in nonconformity at the accession of George I. Only the baptists lacked the support of substantial families in 1714, drawing their strength mainly from tradesmen. By 1760, however, this was also true of other congregations, which had lost many genteel worshippers. The loss of gentry support led to some attrition of dissent in the countryside, and concentration in towns, a trend which made the erosion of the dissenting interest appear even more spectacular at the time than in retrospect. Yet as early as 1710 it could be said, somewhat exaggeratedly, that 'they that think the church is in danger, don't consider the vast disproportion of numbers. The nobility and gentry are all of the church, and above nine parts in ten of the tradesmen, and the rest of the people of England are so.'[12]

The dissenters also suffered from a dispute about dogma under George I which left them much weakened. Dissenting ministers, led by James Peirce, a presbyterian preacher in Exeter, began to entertain scruples about the doctrine of the trinity. Peirce, of whom a hostile observer commented that he 'uses the word of God as men do their tobacco, he chews it without the grace of digestion and spits it out again', became so heterodox that he was accused of arianism and expelled from his ministry. His expulsion provoked such an outcry that a conference was held in Salters' Hall, London, in 1719 to determine the doctrinal position. The meeting revealed division in the ranks of the dissenters and bitterness over the treatment of Peirce. It was said, 'surely such a bear garden synod was never heard of?'[13] A majority of the delegates came out on Peirce's side, and about sixty preachers refused to subscribe to the doctrine of the trinity. This public spectacle of rancour and division was extremely damaging to the cause of dissent. As Strickland Gough, the author of *An Enquiry into the causes of the decay of the dissenting interest*, put it in 1730: 'The unhappy difference at Salters' Hall injured the dissenting interest more than all their enemies together.' Those who were troubled about the breach with orthodoxy were ripe for conversion by the methodists. In Newcastle upon Tyne it was reported in 1743, after John Wesley had started his mission there, that 'one presbyterian meeting is quite deserted and others of them very much thinned.'[14]

Among other causes of decay discussed by Gough was 'the lenity of the government, the want of a persecution to keep us together'. It was paradoxical that dissent throve through the periods of proscription under Charles II and Queen Anne and declined under the benign administration of the Hanoverians. In 1718 Edmund Calamy conceded that, in the thirty years since the Toleration Act, double the number of dissenters had gone over to the Church of England than ever were prevailed upon before.[15] In 1719 the Occasional Conformity and Schism Acts were repealed, and through the Corporation and Test Acts remained on the statute book, under Walpole annual indemnity acts secured the dissenters against malicious prosecution. In 1722 the quakers' objections to the terms of earlier legislation enabling them to affirm rather than to swear oaths were satisfied by statute. Yet the paradox of the decline of dissent when it was tolerated was what low churchmen had predicted. Their whole approach to dissenters was conciliatory in hopes of wooing them over to the established church. After 1714 this approach worked. Many dissenters went over to the Church of England, among the most prominent being Joseph Butler, who became bishop of Durham, and Thomas Secker, who became archbishop of Canterbury.

The absolute number of catholics, on the other hand, appears to have risen from about 60,000 in 1710 to around 80,000 in 1770. This might have stimulated the fears expressed by contemporaries that popery was rampant, though such hysteria does not need statistical data to feed it. Some catholics were themselves convinced that they were on the decline. Joseph Berington, a catholic priest, claimed in 1780 that 'within the present century we have most rapidly decreased.' The explanation of these contradictory impressions is probably that, as Berington demonstrated, the traditional leaders of the catholic community, the peers and gentry who had remained loyal to the old religion since the Reformation, were dwindling, either because their families were becoming extinct or through conversions. In 1780 he estimated that there were only eight peers, nineteen baronets and about 150 landed gentry in their ranks. Unlike dissent, which appealed increasingly to tradesmen, there were hardly any catholics in trade. Indeed Berington thought that there were not 'more than two catholics of any note . . . engaged in mercantile business.'[16] The number of catholic priests also dropped from over 500 to under 400 between 1710 and 1770. However, there had been an increase in the numbers of catholic labourers and their families due to an influx partly from the continent but mainly from Ireland. Consequently, though catholicism was probably increasing among the labouring poor, it was slowly decreasing among the landed classes which were in a position to offer a threat to the establishment.

Yet so seriously was this threat taken that during the rebellions of 1715 and 1745 prominent catholics were taken up and confined by the militia. The association of catholicism with Jacobitism was the justification for imposing an extra levy of taxation on the catholic community in 1722, after the Atterbury Plot. It was argued that it was only right that those elements which presented a danger to the state should be taxed to pay for their suppression. It might seem from such treatment and from the fact that not a single penal law against catholics was repealed that, unlike the dissenters, they declined at least in high places because they were persecuted and not because they were treated leniently. They were, after all, debarred from office locally and nationally by the Corporation and Test Acts and subject to double taxes. However, it appears that apart from times of acute anxiety, such as 1715, 1722 and 1745, the laws were laxly enforced, and the catholics allowed to live in peace. One reason why they declined, according to Berington, was 'that general indifference about religion which gains so perceptibly on all Christians'.[17]

Increasing indifference concerned other believers. Warburton lamented that he 'had lived to see . . . that fatal crisis when religion hath lost its hold on the minds of the people', while a tract of 1730 asserted 'Tis plain and indisputable that Christianity in this kingdom is very much declining.'[18] Religious indifference was particularly

noticeable among the upper classes: 'the generality of the rich and
great', according to a sermon of 1750, 'never frequent the church of
God . . . and deride as superstition the very asking his blessing.'[19] The
growth of indifference among the elite was not a little owing to the
controversy between the church and the deists. Deism came into its
own with the lapsing of the Licensing Act in 1695, when its advocates
could publish their views without the prohibition of the church. It is
significant that two of the more celebrated works in the ensuing
controversy, Locke's *The Reasonableness of Christianity* and John
Toland's *Christianity not Mysterious*, first appeared immediately after
the act expired. As their titles imply, these works argued that none of
the essential doctrines of Christianity were repugnant to reason.
Neither author was an extreme deist and indeed both were at the
time members of the established church, though the Christianity they
acknowledged stripped anglican theology of all but its barest
essentials. A much more thorough-going deist was Matthew Tindal
who, in *The Rights of the Christian Church* and *Christianity as old as
creation*, attacked revealed religion as a bogus system of belief foisted
upon the world by priests. The clergy were regarded by deists and
freethinkers as being involved in a plot to perpetuate their own
undeserved power, and 'priestcraft' became the most pejorative term
in their vocabulary. One of the most outspoken among a host of
anticlerical writings was Anthony Collins's *Discourse on Freethinking*.

Churchmen responded to these attacks upon revealed religion and
the anglican church in innumerable sermons, pastoral letters,
pamphlets, treatises and tracts. Their finest talents were deployed to
meet the objections of deists and freethinkers. Thus Swift ridiculed
both in *An Argument to prove that the abolition of Christianity might . . . be
attended with some inconveniences* and *Mr Collins Discourse on Freethinking
put into plain English . . . for the use of the poor*. The most serious
refutation of deism was Joseph Butler's *Analogy of Religion*, published
in 1736. Butler argued that natural and revealed religion, far from
being at loggerheads, mutually supported each other. This was the
last serious round in the controversy between Christianity and deism
in the early eighteenth century. Bolingbroke's posthumously published writings produced a mild stir when they revealed an essentially
deist attitude after a lifetime's posturing as an anglican, but
otherwise the controversy was closed with Butler's refutation of
Collins. Thereafter both found themselves under assault from the
scepticism of David Hume.

The absorption of the church in the deist controversy conditioned
the religious climate of the times. Among the leading anglican
apologists, latitudinarian attitudes became dominant. These had
been formed, as we have seen, in the earlier controversies between

anglicanism on the one hand and dissent and catholicism on the other. Latitudinarianism answered what its advocates held to be fanaticism with sweet reasonableness and common sense. Thus where the puritans saw God as the jealous god of the Old Testament latitudinarians regarded him as the reasonable father of mankind. Again, in contrast to the puritan view of man as an incorrigible sinner, they saw men as reasonable beings who could at least begin to work out their own salvation. Nor was the road to heaven held to be too strait and narrow, for reasonable men acting in accordance with rational precepts could entertain hopes of a place there.

These views found expression in the stock sermons of the Hanoverian church which were strongly influenced by those of John Tillotson, archbishop of Canterbury in the reign of William III. According to Burnet 'his sermons were so well heard and liked, and so much read, that all the nation proposed him as a pattern and studied to copy after him.'[20] At the time Tillotson's sermons were regarded as models of clarity and lucidity after the over-elaborate discourses of his predecessors. They appealed because they were addressed to men's reason rather than to their passions. As G. R. Cragg observed, 'because the heroic note has vanished there is no deep sense of urgency in Tillotson, his sermons now dismay the reader by their uninspired repetition of arguments directed to an unimaginative common sense.'[21] But it was this very quality which made them attractive to Augustan churchmen. They were convinced that fanaticism in religion had done more harm than good, especially in the previous century, when puritanism and catholicism had threatened to destroy the very fabric of society. Thus on 20 January 1715, the day set aside for thanksgiving for the Hanoverian succession, the bishop of Gloucester preached a sermon maintaining that religious zeal was responsible for 'more cruelty, wars, massacres, burnings, more hatred, animosity, perverseness and peevishness than . . . any or almost all other accounts whatsoever. This has brought a great scandal upon the Christian religion, and probably is one great cause of the infidelity so much complained of both here and in other countries.'[22] People in the early eighteenth century were tired of excesses of zeal. They shuddered at anything which smacked of fanaticism in their own day, dubbing it enthusiasm. Enthusiasm strictly meant, in Locke's words, 'immediate revelation' or, as Dr Johnson defined it, 'a vain confidence of divine favour or communication'. It tended, however, to be used of excessive zeal of any kind. In his *Letter Concerning Enthusiasm* the third earl of Shaftesbury said that he preferred good humour and good manners to zeal.

The antidote to enthusiasm was to play down the apocalyptic themes of the fanatics, with their emphasis on conversion, salvation, heaven and hell, and to concentrate on inculcating good manners. Pope recorded that the dean of Gloucester, preaching at court, 'threatened the sinner with punishment in "a place which he thought it not decent to name in so polite an assembly"'. Moreover, the moral code was not held to be very demanding. The most popular of Tillotson's sermons was on the text 'his commandments are not grievous', while another favourite text was 'be not righteous overmuch'. John Wesley actually heard a sermon preached in 1740 on the 'duty of getting a good estate and keeping a good reputation'. Wesley, of course, was branded as a wild enthusiast, and his comment on this sermon was 'is it possible to deny (supposing the Bible true) that such a preacher is a "blind leader of the blind"?'[23] George Whitefield, the other great leader of the methodist revival, also disdained the fashionable mode in sermons, once saying of Tillotson that he 'knew no more of true Christianity than Mahomet'.

The early methodist notion of what constituted 'true Christianity' was close to that described by the nonjuror William Law in *A Serious Call to a Devout and Holy Life*, which he published in 1729. Law's *Serious Call* was directed primarily against those who were 'strict as to some times and places of devotion, but when the service of the church is over, they are but like those that seldom or never come there.' His solution was to urge Christians in their private lives to demonstrate a piety that would set them apart from non-believers. 'This consider-able writer' claimed the methodist Thomas Coke, 'was the great forerunner of the revival which followed, and did more to promote it than any other individual whatsoever'. When they were at Oxford John and Charles Wesley used to visit him at Putney, and in 1760 John wrote in his journal 'that Mr Law, whom I love and reverence now, was once a kind of oracle.' Wesley certainly agreed with Law's distinction between nominal and true Christians. Thus in his *Character of a Methodist* he objected to the name as having been 'fixed upon them by way of reproach' and insisted that 'from real Christians, of whatever denomination they be, we earnestly desire not to be distinguished at all.' Yet he did wish to be distinguished from 'her who fancies herself a virtuous woman, only because she is not a prostitute: or him who dreams he is an honest man, merely because he does not rob or steal. May the Lord God of my fathers preserve me from such a poor starved religion as this! Were this the mark of a methodist, I would sooner choose, to be a sincere Jew, Turk or pagan.' Again in his sermon, *The Almost Christian*, he argued that honesty, sincere morality and assiduous religious practices could only make a man an 'almost Christian'. Real Christians needed faith, which to Wesley meant the assurance of salvation.[24]

Wesley set out along the road to salvation in the company of high churchmen. His tory father sent him to Christ Church, Oxford, the home of the lost cause of high-church toryism in the early eighteenth century. Oxford was regarded as high church to the point of rank Jacobitism under George I. During the Fifteen it had been found necessary to quarter a regiment of foot there and to arrest several suspects. Notwithstanding the vigilance of the authorities Jacobite riots were a regular feature at the university in the decade after Anne's death. The government was so resentful of the disaffection of both Oxford and Cambridge that between 1717 and 1719 it actively contemplated an act of parliament authorizing an official visitation of the universities, coupled with measures to take appointments out of the hands of the colleges and place them in the control of the king. Although this extreme proposal was dropped, George I did inaugurate regius professorships of classics, divinity and modern history at the universities in 1724, the year John Wesley took his bachelor's degree at Oxford.

Such was the university which Wesley attended. It is sometimes asserted that he found the atmosphere there uncongenial, but he seems in fact to have been very attached to it. He became fellow of Lincoln College in 1726 and acted as tutor there from 1729 to 1735. In later life he commented 'what is wanting but the love of God to make this place an earthly paradise?' Wesley tried to supply the lack when he was there along with a group of fellow Oxonians who became known as the Holy Club. It was of this group that the word 'methodist' was first used. As a sympathizer explained:[25]

> The exact regularity of their lives, as well as their studies, occasioned a young gentleman of Christ Church to say 'Here's a new set of methodists sprung up', alluding to some ancient physicians who were so called. The name was new and quaint; so it took immediately, and the methodists were known all over the university. They were all zealous members of the Church of England, not only tenacious of all her doctrines, so far as they knew them, but of all her discipline, to the minutest circumstance.

So methodism was born in the milieu of the most uncompromising high churchmanship.

It was probably Wesley's high-church principles which persuaded General Oglethorpe, the tory founder of the colony of Georgia, to ask him to go there in 1735. Wesley consulted William Law, and his own mother Susannah, about the mission and both gave it their blessing. Georgia was then very new. It had only been founded in 1733, and Wesley sailed on the fifth voyage of colonists. Even so, it was surprisingly cosmopolitan. Apart from the Indians, whom he hoped to convert, it contained a few years later 'above seventeen hundred white people in an industrious way, and about four hundred negroes'. These were scattered in settlements and villages, though already there were 'three pretty considerable towns . . . two of which have churches and ministers of the Church of England . . . and the third is composed of German protestants from Saltzburgh.'[26] There was even a group of Piedmontese silk workers. One of the 'pretty considerable towns' was Savannah, which had about two hundred houses in it when Wesley arrived there, and a court house which he was to use as his church. Here Wesley instituted the most rigorous high-church rule, insisting that none should be allowed to take communion unless they had first been baptized according to anglican rites. As he himself was to say years later, 'Can any one carry high-church zeal higher than this?' His decision to reject one of the colonists from communion because she had not given previous notice of her desire to communicate caused such an uproar that he decided to return to England. The fact that he had once courted the lady in question and still wrote to her after she married another might well have contributed to his annoyance at her behaviour. But the main reason for the failure of his Georgian mission was that he tried to treat the colonists as though they were members of his Holy Club in Oxford. He was still too much the high-church Oxonian.

When Wesley returned to England, however, other influences made themselves felt. As Warburton put it, 'Mr William Law begot methodism, and Count Zinzendorf rocked the cradle.'[27] Zinzendorf was the leader of a community of moravians at Herrnhut in Upper Lusatia. Their theology stressed Christ more than the Father and the Holy Ghost, for they held that 'whoever believes in Christ, though he knows nothing more of the Godhead, will be saved.' Salvation came from a new birth in Christ, which was a sudden, miraculous regeneration: 'one moment is sufficient to make us free to receive grace, to be transformed to the image of the little lamb.' They worshipped Christ in their agapes or love feasts, and sang hymns, many written by Zinzendorf himself, some of which had a morbid and even Freudian obsession with the saviour's wounds.[28] They were also great missionaries, expecially in the New World, and it was on board the ship sailing for Georgia in 1735 that John Wesley first met them and was impressed by their indifference to the threat of death during the storms they encountered. He kept in touch with them in the colony. Once, in conversation with a moravian pastor, he was asked a question which deeply disturbed him: 'Do you know Jesus Christ?' In Wesley's own words, 'I paused and said, "I know he is the saviour of the world." "True, he replied, "but do you know he has saved you?" I answered, "I hope he has died to save me." He only added, "But do you know yourself?" I said, "I do." But I fear they were vain words.' Wesley was to discover what the man was driving at on his return to England in 1737, when he met Peter Böhler and learned what he termed 'a new gospel'—'Dominion over sin, and constant peace from a sense of forgiveness'. Wesley himself did not experience this sense of forgiveness for his sins until 'about a quarter before nine' on 24 May 1738, when at a religious society meeting in Aldersgate Street, London, he felt his heart 'strangely warmed': 'I felt I did trust in Christ, Christ alone for salvation; and an assurance was given me, that he had taken away *my* sins, even *mine*, and saved *me* from the law of sin and death.'

Early methodism owed much to the moravians. Perhaps their most important contribution was their stress on the new birth which converted men from nominal to real Christianity, although others prominent in the revival stressed this independently of moravian influence. George Whitefield preached a sermon in 1737 on *The nature and necessity of a new birth in Christ Jesus in order to salvation*. The moravian stress on the intercession of Christ, however, did have a direct impact on the revival. The early methodists dwelt more on the New Testament than on the Old, in contrast with earlier puritans, and unlike their puritan predecessors emphasized the love of Jesus rather than the wrath of Jehovah. More peculiarly moravian were the agapes or love feasts, which Wesley introduced to a religious society in Fetter Lane after a visit to Herrnhut in 1738. Another vital aspect of their worship was hymn singing, which also played an essential part in methodist services. Charles Wesley, of course, wrote many of these, though several were translated from German hymns made use of by the moravians.

In 1740, however, the Wesleys broke with the moravians, because some began to insist that those who had assurance of salvation had no need of such means of grace as prayer, Bible reading and good works. They adopted a completely passive attitude towards religion, waiting for inspiration from the Holy Spirit. To Wesley, a man of action as well as a man of God, such 'stillness' was intolerable. He therefore moved his own followers, who numbered eighteen or nineteen, from the Fetter Lane Society to the Foundery. The Foundery, which had been disused for years following a devastating munitions explosion, was refurbished and became the centre of Wesley's movement until the City Road Chapel was built in 1778.

The year 1739 had witnessed the beginning of a more serious split among the early methodists when the Wesleys disagreed with George Whitefield on the issues of predestination and free will. Whitefield had known them since 1735, when he had joined the original methodists in Oxford. They had worked together in Bristol after John's return from Georgia. But though they had much in common, Whitefield was a calvinist who believed that only the elect were predestined to salvation. The Wesleys, on the other hand, were arminians, believing that Christ had died for all men. The breach widened in 1740 when John Wesley published a sermon on *Free Grace* to which Charles appended a hymn which included the lines:

> And shall I, Lord, confine Thy love
> As not to others free?
> And may not every sinner prove
> The Grace that found out me?

This arminianism of the Wesleys owed much to the high-church tradition, while Whitefield was more in line with earlier puritanism. Not that the Wesley brothers were uninfluenced by puritan thought; on the contrary, although they remained high-church in theology, they were more and more drawn to puritan views. After his return from Georgia John began to read the works of eminent puritan divines of the previous century, and eventually incorporated many into his *Christian Library*, which consisted of extracts from 'the choicest pieces of practical divinity which have been published in the English tongue'. Of some sixty English authors whose works were condensed in this massive edition no fewer than twenty-six were nonconformists, including John Bunyan and Richard Baxter. There were also catholic works, including translations from Fénelon and Pascal—Wesley's theology was nothing if not eclectic.

An aspect of methodism which reflected more obviously the low-church and dissenting tradition rather than the high-church heritage was the system of organization. When it came to the task of coordinating the efforts of his followers, Wesley found a pattern was to hand in the example of the religious societies which had sprung up in the late seventeenth century.[29] Some were merely semi-formal clubs of devout Christians who met together for prayer and Bible reading. Others were more elaborately organized societies for the reformation of manners, which systematically prosecuted people who broke the laws against immorality. The efforts of both had been coordinated by the Society for Promoting Christian Knowledge, established in 1698. Whitefield had turned to the societies when he was debarred from preaching in churches and Wesley was familiar with their organization. The Holy Club at Oxford was a type of society, while in Georgia he had advised 'the more serious' believers in Savannah to 'form themselves into a sort of little society, and to meet once or twice a week in order to reprove, instruct and exhort one another'. It was in a religious society that he was converted in 1738.

The methodists were organized originally on similar lines. Devout followers were divided into 'bands' of between five and ten people, composed of either men or women further divided into married and single methodists. These met regularly for prayer, study and censorship of each other's morals. At the end of 1738 Wesley drew up rules for the bands, incorporating eleven questions for those seeking membership, and five for members. Thus every week members had to answer a set of queries beginning 'what known sins have you committed since our last meeting?' The more pious members of the bands constituted select societies, while less zealous members were organized into united societies, first established in Bristol and London in 1739. The united societies sent delegates to the annual conference, the first of which was held in 1744.

Fund raising for paying preachers and for charity required tighter organization, and this resulted in the unique methodist institution, the class. The first class was formed in Bristol in 1742 at the suggestion of a Captain Foy. It consisted of twelve members under a class leader, who collected one penny a week from those in his charge. These leaders at first undertook to visit members to receive the pennies and to give them to the steward of the local society every week. The system extended immediately to London, where sixty-six classes of around six members were formed and became widespread throughout the movement by 1746. Classes became a far more vital part of the methodist organization than mere money raising machines, especially when the class leaders began to meet the members altogether instead of visiting them separately. The classes then met weekly for fellowship as well as funds. Wesley recognized them as the focus of methodist life and maintained a tight control over them, nominating their leaders and catechizing their members 'to separate the precious from the vile'. The vile were purged from the movement, while the precious were given class tickets which permitted them to attend love feasts, society meetings and other functions. This personal control was entirely in line with Wesley's authoritarian attitude to government. He had no time for democracy, for in his view 'the greater the share the people have in government, the less liberty, civil or religious, does a nation enjoy'. He once rebuked methodists, who took what he considered to be undue initiatives, by reminding them how authority radiated outwards from himself: 'In the methodist discipline, the wheels regularly stand thus: the assistant, the preachers, the stewards, the leaders, the people.' He was so autocratic that his opponents called him 'Pope John'.

It became necessary to have a sound organization to hold together the growing number of methodists, for the revival spread throughout the British Isles. Too often methodism is described as a crusade by the Wesley brothers and Whitefield when they were but the most conspicuous among a large number of like-minded men. In Wales, for instance, three ministers, Howell Davies, Griffith Jones and

Daniel Rowlands, and a schoolmaster, Howell Harris, became
itinerant preachers before Wesley began his ministry in England. In
the West Riding of Yorkshire, William Grimshaw and John Nelson
developed societies on similar lines to the methodist societies which
were simply absorbed into Wesley's system. The work in the localities
depended on the zeal of men like Grimshaw who, when he became
curate of Haworth, found but twelve communicants, and at the end
of his curacy had 1,200, requiring thirty-five bottles of communion
wine. What the Wesleys did, with their indefatigable energy, was to
coordinate and control these efforts. Although the Welsh revival
went its own way, they did integrate the early English methodists
into a system. The Wesleys personally kept in touch with their
followers by dint of a staggering amount of travel, John covering a
computed 250,000 miles mostly on horseback in the course of his
ministry. At first they concentrated on an axis bounded by London
and Bristol, until in 1742 John visited Newcastle upon Tyne and the
following year established the orphan house there. London, Bristol
and Newcastle then became the points of a triangle marking the
Wesleys' personal connection. A more impersonal system was
devised at the third annual conference in 1746, which organized
seven 'circuits' around which at least a dozen itinerant preachers
travelled. By 1753 there were eighty-five such preachers travelling
twelve circuits.

The use of itinerant preachers and field preaching enabled the
methodists to reach whole masses of people who simply were not
being catered for by the establishment. One of the difficulties which
faced the anglican church in the eighteenth century was that the
growth of population and internal migration to industrial areas put
too much pressure on a medieval administrative system based on
parishes. Some of the newer industrial areas had several thousand
people living within a single parish. Manchester, for example, with a
population of at least 20,000 by 1750, had only one parish church.
Short of wholesale reform of church government, for which the will
was lacking, the church could only proceed piecemeal with this
problem since it required a special act of parliament to create a new
parish church. Thus in 1711 an act was passed authorizing the
building of fifty new churches in London alone to meet the estimated
needs of the enlarged capital. In the event, however, only twelve of
them were ever built. Not that there was a complete standstill in
church building, as is often asserted. In Cumberland, for instance,
seventeen churches were newly built or rebuilt between 1702 and
1768. Even when they were not freshly constructed or structurally
altered, many churches were refurbished, for example with galleries

and pews. Nineteenth-century 'restoration' removed much of the evidence for this, though some have survived more or less as they appeared in Wesley's day, for example St Mary's, Whitby.

The ways in which churches were built or altered, however, reveal that to some extent priorities were social rather than spiritual. Only twelve out of the projected fifty churches in London were built, because the commissioners responsible for their construction chose the most elaborate and expensive design. The beauty of holiness thus took precedence over the pastoral needs of the London poor. Pews were also socially divisive, separating the more affluent members of the congregation who paid pew rents from the poor. Whether it was a lack of means or will, the end result was the same. The Church of England catered for the comfortably-off in the eighteenth century. Maybe it had never really made contact with the poorest classes but the gap, however great, was growing, especially in the expanding industrial areas.

Methodism deliberately set out to meet these people. Preaching in the open air made initial contact with thousands, and when eventually chapels were built Wesley was adamant that they should be 'plain and decent: but not more expensive than is absolutely necessary', while he banned pews and ordered that seating should be on the basis of first come, first served. His appeal was particularly strong in industrial communities; indeed methodism made relatively little progress in agricultural areas. In Cornwall, it noticeably established itself in places where tin mining and fishing were the main industries and not agriculture. The counties of Surrey, Hampshire and Wiltshire became known as the methodist wilderness and Wesley spent very little time in them. On the other hand, counties with growing industrial areas, such as Staffordshire, Lancashire, Yorkshire, Durham and Northumberland, became strongholds of methodism. By 1767 over a fifth of the members of the methodist societies lived in Yorkshire, mostly in the manufacturing districts of the West Riding.

It was also noticeable that the Methodist converts were 'chiefly the poorer people'.[30] One of Wesley's critics described his followers as 'a ragged legion of preaching barbers, cobblers, tinkers, scavengers, draymen and chimney sweepers'.[31] However, this was typical of the eighteenth-century habit of denigrating any movement, political as well as religious, by associating its members with the rabble. Closer investigation reveals that methodism struck roots at various levels of English society.

There were a number of upper-class supporters, especially among Whitefield's admirers. Perhaps the elite were more responsive to his calvinism than to Wesley's arminianism because they could more

readily accept the notion that they were also the elect. The most
celebrated was Selina, Countess of Huntingdon, whose protegé,
William Romaine, preached at the fashionable church of St
George's, Hanover Square. Her sister-in-law, Lady Margaret Hast-
ings, scandalized polite society in 1741 by marrying Benjamin
Ingham, an itinerant preacher. Lady Margaret's pious namesake,
Lady Elizabeth Hastings, was an early sympathizer with methodism.
She lived at Ledstone House all her life, and had an estate worth
£3,000 a year, from which she endowed over sixty perpetual charities
including nine charity schools and a scholarship at The Queen's
College, Oxford. The Hastings scholarship originally included an
element of chance in the form of a lottery, which even Lady Elizabeth
owned 'may be called by some superstition or enthusiasm'.[32]

Wesleyan methodism, however, did not attract many of the upper
classes. John Wesley himself once said 'to speak the rough truth, I do
not desire any intercourse with any persons of quality in England',
while Charles wrote a hymn which contained the lines

> The rich and great in every age
> Conspire to persecute their God.

Among the rules for methodist preachers was one which said 'do not
affect the gentleman. You have no more to do with this character
than with that of a dancing master.' Although the preachers were not
gentlemen, neither were they for the most part from the very poor.
There is abundant biographical information about the early
preachers which shows that the majority of them came from the stock
of tradesmen, craftsmen and farmers. These groups provided the
bulk of the class leaders and indeed of methodists active in the early
organization. Between the arrival of a field preacher in a district and
the building of a chapel, of which there were only forty by 1760, a
zealous convert would make his house available for worship and
meetings. These people were often more substantial than labourers.
It seems likely that many of the activists in early methodism came
from precisely the same ranks in society as those which had formed
the religious societies, such as those for reformation of manners,
which originated in the late seventeenth century and petered out in
the late 1730s. It is to say the least an odd coincidence that the last
mention of the societies for reformation of manners is in 1739, the
year after Wesley's conversion. The societies looked for a lead in their
fight against vice to the upper classes, arguing that corruption
percolated down from the top of society to the bottom and that
reformation of corrupt manners must follow the same route. They
had of course been bitterly disappointed. Timothy Jollie, in the last
sermon known to have been preached to the London societies,
lamented the lack of support from magistrates, complaining 'how few

seem willing, heartily, to engage in the design.'[33] Wesley did not make the same mistake. He claimed 'that all religious movements for reform began among the poor, moving slowly up the social ladder until finally, in the millenial day, they touched the nobility.'[34]

The appeal of the religious societies and of the methodists to craftsmen and tradesmen was no doubt primarily spiritual. Yet at the same time strong social pressures can be detected behind their enthusiasm. Personal discipline was an important ingredient in commercial and thereby social success. A reputation for drunkenness, swearing and immorality, whether among masters or their journeymen and apprentices, was simply bad for business. The suppression of such activities was the prime aim of the societies for reformation of manners. Methodism not only took over these attitudes but adopted a more positive approach to business. Where the societies had attacked Sunday trading the methodists went further, urging upon their followers in general and tradesmen in particular the most scrupulous standard of fair dealing. Among the 'Rules of the Society of the People called Methodists' issued in 1743 were prohibitions upon 'using many words in buying or selling . . . giving or taking things in usury . . . borrowing without a probability of paying for them'. Methodists were also urged to assist each other by 'buying one of another, helping each other in business'. Tradesmen were enjoined not to sell below or above the market price, nor to 'study to ruin our neighbour's trade, in order to advance our own'. Bankrupts were expelled from the society, though this did not happen very often, and methodists boasted that tradesmen in their midst prospered because of their business ethics. Those that did, however, were supposed to give all that was not necessary for subsistence to the poor.

If the officers of the methodist army consisted primarily of tradesmen, craftsmen and farmers, the rank and file was made up of the labouring poor. Methodism appealed especially to miners, those in the Kingswood colliery near Bristol and those on Tyneside being prominent converts. Insofar as these had any previous religious affiliation at all, it had been to the high-church rather than to the low-church or dissenting tradition; at least, the Kingswood miners had demonstrated in support of Dr Sacheverell in 1710 and were suspected of Jacobitism under George I.[35] But religion of any kind probably sat very lightly on the labouring poor before Wesley and his itinerant preachers addressed them. Among the masses superstition flourished long after the decline of magic had set in among the educated classes. At the lower levels of English society primitive beliefs in witches, devils and magic continued to hold sway at a time when they were ridiculed in higher circles.

Henry Bourne, curate of All Saints, Newcastle upon Tyne, described some of these popular superstitions in *Antiquitates Vulgares*, which he published in 1725. In the preface he claimed that 'though some of them have been of national and others perhaps of universal observance, yet at present they would have little or no being, if not observed among the vulgar.' The practices included the observation of omens, such as a hare crossing one's path, crows and owls screeching, spilling of salt and the chattering of magpies and crickets, which were all regarded as evil portents. Bourne thought that these beliefs were 'sinful and diabolical'. Among instances of practices regarded as producing beneficial results he noted watching the sun rise on Easter Day and the first day of May. Bourne was convinced that these superstitions were relics of popery from before the Reformation. Thus on belief in ghosts he observed that 'tis common for the present vulgar to say, none can lay a spirit but a popish priest.' Superstition among the masses made them peculiarly susceptible to conversions by enthusiastic preachers, many of whom shared their beliefs, and were widely suspected of being crypto-catholics, if not papists. Wesley believed in witches and practised the *sortes liturgicae*, even opening the Bible at random to discover whether God wished him to go to Bristol from London. He and his followers were frequently accused of being emissaries from Rome, and at the height of the Forty-Five of being agents of the Pretender.

The only members of the lower classes that the revival failed to touch in any significant way were farm workers. Otherwise they appealed to labouring people of all kinds, and especially to their wives and children. Wesley's concern for children found expression in the establishment of schools in Bristol and Newcastle; there was no provision for play or games, since he believed that 'he who plays when he is a child, will play when he is a man.' Wesley, although he approved of cheerfulness, disapproved of levity and mirth and one of the rules, headed 'Be serious', exhorted methodists to 'avoid all lightness as you would avoid hell-fire: and laughing as you would cursing and swearing'. This was very far from the good humour and good manners which Lord Shaftesbury advocated as an antidote to enthusiasm.

Indeed in almost every respect the whole spirit of the methodists was so far removed from that of the establishment that it is not surprising that they were decried as enthusiasts. Where the prevailing religion of the upper classes hardly measured up to Wesley's criteria for nominal religion, being little more than a code of good manners, methodists were consumed with a burning conviction that man was sinful and that only a new birth in Christ could wash his sins away. Where the established clergy appealed to reason, they appealed to the passions. Where the sophisticated accepted scientific explanations of the workings of the universe which left little role to God or providence, Wesley put divine intervention at the very heart of human affairs. Wesley's intensely personal religion, his appeal to the emotions and his superstitious beliefs alienated him from most of the upper classes, but helped him to strike a response among the lower classes where the establishment had failed.

Not that his reception from the poor was unreservedly favourable, for he frequently had to face hostile crowds, especially in the early days of his ministry. There were particularly violent demonstrations against him in Staffordshire in 1743, Cornwall in 1745 and Lancashire in 1748. When he did not attribute these to the devil, then in typical eighteenth-century manner he saw in them the work of discontented upper-class elements. Thus a mob attack on a supporter in Gloucestershire in 1743 was instigated, according to Wesley, by 'many of the baser sort, privately encouraged by some of a higher rank'.

There is some evidence that this was so. Certainly landlords and brother clergymen had occasion to stir up demonstrations against the methodists. Landlords and others who employed servants initially viewed them with concern, for however conservative they later became, at first they appeared to be social revolutionaries. The author of *An earnest call to a National Reformation*, published in 1746, who thought that the methodists were 'disorder'd in their senses', nevertheless argued that

> Mr Whitefield's scheme of religion is well adapted for a punishment to those who will not give their servants time and opportunity to serve the Lord on his own day, but make the sabbath as much a working day as others . . . for was his doctrine to take place, they would have nobody to work for them on any day.

Preaching the equality of all believers made the methodists appear to be urging insubordination and led masters of households to feel threatened. Many clergymen who failed to satisfy their criteria of what constituted a good preacher objected to being called 'dumb dogs' or being accused, as they were by Whitefield, of 'only seeking after preferment . . . either to spend on the pleasures of life, or to gratify their sensual appetites'.[36]

But there is no need to look for a superior lead to account for the hostility which methodists often encountered from mobs. There was plenty of spontaneous objection to be made to evangelical preachers who denounced as the work of the devil bull-baiting, cockfighting, dancing and drinking, some of the few pastimes which made the labourer's lot tolerable in those days. Indeed it might be wondered why methodism appealed at all to the masses. In one light, all it seems to have offered them was a reward in heaven for contentedly accepting their lot in this life and working hard to improve the few talents they had been given. Methodism preached that the social hierarchy was divinely ordained and that workers should be inured to hard labour and should avoid idleness, since the devil found work for idle hands. If they were occupied in gaming, drinking, dancing and other prophane diversions, then eternal punishment would be the inevitable fate. On the other hand acceptance of a new birth in Jesus Christ ensured a heavenly reward.

However, methodism offered to the poor more than a reward hereafter. It also held out the prospect of alleviating their lot on earth—a notion at loggerheads with current attitudes towards poverty, which either accepted it as inevitable or blamed it upon the idleness of the poor. Wesley was convinced that a fairer distribution of goods could alleviate hardship, and opposed as 'wickedly, devilishly false' the idea that the poor were poor merely because they were idle. He exhorted the more affluent methodists to give their surplus earnings to the poor and this was done on such a scale that the movement became virtually self-sufficient, boasting that few if any of its poor were a burden to the parish system of relief. Charity went further than relieving poverty, for in 1746 a fund was established to provide capital for methodists to set themselves up in trade. Among the more spectacular beneficiaries of this fund was James Lackington, who received £5 and became a very prosperous bookseller, admitting in later life that, if he had never heard of the methodists, he would have remained 'a poor, ragged, dirty cobbler'.

The Methodists also looked after their sick. Wesley was particularly interested in medicine and issued *A collation of receits for the use of the poor* in 1745 and *Primitive Physick, or an easy and natural method of curing most diseases* in 1747. It must be admitted that he was something of a quack, for in 1756 he used an electrical healing machine which, he claimed, 'by electrifying in a proper manner cures St Anthony's fire, gouts, headache, inflammations, lameness, palpitations of the heart, palsy, rheumatisms, sprain, toothache, sore throat and swelling of all sorts'. Still, it could have done no worse than many of the cures recommended by professional physicians in those days. Education helped to improve the life style of poor Methodists, not only in the schools, but through the distribution of vast amounts of cheap and sometimes free literature. Indeed it could be said that Wesley invented the commercialization of religion. Not that all the tracts and books which poured from the Methodist press were purely religious. Methodist publications 'included biography, poetry, travel, subjects of daily utility, etiquette, school books, Christian casuistry, the writings of Locke, Spencer, Shakespeare and Malebranche as well as explicitly religious works'.[37] The most enduring literature of methodism, however, was not John's tracts but Charles's hymns: the methodist hymnal of 1780 contained no fewer than 480 composed by John's brother.

John and Charles Wesley remained members of the Church of England all their lives, although there was friction between them and fellow anglicans from the start. Even sympathetic clergymen, such as Thomas Adams of Wintringham, James Hervey of Weston Flavell and Samuel Walker of Truro, censured their employment of itinerant lay preachers, their recourse to field preaching and the construction of separate chapels. Such activities kept these early evangelicals aloof from methodism proper. They also caused trouble with the authorities. Field preaching and the erection of chapels created problems under the Toleration Act. According to the strict letter of the law this only tolerated separate conventicles for dissenters from the Church of England, and Wesley's antagonists in the establishment insisted that he should apply for licences for them as a dissenter. Wesley fought a long legal battle for the right of his followers, as anglicans, to worship in their own chapels without the need for a licence under the act.

The debate over ordination, which was eventually to cause the secession of the Wesleyan methodists from the established church, also flared up before 1760. A number of lay preachers began to administer the sacraments and to request ordination from Wesley, which threatened, in Grimshaw's words 'a manifest rupture with the established church. We must then be declared dissenters.' Wesley read a paper 'Ought we to separate from the Church of England?' at the annual conference held in Leeds in 1755. After three days of debate the conference resolved that separation was 'no ways expedient'. Next year a less ambiguous decision was reached, when the Wesleys 'ended the conference with a strong declaration . . . to live and die in the communion of the Church of England.' Despite this some lay preachers continued to administer the sacraments, even taking out licences as dissenting ministers to legalize their position. Charles forced a somewhat reluctant John to come to grips with this challenge to the movement at the Bristol conference in 1760, when those preachers who had licensed themselves were disavowed and Wesley refused categorically to ordain a separate ministry. The crisis of separation from the Church of England was thus evaded for the next twenty years.

# 5 The Economy of Early Hanoverian Britain

In his *Tour through the whole island of Great Britain*, first published between 1724 and 1726, Daniel Defoe set out to provide not merely a tourist guide for the early Hanoverian traveller but an economic dissertation. One thesis he advanced was that there was a national economy over and above the regional economies and local markets of England, Wales and Scotland. This national economy was sustained by demands generated in London for consumer goods which were supplied from every corner of the island: 'this whole kingdom, as well as the people, as the land, and even the sea, in every part of it, are employed to furnish something, and I may add, the best of everything, to supply the city of London with provisions.'[1] Another notion which informs almost every page of Defoe's *Tour* was that the British economy was growing. Practically everywhere he went, or said he had been, he claimed to have seen evidence for increasing manufacture, expanding trade and a general rise in affluence.

Such conclusions would not find general agreement among modern economic historians. Some would object to the notion of a national economy in early eighteenth-century Britain, insisting that economic life was still mainly regional in character, dominated for the most part by local market conditions. Thus it has been argued that there were at least six areas in which the price of grain, a staple commodity, varied in response to local rather than to national conditions. Nor would Defoe's notion that the British economy was rapidly growing find a consensus of opinion. Some historians, impressed by rates of growth occurring in the Industrial Revolution, have suggested that the pre-industrial economy was sluggish if not stagnant. It has even been asserted that the English economy was actually slowing down in these very years. Others have maintained that different branches of the economy varied significantly in their long and short term tendencies, and that even in one industry there could be diverse trends. For example, in textiles the 'old draperies' declined while the worsted industry prospered.

Yet if we set out in Defoe's footsteps and try to examine economic conditions in early Hanoverian Britain without the disadvantage of post-industrial hindsight, we might, like him, be more impressed by the evidence for growth than by signs of decay. We might not share his overall optimism, but in most parts of the island we should notice a quickening of the pulse of economic life. Above all his thesis that London was the great motor which generated economic growth can survive critical scrutiny.

London itself was growing, both physically and in the number of its inhabitants. As an observer noted in 1722, 'The increase of the city of London in all sorts of inhabitants is visible from the increase of buildings in the outparts.'[2] Around the beginning of the century the built-up area stretched along the river from Westminster to Wapping, and north and south from Clerkenwell to Kennington. By 1760 it took in Hyde Park and Mile End and reached as far north as St Pancras.

Already the social structure of the capital had been laid on end, as it were, from west to east. Westminster had become the fashionable end of town, the City was the centre of its financial and business life, some of the newer suburbs in the East End, such as Deptford and Islington, housed merchants, shipbuilders and professional men, while dockyard workers and sailors dwelt along the river in Wapping and Rotherhithe.

The most fashionable part of the West End was the court, which was held in St James's and Kensington Palaces. Here were gathered about 1,000 people who waited upon the king—the peers and gentlemen who fulfilled the formal or honorary functions, such as the lord chamberlain, the groom of the stole and the master of the horse; the gentlemen of the bedchamber and ushers who were in daily attendance; and the grooms and footmen, chambermaids and kitchen staff who undertook the more routine functions. The royal household was but the most conspicuous of a number of similar establishments, and its nearest rival was that maintained by the princes of Wales at Leicester House from 1717 to 1720, and again from 1737 to 1751, when they quarrelled with their fathers. Aristocratic town houses which followed the social pattern set by the court were situated in the West End, such as Marlborough House in Pall Mall, Burlington House in Piccadilly, Powis House in Great Ormond Street and Montagu House in Russell Street. These noble households were probably the biggest employers of labour in Westminster, perhaps a third of their inhabitants being domestic servants. Today one of the largest employers is the government, but this was not so during the eighteenth century. Although the chief departments of state, the admiralty, the treasury and the offices of the two secretaries, were situated in Whitehall, they were very small

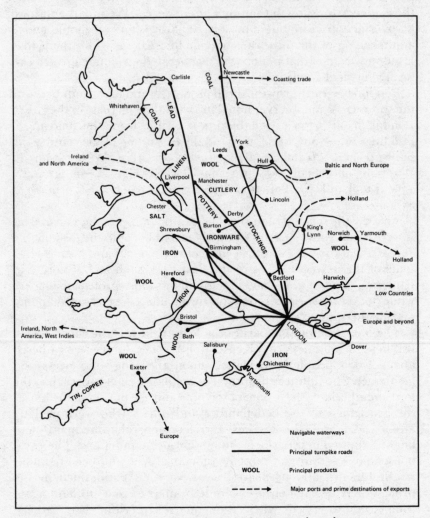

Map 2  England and Wales, showing principal routes and products.

establishments. The secretaries' offices, for instance, housed in a rabbit warren of a building called the Cockpit, had a complete staff of only twenty-four in 1726. Other important departments, the customs house, the excise office and the post office, were in the City, thus bridging the gap between Whitehall and London. The gap anyway was becoming symbolic rather than physical during the period, as the removal of the City gates in 1760 demonstrated.

There were fashionable and unfashionable parts of London, too. As Sarah Fielding put it 'the manner of living of the inhabitants of every different part of this great metropolis varies as much as that of different nations.'[3] Cheapside and Cornhill, for instance, were centres for such luxury trades as jewellery and porcelain. Less fancy trades settled elsewhere. The purlieus of St Paul's contained many booksellers, mercers were to be found in Gracechurch and Lombard Streets and Ludgate, shoemakers in St Martin's and Shoemaker Row. During the eighteenth century watch-makers established themselves in Clerkenwell and the neighbouring parish of St Lukes's. Watch-making was an early example of an industry organized on the principle of the division of labour, some making the dials, others the cases, others the wheels and yet others the springs. About 120,000 clocks and watches were produced in London every year. Less fashionable trades, especially if, like dyeing, tanning or brewing they produced industrial pollution, were as far as possible relegated south of the river to Southwark.

London, of course, was primarily not an industrial but a financial and commercial centre. It had established itself as the nation's financial capital before 1714 for it was in the late seventeenth century that the expression 'the City' first came into use as a term meaning the area around Threadneedle Street and Cornhill where bankers and financiers held sway. Stockbrokers, ejected from the Royal Exchange, took up their abode in Jonathan's Coffee House, which became known as the Stock Exchange in 1773. Hoares, Childs and Goslings banks were established in Fleet Street. The City also housed the first insurance companies, such as the Sun Fire Office, London Assurance and, above all, Lloyds, originally a coffee house in Tower Street. And it was in the City that the effects of the so-called financial revolution were most keenly felt.

The financial revolution was the product of the unprecedented needs for borrowing money which arose after 1688, when William committed England to major wars against France. Where the total revenues granted to Charles II and James II were £1,200,000 and £2,000,000 respectively, the wars against Louis XIV between 1689 and 1713 cost Britain £5,000,000 to £7,000,000 a year. Initially they were financed from current taxation, the land tax, the customs and excise, and fancy taxes like the window tax. Even these had to be anticipated in the form of loans. Thus when the land tax was assessed at four shillings in the pound, as it was for most of the war period, it produced approximately £2,000,000; as soon as the annual bill authorizing its collection had received the royal assent, the treasury arranged to raise £1,800,000 in anticipation of its receipt, largely in the form of subscriptions from private individuals. As the wars went on and became more expensive, however, the government had to borrow on future taxes and even on public credit alone. By 1711 the unfunded debt stood at £9,000,000, out of a total national debt of £36,000,000.

Besides borrowing directly from private citizens, the government created a new machinery of public credit based on three institutions, the Bank of England, the East India Company and the South Sea Company. The Bank owed its charter of 1694 to a loan of £1,200,000 to the government, and it lent a further £2,900,000 in 1709 in return for the authority to increase its capital. The United East India Company, founded in 1709 by the merging of two rival companies, advanced £1,200,000 to the state during the negotiations leading to its incorporation. The South Sea Company was established in 1711 to convert the £9,000,000 of unconsolidated debt into stock in the new company. By 1720 the three great corporations were responsible for about £19,000,000 of the total national debt of about £50,000,000 in that year. It was the South Sea Company's attempt to convert the remaining £31,000,000 into its stock which caused the Bubble. After the South Sea Bubble of 1720 recourse to the three great financial corporations for handling public credit became, not surprisingly in view of that unhappy experience, rather less frequent, and by 1749 they were responsible for only about a quarter of the total debt. Nevertheless they continued to take the lead when the government resorted to the money market. 'In 1759–60, for instance, when what was then the large sum of £8,000,000 was to be borrowed there stands before the names of the nineteen private applicants, "Mr Burrell for the Bank of England £466,000, Mr Bristow for the South Sea Company £330,000, Mr Godfrey for the East India Company £200,000."'[4]

The South Sea and East India Companies, of course, were not just financial corporations but had important trading connections with Africa, South America and the far east. Although trade was less significant than finance to the first, it was more important to the second. The terms obtained from the Spanish government in the negotiations connected with the Treaty of Utrecht had been disappointing to those who had hoped that the South Sea Company would be permitted to play a major role in trading with Spain's overseas possessions. In fact the Company had been allowed to share in the Assiento, or slave trade, and to send one ship a year directly to Spanish colonies in South America. Even these limited concessions were not fully exploited under George I, while the Assiento contract was surrendered in 1750. The East India Company, on the other hand, continued to expand its trading interests with the Far East throughout the period. Since they were worth an estimated £2,000,000 a year, the company's monopoly of these interests was twice challenged under the first two Georges. In 1730 there were complaints against the renewal of its charter, though Walpole extended it to 1766. More serious opposition was raised in the years 1758–9 when the elder Pitt supported objections to the high price of tea imported into England by the Company. It was anomalous in some ways that the Company kept its privileges, for other monopoly trading companies lost their rights during the period. The Royal African Company was wound up in 1750, while the monopoly of the Levant Company came to an end in 1753. The attacks on the London-based chartered companies came to a large extent from merchants in other ports. Significantly the growing trade with the American colonies, which in these years benefited western ports such as Bristol, Liverpool, Whitehaven and Glasgow much more than London, was handled by individual traders rather than by bodies politic, the Hudson's Bay Company being the only one of its kind to operate in North America.

Nevertheless, London remained far and away the most important commercial centre in England. In 1760 the port of London was still handling seventy-two per cent of English imports, seventy-three per cent of her exports and seventy-five per cent of her re-exports. Foreign trade took ships from London to every part of the known world. Their cargoes varied according to their destinations. Woollen cloth destined for northern, western and, increasingly, southern Europe filled the holds of many vessels, for cloth still dominated the export market. Where in the early seventeenth century, however, between eighty and ninety per cent of all exports had been textiles, by the beginning of the eighteenth century cloth had dropped to forty-eight per cent, and by 1750 was down to thirty-three per cent. Indeed, but for the Methuen Treaties of 1703, which gave England a favourable trade with Portugal whereby cloth was exchanged for wine and precious metals, exports of woollen textiles to Europe might well have encountered a severe recession in the eighteenth century. Fortunately for the English cloth industry there was a dramatic growth in exports to Portugal between 1700 and 1760, which ensured that on the whole trade to Europe in woollens remained stable in these years.

During the seventeenth century the share of exports held by cloth had lost ground to the re-export of extra-European products, especially sugar, tobacco and calicoes, most of which were bound for Europe. The ratio of re-exports to exports, however, did not continue to expand during the eighteenth century, remaining static at around thirty per cent. Sugar re-exports actually declined as the French developed their own sources of supply in the West Indies. The export of native raw materials on the other hand, such as coal and corn, was growing. During the century England became a corn exporter on an ever increasing scale until domestic demand caught up with supply some time after 1760.

The truly remarkable growth in exports was that of manufactured goods, especially metalware, though including cotton and linen, whose share rose from eight per cent in 1700 to twenty per cent by 1750. Of the 120,000 clocks and watches made in London each year, some 70,000 were exported, mainly to Europe. Most other manufactures found their way to markets outside Europe, to colonies in the West Indies and above all to the North American mainland and to Africa where they were exchanged for slaves. Manufactured goods were increasingly exported to the Far East, though the main demand from India, China and the spice islands was for metals, and especially for precious metals, which meant a drain of gold and silver from England to pay for the tea, calicoes, spices and luxuries of the East. Extra-European produce such as sugar, tobacco, tea, coffee, rice, spices, silks and raw cotton, loomed increasingly large in Britain's imports, though as late as 1750 over half of all imported wares came from Europe. Although imports of European manufactured articles declined during the century, there was a growing demand for such materials as flax and hemp, timber and iron, wool and linen yarn, a demand met mainly from the Baltic and Mediterranean areas. Most of this trade with Europe was channelled through London.

One important branch of overseas trade which did its best to stay away from London and the vigilance of the customs house, however, was that which involved smuggling. Estimates of the scale of smuggling are of necessity difficult to calculate, since smugglers covered up their tracks too well. It would seem that possibly a third of all trade with France was conducted clandestinely, imported French brandy being exchanged for English wool, the export of which was illegal. The possibility of illegal trade being on this scale casts doubts upon some of the data on which long term trends are based, much of it from customs records which are in themselves difficult to interpret. If they record only a fraction of the real volume of trade—and some historians reckon that three quarters of all tea imported into England during the century did not pay duty—then we are really in the dark about the true commercial pattern in these years. However, this has not deterred some historians from describing as a, if not the, commercial revolution the shift from trade based primarily on the exchange of cloth for European produce to trade in which the re-export of extra-European products and the export of manufactured articles were the dynamic elements. An increase in the rate of growth in overseas trade from one per cent per annum between 1700 and 1740 to 1.9 per cent in the decade 1750 to 1760, was indeed revolutionary for a pre-industrial economy.

The chief beneficiary of this revolution was London. At least a quarter of the 575,000 people who lived there in 1714 and of the 675,000 inhabitants in 1760 were directly employed in port trades. Most of the rest were involved in distributive trades and service industries which provided an infrastructure for this prime commercial activity. Since the capital contained between eight and nine per cent of all the people in Britain during this period, most of them not directly engaged in the production of food or goods, London was far and away the most important market in the country. Its demands for food and manufactured articles had a decisive impact on the national economy.

London had a voracious appetite for food. In 1725 alone it 'consumed 369,000 quarters of flour, 60,000 calves, 70,000 sheep and lambs, 187,000 swine, 52,000 sucking pigs, 115,000 bushels of oysters, 14,750,000 mackerel, 1,398 boatloads of cod, haddock and whiting, 16,366,000 lb of butter, 21,066,000 lb of cheese, 5 million gallons of milk'.[5] Apart from the milk, which had to come from the vicinity if it was to stay fresh and was in fact largely supplied by dairy farmers in Islington, these products were not local in origin. The fish could not come from very far away, as it too had to be reasonably fresh, and most of it came from the fishing ports of Essex, Kent and Sussex, although around 1760 some seventy-one tons of sole were sent annually from the Devon port of Brixham to the capital. But the cheese came from Cheshire, Gloucester and Somerset, while mutton was conveyed from Lincolnshire and Leicestershire, and beef from Scotland and Wales, on the hoof. The wheat for the flour came from an ever-expanding area, radiating in all directions to take in the home counties, with the exception of Middlesex which did not produce much, Kent, East Anglia and the midlands.

British agriculture not only managed to supply the increasing demands of the London food market during these years but actually outstripped it, expanding production until in the years 1730 to 1750 prices fell. The increase in the production of wheat was so great that for a few decades England had a substantial surplus to export, by

1750 perhaps a quarter of the crop. As for meat, an observer in 1736 commented that[6]

> we have of late years greatly increased in the breeding of live stock of all kinds, and the great supply from the northern parts of England and Wales have glutted the London markets. . . . This great increase has of late supplied the London markets with meat far beyond its consumption, and therefore lowered the price, so that the best or middling pieces have been sold cheap enough to be within the reach of common people, therefore common pieces have not had so ready a vent as usual.

The striking increase in agricultural production in the period before 1750 can be attributed to a variety of causes. The weather must not be ignored, for there seems to be little doubt that wheat prices were mainly affected by a run of good harvests in the second quarter of the eighteenth century, after indifferent or even bad summers in the first. A minor cause was the extension of the area under cultivation, for example, the fens changed into farms by improved drainage in Bedfordshire. Gregory King reckoned that there were ten million acres of waste in England and Wales around 1690, while in 1795 the board of agriculture estimated eight million. Although neither estimate was accurate and probably both exaggerated, the area under cultivation perhaps increased by ten per cent between 1700 and 1760, contributing not a little to the increase in agricultural production. At the same time there must have been an improvement in productivity. 'All history cannot furnish twenty such years of fertility and abundance as from 1730 to 1750 when the average prices were the lowest ever known' claimed one who lived through them, adding 'another reason we assign to the fall of price, is the great improvements made in agriculture in the last fifty or sixty years.'[7]

To appreciate these improvements requires some understanding of the agricultural industry before 1714 or rather, of the agricultural industries, for English farming displayed infinite variety at all times, depending upon such variables as rock, soil, altitude, crops, livestock, the pattern of landholding and even the notoriously fickle weather.

England and Wales can be divided into myriad regions on the basis of agricultural geography but three main areas should at least be distinguished—the hilly parts of the north of England and much of Wales, with thin soils covering millstone grit, limestone and basalt; the heavy clay soils of the midlands plain; and the lighter soils of the east and south, especially in chalk country which stretches from the East Riding of Yorkshire down to the white cliffs of Dover, and across southern England to Dorset and Wiltshire. These geographical features to some extent dictated the kind of agriculture in different areas, though there was mixed farming everywhere with pasture and arable in all parts of England and Wales. In the northwest and Wales the hills were much more suitable for raising cattle and sheep than for growing crops, while the midlands were primarily a wheat growing area, and the south and east concentrated on barley and sheep. Within these general areas there were districts of more specialized agriculture. Kent was already famous as a hop-growing county and apples were associated with Worcestershire, Somerset and Devon. Changing market conditions also affected the produce of a region. The Thames valley, for instance, developed market gardens to feed the growing population of London, and similar developments can be seen in the hinterlands of the larger ports and expanding industrial towns. During the eighteenth century the area under cultivation grew at the expense of pasture in East Anglia, whereas the reverse was the case in Leicestershire and Northamptonshire.

The extent to which land had been enclosed also varied regionally. By 1700 much of the northeast, southeast and southwest had already been enclosed, while elsewhere, and especially in the midlands, the open field system survived. Here village land was divided into two or three huge fields of hundreds of acres, which were subdivided into strips. The strips were directly farmed either by freeholders or tenants who, except perhaps at haymaking and harvest time, managed with the labour of their own families. One farmer in Buckinghamshire, to give an extreme instance, farmed twenty-six and a half acres which were divided into twenty-four strips.

It used to be maintained that such farming was very inefficient and increased productivity was only looked for on the enclosed farms. However, even in the open field areas dramatic improvements are discernible in the years before 1750. In particular more widespread recourse to alternate, or 'up and down' husbandry could produce striking results even on the midlands plain. This was a practice whereby fields were laid down to grass for grazing from anything between six and twenty years, but usually from seven to twelve, and then ploughed in order to grow oats, followed perhaps by barley or wheat, and peas, beans and other crops for about five years before reverting to pasture. The result of this was substantially increased crops of corn and grass for the same acreage, which meant that, without expanding the area under cultivation, many more people and beasts could be fed. Another innovation which pre-dated the eighteenth century was the floating of water meadows, a method of controlled flooding in the late winter which led to earlier growth of grass in spring, thus enabling farmers to feed their livestock on fresh rather than winter fodder weeks before they normally could have done so. The result was that many more beasts were kept alive through the winter instead of being slaughtered at Christmas, with a corresponding boost to the production of meat, milk, leather and wool. All the methods of enriching soil with natural fertilizers such as manure, marl, lime, chalk and seaweed were known and extensively practised in England before 1700. Also before that date crops such as sainfoin grass, clover, potatoes and turnips had made their appearance. The heavy midlands soil, however, was largely unsuitable for root crops, and it was in East Anglia that the turnip had a dramatic impact. Its cultivation there made possible a four-year rotation of crops known as the Norfolk cycle, whereby wheat, turnips, barley and clover were grown in successive seasons, dispensing with the old practice of leaving fields fallow.

Although all these developments can be discerned before the eighteenth century, they did not become widespread until after 1750. A variety of agencies led to their extension. In some instances improving landlords, like Coke and Townshend in Norfolk, took the lead and insisted that their tenants adopted the new methods, sometimes, though not as frequently as has been suggested, including terms to that effect in leases. Elsewhere, farmers were the innovators. Jethro Tull, for instance, an Oxfordshire farmer, invented a seed drill in 1700 which improved methods of sowing. His more celebrated practice of 'horse hoeing husbandry' was in fact much less influential. It sprang from an obsession with hoeing which Tull picked up from a study of French viniculture, and was really impractical for most forms of English agriculture. Robert Bakewell, a Leicestershire farmer, made the first significant advances in the scientific breeding of animals through his experiments with horses, cattle and sheep. He was most successful with sheep and by 1770 could earn 3,000 guineas a season from letting his rams to other breeders. Such experiments were partly responsible for the improvements in the weight of cattle and sheep during the eighteenth century, which both increased by about a quarter between 1732 and 1795. How far they improved the quality of meat, milk or wool, however, can be doubted. It was not until the nineteenth century that scientific breeding had a significant effect on breeds as distinct from individual animals or herds. The diffusion of agricultural knowledge was achieved also by literature on the subject, such as Bradley's *Complete Body of Husbandry*. Even itinerant farm labourers could spread new methods from area to area. The incentive to adopt them in this period was not the attraction of spectacular increases in rents or profits so much as the prospects of improving efficiency, especially during the period 1730 to 1750 when good harvests, high yields and low prices squeezed profit margins.

Enclosures were at once the cause and effect of agricultural improvements. It is impossible to measure exactly how much land was enclosed in 1700, so that estimates vary from between a quarter and a half of all land under cultivation. The uncertainty is due to the existence of various methods of enclosing land. One was by common agreement, another was by enrolment in Chancery, a third was by act of parliament. Of these methods only parliamentary enclosure has left anything like a systematic record. Before 1714 there was scarcely any recourse to legislation for enclosure, but it became more popular under the Hanoverians. In the reign of George I some 17,960 acres were enclosed by statute, in the reign of his successor 318,778. The importance of enclosure can be exaggerated. Merely erecting a fence or wall, digging a ditch or growing a hedge round land does not automatically improve it. However, the improving landlord or farmer could experiment far more easily with crops if they were not grown in scattered strips, or with animals if they did not have to mingle with his neighbour's beasts on the common pasture. Enclosure made for more rational division of the land, and this in turn helped to make farming more efficient.

This was certainly true in Scotland, where enclosures helped in the reduction of run-rig farming, which had hindered agricultural improvement. Land was generally divided for husbandry into an outfield, used mainly for oats, which surrounded an infield where other crops were grown. Infields were divided into rigs, not unlike the strips of the English open fields, though they were farmed by groups of farmers rather than by individual families. Run-rig husbandry produced barely enough for subsistence and in the late 1690s harvest failure led to famine and starvation in Scotland. After 1700 conditions slowly improved. The union with Scotland of 1707 stimulated the cattle trade, since the sale of black cattle to England became a foundation of the Scottish economy. Consequently much arable land was converted to pasture, a process which, as in sixteenth-century England, led to many evictions and much discontent. In the 1720s 'Levellers' made their appearance in the lowlands, just as they had done in England a century earlier. Nevertheless the process went on, and the production of beef for the English market became a staple of Scottish agriculture, although there are signs after 1760 of livestock owners turning from cattle to sheep to meet an increasing demand for wool from England's textile industry. Meanwhile arable farming was being improved as landlords encouraged the abolition of run-rig and the introduction of enclosures which, as in England, were accompanied by better drainage, more rigorous crop rotation and more efficient use of fertilisers. Yet despite the enthusiasm of projectors, who formed a Society of Improvers in the Knowledge of Agriculture in 1723, 'of the actual *work* of improvement only a bare beginning had been made and progress was not really rapid or widespread until after 1760.'[8]

The same cannot be said of England, where the so-called

agricultural revolution of the late eighteenth-century was well under way when George III came to the throne. The output of corn, for instance, probably rose from 14,770,000 quarters in 1700 to 16,468,000 by 1760, most of the increase coming after 1740. This led to a significant fall in food prices, despite some increase in domestic demand and the fact that more and more grain was exported during the early eighteenth century. The increased output from agriculture is reflected in falling wheat prices especially in the south, where they fell between twenty and thirty per cent in these decades. Such a fall would have a bigger impact in London and the southeast than in any other part of the country, since ninety per cent of the population ate wheat bread there, compared with seventy per cent in the west and only thirty per cent in the north. The rest of the population in those areas, and almost all in Wales, ate bread made from barley or rye. The price of a quartern loaf in London fell below $4\frac{1}{2}d$ three times between 1714 and 1760—in 1718, from 1729 to 1732 and again from 1742 to 1744. These were direct reflections of the yields of wheat in the previous harvests.

Falling food prices left a surplus between income and expenditure on subsistence which produced a rise in real wages, in urban areas at least. Thus where the rural economy was hard hit by the depression in agricultural prices, towns, and especially London, could actually benefit from them. Even the lowest-paid workers in the capital found extra money in their pockets, which could be used to purchase articles previously considered to be luxuries. Some preferred to spend it on gin. Others could afford to buy modest consumer goods such as cups and saucers, which sold for only $1\frac{1}{2}d$ a set in the 1730s and 1740s. Apart from real luxury goods, few manufactured articles were produced in London itself, so that the increased demand stimulated industry elsewhere. The market for cheap pottery, for instance, helped the growth of the industry in and around Stoke on Trent. There was a tenfold increase in the number of kilns in Staffordshire in the first half of the eighteenth century.

Domestic demand was not the only stimulus to industry generated by consumers. To some extent expanding markets overseas, and above all in North America, stimulated industrial growth. Nevertheless, home demand for manufactured articles was almost certainly more important than overseas markets in stimulating industrial production. Around 1714 it probably accounted for some two thirds of the output of British industry. In 1736 William Allen asserted that 'the home consumption of our manufactures is much greater than our exportation'.[9]

At the outset of the eighteenth century manufacturing was to be found all over England and Wales, for industry was still primarily domestic. Even before 1760, however, the process whereby certain industries became located in particular centres was well under way. The main industry was still the production of woollen cloth, which was scattered throughout the country but principally in the western counties, East Anglia and the West Riding of Yorkshire. Devonshire, Gloucestershire and Wiltshire could be described as being 'inhabited by numerous clothiers and manufacturers' in 1721, while nearly 1,200 worsted weavers voted in Norwich in the general election of 1715.[10] Already, however, the production of 'old draperies' fabricated from short wool was in serious decline, to the detriment of the clothing areas of the west country which entered a recession in the 1720s and gradually became more and more depressed until they collapsed before the end of the century. The 'new draperies', by contrast, principally worsteds from long wool, continued to make progress in East Anglia and above all in the West Riding. It was during this period that Halifax, Wakefield and Leeds established their ascendancy in the woollen industry.

The iron industry was also undergoing a regional transformation. The Sussex Weald, previously its most important location, and within easy access of London, was in decline, while other areas, particularly the west midlands and the Welsh border counties, witnessed the establishment of new furnaces and steady expansion. This benefited the nail industry which, like the manufacture of cloth, was largely domestic in this period and therefore scattered throughout the counties around Birmingham. Birmingham itself had long been noted for its metalware, but grew and prospered on the manufacture of nails, guns, axes and other utensils. A visitor to the town in 1755 was taken to see 'the manufactory of Mr Taylor, the most considerable maker of gilt-metal buttons and enamelled snuff boxes. We were assured that he employs five hundred persons in those two branches, and when we had seen his workshop we had no scruple in believing it. The multitude of hands each button goes through before it is sent to the market is likewise surprising ... they go through seventy different operations of seventy different work folks.'[11] This was a far greater division of labour than Adam Smith observed in pin-making, another midlands industry. It was also a bigger factory than John Lombe's famous silk mill at Derby, which until it failed in the 1730s had employed over three hundred women and children. Both were exceptions in days of cottage industries, as were the Crowley ironworks at Winlaton, near Newcastle, 'supposed to be the biggest manufactory of the kind in Europe'.[12]

Brewing on a small scale was a cottage industry to be found all over the country but on a large scale it demanded relatively substantial

capital investment and indeed technological expertise. It was in this
period that such eminent breweries as Barclay's, Truman's and
Whitbread's were founded in London. Like other industries, however, brewing established itself away from the capital during this
period, and it is in these years that the Trent Valley became a
celebrated centre for beer, Worthington's brewery being founded at
Burton in 1744.

There were many reasons why industry developed in the provinces
during these years. Proximity to raw materials is a partial explanation, especially in the case of the iron industry. Natural resources
helped to stimulate the woollen industry in Yorkshire and the
development of the cotton industry in Lancashire. Another cogent
cause for planting manufacturing in places away from long-settled
centres was the desire to escape the gild restrictions which obtained in
'medieval' towns. But perhaps the most pressing reason as far as
entrepreneurs were concerned was that wages were lower in the
provinces than they were in London. In 1700 average annual
earnings in the capital were £25, compared with £17 10s in the west
country and £11 5s in the north. By 1750 they were £30, £17 10s
and £15 respectively. Despite the significant improvement in
northern wages, which by the end of the century had outstripped
those in the west and were almost equal to those in the capital,
London labourers were paid substantially more than workers
elsewhere under the first two Georges.

The gap between northern and London wages was narrowed
primarily because of the progress of industrialization in the north.
The extent to which industry as a whole expanded in this period is
problematical. Growth rates in many industries are so spectacular
after 1780 that some historians see the Industrial Revolution as a
sudden development after that date and regard England under the
first two Georges as pre-industrial. Yet the idea that the eighteenth
century was industrially stagnant until the last two decades, when a
great leap forward occurred, is too melodramatic. There was, it is
true, little technological progress. Newcomen's steam engine, designed in Anne's reign, probably had the greatest impact, being used
extensively to drain mines very soon after its invention. About the
same time Abraham Darby discovered the use of coke as an
alternative to charcoal in the smelting process, though this was not
widely available to the iron industry until after 1760, when there
were only seventeen coke-fired furnaces. John Kay invented the
flying shuttle, which could double a weaver's productivity, in 1730,
though again it was not extensively used in the textile industry until
later. Nevertheless, there was development in manufacturing industry between 1714 and 1760 and especially in the years after 1740.

The consumption of raw cotton by British manufacturers doubled between 1700 and 1750. The output of coal more than doubled during the same period. The rate of growth of the woollen industry was about eight per cent per decade from 1700 to 1740, and thirteen or fourteen per cent between 1740 and 1770. The increase in the rate after 1740 was parallelled in other industries, to such an extent that the origins of the Industrial Revolution have been 'sought in the remarkably pervasive if sometimes unobtrusive stimuli which seem to have influenced practically every sector of the industrial economy in the 1740s'.[13]

One of the obstacles to the progress of industry was the state of communications. The easiest way of conveying goods to any market, and particularly to London, was by water. At any time during the period something like half the ships in the outports were engaged in domestic rather than overseas trade. One of the leading branches of the coasting traffic was the Newcastle coal trade. In 1731 some 742,000 tons of coal were shipped from Newcastle upon Tyne to fifty-four British ports, from Aberdeen and Dundee in Scotland to Fowey in Cornwall, though most of it, some 575,050 tons, was sent to London. Another extractive industry which shipped to London was the tin mining of Cornwall, the bulk of tin shipments from Cornish ports finding their way to the capital. Agricultural produce also reached London in ships. In 1735 King's Lynn shipped over 60,000 quarters of corn there. Finally a great variety of manufactures, Colchester cloth, Yorkshire ironmongery, Portsmouth paper, for example, were sent to London by the sea and the Thames rather than by road.

Much freight was carried by water because it was cheaper than taking it by road. Contemporaries reckoned it was twenty times cheaper to transport goods from Newcastle to London by sea rather than by road. Moving goods along the highways of mid-eighteenth century Britain could be prodigiously expensive. Thus it cost about two pounds to transport a ton of merchandise from Liverpool to Manchester, a journey which by river cost twelve shillings. Fortunately England was equipped with an extensive system of navigable rivers. Nature alone provided some seven hundred miles of such waterways, and the efforts of man had added a further three hundred miles by 1700. Improvements continued to be made throughout the eighteenth century. Defoe estimated that there were 1,160 miles of navigable rivers by the 1720s, and this figure probably reached 1,400 miles by 1760. But the most dramatic exploitation of navigable waterways came with the construction of artificial canals towards the end of our period. The first of these was undertaken in 1759 by James

Brindley, who engineered a canal to take the duke of Bridgewater's coal from his mines at Worsley into Manchester. When the Worsley Canal was completed in 1761 it so lowered the cost of transporting coal from Bridgewater's mines that he was able to halve its price in Manchester. Such economies were a big attraction to investment in canals. Brindley led the way, backed by the enthusiastic duke, and by 1767 had constructed a canal linking Manchester with Liverpool which enabled goods to be conveyed between the two towns for six shillings a ton, half the price charged by the Mersey Navigation Company and fifteen per cent of the cost of sending goods by road. The attractions of cheap transportation were not lost on the mineowners and manufacturers of England, and the closing decades of the eighteenth century witnessed a spate of canal construction until by 1800 a virtually complete network linked the industrial areas of the midlands and the north with London and the ports.

While economic historians have sung the praises of the entre-preneurial and engineering achievements of canal construction, they have on the whole condemned the state of the roads in the eighteenth century. Their condemnations can be supported by passages from the two great travellers of the period, Defoe and Arthur Young, and from the preambles to turnpike acts. Defoe was particularly critical of roads which crossed the midland clay. Thus his description of the road from London to Leicester records that 'on this road after you are passed Dunstable ... you enter the deep clays, which are so surprisingly soft that it is perfectly frightful to travellers.'[14] Young, who travelled round the southern counties in 1767 and more extensively round the north in 1768, was far more outspoken. Nor were his strictures confined to the roads which crossed the midlands clays. Writing of Norfolk he complained, 'I know not one mile of excellent road in the whole county;' of the road between Chepstow and Newport, 'mere rocky lanes, full of huge stones as big as one's horse, and abominable holes'; and of the road from Liverpool to Wigan, 'Let me seriously caution all travellers who may accidentally purpose to travel this terrible country to avoid it as they would the devil: for one thousand to one but they break their necks or their limbs by overthrows and breakings down.'[15] The language of the turnpike acts tends to be more prosaic but tells the same story. That for repairing the roads from Leeds to Ripon, passed in 1752, described their existing state as 'so very ruinous and bad, especially in the winter season, that travellers cannot pass without great danger'.

Defoe held out great hopes of the turnpikes, which relied on tolls levied on road users rather than on the statutory obligations laid on parishes for repairing roads. The first of these had been administered by justices of the peace along a stretch of the Great North Road running through Hertfordshire, Cambridgeshire and Huntingdon-shire. They had obtained a private act of parliament for the purpose in 1663. The first turnpike to be run by a trust of private citizens rather than by JPs was established in 1706. By the 1720s many stretches of highway were administered by such trusts, and Defoe was very enthusiastic about the improvements they had made and the prospects of further progress. He noted of the highway from London to Holyhead, 'upon this great road there are wonderful improvements made and making, which no traveller can miss the observation of, especially if he knew the condition these ways were formerly in;' and he predicted that 'this custom prevailing, 'tis more than probable, that our posterity may see the roads all over England restored in their time to such a perfection, that travelling and carriage of goods will be much more easy both to man and horse, than ever it was since the Romans lost this island.'[16]

When the system was complete, it significantly reduced the costs of road haulage. For example, in 1710 the justices set the rates from Northampton to London at 4s per hundredweight; in 1743 it was reduced to 3s 6d. Rates from the North Riding to the capital dropped from 16s per hundredweight in 1727 to 10s in 1758. As a contemporary noted in 1752, 'carriage in general is now thirty per cent cheaper than before the roads were amended by turnpikes.'[17] Too much has therefore been made of the high cost of moving freight by road. Although it was still considerably higher than water transport, even when the turnpikes had improved matters by increasing the size of loads and cutting down the time of journeys, this only made the conveyance of cheap raw materials prohibitively costly. It did not make much sense to send coal by road in the mid-eighteenth century. But it made increasing sense to send expensive manufactured and luxury articles. Transporting steel from Birmingham to London probably added only five per cent to the delivered price. An advantage of road transport over water was that it was considerably quicker. It usually took a month and sometimes six weeks to carry goods from Bristol to London by sea. A voyage of only one week was regarded as prodigious. Fish sent from Devon to London consequently went not by sea but by road and, although the journey took between thirty-six and forty-eight hours, it was still sold as fresh in Billingsgate for roughly twice its price when landed.

The 'fresh' fish arriving in Billingsgate from Brixham is perhaps the most striking proof of Defoe's assertion that the whole kingdom was employed in supplying goods to London. Before the growth of population and the mechanization of production the capital was the only market which could generate mass consumer demand. The impact on the economy of its consumption of agricultural produce and manufactured articles was the most dynamic element in the generation of economic growth before the coming of industrialization.

Defoe might applaud the dominance of London in the national economy, but it gave rise to concern in others. It seemed for one thing that the city was simply too big, a gigantic growth, the notorious 'great wen'. This made it a prodigious consumer, of money, of goods, even of men, without being a producer. Its reputation for unrestrained hedonism alarmed some economists as well as moralists, for the effect of vice was considered as detrimental on the economy as on individuals, and London seemed to epitomize all that was vicious in society. The economic effects of vice were summed up by Josiah Woodward when he wrote:[18]

> There is a natural tendency in vice to ruin any person, family, city, or nation that harbours it. It engenders sloth, variance, profuseness, pride, falsehood, violence, and a neglect and betraying of the publick good: it dulls the understanding, takes away the sense of honour, despirits mankind, cuts the nerves of diligence, and destroys the true principles of commerce and just dealing. And by these means it directly tends to undermine and overthrow the prosperity of any nation, city, or public body.

Sloth does not appear first in Woodward's list of vices by accident, for it was held to be the cardinal sin of the century. Its economic effects were allegedly most disastrous among tradesmen and labourers because it adversely affected production. Profuseness was another name for luxury, which was perhaps the second most notorious vice of the period, though pride ran close. Both were held to be particularly bad for the economy because they led to the consumption of useless luxuries, worse still, fripperies imported from abroad. This offended against the prevalent view, later dubbed mercantilist, that the country should build up a favourable balance of trade by exchanging its manufactures for primary produce and above all precious metal.

Bernard Mandeville disagreed with the whole thesis, arguing in *The Fable of the Bees* that the seven deadly sins, far from being detrimental to the economy, stimulated economic growth. Luxury, he insisted

> Employ'd a million of the Poor,
> And odious Pride a Million more.

Mandeville in fact sought to divorce ethics and economics. Moralists might seek a virtuous England, and economists a prosperous one. But they could not have both.

> T'enjoy the world's conveniences,
> Be famed in War, yet live in Ease
> Without great Vices, is a vain
> Eutopia seated in the Brain.

Critics of Mandeville attacked his assumptions and reasserted the bond between economics and morality. Swift ridiculed Mandevillean economics in the fourth voyage of Gulliver, when he got the Captain to explain to his Houyhnhnm host how, 'in order to feed the luxury and intemperance of the males, and the vanity of the females, we send away the greatest part of our necessary things to other countries, from whence in return we brought the materials of diseases, folly and vice, to spend among ourselves.' Pope faced up to Mandeville more directly in his *Epistle to Burlington*. He conceded that Timon's pride and luxury created employment and recycled his wealth.

> Yet hence the Poor are cloath'd, the Hungry fed;
> Health to himself, and to his Infants bread
> The Lab'rer bears: what his hard Heart denies,
> His Charitable Vanity supplies.

This is often taken to be a capitulation rather than a concession to Mandeville, but it is not. The poem proceeds immediately to assert that:

> Another Age shall see the golden Ear
> Imbrown the Slope, and nod on the Parterre.
> Deep harvests bury all his pride has plann'd,
> And laughing Ceres re-assume the land.

For pride's plans to be buried in deep harvests represents the triumph of a moral economy over a system which divorced morals from economics. Pope accepts that pride can create wealth, but it is artificial wealth, a paved parterre. Natural wealth was not only morally but economically better. To create it necessitated acting in conformity to nature and above all to the law of nature. The moral is drawn in Timon's opposite, Pope's Man of Ross, John Kyrle, whose use of riches is better than Timon's both morally and productively, even though he is far less rich, because he employs it naturally and virtuously. Thus water is used not to make ostentatious and useless fountains but to quench thirst, while Kyrle's generous heart provides charity which Timon's hard heart denied.

Mandeville, however, was on the winning side, historically if not logically. His views were to be largely confirmed by the century's greatest economist, Adam Smith. It is not altogether true, though it is often asserted, that Smith himself separated the moral from the economic world. On the contrary, his first major work, *The Theory of Moral Sentiments*, which appeared in 1759, revealed a man profoundly concerned that society should conform to moral norms. However, his view in *The Wealth of Nations* that 'the uniform constant and uninterrupted effort of every man to better his condition' was the great motor of economic progress is much closer to Mandeville than to Pope, even though his notion that 'the hidden hand' would harmonize interests is curiously similar to some of the sentiments in *The Essay on Man.*

Smith is so often regarded as advocating *laissez-faire* to the point where the state had little if any economic role in his theory that it is odd to find him maintaining that 'from the beginning of the reign of Elizabeth . . . the English legislature has been peculiarly attentive to the interests of commerce and manufactures. . . . Commerce and manufactures have accordingly been continually advancing during all this period.'[19] Certainly in the eighteenth century, politicians of all parties were to be found asserting that England was a trading nation and urging the primacy of protecting and expanding trade in the conduct of her foreign policy. How far the state did affect economic growth in this period, however, is uncertain. The navigation acts, of which that of 1661 was the most significant, and the board of trade and plantations, set up in 1697, were devised to stimulate commerce, manufacturing and shipping by protecting trade and especially colonial trade from foreign competition. There was an increase of about thirty per cent in the tonnage of shipping, from 323,000 tons in 1702 to 496,000 by 1763 and exports to North America more than doubled in the period; but to what extent this expansion was due to these measures rather than to 'natural' growth is perhaps an insuperable problem. Again, the corn laws protected grain producers from imports unless prices reached a certain limit and encouraged exports with bounties when prices were low; yet the weather almost certainly provided a greater stimulus to agricultural production than the government during these years.

However, even the purest of pure economics cannot ignore the role of the state in the economy of Scotland during these years. For the Act of Union of 1707 was a major landmark in Scottish economic history. By that date a Scotland economically independent of England was scarcely viable, as the English threat to cut off the trade in black cattle, the main Scottish export, revealed. Scotland benefited from admission into the colonial trade and from the protection of the navigation laws. Although there was no immediate economic miracle, as some of the more enthusiastic advocates of union, including Defoe, had forecast, nevertheless by the middle of the eighteenth century the lowlands economy at least was sharing in the commercial and industrial boom which England was experiencing. Glasgow in particular profited from the rapid expansion of North American trade after 1745.

The main impact of the state upon the economy was caused by its involvement in foreign wars, yet it is still debatable whether these helped or hindered long-term economic trends. In the short run the wars of 1739 to 1748 and 1756 to 1763 dislocated the economy, disrupted trade, and diverted investment into the war effort, raising the national debt to £76,000,000 by 1748 and £132,000,000 by 1763. The land tax and excises were mainly used to finance the wars. At four shillings in the pound, the land tax brought in about two millions. As the cost of war soared this proved less and less adequate to meet the requirements of the state, but no more could be squeezed from direct taxation. Instead politicians exploited the excise duties, the revenue from which rose from £849,000 in 1700 to £1,600,000 by 1760. The main burden fell on malt throughout the period, though as tea became a popular drink and ceased to be a luxury its share rose rapidly. The growing range of articles subject to excise caused a tract of the times to complain:[20]

> The excise man is our companion from the crown of our head to the soal of our foot. If we clean our hair, he examines the powder, even the washing the ladies' linen does not escape inspection. He walks abroad in our shoes, at our tables he seasons our meat, and he drinks so deep in our cup, that he has a larger portion than the owner of the land, which sowed the barley for the malt, through the various payments of land tax, malting and brewing. Is it daylight? He peeps in at our windows. Is it night? He shines in our candles. Have we sweets or sours, light or darkness, the custom house officers or excise men are our constant attendants.

The excise probably depressed the production of such products as beer, spirits, soap and leather, whose output increased only fourteen per cent between 1700 and 1760, while manufactures not subject to excise on the whole fared much better. Starch was an exception which, despite being subject to excise, increased its output from 2·5 million pounds in 1714 to 3·6 million in 1763. Surplus capital for investment possibly found its way into the national 'funds' rather than into river improvements, turnpike trusts, and other 'local' enterprises, though there is some evidence that the two markets were quite separate, with different investors in each. Moreover, tax collecting actually stimulated the development of country banks, especially during the Seven Years' War when local receivers deposited their receipts with them, partly for personal profit, partly for security. By 1760 there may have been as many as five hundred banks outside London.

The disruption of trade by warfare undoubtedly held up supplies of timber vital for the building industry. At the same time the wars were ostensibly fought, in part at least, to protect and even to expand trade, and did eventually yield new colonies and markets for British merchants and manufacturers. They also stimulated certain industries, such as shipbuilding, iron and textiles, with orders for ships, guns and clothing for the armed forces.

Government intervention in economic affairs, whether for pacific or bellicose purposes, fostered the development of a national economy. The policy of economic nationalism in foreign relations itself stimulated the notion of a British economy with its own independent interests, while government finance affected prices and profits in a whole range of enterprises, agricultural, commercial and industrial. This brought home to the remotest part of the realm the truth of Defoe's contention that activities in London had an economic impact throughout the whole island of Great Britain.

# 6 The Making of the English Ruling Class

During the period between the death of Queen Anne and the accession of George III, England's governors came from a very narrow social stratum. The levers of power, both at the centre and in the localities, were in the hands of a few hundred families who between them controlled the machinery of government.

Both houses of parliament were occupied by men at the very top of English society. Fewer than two hundred hereditary peers were regularly summoned to the House of Lords under the first two Georges. This landed aristocracy was dominated towards the end of George II's reign by a tiny elite, of whom the dukes of Bedford, Devonshire and Newcastle and the marquis of Rockingham were the foremost. Their type constituted what Disraeli was to term the 'Venetian oligarchy'. By an act of 1711 members of parliament for England and Wales had to own property to the annual value of £600 to represent a county, £300 to sit for a borough. These property qualifications virtually ensured that the lower house was inhabited almost exclusively by country gentlemen, prosperous businessmen and leading professional men. 'We know that the British House of Commons, without shutting its doors to any merit in any class' wrote Burke in 1789, conveniently overlooking the 1711 act, but continuing more realistically, 'is, by the sure operation of adequate causes, filled with everything illustrious in rank, in descent, in hereditary and in acquired opulence, in cultivated talents, in military, civil, naval, and politic distinction, that the country can afford.'[1]

By far the most numerous group in the Commons were the landed proprietors, those whom Burke called 'the ballast in the vessel of the commonwealth'.[2] These always comprised over half the house. Although they were socially inferior to the peerage, economically they were part of the same class. Indeed about a fifth of the Commons consisted of either Irish peers or sons of English peers. It was regarded as part of the natural order of things in England that the heirs of aristocrats should sit in the Commons; so much so that the Property Qualifications Act contained a clause exempting them from its provisions, though curiously the eldest sons of Scottish peers were not allowed to sit for any constituency in Scotland. Whether related or not, the country gentlemen and the Lords had a 'natural' interest based on property. Large estates made them powerful forces in county elections, while country houses in the immediate vicinity of parliamentary boroughs gave their inhabitants enormous electoral influence in small constituencies. Most landed proprietors in the Commons were consequently either knights of the shire, sitting for counties in their own interest combined with that of peers and other local gentry, or country gentlemen who so dominated a tiny borough that they virtually returned themselves.

Most of the businessmen, by contrast, operated their businesses in the City and spent much of their time in the capital. Of the sixty-one businessmen in parliament in 1701, thirty-nine were London merchants, fourteen of whom were strangers to the constituencies which they represented. In 1754 only five were based in the provinces, out of a total of about sixty. So low a figure in comparison with the numbers of landed men might seem surprising, especially considering that there had been as many as fifty-five merchants among the original members of the Long Parliament and that between 1640 and 1714 English commerce expanded considerably. Commercial representation was to remain relatively low, however, throughout the eighteenth century, sixty being the usual number of businessmen returned to the house after each general election. Some were carpet baggers who debauched venal voters in small boroughs with bags of City gold; East India merchants were notorious for this practice throughout the period. Most, however, obtained their seats by cultivating alliances with borough patrons who brought them into parliament. Only four could represent the City of London itself.

The law was as well represented as trade, there being approximately sixty members of the legal profession in any parliament, about half of whom were barristers. Others were law officers of the crown or Welsh judges. Few were mere attorneys. Lawyers made good MPs for the simple reason that the chief function of the House of Commons was to legislate, a task for which men with legal training were eminently suited. They could help or hinder the government in the drafting of bills and in their passage through committee. They could also be called upon to employ their skills in advancing private measures in parliament, and this was a most valuable asset at a time when, quite unlike today, private bills outnumbered public. Lawyers were often the most useful representatives a borough could have for promoting private bills affecting the constituency as a whole, or individual constituents, and their services were often eagerly sought.

The armed forces had a sizable muster in the house, with thirty-nine army officers and nine naval officers in 1701, and forty-nine and twenty-two respectively in 1761. The number naturally fluctuated with the size of the forces, which in turn depended upon whether or not the country was at war. As far as their parliamentary functions were concerned, however, contemporaries saw very little difference between army officers and any other government officials. In the House of Commons they were usually identified with the ministers of the crown who together made up the large and growing Court and treasury party.

Finally there was a sprinkling of individuals who defy classification. What are we to make of Joseph Addison, for instance, who sat for Malmesbury from 1710 to 1719? Was he an essayist, playwright, poet or placeman? Or Edmund Burke, returned for Wendover in 1765? Was he a lawyer, a pamphleteer, a politicians's secretary or a philosopher? These extreme cases reveal the ultimate absurdity of rigid categorization, for the ruling class was not made up of entirely self-contained units. On the contrary, there were many links binding together its component parts.

Not all the country gentlemen lived wholly off the proceeds of their estates, whether in the form of rents or the exploitation of mineral deposits. Some invested money in the City and other enterprises. Merchants and professional men bought land: indeed after 1711 they were obliged to possess real estate in order to stand for parliament. Most members therefore owned country houses which represented values and symbolized their status. When an army officer like Thomas Erle visited his house at Charborough Park, Dorset, or a minister like John Aislabie was at home in Studley Royal, Yorkshire, or a banker like Henry Hoare was in the country at Stourhead, they would be indistinguishable from the country gentlemen around them.

These links between various social units were reinforced by kinship. The ruling class was criss-crossed with a vast network of family ties. As we have seen, about a fifth of the Commons was related to the peerage, itself closely bound by ties of marriage. When George Granville wrote to an assembly of the gentry of Cornwall in 1710 to solicit their votes he could boast, 'I have nothing to value myself upon but having my veins so full of Cornish blood as to have the honour of being related perhaps to every one of the gent[lemen] to whom you may have an opportunity at this time to communicate my sentiments.'[3] The upper ranks of English society were so riddled and honeycombed with genealogical relationships that the ruling class sometimes gives the impression of having been one big, if rather unhappy, family.

The counties were microcosms of the country, where the leading landed families held sway. At the top of county society was the lord lieutenant, almost invariably a peer and usually from the front rank of the peerage. His deputy lieutenants in the county militia were also drawn from the principal aristocracy and gentry of the shire. Then the commission of the peace, the most active agency of county government, was composed of substantial country gentlemen. Although by an act of 1689 they had to be worth only £20 a year, statutes of 1731 and 1744 imposed a property qualification on justices of the peace of £100 per annum in lands within the county.

Although aristocrats and gentlemen dominated the commanding heights of government in the country, as in parliament there were other elements with whom they had to share power. Clergymen, for instance, became increasingly active on the commissions of the peace. In corporate boroughs the commercial community formed part of the governing body, providing mayors, aldermen and common council men. Although in small boroughs they tended to be dependent upon the local gentry, in larger towns they were virtually autonomous. This was particularly true of cities such as Bristol and Norwich and, above all, London which was almost a separate estate of the realm. Yet even including the business and professional men with whom the landed proprietors had to share power, those who controlled the machinery of government both national and local seem to have represented a narrow oligarchy, forming a homogeneous, not to say, monolithic, ruling class.

At the outset of the eighteenth century, however, this was not the case. In 1714 the ruling class was so bitterly divided that many feared a civil war might break out on Queen Anne's death. Both houses of parliament were locked in angry debates, and the constituencies in frequent disputes. In 1715 there were at least 110 contested elections in England and Wales, and 156 in 1722. The lord lieutenancies, county militias and commissions of the peace were purged and purged again. The bishops and inferior clergy were frequently at loggerheads in convocation and in the dioceses. Mayoral, aldermanic and council elections were rent by bitter feuds; Bishop Burnet could observe in 1708 that 'the parties are now so stated and kept up, not only by the elections of parliament-men that return every third year, but even by the yearly elections of mayors and corporation-men, that they know their strength; and in every corner of the nation the two parties stand, as it were, listed against one another.'[4] Society was then so divided that even social life was disturbed, men being distinguished in their very diversions. There were tory and whig coffee houses, theatre crowds, horse races, literary and social clubs, newspapers and assemblies.

On George II's death all was changed. In 1760, according to the historian of the opposition, 'ministerial policy was rarely attacked. Parliamentary attendance was thin, and divisions were few.'[5] General elections were rarer, since under the Septennial Act they need only occur every seven years and the first two Georges by and large let parliament run the full term. Even when elections were held, the number of contests was low. In 1754 there were only sixty-six, and in 1761 a mere fifty-seven. After 1730 few political changes occurred in the composition of the county militias or the commissions of the peace. The anglican clergy were politically united in support of the dynasty and the regime. Partisanship in leisure pursuits had declined considerably. Tory coffee houses had dwindled to one, The Cocoa Tree. After the earlier wave of politically committed plays, which led to the Licensing Act of 1737, the theatre was in the mid-century doldrums of masquerades and pantomimes from which it was to be rescued by Garrick and Goldsmith. Gambling, the ruling passion of the upper classes, was not politically divisive. Peers and gentlemen of all persuasions lost and won vast sums at White's. Even in the provinces, where older attitudes lived longer and died harder, the partisanship of Anne's reign gradually ceased to divide men in their social activities. There had been, for instance, two assemblies at York, one whig and one tory, but as early as 1724 they made overtures towards a reconciliation.[6]

The process by which the friction of two power elites was transformed into the rule of a governing class was one of the most crucial developments of eighteenth-century England. Its causes were complex. Perhaps the most important was the decline in the intensity of the political issues which had divided the ruling class into the tory and whig parties since the Exclusion Crisis of Charles II's reign. At the same time divergent social and economic interests which had created tensions within the ruling class were removed or reconciled under the first two Georges. Administrative developments facilitated the extension of patronage, while oligarchy finally triumphed over party in many constituencies. There are even some signs of a closing of class ranks to protect the interests of property owners in response to threats, real or imagined, from below. All these trends coincided in the years 1714 to 1760 to transform a divided elite into a ruling class.

During the general election of 1715 the electorate was invited to peruse a remarkable tract, some forty pages long, with the title *A Collection of White and Black Lists*. It was subtitled *A view of those gentlemen who have given their votes in parliament for and against the protestant religion and succession, and the trade and liberties of their country, ever since the Glorious Revolution to the happy accession of King George*. There were nine lists in it, all purporting to record divisions in the House of

Commons, from those who were against putting William and Mary on the throne in February 1689, to those who voted for the expulsion from the house in March 1714 of Richard Steele, as the author of *The Crisis* and *The Englishman*, two pamphlets in which he had argued that the succession of the house of Hanover was in danger under Anne's last ministry.

The lists record the degree to which members of parliament had become polarized into whigs and tories between 1689 and 1714. In Anne's reign some 1,220 men had been returned to the Commons, and the names of over a thousand occur in the *White and Black Lists* or in similar compilations. When collated they reveal that 495 voted consistently tory, 439 divided only on the whig side, while a mere 130 wavered in their party allegiances. The names with the longest voting records read like a roll call of the party stalwarts on both sides of the house. On the tory side members like William Bromley, who sat for Oxford University, and Sir John Pakington, knight of the shire for Worcestershire, who were to be prominent tories in the reign of George I, had already recorded a high degree of consistent voting on that side under his predecessors. Among the whigs William Pulteney and Robert Walpole had solid voting records for that party long before 1714. The whigs were in fact the more well disciplined party for most of the 130 waverers were tories who lost their nerve in the last years of Anne's reign; no fewer than fifty-nine of them were 'whimsicals' voting against the treaty of commerce with France in 1713, with Sir Thomas Hanmer, another politician who led the tories into the wilderness under George I, the most prominent.

The voters in 1715 were not, of course, asked to choose between the voting records of peers, though a perusal of them could have produced an aristocratic collection of white and black lists, for the Lords were just as polarized as the Commons. Of 182 lay peers who feature on parliamentary lists in Anne's reign, only forty-one appear across party lines. As in the lower house so in the upper the whigs were the more united party, for two thirds of the inconsistent peers were tories, most of whom either occasionally voted with the Court even when the whigs were in power or became anxious about the succession in the last years of the reign. The most stalwart of all were the five whig lords known as the Junto, the leaders of the party at the time of Anne's death—Halifax, Orford, Somers, Sunderland and Wharton. Between them they appear on the lists twenty-nine times out of a possible thirty, invariably on the whig side.

The compiler of the *White and Black Lists*, himself clearly a whig, indicated the kind of issues which divided tory from whig in 1715. He gave priority to the protestant religion, a reminder that at bottom the party strife was primarily religious. Tories regarded the Church of

England with more reverence than the monarchy, and strove as far as possible to preserve the unique position which it had acquired in English life at the restoration of Charles II. They considered that insofar as the church no longer enjoyed a monopoly of worship or political power, it had been undermined by the dissenters, and they were increasingly concerned at the infiltration into borough corporations of nonconformists practising occasional conformity in order to qualify for local office. In Anne's reign the tories had retaliated by introducing bills to outlaw the practice, and when a bill became law on the fourth attempt it penalized dissenters who qualified for office by taking communion in the Church of England. Finally in 1714, the tories passed the so-called Schism Act. The whigs on the whole had opposed these measures. It was due to their efforts that the occasional conformity bill did not get through both houses of parliament until 1711, while they came out strongly against the schism bill. They thus tried to defend dissenters against tory attempts to undo the consequences of the Toleration Act.

Only in 1711 did the whigs reluctantly acquiesce in the passing of the occasional conformity bill, being criticized by dissenters for this betrayal. The whigs' excuse was that this was the necessary price for the support of a handful of renegade tories, mainly in the Lords, prepared to vote against the preliminaries of peace with France. The negotiations leading to the Treaty of Utrecht in 1713 were held by the whigs to be a much greater betrayal of the protestant interest by the tories than their own acquiescence in the occasional conformity bill. Certainly unilateral talks with France were a breach of the spirit if not of the letter of the Grand Alliance. At that time the tory government was prepared to drop allied war aims to reach agreement with France, and rallied its supporters by having Swift denigrate England's partners in *The Conduct of the Allies*. The whigs, on the other hand, identified themselves fully with the war effort, and particularly with the allied policy of ensuring that the Habsburg claimant to the Spanish empire ousted his Bourbon rival from the throne of Spain itself. The readiness of the tories to recognize the Bourbon candidate as Philip V of Spain was the most controversial of the preliminaries and, rallying to the slogan 'no peace without Spain', the whigs voted against them in parliament. They were easily outvoted in the Commons, but had a narrow majority in the Lords. The tory government overcame this obstacle by the dubious device of creating twelve peers at a stroke in 1712, but the whigs opposed the moves towards peace at every opportunity. It was their tenacious opposition which later led Swift to claim that in the last four years of Anne's reign the party conflict was really between lovers of peace and lovers of war.

Once peace was signed, however, fears for the succession began to dominate the party struggle. As far as the whigs were concerned the main threat to the protestant interest lay in the possibility of a Stuart restoration. Their identification of protestantism and the house of Hanover was underlined by the whig compiler of the *White and Black Lists* who bracketed together 'the protestant religion and succession'. Where many tories stressed the divine right to succeed and with it the doctrines of passive obedience and non-resistance, the whigs emphasized the contractual theory of monarchy and insisted that there had been justifiable resistance in 1688. Dr Henry Sacheverell's sermon, *The perils of false brethren*, reiterating the traditional tory view and challenging the whig interpretation of the Revolution, led the whigs to impeach him in 1709. The subsequent trial in 1710 brought out their basic differences in attitude to the succession, the whigs stressing Anne's parliamentary title, the tories her hereditary right to the throne. Both were adopting extreme positions, for the logical extension of the tory case was Jacobitism, which only a minority of them espoused, while a corollary of the whig case was elective monarchy, which none in fact advocated. Instead the majority in both parties was committed to the principle of hereditary descent through the protestant line. Yet there was a vital difference in attitude. The tories looked forward to the accession of George I with foreboding, while the whigs anticipated it with enthusiasm. For most tories the Hanoverian succession was the gravestone of their philosophy, for most whigs it was the copingstone of the Revolution settlement.

Between 1710 and 1714 apprehensions about the succession divided the tories and at the same time united the whigs more firmly than ever. The tory split can be detected as a hairline crack as early as the vote on the peace preliminaries in 1711. After the Peace of Utrecht it widened into a fissure in the vote on the treaty of commerce with France, which saw the secession of enough 'whimsical' tories in conjunction with the whigs to defeat the measure in June 1713. Although the basic issue involved trade, these tories were also concerned about the succession, for closer economic ties with France seemed to presage political links and possibly French aid to secure the restoration of the direct Stuart line. The 'whimsicals' thus formed the nucleus of those Hanoverian tories who were convinced that a plot was on foot to put the Pretender on the throne when Anne died. The whigs, even more prepared to believe that such a plot existed, made contingent plans to defend the protestant succession with military force if need be. Such fears and preparations made many anticipate a civil war on the Queen's death.

Yet in the end George I succeeded peacefully. Moreover, during his reign the great issues gradually cooled down, until by 1727 they were of relatively little account. Religious animosities faded so quickly that it was almost as if they had burned themselves out in the heat of party violence before 1714. The Bangorian controversy led to a revival of moderate churchmanship and the decline of high-and low-church partisanship, while the silencing of convocation removed a potent engine of faction from ecclesiastical politics. Although the Occasional Conformity and Schism Acts were repealed, this was not done until 1719, and then some whigs who had opposed them previously were against their repeal on the grounds that they did not want a revival of the animosities which they had kindled. A consensus was already being reached on church matters. There were to be no major concessions to dissent under the Hanoverians, certainly no serious move to repeal the Corporation and Test Acts. The cry 'the church in danger', so potent under Anne, was rarely heard after 1720, despite the almost annual indemnity acts protecting dissenters against malicious prosecutions for breaches of the two acts. As the years went by, the ruling class grew increasingly indifferent to religion and, apart from odd crises such as those provoked by the tithes bill in 1736 and the Jewish naturalization act of 1753, religious disputes rarely ruffled the surface of Hanoverian politics. As John Brooke observed, 'no one could describe the latter half of the eighteenth century as an age of religious zeal or bigotry: the ruling class valued religion as a restraining and civilizing force in social life rather than as a revelation of man's nature and destiny.'[7]

Foreign policy ceased to be a source of friction between the tory and whig parties very soon after the Hanoverian accession. Franco-phobia received a setback with the death of Louis XIV in 1715, and during the subsequent regency the whigs came to accept the tory Treaty of Utrecht as the cornerstone of their diplomacy. This nullified their previous opposition to it, as their failure to follow up the impeachment of the earl of Oxford virtually admitted in 1717. Walpole's pacific foreign policy made Britain's role in Europe a relatively low-key issue during his ministry. Although the wars between 1739 and 1748 and 1756 and 1763 imposed great strains on the political system they were nothing like as divisive as the War of the Spanish Succession. There was less of a consensus on foreign policy than there was on religious issues, but by and large the ruling class was united over what constituted Britain's interests in inter-national relations. Friction arose over the best way of safeguarding British interests or the extent to which they were in conflict with those of the electorate of Hanover; but serious though this was, it did not reproduce the fundamental rift, dividing tory from whig in the last four years of Anne's reign, over whether Britain should be involved on the continent at all.

The succession problem survived Anne's death to plague British politics in one form or another until the final defeat of the Jacobite rebels in 1746. Yet after the Atterbury Plot of 1722 Jacobitism was not a serious threat to the stability of the political system, despite all Walpole's attempts to claim that it was. Some historians have tried to identify almost the entire tory party with the Jacobite cause in these years, but this is even more far-fetched than the wildly optimistic hopes of the Pretender's genuine adherents on whose wishful thinking most of the identifications are based. In fact most tories were loyal to the Hanoverian dynasty and became increasingly so, until the Pelhams could even think of admitting them into a share in government both local and national in 1744, ironically on the very eve of the 'Forty-Five'. In that year most of those who drank to the Pretender in their cups acted like their predecessors in 1715, when a genuine Jacobite caustically observed of the high-church tories.[8]

> That party . . . are never right hearty for the cause, till they are mellow, as they call it, over a bottle or two . . . they do not care for venturing their carcases any further than the tavern. There indeed . . . they would make men believe, who do not know them, that they would encounter the greatest opposition in the world; but after having consulted their pillows, and the fume a little evaporated, it is to be observed of them that they generally become mighty tame, and are apt to look before they leap, and with the snail, if you touch their houses, shrink back, and pull in their horns.

To some extent the tory and whig philosophies of the post-Revolution era could be regarded as the ideologies of rival social interests. Insofar as the tories projected themselves as the party of the landed interest and were regarded as being for the most part country gentlemen, the hereditary principle can be seen as the natural justification for those who inherited landed estates. At the same time the whigs were identified with the business and professional classes, those interests which recruited the younger sons of the gentry, to whom contract was a more obvious legitimizing device than inheritance.

Of course severe qualifications must be made to such sweeping generalizations. For one thing the anglican clergy, younger sons almost to a man, were even more vehement in their toryism than the gentry, though it is interesting that the high-church clergy laid great stress on the apostolic succession, regarded the hereditary principle as literally sacrosanct and considered the notion of a solemn league and covenant anathema. A more serious criticism is that any investigation of the social background of tories and whigs in the early eighteenth century reveals that they drew their support from all sections of society. Country gentlemen, as we have seen, formed the bulk of the House of Commons and wielded enormous influence in the provinces. Without substantial numbers of them backing the whigs, the party would have made no headway at all, much less win elections as it did in 1708 and 1715. Moreover there were tory merchants, lawyers and army and naval officers in any parliament of Anne's reign.

Nevertheless, the generalizations can survive the qualifications. The bulk of the gentry and clergy were tories, while the majority of business and professional men were whigs. One contemporary rightly observed that 'the majority of the gentry upon a poll will be found tories', an observation borne out by the fact that the tories could count on eight times as many county seats as their rivals at every election throughout the years 1701 to 1715, while the whigs often found it difficult to replenish the commissions of the peace from their own ranks.[9] Poll books for parliamentary elections record that the overwhelming majority of the clergy voted tory. On the other side the Bank of England and the United East India Company were both whig institutions. Although Robert Harley drew on tory merchants to launch the South Sea Company in 1711, it is significant that he kept the right to nominate its governing body in the hands of the Queen, while the whigs tried to vest it in the principal shareholders. They knew that if they could win this concession then the company would be whig-dominated from the start, as indeed it was to become soon after Anne's death. As for the professions, the tories were so short of lawyers that they had difficulty filling the great legal offices of state when they formed an administration, while the whigs had a positive embarrassment of talented gentlemen of the long robe.

Whatever the underlying reality, a party's 'image' can have a social identity of its own anyway. In modern Britain the conservative and labour parties are identified with businessmen and workers respectively, despite the fact that many businessmen are not tories while by no means all workers vote labour. In the political propaganda of the early eighteenth century the tories both saw themselves and were seen as the spokesmen of the gentry and clergy, while the whigs were similarly regarded as the party of commerce and the professions.

Between the Revolution and the death of Anne these different social interests were thought to have undergone distinct economic experiences. The landed proprietors and the clergy were alleged to have fared badly, while merchants and above all financiers were held to have done well. The preamble to the act lowering the rate of interest in 1714 gives the tory view of the fate of the landed interest in the years since William's accession: 'the heavy burden of the late long and expensive war hath been chiefly borne by the owners of the land of this kingdom, by reason whereof they have been necessitated to contract very large debts, and thereby and by the abatement in the value of their lands are become greatly impoverished.' Whether or not this was true depended upon a great many considerations. The chief form of direct taxation during the wars was the land tax, levied at a wartime rate of four shillings in the pound on an assessment of rental values made in 1693. The actual incidence of this tax, however, varied greatly. In the home counties and East Anglia where the assessment had been reasonably accurate, it really could mean a twenty per cent tax on rents. Elsewhere the assessments tended to undervalue rentals, so that in the furthest provinces of England the real rate was less than one shilling in the pound. But there can be little doubt that landowners thought their estates greatly encumbered by the land tax, especially since it had only become a regular levy on their rents since the Revolution. Whether or not they had incurred debts or had become impoverished by a drop in the land market could again depend on where their estates lay and even on their efficiency as estate managers. On the whole it seems that rents, and therefore market values, at best remained steady and at worse declined under William and Anne. Many landowners certainly found the going tough. Few had surplus capital to invest in non-landed securities for hardly any were active on the stock market in these years.

The tory view of the economic effects of the stock market is also conveyed in the preamble to the act lowering the rate of interest, which claimed that 'by reason of the great interest and profit which hath been made of money at home, the foreign trade of this nation hath of late years been much neglected.' This too was an exaggerated claim. Warfare itself had jeopardized commerce as merchant shipping had to run the gauntlet of French privateers. Their activities particularly affected the re-export of colonial produce, which significantly declined during the War of the Spanish Succession. Indeed this sector alone accounted almost entirely for the alleged neglect of foreign trade for imports remained relatively buoyant while exports of British merchandise to Europe generally increased in the years after 1700. Moreover, not all or even a majority of merchants were investing in the stock market during the war years, though one tory complained in 1702 that 'a merchant finds a better return between the exchequer and the exchange than he makes by running a hazard to the Indies.'[10] The investing public under Anne numbered around ten thousand and included professional men as well as businessmen, though significantly few landlords. The typical investor derived his livelihood from non-landed sources in London and the home counties. These on the whole profited from their investments in 'the funds', as they were known. This expression referred to the new machinery of public credit which had been constructed since the accession of William and Mary during the financial revolution, and especially the stock of the Bank of England, the East India Company and the South Sea Company. The stocks of these three corporations were the most coveted in the market, and confidence in them was justified for in the twenty years between the establishment of the Bank of England and the accession of George I there were fifteen during which the price of its stock was above par. Apart from the year 1696 when no dividend was declared, the lowest dividend was seven per cent and the highest sixteen.

The fiscal needs of government in wartime therefore affected sections of society very differently. Landowners, including clergymen, found themselves paying unprecedented sums in direct taxation, while the investing public, composed mainly of London-based merchants and professional men, made profits in the funds. Tories feared that the new monied interest would actually come to rival the landed interest itself. As Henry St John, later Lord Bolingbroke, put it in 1709, 'a sort of property which was not known twenty years ago is now increased to be almost equal to the terra firma of our island.'[11]

It is not surprising that the animosity between the landed and business interests reached its height in these years. Although the more discerning tory apologists, such as St John and Swift, drew a distinction between the investments of merchants engaged in overseas trade and the speculations of monied men who made money make money, their less discriminating followers linked both types together in a City conspiracy against landowners. Addison caught their blanket condemnation of business activity when he caricatured a tory landlord, 'Foxhunter', who 'expatiated on the inconveniences of trade, that carried from us the commodities of our country, and made a parcel of upstarts as rich as men of the most ancient families of England'. When charged with this assertion 'he replied, with some vehemence, that he would undertake to prove, trade would be the ruin of the English nation'. His 'proof', however, consisted of 'affirming it more eagerly, to which he added two or three curses upon the London merchants, not forgetting the directors of the Bank'.[12]

After 1713 the stresses and strains produced by the wars against France were gradually eased. The ending of the War of the Spanish Succession and the subsequent lowering of the land tax brought immediate relief to landowners. The early Hanoverians took pains to keep the rate low, and until war broke out in 1739 they by and large succeeded. Even when the War of the Austrian Succession forced the government to raise the tax to four shillings in the pound the burden was by no means as heavy on the landowner as it had been in the wars

against Louis XIV. This was because the rate was still levied on the
assessment of 1693, and by 1740 rents had on the whole risen since
William's reign. As soon as war ended in 1748 the rate was again
reduced. The result of these fiscal policies was, to quote Henry Pelham,
that 'his majesty's administration had gained the favour and esteem of
the generality of the landholders of England.'

Trade also expanded between 1714 and 1760. Exports rose by
eighty per cent, re-exports by nearly fifty per cent and imports by forty
per cent, though much of this expansion occurred after 1740.
Nevertheless, under Walpole the value of exports rose by one third and
that of imports by just over a fifth. Meanwhile the 'funds' had become
relatively less attractive. This was partly due to the lowering of the
official rate of interest from five to four per cent in 1727 and again to
three per cent in 1751, but mainly to the South Sea Bubble, which was
a disaster for investors of all kinds.

Where under Anne the investing public had been very restricted, in
1720 speculation involved 'all ranks of men and women too';
according to the bishop of Norwich, 'more families and single persons'
were 'undone and ruined than hardly ever were known to have been
so, by the most tedious and lingering war'.[13] Country gentlemen,
anglican clergymen including Oxford and Cambridge dons, provincial merchants, professional men and country tradesmen speculated in stock in that year. When the explosion came many had their
fingers badly burned. They were determined not to burn them again.
Landed men stopped investing in the funds. Thomas Coke of
Holkham, for example, who had invested £58,300 in South Sea stock
in 1720, and who lost £37,928 'never plunged again into the stock
market; never again bought securities to more than a negligible
amount'.[14] Those with surplus capital to invest now rushed to place it
in the less profitable but more secure investment of land. 'In the
eighteen months after the Bubble burst [Lord] Cowper spent £12,998
on lands, almost as much as in the previous thirteen years.'[15] The result
was that the price of land held its own in 1720 when the bottom fell out
of the stock market. Contemporaries dated the upturn in the value of
lands from 1720. Never again did the monied interest appear to be a
rival on an equal footing with the landed interest. The spectacular
growth of the investing public, from 10,000 under Anne to 40,000 by
1720, eased off, reaching only 60,000 by 1760.

The tory division between the landed interest on one side and the
business, professional and monied men on the other no longer seemed
to make sense even in political propaganda. It was replaced in
Country rhetoric by a division between a narrow financial interest and
the rest of the country. As Sir John Barnard put it in 1737, 'the publick
funds divided the nation into two ranks of men, of which one are

creditors and the other debtors. The creditors are the three great corporations and others, made up of natives and foreigners: the debtors are the landholders, the merchants, the shopkeepers and all ranks and degrees of men throughout the kingdom.' 'Foxhunter' had not put it that way in 1716. Then it had seemed that the landholders were beleaguered by the other interests.

After 1720 the monied interest seemed a relatively small, if parasitic, minority. The plutocrats among them were prime targets for Country propaganda, especially since Walpole had screened so many of them after the Bubble, and remained financially dependent upon them during his ministry. It was these whom Bolingbroke attacked as the 'principal men in our great companies who, born to serve and obey, have been bred to command even government itself'. The charge of low birth was vital to his case, for he argued that such men were usurping the traditional role of the ruling class. How much truth there was in this propaganda is another matter. Men like Sir Peter Delmé and Sampson Gideon really did wield disproportionate power in the financial world, while the bulk of the big investors were predominantly a bourgeoisie resident in the vicinity of the capital. Below them, however, were thousands of small investors, especially in South Sea stock, including even the poor clergy of the Church of England. As the historian of the financial revolution has observed, 'by the severest tory standards these accounts were for admirable causes, and could not plausibly be fitted into the picture of a sinister plutocracy.'[16] As with so much of its propaganda the Country opposition lived in a dream world far removed from the reality of social and economic life at the time.

Walpole was much more in touch with social realities. He realized that the tensions created by the commercial and financial revolutions were being absorbed and the resulting conflict of interests was dying down. Indeed he did much to reconcile them. A country gentlemen who ostentatiously ate Norfolk apples in the Commons and boasted that he read the letters of his steward before official despatches, and who at the same time had the reputation of being the shrewdest financier in politics, Walpole symbolized in his own person the reconciliation of interests. He also sought to benefit both landed men and merchants. Walpole was primarily responsible for holding down the land tax, even reducing it to one shilling in the pound from 1731 to 1732, and hinting at the possibility of abolishing it altogether. As for trade, as early as 1721 he had inserted in the king's speech to parliament a passage on the importance of 'extending our commerce, upon which the rich and grandeur of this nation chiefly depend'.[17] To facilitate trade he abolished export duties on nearly all manufactures and gave bounties to encourage the export of grain, spirits, silk, sail cloths and sugar. He also reduced or removed import duties on raw materials but placed high duties on such foreign manufactured articles as linen and silk. By these measures he hoped to bring about a favourable balance of trade. Finally he earned the reputation, rightly or wrongly, as the man who rescued public credit from catastrophe and restored it to a flourishing condition.

The opposition vied with Walpole for the merit of being more concerned with the prosperity of landed men and merchants. Country ideology appealed especially to landowners, mere country gentlemen and backwoods gentry in the shires and the inferior clergy. But it also made a bid for the support of the commercial community. Opposition writers never missed an opportunity to complain that Walpole was not really assisting English commerce and that in fact trade was languishing because of the inept measures of his ministry. In 1729 the *Craftsman* bemoaned how England was 'from a rich and flourishing condition daily declining in its wealth [and] power'. Its espousal of trade was truly remarkable for a self-styled 'country journal'. In 1732 it extolled the 'trading part of the nation' to whose 'labour and industry it is owing that this country is raised from a wild uncultivated desert to its present height of riches, grandeur and strength' and flattered merchants as being 'the heart-blood of the body politick'.[18] This contrasts sharply with Atterbury's description of the landed interest in 1715 as 'the political blood of the nation'.[19]

The Country opposition's espousal of merchants compares oddly with the animosity to the City formerly displayed by foxhunting tories. Of course enlightened tory leaders had not made the distinction between the landed and the trading interests which their more backwoods supporters had done. In office under Anne tories like Lord Rochester and even Bolingbroke himself had advocated that trade should be a prime aim of foreign policy, and therefore of military strategy in the War of the Spanish Succession. But there was far more to the Country wooing of merchants than the old tory 'blue water' policy. In their anxiety to construct a genuine Country platform from tory and whig materials, opposition leaders realized that they must play down tensions within the ruling class and play up the degree to which it had mutual economic interests. The ultimate irony perhaps came in the Excise Crisis of 1733, when Walpole's attempt to shift taxation from land to consumer goods caused the opposition to accuse him of reviving the 'invidious distinction of the landed and trading interest, which in reality are always united; the annual rent of lands and the number of years purchase being generally increased or decreased as trade hath been more or less flourishing'.[20]

The attempt of the Country opposition to make common cause with commercial elements against the Robinocracy met with some success, particularly in the City of London. Here Walpole's opponents were able to exploit the fact that he favoured the more substantial citizens, both economically and politically. Thus his financial policies led him to ally with the Bank, East India and South Sea Companies against those who wished to break their monopolies, while he favoured the aldermen in their long-standing battle with the Common Council over whether the aldermanic bench could overrule decisions made by the councilmen. In 1725 he was instrumental in passing the City Elections Act, which circumscribed the powers of the Common Council and recognized the aldermen's right of veto. Such actions alienated the liverymen who formed the parliamentary electorate of London and incidentally chose the sheriffs of Middlesex, so that the City's four MPs and the shrievalty of the county were usually in opposition to the Walpole ministry.

These tensions held up the consolidation of the economic interests of the ruling class for another generation. Under Pelham, however, and especially under Pitt, the friction between the great financial corporations and the less powerful business interests in the City, and between the aldermen and Common Council, was gradually relaxed. Henry Pelham relied much less than Walpole had done on the three great corporations for loans and repealed the City Elections Act in 1746. The elder Pitt cultivated the 'Country' elements in the City, backing up their demands for the suspension of the East India Company's charter in the late 1750s. The formation of the Pitt-Newcastle ministry in 1757 symbolized the reconciliation of the whig oligarchy with the City. They had become reunited in the common interests of the ruling class.

One source of conflict which was never quite resolved in this way was the executive. Indeed the proliferation of places in the administration and the systematic use of patronage by the court to distribute them to its supporters, replaced the earlier party issues as the greatest grievance keeping an opposition alive during the Walpolian era. Yet paradoxically the growth of the executive contributed not only to the establishment of political stability but also to the making of the English ruling class.

Before 1714 no party gained complete control of patronage, and the result was that a spoils system operated in English politics, 'the places of trust and profit', as Abel Boyer observed, 'being . . . in a perpetual fluctuation according as either of the two parties that divide this nation prevails'.[21] In a desire to protect certain departments, the treasury and the navy board for instance, from the effects of this instability, attempts were made to preserve continuity of personnel and there was even an embryo notion of a non-political civil service. In the last years of Anne's reign, however, when the tories were in the ascendant and

party rage was at its height, these broke down. At one level the fight
between Bolingbroke and Oxford was over the use of patronage, for
the lord treasurer was determined to keep some whigs in office while
Bolingbroke was bent on driving them out of every post 'down to the
meanest'.[22]

After Anne's death the triumphant whigs were able to implement
this programme in reverse, until by the mid-1720s the administration
was thoroughly whig from top to bottom. Moreover, by that time it
had become clear that the only way to get promotion lay through
support of the whig ministers. The result was that any family which
entertained hopes of dipping its bread in the gravy of court patronage,
even if previously it had been rabidly tory, had to go over to the side of
Walpole. The exiled Atterbury himself was prepared to admit in 1727
that 'the great tories, who have hitherto stuck out, are going in apace,
and as ready as any to make their court.'[23] By then, as J. H. Plumb
observes, 'it was a well-trodden route—the Finches, the Foxes, the
Winningtons, Chetwynds and Legges, had all made their peace and
pocketed their perquisites.'[24]

Patronage was used most directly, of course, to build up a power
base in parliament. Peers and commoners were rewarded for
supporting the government with places and pensions. The relative
number of placemen and pensioners was always far higher in the upper
house than in the lower. Even in Anne's reign there had been towards
the end some eighty-seven peers with places or pensions or both, a
slight majority of all the Lords and an overwhelming majority of those
who regularly attended debates. Under the first two Georges the Court
improved its grip on the Lords, not so much because it deployed more
patronage but because, as party issues cooled, the votes of peers with
some dependence upon the Court became much more reliable. This
was particularly noticeable of the bishops, whose whiggishness had
made them notoriously unreliable under Anne. By 1730 all twenty-six
could normally be depended upon to support the Court in any
division.

The extension of control over the lower house was more spectacular.
Under Anne about 120 members could be described as 'Queen's
servants', but the party commitments of many were so great that the
votes of only half could be completely relied upon. During the reigns of
the first two Georges the numbers steadily grew as patronage was more
systematically employed for this purpose, rising soon after Anne's
death to about 160, to become as high as 220 by 1760. As in the Lords,
their votes became more dependable with the waning of party issues.
Towards the end of George II's reign, therefore, some forty per cent of
the whole House of Commons was dependent upon the Court, which
meant a comfortable majority of those who regularly attended.

The network of influence produced by patronage extended far beyond Westminster, as it was used to reward not only politicians but their relatives, friends and constituents. It thus built up and consolidated the interests of Court supporters throughout the land. This was especially obvious in the parliamentary constituencies. The Court itself had an electoral influence in some boroughs which it used to create a body of support in the Commons. For example, the garrison at Sheerness gave the army a dominant interest in the nearby constituency of Queenborough, while the Chatham shipyards similarly enabled the admiralty to exert influence in Rochester elections. This ensured the return of four government supporters from these two Kentish constituencies throughout the period, except in 1727 when a tory was returned for Queenborough. His timely death in 1728 enabled the Court to return a candidate at the subsequent by-election. The admiralty also had a preponderant interest in Plymouth and Portsmouth, guaranteeing a further four members for the administration.

The extent of the government's direct influence can, however, be exaggerated. It certainly was by the *Craftsman* in 1729, which made the claim that 'it would be no difficult task to specify some . . . ministers, who by the absolute power of opening the floodgates of the treasury and of disposing honours and employments, have sat in their closets and nominated the members of above half the boroughs and corporations in the kingdom.'[25] Even now it is sometimes asserted that the government could directly influence the outcome of elections in many constituencies, including all the boroughs in the Isle of Wight, and all the Cinque Ports. In fact only four of the six Isle of Wight members were regularly returned on the Court interest, while only ten of the sixteen barons of the Cinque Ports, as they were called, owed their returns directly to the influence of the government throughout the period. The total number of members of parliament which the Court could absolutely guarantee to return was about twenty-five from some thirteen boroughs.

Far more important to the creation of a block of Court supporters in the Commons through the exploitation of electoral interests was the cultivation of borough patrons. The attraction of bringing the duke of Newcastle into office in 1724 was not primarily his administrative ability but his possession of extensive interests in constituencies in Nottinghamshire, Sussex and Yorkshire. Newcastle presided over the biggest electoral empire of the period. It had been built up in the early eighteenth century not without a struggle with local tories. For instance, Newcastle found that he had to compete with Sir Bryan Stapleton, a tory landowner in Boroughbridge, before he gained complete control of that borough. Many constituencies witnessed

conflicts between rival tory and whig interests in Anne's reign which
had resulted in whig victory by the accession of George I or were to do
so during his reign. In Brackley and Bury St Edmunds, for example,
the whig lords Bridgewater and Hervey fought local tory interests
throughout Anne's reign before they obtained the nomination to both
seats in each borough in 1715.

These rival local interests were usually based on country houses in
the immediate neighbourhood of a borough, such as Lord Hervey's at
Ickworth just outside Bury, the duke of Marlborough's at Blenheim on
the doorstep of Woodstock and John Aislabie's at Studley Royal near
Ripon. They rarely reflected a conflict between a resident commercial
and professional bourgeosie resisting the infiltration of their borough
by outside landed interests. Bridgewater and Hervey were engaged in
struggles not with the tradesmen of Brackley and Bury but with tory
landlords like the bishop of Durham and Sir Robert Davers. Unable to
agree to share power in their local constituencies, landowners vied
with each other for the support of the electorate below them. During
Anne's reign the voters themselves were as partisan as the political
magnates, which made the struggle between interests more than a
crude exploitation of the economic powers of landed proprietors.
However, when party passions died, material interests came to the fore
in the battle for electoral support. To some extent this is reflected in the
inflation of election expenses which occurred during the period.

The trend of rising expenses began before 1714, though there were
few constituencies where the cost came to more than two or three
hundred pounds. The turning point was the Septennial Act of 1716.
Men had been reluctant to invest sums in seats which gave only three
years' tenure in theory, and only two on average, in practice. Once
they were assured of six or seven years' tenure the price of elections
began to soar. Several hundreds of pounds, even sums over a thousand,
became commonplace. These figures were enough to exclude many
landed families who could not afford them and to frighten others,
especially tories, even if they could. For their part the electors, now
that issues no longer acted as a barrier against venality, sold out to the
highest bidder. In many boroughs the consolidation of the whig
interest represented the triumph of the magnate with the longest purse.

Material considerations in the growth of oligarchy were not
necessarily so crude. Country houses gave their proprietors a 'natural'
interest in a borough, based on the deference paid to the aristocracy
and gentry by tradesmen and professional men in an intensely
hierarchical society. Add to this the dependence which people in trade
had on the services required by a substantial household in the
neighbourhood, supplying food and raiment, even daughters and sons
for domestic service, and the respect paid to the political views of the

owner of a big house by his immediate neighbours is perfectly understandable. These social and economic considerations could be exploited to give complete control of a small constituency to a local magnate and create a propertied ruling class on the basis of a federation of country houses. In the early eighteenth century this development was held up by the rivalry of local landed families on the lines of whig and tory partisanship. This brought national politics into local affairs in most parliamentary boroughs throughout the nation.

Government influence could tip the seesaw of local interests decisively one way or the other. The jobs which the whig Lord Wharton and the tory Lord Thanet could obtain for the burgesses of Appleby, when their party was in the ascendant at Court, played a crucial part in their struggle to control one of the borough's seats, and this pattern could be repeated across the country. It was probably the most influential consideration in the rivalry between the tory George Granville and the whig Hugh Boscawen who influenced elections in many Cornish boroughs. When the balance went in favour of the whigs in 1715 Boscawen was able to transform a tory majority of thirty-four to eight into a whig lead of thirty-two to ten in Cornwall.

After 1715 the whigs finally gained the advantage and the resultant consolidation of the whig interest can be measured to some extent by the decline in the number of contests in the constituencies. Twenty-nine boroughs went to the polls in 1715 or 1722 for the last time until after 1761, in most cases until well after. The first two elections held under George I set the seal on the ascendancy of the whig interest and led to the withdrawal of tories from contests they could no longer expect to win or, even if they won, to recoup the outlay of election expenses by obtaining a post in the government.

In some constituencies the failure to go to the polls under the first two Georges, after a succession of contests in Anne's reign, represents an agreement between the rival interests to share the representation by nominating one each to the two seats. Partly this was a product of financial exhaustion, though it also testifies to the diminution of party passions. Since no burning issues were at stake to prevent the tory and whig interests reaching an agreement, then they could resolve their differences and save their money by sharing the seats. This was certainly the case in many counties, where the incidence of contests shows the most dramatic fall of all. In the general election of 1705, twenty-six out of forty English counties were contested, a record for the century, although that of 1710 came close when twenty-three went to the polls. As late as 1722 there were seventeen county contests. Thereafter the total drops dramatically, down to four in 1741, three in 1747, five in 1754 and four again in 1761.

This is the most compelling evidence that the political elites of England fused into a homogeneous ruling class in the central decades of the eighteenth century. No longer riven by bitter party strife or rent by conflicting economic interests, the aristocracy and gentry, together with merchants, plutocrats and leading professional men, amalgamated to form a narrow oligarchy which controlled all the levers of power, at the centre and in the provinces. Parliamentary debates became more like family bickerings than the shouts which presage civil war. Constituencies became quiet backwaters as the ruling class dropped its need for the support of the electorate and either controlled it or evaded it. The oligarchs cemented their hold on some boroughs by reducing the size of the electorate to a more manageable level. Admissions of freemen were carefully regulated to secure a select number, or the right to vote of inhabitant householders was restricted by insisting that they should not be in receipt of alms or charity, and even that they should be rated to church and poor.

Once in power it seemed as though the whigs were anxious to eradicate all signs of their earlier connection with urban mobs and popular politics and to project a new image of respectable oligarchy. The speed with which they repudiated their association with the whiggery of the Exclusion Crisis was remarkable. The cry for frequent elections was replaced by the Septennial Act. Habeas Corpus was suspended in every Jacobite scare. The Riot Act made assembling for political as well as for other purposes a potentially capital offence.

Other legislation which followed the accession of George I also seems to betray a concern to defend the interests of the ruling class against the lower classes. The so-called 'Act to encourage the planting of trees', passed in 1716, made it a capital offence to mutilate 'rows and walks of young trees planted by gentlemen for ornament about their houses'. An act of 1721 forbade combinations among journeymen tailors for the purpose of raising wages. In 1723 another act empowered local authorities to erect workhouses for the poor on parochial relief, with the avowed aim of lowering the burden of the poor rate. Perhaps the most glaring example was the notorious Waltham Black Act of 1723 which, though primarily directed against poachers in game parks, incidentally created about fifty new capital offences, including that of appearing in disguise on the king's highway.

Such legislation embodied the ideology of the ruling class. Soon after the triumph of whiggery the philosophical defence of 'liberty and property' narrowed down to the protection of property even at the cost of infringing liberty. This was to do no real violence to Locke or his popularizers, for their philosophy was socially very conservative. Although they talked about the rights of the people, it soon becomes very clear that they did not include everybody in that concept. On the contrary, the rude multitude, the vast majority of the population, were excluded and servants and labourers were not regarded as freeborn Englishmen unless they were independent householders, which few were. Moreover, Locke drew a distinction between liberty and licence, the definitions of which were very much those of the ruling class. Emphasis on the conservative aspects of whig political thought, however, probably reconciled to the rule of the whig oligarchy a great many who might have feared the social effects of the overthrow of divine right theories. As far as the justification of the right to rule was concerned, the ruling class was thoroughly Lockean by the middle of the eighteenth century.

Nor should much be made of the apparent unwillingness of tory justices to convict under the new legislation. It was not that the Country opposition adopted a more paternalistic philosophy so much as the natural reluctance to visit the full powers of the law upon specific examples. Thus the penal laws against catholics were happily heaped up in parliament but were rarely enforced on individual recusants. There is no evidence that the passing of legislation creating new capital offences caused a debate, let alone a division, between Court and Country. Furthermore, the insistence upon property qualifications for MPs and JPs alike, which were the hallmark of ruling class attitudes, was primarily Country-inspired.

At the same time it would be a mistake to consider all these developments as a crude protection of its own interests by a narrow ruling class. The defence of property was an interest common to tradesmen and even labourers in addition to landed proprietors, as surviving inventories eloquently testify. The modern slogan 'law and order' might, as radical critics insist, merely veil white racist demands for tougher law enforcement against black criminals. Yet they should not overlook that fact that most victims of black criminals are black themselves. By the same token the defence of property in the eighteenth century might have been, and in some cases like the game laws patently was, the embodiment of narrow class interests. Nevertheless the law did protect, insofar as legislation alone could, the interests of shopkeepers even more than of landlords. The recourse to capital punishment as a defence against attacks upon property rightly calls for comment in any discussion of the relationship between politics and society under the first two Georges. It should be balanced by the reluctance to employ a police force to enforce the legislation, a reluctance which stemmed as much from the respect for liberty as the legislation did from the desire to defend property. The ruling class was perhaps only lukewarm in its defence of liberty, yet it did pay more than mere lip service to it. Its members might shout about the defence of property but they did not whisper about liberty. They were more careful of the liberties of the individual than the Pretender would have been had he succeeded in his designs. For all the talk of popular Jacobitism there is precious little evidence for it, in England at any rate, possibly because the bulk of the population accepted that they were better off under the whig oligarchy. When a French invasion seemed imminent in March 1756 the *Sherborne Mercury* published the following advertisement, without hint of irony, appealing for recruits to join a regiment being raised at Salisbury. It addressed itself to

> the bold, the hardy, the brave, to those enured and seasoned by rustic labour; to those honest fellows, though in a lower degree of life, who have too much true English courage left, to sit down unconcerned when a cruel enemy is almost at their doors ... we know that these have wives, or children, or possessions, or at least precious liberty, which they prize—These have all at present their peaceful and free habitations, where they feel an enjoyment after each day's labour equal if not superior to that of kings.

The English ruling class, therefore, did not become alienated from the rest of the community as continental aristocracies did in these years. On the contrary, as it entrenched its hold on the country so it appropriated patriotic symbols to reflect its own image. John Bull, 'the picture of the plain country gentleman', established himself in these very years as the embodiment of the English virtues.[26] Commonsensical, complacent and self-confident, his very solidity depicted the assurance of the ruling class that the divine right to rule had passed from the Stuarts to themselves.

# II  Strife

# 7 The Establishment of the Hanoverian Dynasty

On the morning of 1 August 1714 the phrase 'Queen Anne is dead' was fresh news. She died surrounded by physicians and politicians, the calm centre of a storm which had been brewing ever since 1701, when the Act of Settlement had taken the succession out of the strictly hereditary line and placed it in the house of Hanover. As many as fifty-eight people could claim closer kinship with the dead queen than George Lewis, Elector of Hanover, who was proclaimed as her successor immediately after her death. Next in line was her half-brother James Edward, son of James II and Mary of Modena, who was at that moment in exile in Lorraine. The fact that the Pretender, as he was called, was geographically nearer London than the successor established by parliament added to the tensions surrounding her deathbed.

The ministers with whom she had worked during the past four years were suspected of Jacobite sympathies, that is of favouring the Pretender. These suspicions particularly attached themselves to Henry St John, Viscount Bolingbroke, who had emerged as the leading minister only in the last few days. For some time there had been a struggle for supremacy within the ministry between him and Robert Harley, earl of Oxford. Oxford, although like many other politicians he took out insurance against a Stuart restoration by corresponding with the exiled Pretender, was a staunch Hanoverian and had fought stubbornly to resist Bolingbroke's moves to keep the option of recognizing James Edward open. As lord treasurer since 1711, Oxford wielded immense power within the ministry, being generally acknowledged as prime minister. He had employed it successfully to scotch his rival's schemes and, while in the end he had been unable to prevent his own dismissal, his fall came on 27 July, too late for Bolingbroke to do anything to put his plans into execution before the Queen died.

What those plans were, indeed if he had any concrete policies beyond taking advantage of events, is now obscure. His strategy remains clear enough: he wished to keep the tory party in power after Anne's death. But the tactics he was prepared to employ to achieve this goal seemed bewildering to contemporaries and now merely confused. At times he appeared to be pandering to the Jacobite wing of the party by making overtures towards the Pretender. Yet when James refused to change his religion by renouncing catholicism and adopting anglicanism Bolingbroke knew that such a game was hopeless. He admitted candidly that the English would sooner prefer the Grand Turk than a papist as their king. At the same time the alternative, the accession of George I, looked grim for the tories. During the past four years they had taken England out of involvement in the War of the Spanish Succession and signed what was to all intents and purposes a separate peace with France at Utrecht in 1713, despite the terms of the Grand Alliance which made allied agreement to negotiations necessary. Among the allies thus aggrieved was the Elector of Hanover, and although as king of Great Britain he might expect to reap any advantages the tories had gained for their country from the French, he refused to see it that way. It was clear from the activities of his representatives in England, who associated almost entirely with whigs, that the peacemakers were to be proscribed when he came to the throne.

In this situation there was little Bolingbroke could do except try to place the tories in so strong a position that the new king would be obliged to come to terms with them. This would have involved a thorough purge of the administration from top to bottom, eliminating whigs and replacing them with tories, a policy which Oxford had stubbornly resisted up to the day of his fall. After his dismissal Bolingbroke apparently realized that there would be no time to implement such plans, and tried to come to terms with the whigs at a bizarre dinner he gave attended by several of their leaders. On this occasion, James Stanhope, one of the prominent whigs invited, turned to him and said bluntly 'Harry! you have only two ways of escaping the gallows. The first is to join the honest party of the whigs, the other to give yourself up entirely to the French king and seek his help for the Pretender. If you do not choose the first course, we can only imagine that you have decided for the second.'[1]

It was because they believed he had decided upon a Stuart restoration that the whigs were most anxious to influence the course of events upon the death of Queen Anne. Consequently when news reached them on 30 July that her life was despaired of, those who were still members of the privy council hastened to Kensington to take their place along with tory councillors in order to arrange for the immediate proclamation of King George as soon as Anne breathed her last.

Although the privy council presided over affairs while the Queen lay dying, as soon as she was dead the chief executive functions were taken over by a council of regency which had been established by an act of

1706. This consisted of seven great officers of state and an unspecified number of individuals nominated by the successor himself. The majority of *ex officio* members were, of course, tory, though one, the now aged Archbishop Tenison of Canterbury, was a staunch whig while another, the duke of Shrewsbury, appointed to succeed Oxford as lord treasurer as the last act of the dying queen, had the reputation of being a whig even though he had fallen in with the measures taken by the tory ministry since 1710. Shrewsbury enjoyed the high offices of lord chamberlain and lord lieutenant of Ireland in addition to the newly conferred lord treasurership. Most of the eighteen added to the regency by George I were also whigs. However, it was noticed that he co-opted a number of Hanoverian tories, including the earls of Anglesey and Nottingham, to the body, and kept out three members of the Whig Junto, Lords Somers, Sunderland and Wharton. This was widely interpreted as a conciliatory measure designed to show that the King was not exclusively attached to the whig party but was prepared to promote any tories who had not supported the obnoxious Peace of Utrecht or flirted with the Pretender. Thus he kept many minor tory officials in his own household, purging only those in high places. Such a policy was not only a magnanimous attempt to unite the nation by repairing the breaches between the parties; it was also a prudential move to prevent himself becoming too dependent upon the whigs.

For this policy to succeed it was necessary to preserve and perpetuate crucial divisions within the tory ranks. At the time of his accession the tories were deeply divided. The making of the Treaty of Utrecht had separated those who went along with it from those who entertained doubts about its implications for the succession, and who were known as the Whimsicals. Since then the enmity between Bolingbroke and Oxford had caused the party to fall further apart, so that on Anne's death there were four major groups of tory MPs. First there was a small but significant group of tories who identified themselves with the intransigent attitude to the peace adopted by Daniel Finch, earl of Nottingham, ever since 1711. Then there were the whimsicals, led by Sir Thomas Hanmer, who had materially assisted the defeat of the treaty of commerce in 1713 and now stood first and foremost for the Hanoverian succession. Thirdly there were Oxford's followers, who like their leader also supported the accession of George I, but whose first loyalty lay with Queen Anne and the defence of her government's policies since 1710. The most outstanding of Oxford's supporters in 1714 was William Bromley, formerly a high churchman, who now enjoyed the post of secretary of state. Finally there were Bolingbroke's cronies, a motley assortment of opportunists, time-servers and Jacobites whose principal concern throughout was how to keep power after Anne died. Leading lights in their ranks were

Sir John Pakington, William Shippen and Sir William Wyndham. George made no secret of the fact that this last group could expect no mercy from him. Bolingbroke was ignominiously dismissed before the new king even arrived in England. But the other elements in the tory ranks were given some encouragement to hope for favours from him. Thus Nottingham was given the post of lord president of the council while Sir Thomas Hanmer was offered the chancellorship of the exchequer. Even the Harleyites were not completely overlooked, for although Oxford himself received a very cold snub on being presented to the King shortly after his arrival in the country, Bromley was offered the treasurership of the chamber.

No decision, not even Bolingbroke's subsequent flight to the Pretender, was more fateful to the tory cause than the refusal of Hanmer and Bromley to accept office under George I. For this left only a handful of tories associated with Nottingham in the government and led the rest to hazard the party's political future on the outcome of the general election of 1715. If they could obtain a majority in the Commons, so they argued, they could force the King to come to terms with them. Pinning their hopes on victory at the polls, the tories declared electoral war on the whigs, rallying to their old battle cry 'the church in danger'. Their chief manifesto, penned by Francis Atterbury, bishop of Rochester, was issued under the title *English Advice to the Freeholders of England* and was 'dispersed throughout the kingdom'. It explicitly attacked the whigs, accusing them of aiming at a new war, the destruction of the church and a standing army. By implication it also criticized George I, particularly with its assertion that foreigners would be given equal employment opportunities with Englishmen at court; and the King was stung into offering a reward of £1,000 for the discovery of its authors, and £500 for the apprehension of its printers and distributors.[2]

It must be admitted that George I and his entourage were wide open to tory libels. George himself was unprepossessing, even vacant, in appearance and, although not as stupid as some historians have made out, he was dull and ponderous. Even his humour was heavy. His manner, in public at least, was formal, stiff and cold, sometimes positively icy. Although he had known for thirteen years that he was heir apparent to the English throne he had not bothered to learn even a smattering of the English tongue. There was also a sinister streak in a man who had divorced his wife and kept her permanently in confinement in Hanover for an alleged affair with a Swedish count, especially since he himself did not scruple to keep mistresses, one of whom, now somewhat superannuated, came across to his court shortly after his accession. This was the baroness von Schulenberg, who was known as 'the Maypole' because she was so thin. In 1719 she was made duchess of Kendal. Robert Walpole thought her 'as much queen of England as ever any was'. Baroness Kielmansegge, who by contrast was so bulky that Horace Walpole remembered as a boy 'being terrified at her enormous figure' was not, as is usually alleged, George's mistress, but his half sister. When she became countess of Darlington in 1721 the patent stressed that she was related to the King. She did, however, have such a reputation for amorous intrigue that her husband gave her a certificate vouching for his faith in her! She also exercised influence at court. John Chetwynd was reputed to have got a place at the board of trade by giving her 500 guineas down, a pension of £200 a year and a pair of fine brilliant earrings.[3]

Other Germans in George's confidence exercised even more power, although by the Act of Settlement they were strictly forbidden to hold office in England. His principal German advisors were Barons Bothmer and Bernstorff, and Jean de Robethon, a cosmopolitan Huguenot who had become his private secretary. Bothmer had been sent to England in June 1714 in order to safeguard Hanoverian interests there. He had quickly acquired influence with the whigs, and his advice had been sought by the regents before George himself arrived. Even after the King landed Bothmer acted as an essential go-between with English politicians, to the extent of advising on ministerial appointments. Bernstorff's knowledge of European affairs was such that the King confided very closely in him during the formulation of foreign policy and the forging of diplomatic relations. Indeed he acted as premier minister for Hanoverian affairs. Robethon, too, was an accomplished diplomat, and became Bernstorff's *alter ego*. These Germans acquired enormous influence at court. British politicians and foreign ambassadors found it to their advantage to cultivate their acquaintance.

The alien nature of the German king's court was a natural target for xenophobic tories. They squeezed every ounce of adverse publicity out of George's personal foibles and entourage, even accusing him of keeping two Turkish servants, Mohamed and Mustapha, who were prisoners from his Turkish campaign, 'for abominable purposes'.[4] Among the libels put out by the tories at this time were two poems on affairs of state: *Pasquin to the Queen's Statue* and *The Blessings Attending George's accession*. The first, addressed to Anne, began:[5]

> Behold he comes to make thy people groan,
> And with their curses to ascend thy throne;
> A clod-pate, base, inhuman, jealous Fool,
> The jest of Europe, and the faction's tool.
> Heav'n never heard of such a right Divine,
> Nor Earth e'er saw a successor like thine:
> For if in sense or politicks you fail'd,
> 'Twas when his lousy long succession you entail'd.

The second contains the lines:

> Hither he brought the dear Illustrious House;
> That is, himself, his pipe, close stool and louse;
> Two Turks, three Whores, and half a dozen nurses,
> Five hundred Germans, all with empty purses.

Such abuse and the whole tory policy of non-cooperation forced George into relying far more heavily on whig support than he had at first intended. The result was a massive transfer of power from the tories to the whigs both at the centre and in the provinces.

At the centre the ministerial changes of 1714 affected the cabinet, the privy council and the departments of state. The cabinet was completely changed for the first time in English history. Even the ministerial revolution of 1710, though Bishop Burnet wrote of it, 'So sudden and so entire a change of the ministry is scarce to be found in our history', had not gone as far as that.[6] Despite the tory changes of that year Harley's cabinet contained four men who had sat in it during the previous ministry. Now in 1714 there was a clean sweep. None of the members of George I's cabinet had held office, much less enjoyed cabinet rank, in the last year of Anne's reign.

George made a break with his predecessor, too, by not appointing a lord treasurer. Instead he put the treasury into commission. The result, as intended, was that nobody succeeded immediately to Oxford's role as prime minister. Lord Halifax, who was made first lord of the treasury, was not a little chagrined at this since he had hoped to play that part. In the event he had a rival in the secretary of state for the south, General James Stanhope, while the northern secretary, Lord Townshend, also challenged his supremacy. Yet another cabinet minister who jockeyed for a leading position was the duke of Marlborough, restored to his post of captain general shortly after the King's arrival. Marlborough's son-in-law, the earl of Sunderland, was made lord lieutenant of Ireland. Lord Somers, a veteran of the Whig Junto like Halifax and Sunderland, but who had been ailing for many years, was honoured by being given a place in the cabinet without office. Lord Cowper, who shared with Somers the distinction of being one of the leading lawyers of the age, became lord chancellor. The remaining member of the cabinet was the only one not a whig, being the renegade tory earl of Nottingham whom George made lord president.

The privy council, too, underwent a drastic change. On Anne's death about eighty men had the title of privy councillor, some forty-two of whom had assembled near the bedside of the dying queen. These, as we have seen, consisted of whigs as well as tories who were anxious to exert some influence at that critical moment. On 1 October

George I reformed the council, reducing it from eighty to thirty-two members. The only tories left in were those few who had voted the previous winter against a parliamentary motion that the protestant succession was not in danger under Anne's last administration. Among the new councillors were the two remaining members of the Junto who had not been admitted to the cabinet—Lord Wharton, now lord privy seal, and Lord Orford, first lord of the admiralty. Their junior colleagues included Robert Walpole, who received the lucrative post of paymaster of the forces.

Whole departments of state were also purged of any tory suspected of being less than enthusiastic for the protestant succession. The treasury and the commissioners of the land tax, customs and excises were all combed, and tories zealous for the previous administration were dismissed, to be replaced by stalwart whigs.

The whig revolution extended from the centre into the remotest provinces. The key officials in the localities were the lords lieutenants of the counties. Two of these were changed by the lord regents before George I arrived in the country. Hampshire was taken out of the hands of the Jacobite duke of Beaufort and placed in those of the duke of Bolton, a reliable whig. Presumably the regency felt that a county which contained such key ports as Southampton and Portsmouth was too vulnerable to the Pretender to be left in charge of a suspect tory. Thus at the same time they replaced the Jacobite governor of Portsmouth, Lord North and Grey, with Thomas Erle, a soldier staunch for the protestant succession. They also appointed a whig to the lord lieutenancy of Lancashire, a post vacant since 1711, no doubt to keep an eye on the many catholics in that county. After his arrival the King continued this policy of putting the counties under men he could trust, changing in all some twenty-two of the forty-two lord lieutenancies in England. Thus the whig earl of Scarborough replaced the tory bishop of Durham as lord lieutenant of Durham and Northumberland, while the whig earl of Holderness took over from the tory duke of Buckingham as lord lieutenant of the North Riding of Yorkshire. Incoming whig lord lieutenants would see to it that there was a purge of tory deputy lieutenants. A similar purge was undertaken of justices of the peace. Under Lord Chancellor Harcourt the commissions had been stocked with tory JPs many of whom, like the chancellor himself, were suspected of Jacobitism. It was said that within two weeks of Anne's death Harcourt had changed the entire commission of the peace in Cumberland, packing it with notorious Jacobites. When Lord Cowper succeeded Harcourt as chancellor this process was reversed and those justices of the peace known to be Jacobites were replaced with staunch whigs, though those only suspected of Jacobitism were kept in on good behaviour.

It was Cowper who had advised George I shortly after his accession that 'the parties are so near an equality and the generality of the world so much in love with the advantages a king of Great Britain has to bestow . . . that tis wholly in your majesty's power, by showing your favour in due time [before the elections] to one or other of them to give which of them you please a clear majority in all succeeding parliaments.'[7] Upon the dissolution on 15 January 1715 George had showed his favour in due time by giving power almost exclusively to the whigs. It remained to be seen what effect this would have at the polls.

Although according to Cowper the result was a foregone conclusion, the tories do not appear to have considered their cause entirely hopeless. Moreover, even if events apparently vindicated his judgement, it was not at all clear on the eve of the polls that his assessment was accurate. For one thing it is hard to see where he got his idea that the parties were about equal. On the contrary, in January 1715 the tories were in an extraordinarily powerful position in the constituencies. At the previous general election they had been returned to parliament in greater numbers than at any time since 1685, when the results of Charles II's borough-mongering and James II's electioneering had achieved the greatest majority the party had ever enjoyed. When the polling was over in 1713 about 364 tory members had been returned to the House of Commons from England and Wales. Since then the number had grown to around 376, partly as a result of by-elections, but mainly as a result of decisions upon petitions relating to controverted elections, leaving the whigs with only 137.

This huge majority was based on three electoral props. First there was a hard core of constituencies where the tory interest was so strong that it could control one if not both seats no matter how strongly the whigs challenged. Then there were the gains made in 1710 and improved and consolidated in 1713 in those constituencies with over 500 voters where public opinion counted, and which had swung to the tories in the previous two elections. Thirdly there was the undoubted influence of the crown which, though it had been sparingly deployed in 1710, had been unstintingly exercised on behalf of the tories in 1713, contributing not a little to the great majority they had achieved at the polls.

The tories could rely on some 114 'safe' seats which the whigs could not possibly take. Some were in tory proprietary boroughs, such as Newton, Lancashire, where the Leghs of Lyme could be relied upon to nominate both members, or Minehead, safe in the tory hands of the Luttrells of Dunster Castle. Some were in boroughs where the tories always nominated one member. Thus the Seymours of Berry Pomery controlled a seat in Totnes, Lord Thanet's proprietorship of Appleby

Castle and several burgages in the town assured one tory member for that borough, while the return of Edward Nicholas for Shaftesbury could be guaranteed thanks to his interest in the borough created by his control of its water supply. Then there were others in large constituencies, such as Devon and Oxfordshire, where toryism was so prevalent that the whigs never stood a chance.

In other large constituencies the outcome of elections seesawed between the two parties. However, the 'swing' to the tories had been so great in 1713 that it would take an enormous reaction to reverse it. Just before the polling began in 1715 they held as many as 160 of the 190 seats in the 105 constituencies with over 500 voters, including no fewer than 79 of the 92 county seats. If by a popular campaign they could retain these seats, then their ascendancy in the new parliament would be guaranteed despite the opposition of the Court. The tories hoped, by playing up the theme 'the church in danger', and by exploiting the apparent unpopularity of the house of Hanover, to survive as the majority party even though the third prop of their electoral success in 1713, the support of the Court, had been pulled from under them.

Probably more important than their previous success in giving the tories grounds for optimism in 1715 was their belief that the tory party had a natural majority in the country. After all, they had won six out of the seven general elections held prior to 1715, one of them in December 1701 against the influence of the Court. The whig victory of 1708 they regarded as an aberration from the norm, an artificial, contrived outcome, the result of over four years' official proscription of the tories and encouragement of their opponents. As Bolingbroke had put it when the tories won again in 1710: 'What a difference there is between the true strength of this nation, and the fictitious one of the whigs. How much time, how many lucky incidents, how many strains of power, how much money must go to create a majority of the latter. On the other hand, take but off the opinion that the crown is another way inclined, and the church interest rises with redoubled force, and by its natural genuine strength.'[8] It was true that in 1715 the crown was again entirely another way inclined, but the other ingredients necessitating a whig victory were apparently inoperative. At least the time factor was lacking, for George had not had six months, let alone four years, to prepare for this election. So unprecedented strength following the 1713 results and confidence in their own natural majority, gave the tories hopes that they would more than hold their own in the ensuing contest.

In the event the whigs transformed a tory majority on paper of 240 into a whig lead of sixty-five, not counting the Scottish seats. This was a much better result than they had achieved in 1708, even though their actual majority was very similar. In 1708 there had been much less

ground to make up, since the parties had been almost equal after the
1705 results and, with electoral petitions bringing in whigs and ousting
their rivals, on the eve of the general election they had actually
outnumbered the tories. The transformation between 1713 and 1715
was much more spectacular, and in bringing it about the whigs
obtained fifty-three seats which they had not won in 1708, twenty-
three of which had not been held by a whig during the whole of Anne's
reign.

The success of the whigs in the popular constituencies was as much
owing to public opinion as to the influence of the crown. Here the
tories cannot have been helped by the declaration which the Pretender issued in November 1714, addressed to his 'loving subjects' and
claiming 'that for some time past he could not well doubt of his sister's
good intentions towards him . . . which were unfortunately prevented
by her deplorable death'.[9] Certainly the tories were embarrassed by
this statement and tried to dismiss it as a whig contrivance. For at the
last election when the succession had appeared to be in danger, in
1708, the electorate returned an unequivocal whig majority for the
only time in Anne's reign. They did so again at the first election held
under the Hanoverians.

After their victory the whigs made the most of their gains. There
were over fifty petitions from defeated whig candidates against tory
sitting members. As many as possible of these were heard and decided
in favour of the unsuccessful candidate; with each decision removing
a tory from the house and adding a whig their majority was increased
by two votes. The parliamentary ascendancy of the whigs ensured
the establishment of the Hanoverian dynasty. Bolingbroke saw the
way things were going and fled to France. 'The grief of my soul is
this', he had written earlier, 'I see plainly that the tory party is
gone.'[10]

So determined were the whigs to ensure their supremacy and
perpetuate the proscription of the tories, that they seized every
opportunity to exploit the humiliation of their rivals. The flight of
Bolingbroke was a godsend, for it enabled them to label as Jacobites
leading men in the late ministry. When the duke of Ormonde joined
him on the continent in July their titles and estates were confiscated by
acts of attainder. Two of their former ministerial colleagues who stayed
to face their accusers, the earls of Oxford and Strafford, were
impeached. The gist of the charges against them was that they had
been guilty of treason when they deserted the allies and made a
separate peace with France. As Oxford riposted in the Lords 'if
ministers of state, acting by the immediate commands of their
sovereign, are afterwards to be made accountable for their proceedings, it may, one day or other, be the case of all the members of this

august assembly.'[11] But his arguments availed him little, and on 27 July he entered the Tower.

Such violent measures produced a desperate reaction. Tories, afraid that there was no political future for them under the new regime, turned their eyes towards the Pretender. It was not that they were all Jacobites; but as Baron Schutz, the Hanoverian envoy, had predicted in February 1714, 'it is certain that of fifteen tories there are fourteen who would not oppose the Pretender, in case he came with a French army.'[12] In this silent majority there was an active minority of tories and their supporters who were prepared not merely to withdraw support from George I but to declare allegiance to James III. These persuaded the Pretender that all that was necessary for his restoration was his appearance. Their optimism was based on pure delusion, especially since their every move was observed by the earl of Stair, the astute and diligent ambassador whom George I sent to Paris in January 1715. Bolingbroke, who since his flight had become James's secretary, tried in vain to inject a little realism into the preparations for an uprising. James had insufficient ships even to establish himself in Scotland and without French help he could not hope to overcome the Hanoverians. Yet Louis XIV was reluctant to give more than promises, and meanwhile the British had a fleet patrolling the northern coast of France and were increasing their armed forces from eight to fifteen thousand men. The final blow to the Jacobite cause was the death of Louis himself in September, an event which, as Bolingbroke agreed, 'rendered vain and fruitless all we had done'.[13] The French government was plunged into the uncertainties of a regency round the infant Louis XV. It could ill afford to back rash ventures in European politics, so that even the hope of assistance from France faded from the Pretender's calculations.

This did not, however, deter his Scottish supporters. The die was cast on 6 September 1715 when the earl of Mar raised James's standard at Braemar. It was no accident that the rebellion began in Scotland. Ever since the union of 1707 there had been discontent in many sections of Scottish society which objected to the consequences of closer ties with England. Whig and tory, Country and Court, no matter what element in English political life had been uppermost, all seemed hostile or indifferent to Scottish interests. Thus in 1709 the whigs had extended to Scotland the harsher treason laws of England. Then in 1712 the tories had passed the Toleration Act, which safeguarded the separate episcopalians from the harassment of the presbyterian establishment, and the Patronage Act which restored the rights of lay patrons over church livings. In the same year opposition elements from both parties had prevented the duke of Hamilton from taking his seat in the House of Lords by virtue of his elevation to the peerage of Great Britain as duke of Brandon, on the constitutional grounds that under the terms of the union only sixteen Scottish noblemen, chosen by their peers, could sit in the upper chamber. Finally in 1712 the Oxford ministry had extended the malt tax to Scotland, although technically this was in breach of the agreement that such a step should not be taken until peace was reached with France. Thus lawyers, presbyterians, peers, farmers and merchants were added to the permanently disaffected Jacobites to make a formidable list of Scots who regretted the Union. As Nicholas Tindal, continuing Rapin's *History of England*, admitted, 'Scotland was generally dissatisfied with the union. They were apt to consider themselves as degraded to a province of England.'[14] There were meetings of Jacobites in the highlands soon after the accession of George I, while even in Glasgow a meeting house was pulled down. In December the Jacobites felt that sentiment was strong enough for them to organize a national address against the union. Mar exploited these sentiments in a proclamation which claimed that the Pretender would restore the 'ancient free and independent constitution' of Scotland. On the Pretender's religious intentions, however, the manifesto was eloquently silent and the prospect of restoring catholicism along with independence ensured that only a handful of lowland Scots rallied to the Jacobite cause.

Even so Mar's call was answered by an impressive array of eighteen lords who rallied to the Pretender's standard, bringing with them some 5,000 men. Since the regular troops in Scotland scarcely numbered 1,500 at the outbreak of the rising, a determined move by Mar at this stage could have been decisive. Instead he delayed, waiting for reinforcements. Although the Jacobite forces swelled to 10,000 by November, this delay proved fatal, for while he waited the government was able to concentrate its efforts on drawing the teeth of Jacobitism in England.

George I's ministers all along regarded the threat from Scotland as less serious than any potential uprising in the south. Evidence of disaffection among George's English subjects early gave them cause for concern and the Jacobites occasion for hope. Popular demonstrations against the regime grew menacingly in the months after the King's arrival. On 20 October, the day of his coronation, there were disturbances in Birmingham, Bristol, Chippenham, Norwich and Reading. Many of the elections held the following February took place in an atmosphere of mob violence, the one for the county of Leicester being so turbulent that the sheriff felt his life threatened and adjourned the poll. Every suitable occasion, from the anniversary of Anne's coronation on 23 April to Ormonde's birthday on the 29th, and from George I's birthday on 28 May to the anniversary of Charles II's restoration the following day, saw Jacobite activity in the capital. On 29th they were so provocative as to burn a bonfire in Chancery Lane. During June and July rioting reached epidemic proportions, especially in Staffordshire, Shropshire and Worcestershire, and the ministry rushed the Riot Act through parliament. It was introduced on 1 July and obtained the royal assent on the 20th. Even so Jacobite demonstrations continued, especially in Oxford which was so disaffected that the King actually refused to receive an address from the university with the retort, 'that as they had shewn a manifest disrespect to his majesty's person and government in all their late proceedings, so his majesty expected they should convince him of their loyalty by their actions and not by words'.[15]

It was against this background of sedition and treason that the authorities learned of the Pretender's plans for an invasion. On 21 July, therefore, the day after the royal assent to the Riot Act, Habeas Corpus was suspended by another act 'to impower his majesty to secure and detain such persons as his majesty shall suspect are conspiring against his person and government'. For the whigs to take such measures shows how rattled they were. The first arrest was made on 2 September, when a lieutenant-colonel in the Guards was taken up for enlisting men for the Pretender. Bigger game were rounded up on the 21st when Lords Lansdowne and Dupplin were apprehended. On the same day a warrant was issued against the earl of Jersey, while the House of Commons consented to the arrest of six members, including Sir William Wyndham and Thomas Forster, knights of the shire for Somerset and Northumberland respectively. Wyndham was implicated in plans for a rising in the west based on Bristol and Bath, which were secured by troops at the end of September. Forster actually led a rising in the north, in conjunction with the earl of Derwentwater. They proclaimed James at Warkworth and Alnwick, but failed to take Newcastle. Thereafter they joined with Scottish Jacobites, some from the lowlands under Lords Kenmore, Nithsdale, Carnwath and Wintoun, and others detached by Mar who were led by MacIntosh of Borlum. After aimless foraying back and forth across the border, they decided to march into Lancashire, hoping that many Jacobites would join them there. Some 1,600 recruits did come in but it was observed that they were for the most part catholics and that hardly any anglican tories were prepared to lift a finger for the Pretender. Forster's forces got as far south as Preston, where they were intercepted by Hanoverian troops under General Wills. Initially the Jacobites kept Wills at bay, but when he was joined by General Carpenter they decided to surrender. On 14 November some 75 English and 143 Scottish officers, and several hundred soldiers, gave themselves up. This left only the rebels in Scotland, and even James's own half-brother, the duke of

Berwick, observed, 'I shall always consider it a folly to think that he will be able to succeed in his undertaking with the Scotch alone.'[16]

In fact the day before Forster surrendered at Preston, Mar had engaged government forces under the duke of Argyll in the battle at Sheriffmuir. Because the ministers had given top priority to crushing Jacobitism in England, Argyll, much to his disgust, had been supplied very sparingly with reinforcements, so that his army only numbered about 3,300. Meanwhile Mar's had been augmented to around 10,000. Argyll, however, had the advantage of a superior position, and he made the most of it, his attack on Mar's left wing putting that section of the Jacobite army to flight. The other wing, meanwhile, led by Mar himself, forced the Hanoverian troops opposite them to retreat. The result was really a draw, though both sides claimed they had won. But, in Sir Charles Petrie's words, 'for James a battle drawn was a battle lost. Argyll had prevented Mar from penetrating into the lowlands, and so the victory was for George.'[17]

James himself was at that moment in St Malo, waiting good news from Britain. He had hoped to hear it from England, but when Ormonde went over in October and lay off the coast of Devon there had been no reply to the signal announcing his arrival, and he had returned. 'In a word', wrote Bolingbroke, 'he was refused a night's lodging in a country which we had been told was in a good posture to receive the chevalier, and where the duke expected that multitudes would repair to him'.[18] Although Ormonde returned to Cornwall, at James's bidding, his second voyage was equally futile. On his return James had despaired of England and instead had to reconcile himself to the now bleak prospect of Scotland. He therefore went to Dunkirk and sailed up the North Sea to land at Peterhead on 22 December. By this time Mar's army was seriously depleted, while Argyll's had been heavily reinforced, with troops which included a Dutch contingent sent across under the terms of a treaty between Britain and the United Provinces for safeguarding the protestant succession. The Jacobites were now entirely on the defensive, and it was only a matter of time before they were overcome. James, realizing that the cause was lost, embarked for France on 4 February, taking Mar with him but leaving most of his loyal supporters to fend for themselves. His cause had really been hopeless from the time in Anne's reign when he refused to change his religion even nominally from catholicism to anglicanism. As Wolfgang Michael put it: 'while his refusal of an interested conversion does him honour, he should have gone a step further, and, being unwilling to conform with the wishes of the nation, he should have accepted the consequences, and renounced all attempts at a restoration.'[19]

The consequences were dire. Nineteen Scottish peerages were

forfeited by attainder, while seven peers captured at Preston were impeached, found guilty and sentenced to death. Only two of them, Lords Derwentwater and Kenmure, were in fact executed: Nithsdale and Wintoun escaped, while Carnwath, Nairne and Widdrington were reprieved. Thomas Forster was committed to Newgate, from which he too escaped. Smaller fry were less fortunate. Twenty-six were hanged, while hundreds were transported to the colonies.

The treatment of the seven lords broke the last frail threads still connecting the crown to the tories, for the earl of Nottingham was appalled at George's initial determination to see them all executed and interceded with him to urge clemency, much to the annoyance of his ministerial colleagues. 'All the trouble we have had in favour of the condemned lords' wrote Walpole, 'arose from that corner.'[20] Although Nottingham's pleas, backed by tory addresses for mercy to be shown, caused the King to back down, the friction led to the earl's departure from the ministry, accompanied by his brother and his son. The flight of Finches from the government in 1716 thus left the whigs in sole charge.

The whigs sought to consolidate, if not to perpetuate, their power by means of the Septennial Act. This controversial measure, replacing the Triennial Act by allowing seven years to elapse between general elections, was introduced into the House of Lords on 10 April. The immediate justification was the continued turbulence in the nation following the Jacobite rebellion, which made the prospect of a general election as early as 1718 appear hazardous. Other reasons given were that frequent elections had fomented feuds, kept up parties, occasioned ruinous expences and consequently corruption, vice and debauchery. Perhaps Lord Islay gave the whig game away when he commented that they also rendered 'government dependent on the caprice of the multitude, and very precarious'.[21] Despite tory protests that the measure was unconstitutional and deprived the electorate of its rights, it went through both houses. Few could have predicted when the whigs came into their own in 1714 that within two years they would pass the Riot Act, suspend Habeas Corpus and replace the Triennial Act with the Septennial Act.

When Francis Atterbury had suggested in *English Advice to the Freeholders of England* that the whigs would repeal the Triennial Act the notion had been ruled out of court by Abel Boyer: 'How can any reasonable man conceive that the whigs, whose characteristic is to be strenuous asserters of liberty, should ever be for pulling down those very fences they have themselves cast up to preserve it?'[22] The whigs were to go much further than this as they moved from the demagogy practised by the first earl of Shaftesbury to the oligarchy presided over by Walpole. Their excuse at the time was that the stability of the

Hanoverian succession was threatened and that these counter-measures were essential to secure its safety. Certainly they served that purpose. As Stanhope boasted in May 1716, 'His majesty's affairs are, thanks be to God, at present in a more settled and prosperous condition than his most sanguine servants could ever have expected.'[23]

# 8 Stanhope's Ministry

With the dynasty secured, the tories cowed if not crushed, and the prospect of a general election in the near future eliminated by the Septennial Act, the triumphant whigs could afford the luxury of disagreement. The resulting whig schism was not merely a blow to the unity of the whig party: it set a new pattern to politics.

There had, of course, been divisions in the whig ranks before. Contemporaries distinguished at all times, even in Anne's reign, between Court and Country whigs, while the Court whigs often disputed among themselves. In the years 1707 and 1708, for instance, there was a serious split between the Junto and Lord Treasurer Godolphin, who both made a bid for the leadership of the party. These splits had been largely cauterized in the heat of party warfare during the last four years of the Queen's reign when the Junto had re-established its grip on the whigs.

After 1714 the Junto disintegrated, even before the deaths of Halifax and Wharton in 1715 and of Somers in 1716 brought about its own demise. Halifax was so chagrined that he alone of the five lords had been left out in the cold, receiving no cabinet office under Anne, that he determined not to lose in the new reign, and shortly after George I's accession he even allied with tories to try to ensure his own position. Somers was a spent volcano on the Queen's death anyway, his own health having collapsed long before he died himself. The earl of Sunderland was a somewhat isolated figure when George arrived, for the new king distrusted him at first, having heard of his reputation as a republican who disliked monarchy. It took all the influence which his father-in-law, the duke of Marlborough, could wield to secure a post for him, and even then he was sent into virtual exile as lord lieutenant of Ireland. Orford became first lord of the admiralty, but was to secede from the government in 1717, having played an important role in bringing about the whig schism. The disintegration of the Junto brought about a vacuum of power at the head of the whig party which younger politicians rushed to fill. Among the leaders were James Stanhope, Charles Viscount Townshend and Robert Walpole.

James Stanhope was forty-one when George I succeeded to the throne. In the previous reign he had acquired a reputation as a resourceful general, being the hero of the capture of Minorca in 1708. Although his military duties had kept his appearances in the Commons rare, he made a big impact when he did appear there. In the session 1705–6 for instance, he emerged, paradoxically for an army officer, as the leader of those Country whigs who tried to ensure that a severer measure against placemen was included in the Regency Act than the clause which was in fact enacted. Unfortunately the general was forced to embark on active duty while the measure was still before the House. In 1710 he was one of the more forceful managers against Dr Sacheverell, describing the doctor in his speech as 'an inconsiderable tool of a party'. When Walpole was in the Tower in 1712 Stanhope virtually took over as leader of the opposition in the Commons. His European experience and facility with languages made him admirably suited for the post of secretary of state for the south in 1714, having according to Horace Walpole a 'fruitful and luxurious genius in foreign affairs'. Although his homosexuality roused public comment in the general election of 1710 it did not impede his political advancement.[1] When at ease he could be a most agreeable companion, but under attack he tended to react violently—hence perhaps his nickname 'Hackum'.[2]

Charles, second Viscount Townshend, was forty in 1714. He had been a peer all his adult life, his father having died when he himself was only twelve. When he first took his seat in the Lords in 1697 he was opposed to the Junto, and protested against the acquittal of Halifax, Orford and Somers when they were impeached in 1701. By 1709, however, he was sufficiently reconciled to them to be sent at their recommendation to the Hague as a plenipotentiary to negotiate first an abortive peace with France and then a treaty with the Dutch guaranteeing them British support in obtaining a number of garrison towns in the Netherlands when the war ended. This Barrier Treaty, as it was called, earned Townshend much tory opprobrium, but helped to secure him the northern secretaryship of state in 1714. Like Stanhope, he had a violent temper, but lacked his colleague's diplomatic ability to control it. Townshend was a political ally of Walpole and had married his feckless sister Dolly.

Robert Walpole was thirty-eight when George I landed in England. During the previous reign he had acquired a reputation as a capable, if apparently corrupt, financial administrator and as the leading light among the third generation of whigs in the House of Commons. His ambition was rewarded after the new king's arrival with the post of paymaster, and his ability when he became first lord of the treasury and chancellor of the exchequer in 1715. Walpole was given many nicknames during the course of his long career, including Brass for his affrontery and Macheath for his unscrupulousness, while by far the most common was 'the great man'. He was great in every sense of the word, with a solid stocky frame, a huge capacity for hard work and hard living and a driving ambition coupled with a sense of political realities which was unrivalled among his contemporaries.

Although the collapse of the Junto was bound to produce collisions among the whigs as the leaders of the new generation rushed to fill the gap created by it, the form which the conflict took was dictated by the new circumstances arising from the Hanoverian succession. Had Halifax, Somers and Wharton died under Anne it would be impossible to envisage the same developments in the whig party; for what finally brought about the split was a dispute over the influence of the electorate of Hanover on the conduct of foreign policy.

In November 1714 Charles XII of Sweden returned to his dominions after five years' voluntary exile in Turkey, and thus precipitated a new phase in the Great Northern War which had been exercising the Baltic powers since 1700. Among those opposed to Sweden were Denmark, Poland, Russia and the Electorate of Hanover. As Elector of Hanover, George was anxious to obtain the secularised bishoprics of Bremen and Verden, former Swedish territories which had been annexed by Denmark in 1712. He therefore allied with Prussia in April 1715 and with Denmark in May 1715, in return for recognition of his claim to those duchies by those two powers. Finally in October 1715 he allied with Russia and declared war on Sweden. The tactics of his allies in that year were to take Stralsund and Rugen from the Swedes as part of a drive to evict them from all German territories. In order to do this they needed naval supremacy over Sweden, and the combined Danish and Russian navies were inadequate for that purpose. The only attraction to them of an alliance with the small Electorate of Hanover was that George as king of Great Britain could bring the British navy into the balance and weigh down the scales.

When George offered to do this, however, he was bound to produce friction between British and Hanoverian interests, for by the Act of Settlement England was not to be involved in war for the defence of territories not annexed to the English crown without consent of parliament. His English ministers, therefore, were reluctant to give wholehearted support to his Baltic schemes for fear of the parliamentary consequences. The most they could commit themselves to was the dispatch of a fleet necessary to protect English trade with Russia, which had been jeopardized by Swedish intervention, and to give the admiral in charge freedom to interpret his instructions as fully as possible in accordance with Electoral policy. Thus four expeditions were sent out between 1715 and 1718, and on each occasion a detachment of ships from it performed combined manoeuvres with the Danish navy. Lord Orford, the first lord of the admiralty, was so disturbed at this surreptitious use of the fleet that in 1715 he threatened resignation before signing even the overt instructions to Sir John Norris, the commander of the first expedition.

Although the Northern War strained relations between the 'German' and the 'English' elements in the cabinet, it was its repercussions in western Europe which stretched them to breaking point. For in 1716 George I's preoccupation with Baltic affairs led to a major change in England's policy towards her European neighbours. Whig foreign policy at the outset of the new reign was to restore the old system of allying with the Dutch and the Emperor against France, which the tories had jettisoned when they negotiated peace with Louis XIV. Thus in February and May 1716 alliances were signed with the United Provinces and Charles VI respectively. Meanwhile the death of Louis XIV had, for the time being at least, completely transformed the situation with regard to France. Louis's successor was a mere child, and this necessitated a regency. Although Philip V of Spain had renounced his claim to the French throne at the Treaty of Utrecht, he showed an active interest in achieving power in France as a regent. This made the duke of Orleans, who emerged as the one and only regent, albeit technically assisted by a council, anxious to keep Philip from interfering. The result of their rivalry was a far more effective separation of the two powers than any clauses in the Treaty of Utrecht could have achieved. The regent was even prepared to negotiate with England in order to protect his position. Such developments suited George I perfectly, since properly used they could eliminate the French threat to his succession and neutralize western Europe, leaving him free to concentrate on the north. They also appealed to Stanhope, whose diplomatic ambitions soared to the height of casting himself in the role of arbiter of Europe. Already he had travelled to Vienna in a premature attempt to reconcile Charles VI to the territorial and political influence which the Dutch wanted to preserve in his newly acquired territories in the Netherlands. Now he was prepared to travel to the Hague and to Hanover to make Europe safe for the protestant succession.

When George left England in 1716 for the first time since his accession in order to visit Hanover, Stanhope went with him. At the Hague and subsequently in the Electorate, in secret conversations with the Abbé Dubois, the obstacles to a rapprochement with France were one by one removed. It was agreed that the Pretender should be evicted from Avignon, where he had settled his pathetic court after the failure of the 'Fifteen', to Italy. Difficulties concerning French plans to build up Mardyke as an alternative to the port of Dunkirk, which they had been obliged to destroy after Utrecht, were also resolved. Indeed Stanhope's ministerial colleagues at home thought that the discussions were dispatched with unseemly haste and suspected that George's fears of Prussian and Russian activity in the Baltic had speeded things up too much. Certainly Bernstorff was very concerned to prevent Prussia and Russia expanding at Sweden's expense and welcomed British alliances with other powers, especially with the Empire, which strengthened Hanover's arm. Already chafing at what they considered to be the undue influence of Hanover over fleet manoeuvres in the Baltic, Townshend and Walpole baulked at the terms of the draft treaty which Stanhope had negotiated. In disgust, Walpole's brother Horace left the Hague where the treaty was to be signed, rather than be a party to it. Townshend as secretary of state clearly protracted the technicalities of signing as long as he could to delay the completion of the treaty. To Stanhope, and even more to George, this procrastination was intolerable. For thwarting his foreign policy the King decided that Townshend should be removed from the post of secretary. Before his return to England, therefore, in December 1716, he demoted him to the office of lord lieutenant of Ireland.

George was the more willing to disgrace Townshend at this time because he was suspicious of the secretary's activities while he himself had been out of the country. When George departed for Hanover in the summer of 1716 he had been obliged to leave his son behind as chief executive during his absence, but the growing estrangement between them had made him reluctant to give the Prince untrammelled power. The King's efforts to circumscribe his son's authority produced friction among British politicians, some of whom had agreed to curb the power of the regent while others had defended the son's right to enjoy them without restraint. Among those who backed the King were the duke of Marlborough and his son-in-law Sunderland. Marlborough's political ambitions were finished by a stroke which incapacitated him in May 1716, but Sunderland's were still to be fulfilled, although his prospects had improved with his promotion from the lord lieutenancy of Ireland to the post of lord privy seal on Wharton's death in 1715. Among the Prince's defenders his champion was the duke of Argyll, his groom of the stole, who on Sunderland's insistence was removed from his posts as colonel of the Horse Guards and governor of Minorca on 29 June. Argyll then appeared ostentatiously at the Prince's court during the King's absence, intriguing against the next session of parliament. Although they vehemently denied being involved in these schemes, and probably with justice, the King suspected Townshend and Walpole of conniving with his son against him.

These suspicions were fed by Sunderland, who went to the continent in August 1716, ostensibly for the sake of his health; once there he made straight for Hanover, where he intrigued with Stanhope against Townshend and Walpole. The ferocity with which Townshend and Walpole later assailed Sunderland and Stanhope in parliament can partly be explained by their rage at the discovery that they had been stabbed in the back by these fellow ministers while they were abroad with the King. Stanhope was a little embarrassed at the role he had played, but not his hard and ruthless accomplice, who was well versed in prising rivals out of office, as he had demonstrated in Anne's reign. From 1706 to 1710 he had been secretary of state, and had been relentless in opposing his fellow secretary Robert Harley until he quitted in 1708. Now Sunderland persuaded the King to dismiss Townshend, and to salt the wound got George to give him the very post of lord lieutenant which he himself had felt to be an insult when he was appointed to it in 1714. Townshend bore the insult for only a few months before demonstrating more publicly his dislike of the way in which British interests were being subordinated to those of Hanover.

The occasion arose in April 1717 when details of a Jacobite plot involving the Swedish minister in London, Count Gyllenborg, were laid before parliament. That Gyllenborg had intrigued with Jacobites, offering the assistance of the king of Sweden, was indisputable. Indeed it would have been odd if he had not dabbled in such intrigue at a time when relations between Charles XII and George I were so strained. Yet the way in which his indiscretions had been uncovered raised the question whether George was anxious to wring every ounce of juice from them, perhaps even to the point of using the plot to get England to declare war on Sweden. Contrary to international convention, Gyllenborg's house was forcibly entered and his papers seized. Selections from his correspondence were subsequently published, which fanned the flames of resentment against Sweden. But when on 9 April 1717 the King asked parliament to support hostile moves against the Swedes, Walpole was reluctant to commit himself and the government's majority in the Commons slumped to four. It was clear that there was a serious split in the ministry between supporters of George's involvement in the Northern War and critics who did not want it to embroil England in a war with Sweden. That very day Townshend was dismissed from the lord lieutenancy. Next day Walpole resigned the chancellorship of the exchequer. They were joined in opposition by Orford, who had been one of the first to feel uneasy at the fleet's role in George's Baltic policy, and a number of close political associates including William Pulteney, Paul Methuen and the duke of Devonshire.

The departure of the Walpole-Townshend group from the ministry produced a new pattern of opposition. It is true that there had been

whigs opposed to the Hanoverian government before this. As early as
13 May 1715, in a debate on the civil list when the tories had opposed
granting £700,000 to the King, they were 'strengthened and backed
by some eminent whigs' and 'a whig member who at this time spoke on
the tory side, made some reflections on the present unthrifty administration of his majesty's revenue'. Again in a debate on pensions 'the
leading men of the tories', supported 'by a great many whigs,
exclaimed against the pensions given by the crown to several persons of
quality'.[3] But this kind of whig opposition was a revival of the older
pattern of Court against Country. It does not appear that the whigs
who spoke out against the civil list and pensions were seeking to get
into the ministry: they were merely voicing backbench complaints.
With the departure of Walpole into opposition, however, the situation
was transformed, for he and his friends were not prepared to rest
content on the backbenches. They were determined to exploit their
nuisance value to get back into power. Moreover, although they had
left office largely on a point of principle, they were not going to let
party principles stand in the way of their return. In this respect their
departure from the ministry differed from that of Lord Nottingham
and his associates in 1704, or even of Harley and the Harleyites in
1708. Although these groups, too, had fought for ascendancy within
the cabinet and had lost, in opposition they preserved some sort of
consistency to tory ideals. Walpole and his supporters, by contrast,
were prepared to vote quite contrary to their previous record, even on
matters involving a clash of party principles, in order to force the
ministry to take them back. This introduced a measure of aggression
and opportunism into their actions which perhaps more than any
other single development corroded the old two-party distinction and
produced the more pragmatic and cynical system which prevailed in
the years after 1720.

Within days of leaving the government Walpole and his friends were
allying with the tories against their former colleagues. Their first
victory was obtained on 29 May when they supported a tory motion to
have a prominent high-church clergyman preach to the Commons,
and thus helped carry it by 141 votes to 131. A few days later, in a
much bigger house, the addition of at least a hundred Walpolians to
the tories, who challenged the ministry over the question of the costs of
transporting Dutch troops to England during the 'Fifteen', had the
government reeling. Only ten votes prevented an inquiry into the
conduct of the minister responsible, who was suspected of fraud. Such
tactics, aimed at embarrassing the ministry, might be considered
legitimate opposition manoeuvres rather than the abandonment of
whig principles.

Walpole's first undoubted apostasy, therefore, was his refusal to support further proceedings against the earl of Oxford. Since he had been among the most enthusiastic advocates of impeachment this was a complete volte face. It helped Oxford to obtain an acquittal from the Lords of the charges brought against him in 1715, and his release after two years in the Tower. In the next session Walpole was outspoken against the standing army, and later spoke against the repeal of the Occasional Conformity and Schism Acts, though he had been violently opposed to these measures on whig principles when they were passed in Anne's reign. Yet in 1718 he told the House of Commons that 'he was turned out for not consenting to the repeal of these bills.'[4] This was so blatantly opportunistic that some of his whig associates could not go along with it.

The ministry which Walpole and Townshend left was dominated by Stanhope, who was raised to the peerage as a viscount, and Sunderland. Stanhope took over as first lord of the treasury and chancellor of the exchequer, while Sunderland became the leading secretary of state, the writer Joseph Addison being the somewhat surprising choice for the other secretaryship. However distinguished as a popular playwright and eminent essayist, Addison was not a successful administrator and was very much Sunderland's junior. Stanhope, on the other hand, was so clearly the leader that until his death in 1721 it is legitimate to consider him as prime minister. Between 1717 and 1720 the Stanhope ministry was responsible for a vigorous foreign policy, a programme of domestic reforms and a financial scheme which brought about the crisis of the South Sea Bubble.

The signing of an Anglo-French treaty in November 1716 opened up a new era in international relations. Stanhope hoped to use it as the foundation stone of a diplomatic structure which would guarantee the Treaty of Utrecht and with it the peace of Europe. In January 1717 he persuaded the Dutch to join, thereby making it a triple alliance. His next step was to get the Emperor to come in and make it a quadruple alliance. This was to be the most exacting test of his diplomatic abilities, for Charles VI had refused to be a party to the Treaty of Utrecht and, although he had made peace with France at Rastadt in 1714, he still refused to recognize Philip V as king of Spain. On his part Philip wished to regain possession of Sardinia, Naples and Sicily, which had formerly been part of the Spanish empire, but which had been detached from it in the peace treaties, Sardinia and Naples going to Charles VI and Sicily to Victor Amadeus of Savoy. In the summer of 1717 Spanish troops invaded Sardinia and Charles VI listened more favourably to Stanhope's overtures. When the following year Spain launched an invasion of Sicily, he agreed to join the alliance and, although Stanhope had to go in person to Paris to obtain the regent's approval, agreement between Britain, France and the Empire was finally reached in August 1718. The Dutch were only nominally contracting parties but the treaty gave rise to what was known as the Quadruple Alliance.

Stanhope, an enthusiast for 'summit' diplomacy, even went to Madrid to get Philip V to join in this guarantee of the settlement of Europe; but Philip, or rather his leading adviser Cardinal Alberoni, refused to accept this blow to his ambitions and to withdraw his forces from Sardinia and Sicily, despite the fact that Stanhope was prepared to give Gibraltar back to Spain. In accordance with the terms of the Quadruple Alliance, therefore, the English navy attacked and destroyed the Spanish fleet at Cape Passaro while Stanhope was actually in Spain, though he left before the news reached Madrid.

On his return to England it took all Stanhope's skill as a parliamentary manager to get the two houses to agree to the consequences of his new diplomatic system. Both the Quadruple Alliance and the naval engagement were denounced by the opposition, among whom Townshend and Walpole were prominent, as contrary to British interests and especially to English trade with Spain. However, the government obtained majorities approving its actions and felt secure enough to declare war on Spain in December.

In the ensuing hostilities Britain engaged Spain in the Iberian peninsula, the Mediterranean and even in Scotland. Thus British troops cooperated with French forces in an invasion of Spain, and the Mediterranean fleet kept Sardinia and Sicily cut off from mainland supplies while Savoyard and Imperial troops fought to retake them. Without this naval assistance it is doubtful if they could have regained the islands, for Spanish soldiers were still present there when war ended in March 1720. Scotland was the scene of a Spanish diversion on behalf of the Jacobites in 1719. Two expeditions set out from Spain to Britain early that year, one consisting of thirty ships and about 5,000 men, the other made up of two frigates carrying about 300 men. The first, bound for Bristol, ran into a ferocious storm off Cape Finisterre and was dispersed. The second reached the Isle of Lewis, then entrenched at Glenshiel on the mainland, putting itself under the command of Lord Tullibardine who brought in a handful of Scots. On 10 June, James Edward's thirty-fifth birthday, this force was beaten by government troops under General Wightman. The Scots fled and the Spaniards surrendered. It was the last military threat to the internal security of the Hanoverian dynasty until the 'Forty-Five'. When Philip V agreed to join the Quadruple Alliance in 1720 the main threat to European peace was also temporarily removed. Thus Stanhope's diplomacy was resoundingly successful in western Europe.

He hoped to achieve a similar success in northern Europe. Like

Townshend and Walpole before him, he began to resent the way Bernstorff tried to keep northern policy in his own hands, particularly when active Baltic and Mediterranean policies involved England in expenses which Stanhope had to justify in parliament. Fortunately in the Baltic the situation was almost completely transformed by the death of Charles XII in 1718. This made a peace settlement inevitable and Stanhope hoped to dictate its terms. His policy was to restore the balance of power in the north by getting Sweden to agree to relinquish its former German possessions in Pomerania to Prussia, and in Bremen and Verden to Hanover, in return for assistance in regaining some of the territories she had lost to Russia, which included the whole of Finland and Karelia, Ingermanland, Estonia and Livonia. Even before the death of Charles XII, Russian ambitions in the Baltic had aroused George's suspicions. Now Stanhope considered them the major threat to a lasting settlement in the north. To achieve his ends he sent Lord Carteret to Stockholm in 1719 and despatched a fleet to the Baltic, this time to deter the Tsar rather than the Swedes. Carteret managed to negotiate a treaty with Sweden in which Hanover's sovereignty over Bremen and Verden was recognized. At the same time Stanhope, now free from German influence over George I, negotiated treaties with Prussia, Sweden, Britain and Hanover guaranteeing the duchies. Nevertheless, in the ensuing peace settlement of 1720 Sweden kept a foothold in Germany, while it proved impossible to deprive Russia of her Baltic acquisitions.

As well as pursuing a vigorous foreign policy, Stanhope's ministry was very active in domestic affairs. Indeed he deserves to be remembered not only as an outstanding diplomat but also for having the most enlightened programme of religious toleration before the nineteenth century. He attempted at a stroke to undo decades of religious bigotry when he repealed the Occasional Conformity and Schism Acts in 1719. These measures had been passed at the height of tory reaction in the last few years of Anne's reign. The Occasional Conformity Act of 1711 penalized dissenters who qualified for local or national office under the Corporation and Test Acts by taking communion in the Church of England and thereafter frequented their own conventicles. The Schism Act of 1714 was intended to prohibit the separate education of dissenters in their own schools and academies. It had been due to come into operation on the very day Anne died and, with the advent of the whigs to power, had not been enforced, though still on the statute book. Neither act was immediately repealed for fear of alienating the Church of England from the new regime. High churchmen regarded them as indispensable for saving the church from danger, while many low churchmen, including several bishops, were anxious not to bring anglicanism back into the political battleground by reviving the bitter debates of Anne's reign.

Not surprisingly the dissenters objected to this reluctance to seize the nettle, and early in 1717 groups of sympathetic MPs undertook to raise the matter at the earliest opportunity. The whig schism and the Bangorian controversy, however, held up the repeal of the acts, and it was not until 1718 that Stanhope felt he could get it safely through both houses. Even so he had to concede more than he wished in order to secure the agreement of enough bishops. The original bill repealing the two acts contained a clause which nullified the effects of the Test and Corporation Acts as far as the dissenters were concerned but, although the King was keen on it, this was considered too far advanced even by his own supporters and was dropped in the House of Lords. Nevertheless Stanhope managed to carry a separate bill which cushioned dissenters against the effects of the Corporation Act by indemnifying them from its provisions if no one took them to court within six months of their election to local office. This was the first in a series of such indemnity acts, which later became annual. Stanhope, whose enlightenment in religious questions went far beyond that of most of his contemporaries, even proposed a measure to give some relief from the penal laws to the catholics, but in the atmosphere of the early eighteenth century this was doomed to failure.

His enlightened religious policy stands in sharp contrast to his proposals for dealing with parliament, where he planned nothing less than the deliberate creation of a permanent majority for his ministry in both houses. His peerage bill of 1719 was designed to prevent any addition to the number of Lords once George had created six new English peers, and the terms of the Act of Union had been altered so that the Scottish nobility, instead of choosing sixteen of their number at every general election, were to be represented by twenty-five hereditary nobles. Thereafter the monarch's prerogative of making peers was to be restricted to filling vacancies created by lines becoming extinct. When this measure was introduced in February 1719 it created such a furore that Stanhope deferred it until the next session. He endeavoured to make it more acceptable to the lower house by offering to repeal the Septennial Act, thereby extending indefinitely the date of the next election.

For the first time Walpole found a real issue on which to oppose his former colleagues in the government, one which could unite all elements of the opposition against the ministry. Among these could now be reckoned the Prince of Wales, who had openly quarrelled with his father in 1717. The occasion of the dispute was the christening of the Prince's son, for George I had insisted that the duke of

Newcastle, who was lord chamberlain, should be godfather, a demand which the younger George found so objectionable that he had publicly remonstrated with the duke. When Newcastle, misunderstanding the Prince's gutteral ejaculation 'I find you out' for 'I fight you', thought that he was being challenged to a duel and in terror reported this to the King, George put his son under house arrest. Soon after the Prince had set up a rival establishment to the court at Leicester House. One of the reasons why the King was prepared to give up his prerogative of creating peers, therefore, was that it would affect his heir much more than it affected himself, while it entered into Stanhope's calculations that he could preserve a majority in his favour in the Lords even if the Prince continued to oppose him on the death of his father. During the estrangement of the two Georges, Leicester House had become a centre for all the politicians who opposed the ministry, and among them Walpole had gravitated into its orbit. By February 1718 'the tories and the Walpolites' were 'blended together and styled the prince's party'.[5] Walpole's resistance to the peerage bill was well received by the prince, since he wished to enjoy all the prerogatives of his father. It was even better received by members of the House of Commons, who did not want to throw away the chance of becoming peers themselves. Walpole exploited these sentiments in two pamphlets and a brilliant speech in which he played on the dreams of the obscurest country gentlemen that their children or their children's children might sit in the House of Lords. Since the peerage bill blasted all such hopes, the backbenchers were roused to oppose it, and it was defeated in December 1719 by the decisive majority of 269 to 177.

To demonstrate their ascendancy in the Commons was one thing, to storm the ministry quite another. Before they could do that Walpole and his associates had to come to terms with George I. At first the King approached other opposition groups, even tories, in order to repair the damage done in parliament, before reluctantly agreeing that a deal with Townshend and Walpole was essential. Meanwhile they assisted their cause by bringing about the formal reconciliation of the King and the Prince of Wales in April 1720. By June the terms were settled, though George I drove a hard bargain. Townshend became lord president of the council, while Walpole accepted the post of paymaster general. Since he had previously been chancellor of the exchequer he still had a long way to go to regain his former prestige, even more to become prime minister.

What finally enabled him to rise to the top was the South Sea Bubble. The origin of the Bubble can be traced back to the foundation of the South Sea Company in 1711. This was a tory corporation set up by Harley deliberately to offset the whiggish Bank of England and East India Company. He had also launched the Company to consolidate some £9,000,000 of national debt which was not secured against the proceeds of taxation, this unfunded debt being changed into South Sea stock. The South Sea Company from the start had thus been principally a financial corporation, and was only marginally concerned with trading activities. Although it had been set up in the anticipation of substantial trading concessions from Spain at the signing of the treaties of Utrecht, the actual terms negotiated with the Spanish government were disappointing. As a financial corporation, however, it was modestly successful and the debt conversion exercise of 1711 worked. It appeared to hold out a more speedy method of eliminating the debt than the sinking fund, a scheme of earmarking surplus revenue for debt redemption devised by Walpole when he had been chancellor of the exchequer, though actually implemented by Stanhope in 1717. In 1719 the experiment was repeated when holders of 1710 lottery orders converted them into South Sea stock. On this occasion the Company made a handsome profit. It took in lottery orders on which the treasury was committed to paying £94,330 a year until 1742. The government valued these at eleven and a half times their annual value and authorized the Company to issue stock to the holders of the orders to the value of £1,084,790. The Company was also allowed to sell new stock in addition to this to the value of £662,034—£117,912 for arrears of interest, £544,142 to be lent to the exchequer. It was on the amount to be lent to the exchequer that the Company made its profit. Instead of raising the whole £544,142 by issuing new stock at par, it found that, since £100 value of stock was selling for £114, it could issue less than this to make up the sum owing to the exchequer. The rest could then be sold on the exchange for its own profit. This was a prelude to the much more ambitious scheme undertaken the following year.

At that time the national debt stood at about £50,000,000. The scheme was to convert into Company stock that part of it, some £31,000,000, which was in private hands in the form of annuities, leaving the rest to the Bank and the East India Company. Holders of the annuities were to be encouraged to transfer them into South Sea stock, on which the government would pay five per cent interest until 1727 and four per cent thereafter. At first the Company proposed to lend the government about £3,000,000 at the time of the conversion, but the Bank got wind of the scheme and insisted that it should be put out for tender. The Company eventually outbid the Bank, by which time it was pledged to advance some £7,500,000 at the time of the conversion. As with the lottery orders scheme of 1719, the company would profit from the project according to the difference between the par value and market value of its stock. Thus if £100 of its stock sold for £200 it need only assign £15,500,000 to the holders of the £31,000,000 of annuities, and sell the rest on the exchange. 'Its profit would come from the difference between the proceeds of this sale and the sum payable to the government.'[6] The Company therefore used all means, both fair and foul, to drive up the market value of its stock.

Prospects of glittering profits to be made from trade with Spanish possessions across the Atlantic were held out as inducements to annuitants to convert their annuities into stock. Some of the promised gains were, to say the least, dubious. Questionable, too, was the way the Company removed several rivals by getting the government to pass the Bubble Act, whereby companies without a charter were declared illegal. This act closed down many companies which had mushroomed at a time when the financial world seemed to have gone mad with projects, and made money which might have been invested in them available for the South Sea Company. Downright corruption was also used, with the allocation of stock valued at over £500,000 for the bribery of politicians who included, among others, the earl of Sunderland, first lord of the treasury, John Aislabie, the chancellor of the exchequer, James Craggs the elder, postmaster general, and Charles Stanhope, junior secretary of the treasury.

These measures worked beyond the wildest dreams of even the South Sea directors—for a while. South Sea stock began the year 1720 above par, £100 of stock bringing £128 on the Exchange. By April it brought over £130; before the end of June it realized £745; in July it peaked at over £1,000. Then the inevitable happened. Big investors who saw that the market had reached its ceiling sold, foreigners apparently being the first to pull out. This precipitated the crash. By mid-September £100 stock was selling for £520. By 1 October it was down to £290. The Bubble had burst.

Many were hurt by the explosion. As Sir John Perceval put it, 'the fire of London or the plague ruin'd not the number that are now undone.'[7] There were a few spectacular bankruptcies. Sir Justice Beck, a city magnate, described by a contemporary as 'a man of considerable capital and of the first credit on the Exchange' was left owing £347,000. As late as 1732 his creditors were being offered a mere five shillings in the pound.[8] James Brydges, duke of Chandos, who had made a cool million as paymaster general to the army abroad in Anne's reign, lost much of it when the crash came. Sir David Hamilton was said to have lost over £80,000, Lord Fitzwilliam and Lord Londonderry £50,000 each. Many country gentry read their correspondence with trepidation in the autumn of 1720, while many merchants faced ruin. 'In early October it was reported from Bristol that "five of the most eminent merchants have failed, which has caused a great consternation."'[9]

The Bubble was the making of Walpole. In 1717 he had resigned the office of chancellor of the exchequer, and although he had rejoined the ministry in June 1720 it was in the post of paymaster general. This was lucrative, and Walpole needed the money after three expensive years in the wilderness, but it did not even carry the prestige of his former post of chancellor. It looked as though he had been bought off by the Court. Yet in April he became again chancellor of the exchequer and in addition first lord of the treasury. His career as prime minister had begun.

There is some debate about the connection between the Bubble and Walpole's promotion from the post of paymaster general to that of first lord of the treasury. Traditionally it was regarded almost as cause and effect. Walpole was seen as the sagacious statesman who stood aloof from the corrupt and crazy scheme, and then as the financial expert who stepped in and saved the country's finances, and with them the regime, from the effects of the crash. As N. A. Brisco put it: 'The bursting of the South Sea Bubble, in September, threw the country into a panic and the people looked to Walpole as the only person able to restore confidence in public credit. He accepted the task, and soon brought harmony out of chaos. . . . He had from the first opposed the scheme, and now when the country needed him, he willingly offered his services.'[10] More recent investigations, however, have found these claims untenable. It is true that Walpole was out of office when the scheme was first proposed to the government, and that he opposed it on behalf of the Bank. But it is not true that he was opposed to it on principle; he applauded the idea while criticizing some details. Nor did he remain opposed to it all along. On the contrary, in June 1720 he himself invested about £9,000 in South Sea stock. He even arranged to spend a further £5,000 on the Company's stock in August, after the slump had started, but was prudently prevented from doing so by his bankers. He was still prepared to invest in the stock as late as 24 August. As Professor Plumb observes, 'These decisions must dispel for ever the old legend that Walpole saw through the South Sea Bubble from start to finish and skilfully exploited it to create a large personal fortune.'[11] So far from making a fortune, Walpole lost by the Bubble, any increase in his private finances in 1720 coming from other sources.

Dr Plumb is also anxious to dispel the notion that Walpole was the saviour of the country's finances. As he sees it, 'Walpole has been inordinately praised for his financial skill at this juncture. Time was the healer, not Walpole. . . . Few reputations have such strange or inaccurate origins as Walpole's. Generations of historians have praised him for repairing his country's ruined finances, yet for this there is no foundation in fact. The finances repaired themselves.'[12] For instance, his scheme to get the Bank and East India Company to take over £18,000,000 of South Sea stock, though authorized by statute, was never put into effect. On the other hand Dr P. G. M. Dickson's exhaustive analysis of the measures taken to retrieve public credit confirmed rather the traditional view than Plumb's. Thus of the act to restore public credit passed in 1721 he wrote:[13]

> There can be little doubt that Walpole was the main architect of these proposals, which applied the harsh cautery of common sense to the soaring dreams and megalomaniac expectations of the South Sea year. The Company was forced to disgorge the surplus stock which it had accumulated at the public creditors' expense, and to give up its claims to be paid in full for the amount it had sold. The public creditors were forced to reconcile themselves to drastic losses of income and capital. The airy fabric of speculative purchase and sales was cut down to a realistic size.

Again, of the measures taken in 1722, whereby the Bank stepped in to put the South Sea Company's affairs back on a sound financial footing, Dickson argued 'that the magnitude of the difficulties which he overcame in resolving the crisis can hardly be overestimated. There is no doubt that the hard, tough men who ran the City and its institutions recognized in his handling of this and subsequent financial issues a competence equal to their own, and not found at the treasury for any length of time since the fall of Godolphin.'[14]

The Bubble was the making of Walpole's political career as well as of his financial reputation. At one time it looked as though the year 1720 would herald a period of political instability such as had obtained in England before 1714. Indeed to some it seemed likely that a revolution might break out. Instead it was to mark the beginning of twenty years of political stability, a phenomenon unknown in England since the reign of Elizabeth.

Perhaps the epitome of the period of political stability was the career of Arthur Onslow, who occupied the Speaker's chair in the House of Commons from 1728 to 1761; he was the first career Speaker, and the longest incumbent of the chair. In 1720 Onslow was in London, and far from anticipating political stability,[15]

> wondered that [the Bubble] did not produce some convulsion in the state. That it did not was certainly owing to people of all denominations thinking of nothing but their own losses and flattering themselves with the hopes of some quick turn in the public credit, as they called it, to recover their late fortunes. If otherwise, or some bold men had taken advantage of the general disorder men's minds were in, to provoke them to insurrection, the rage against the government was such for having as they thought drawn them into this ruin, that I am almost persuaded, the King being at that time abroad, that could the Pretender then have landed at the Tower, he might have rode to St James's with very few hands held up against him.

Fortunately for George I the Pretender did not take advantage of this opportunity, apart from issuing a proclamation in October. Meanwhile the King hurried back from Hanover, arriving in England in November. The dynasty was saved from disaster.

The fate of the ministry, however, was still in the balance. The earls of Stanhope and Sunderland, after all, had been responsible for giving the government's backing to the South Sea scheme. Stanhope defended himself so vehemently in the House of Lords that he burst a blood vessel and died. John Aislabie, James Craggs senior and Charles Stanhope were even more seriously implicated in the Bubble because they had accepted bribes from the Company. The ruined and disappointed investors in South Sea stock were looking for somebody to blame. Indeed the very term Bubble was used by contemporaries to mean fraud or cheat. At first their wrath was directed against the Company directors. Thomas Gordon demanded their execution in *Cato's Letters*, which first appeared in November 1720 'to call for public justice upon the wicked managers of the . . . South Sea Scheme'. Instead, their assets were confiscated to the tune of £2,000,000 to compensate ruined creditors. But before long the finger of accusation was being pointed at the government itself. Investigations into the activities of certain members of the government brought some very murky transactions to light in the House of Commons. Aislabie, Craggs and Stanhope were accused of corruption by the committee set up to probe the affair. Charles Stanhope was acquitted of these charges by a mere three votes, which everyone took for a virtual verdict of guilty. Craggs died in mysterious circumstances while his part in the scheme was being examined, probably committing suicide. Aislabie was expelled from the house and sent to the Tower.

Walpole's role in these proceedings was remarkable. Pressing home the investigations as hard as he could would seem to have been the best way to discredit his ministerial colleagues and thus clear the path to power himself. Instead, he tried to stave off the full force of the attacks. The reason for this course of action was simply this: joining in the hue and cry against the guilty ministers would have made him  popular with the backbenchers in the Commons, but it would not have endeared him to the King, whose closest friends and mistresses were involved in the shady transactions under investigation. Since the way to win power was not to court popularity but to gain the confidence of the King, Walpole deliberately alienated popular support by defending the ministers. He earned himself the contemptuous nickname of 'the screen master general', or simply 'the Screen', because he tried to protect the court from the charges of corruption. He even screened the earl of Sunderland, his deadly rival within the ministry. On 15 March 1721 Sunderland was acquitted by 233 votes to 172. A few days later Walpole got his reward when he was made chancellor of the exchequer and replaced Sunderland as first lord of the treasury.

Walpole's promotion to these posts did not automatically ensure his ascendancy. Although Stanhope's death had removed the greatest obstacle to power, he still had to reckon with Sunderland until he too died in April 1722. Thus he had to take account of Sunderland's continuing influence with George I in his new post of groom of the stole, and of his retaining control of disbursements of secret service money. Sunderland was clearly attempting a come-back in the general election of 1722, exerting every ounce of interest he could muster against Walpole, even to the extent of intriguing with tories and Jacobites. Only his sudden death from pleurisy, which occurred as the results of the elections were still coming in, removed the last rival under George I who could challenge Walpole's position as prime minister.

The general election of 1722 was the most hotly contested of the entire eighteenth century. At least 138 constituencies in England and Wales went to the polls in that year, and a further twenty in Scotland. When the polling ended there were approximately twice as many whigs as tories returned to the new House of Commons. However, this did not mean a two to one majority for the government, since by 1722 the party situation was more complex than it had been in 1715. For one thing the ministry itself was divided on the eve of the polls, with Sunderland making interest against Walpole. Although Sunderland's death left Walpole in the ascendant, he still had to reckon with several supporters of the dead minister, including Carteret in the cabinet and a number of tories in the Commons. More significant than the split in the government was the rift in the ranks of the whigs. This had now become so serious that in over a dozen constituencies the main contest had been between rival whig candidates rather than between whigs and tories.[16] By 1722 the whig party was irreconcilably split into Court and Country segments.

# 9 The Robinocracy

Walpole's uninterrupted run of twenty years as prime minister is rightly regarded as one of the major feats of British political history, and explaining it has absorbed the interest of historians for over two centuries. Explanations are usually offered in terms of his expert handling of the political system after 1720, his unique blending of the surviving powers of the crown with the increasing influence of the Commons. If the answer to his success is to be found in his own political skill, however, then it seems legitimate to ask how he acquired it? To find out it is necessary to go back beyond the accession of George I for, when Queen Anne died in 1714, Walpole had already been in parliament nearly fourteen years. He was thus an old hand at politics long before the South Sea Bubble, serving his political apprenticeship in the years 1701 to 1714. It was during Anne's reign that he developed his political philosophy and acquired his masterly understanding of the workings of politics.

His political philosophy was that of a whig. Upon first entering parliament in January 1701 he immediately identified himself with the whig party, championing the Revolution Settlement and the protestant succession in the house of Hanover. In 1710 he was one of the whigs selected to act as a manager for the House of Commons in the impeachment of Dr Sacheverell, and in his speech at the trial he upheld the right to resist in defiance of high-church theories of passive obedience and non-resistance which, he claimed, were 'first invented to support arbitrary and despotic power'. He also supported the Toleration Act, and opposed attempts to penalize dissenters for occasional conformity. Finally he was a thoroughgoing whig in his complete commitment to England's role as a principal in the War of the Spanish Succession, and his opposition to the tory peace negotiated between 1710 and 1713. Addressing his constituents in King's Lynn during the general election of 1713 he affirmed that 'had the king of France beaten us, as we have done him, he would have been so modest as to have given us better terms than we have gained after all our glorious victories.'[1]

Support of the war first brought Walpole into office. In 1705 he was made a member of the peculiarly constituted council of admiralty presided over by Anne's husband, Prince George. Three years later he replaced Henry St John as secretary at war, and in 1710 he became treasurer of the navy. Acceptance of office by whigs, however, had created strains within the party since the Revolution. The whigs had started life during the Exclusion Crisis as an opposition party, and when some of their leaders went into the ministry under William III not all the rank and file could go along with it. On the contrary, a substantial number regarded whig government as a contradiction in terms and upbraided these leaders as apostates, men who had been bought off with the bribes of office. They particularly complained about the willingness, even eagerness, to accept office of the Junto lords, Halifax, Orford, Somers and Wharton. These attitudes divided the whig party into two elements, the Court whigs, who were prepared to support a whig ministry dominated by the Junto; and the Country whigs, who stayed in opposition even when the government consisted overwhelmingly of whigs. Some of the most bitter denunciations of the Junto came from Country whigs who held that their cause had been betrayed. They continued to campaign hard for issues dear to the hearts of the old exclusionists, like frequent and free elections and the elimination of placemen from the House of Commons.

The campaign against placemen reached its height in the very first session of Walpole's parliamentary career, when a clause was added to the Act of Settlement which, had it become operative, would have eliminated them from parliament altogether. In fact the clause never did come into use, since like most of the provisions of the act it only became law on Anne's death; during her reign the opportunity was taken with the passing of the Regency Act in 1706 to repeal the clause and to replace it with a milder measure to deal with the problem of placemen.

Walpole was opposed to the complete proscription of placemen when it was first inserted in the Act of Settlement, and he supported the repeal of the measure. By 1706, of course, he was himself in place as a member of Prince George's council of admiralty, and had therefore a material motive for objecting to the removal of placemen from the Commons. However, except when he was in opposition and for tactical purposes prepared to support place bills to embarrass the government of the day, there can be no doubt that, insofar as this issue divided Court whigs from Country whigs, Walpole came down heavily, not to say with all twenty stones of his immense frame, on the Court side of the fence.

This was true even when he was out of office, as he was from 1701 to

1705, from 1711 to 1714, and again from 1717 to 1720. For the basic attitude of a Country whig was essentially that of a permanent backbencher, not that of an ambitious politician aching to achieve power. Country whigs were suspicious of the executive, regarding all government as essentially corrupt. They were anxious at the increase of government dependants in the lower house because they feared that the Court would use these to build up a party of 'yes men' in the Commons, and thus render parliament a rubber stamp of the executive. As *The Danger of Mercenary Parliaments*, a Country whig tract of the 1690s, put it:

> What points might not such a number carry in the house, who were always ready and constantly attending with more diligence to destroy our constitution than the rest were to preserve it? Who represented not their country but themselves, and always kept together in a close and undivided phalanx, impenetrable either by shame or honour, voting always the same way, and saying always the same things, as if they were so many engines merely turned about by a mechanic motion, like an organ where the great humming bases as well as the little squeaking trebles are filled with one blast of wind from the same sound board?

Walpole by contrast was a man of immense ambition. He wished to be not just a little squeaking treble, but a great humming bass. Indeed he wanted to become the organist.

To be a Court whig in William's reign meant enlisting as a lieutenant of the Junto. In Walpole's first session of parliament the Junto came under heavy attack for having given William III a virtually free hand to conduct diplomacy with a view to averting the War of the Spanish Succession. These attacks culminated in articles of impeachment being exhibited against three of the Junto lords, Halifax, Orford and Somers. Walpole sprang to their defence. As J. H. Plumb wrote, 'why Walpole supported the cause of the impeached ministers can only be surmised, but almost certainly it was due to his friendship with Lord Orford, the victor of La Hogue, and one of the accused ministers. Until Orford died in 1727, Walpole remained his close friend, staying often at his house.'[2] It is also significant that when Walpole was eventually raised to the peerage himself in 1742 he took his late friend's title of earl of Orford.

Not that the Junto were Walpole's only patrons, which was just as well for his political ambitions since they were eclipsed by the tories on Anne's accession. Those who were members of the privy council, including Orford, were subjected to the indignity of being struck off by the new monarch. They remained beyond the pale until 1708 and Orford himself did not return to office until 1709. Meanwhile Walpole had become a member of the Prince's council. He owed this advancement not to his alliance with the Junto but to his friendship with the dukes of Devonshire and Somerset, an association strengthened in 1702 when Walpole used his influence in the Norfolk borough of Castle Rising to bring into parliament first Devonshire's son, at a by-election, and then Sir Thomas Littleton, client of Somerset and treasurer of the navy, in the general election. These connections were invaluable, for Devonshire and Somerset were the only whigs in the cabinet to survive the purges of Anne's accession, apart from the archbishop of Canterbury. They were presumably instrumental in obtaining his admiralty post for him three years later.

His promotion was a significant manifestation of the prevalent policy of moderation. By 1705 the government was embarked on a scheme to govern with the support of moderate tories and whigs who were not bound to follow the lead of the high churchmen on the one hand or the Junto on the other. The high-church tories whom Anne had appointed to cabinet posts in 1702 had discredited themselves by factious support of ecclesiastical measures, such as bills to suppress occasional conformity, even to the point of jeopardizing war finance and with it the war effort. Since the direction of the war was the chief objective of the duke of Marlborough and Lord Treasurer Godolphin, they had persuaded the Queen to dispense with the services of these obstructionist colleagues. At the same time the two ministers, in conjunction with Robert Harley, the secretary of state, were attempting to manage parliament by building up a Court party of moderate tories and whigs who would offset the more zealous partisans on both sides. To achieve this they kept in service many moderate tories, and turned to moderate whigs like the dukes of Devonshire and Somerset for advice in filling vacancies. Walpole was a beneficiary of this policy when in June 1705 he was appointed to the Prince's council.

One of the first overt manifestations of the policy of moderation was the selection of a Speaker after the opening of parliament in October 1705. The Court nominated John Smith, a moderate whig, and it was noteworthy that Walpole and his associates in the Commons were the chief managers for the ministerial side in the debate on the Speakership.

From 1705 to 1708, therefore, so far from being a Junto protégé Walpole was identified with those Court whigs who were defending the policy of moderation. By the winter of 1707–8 these had acquired a definite identity, being so closely associated with Godolphin's ministry that they were called 'the lord treasurer's whigs'. During the parliamentary session of that winter the new scheme came under fierce attack from party leaders on both sides: Walpole found himself having to defend the Prince's council from accusations that the admiralty had grossly neglected the protection of commerce, to the no small detriment of the merchant marine which had suffered severe depredations. The fiercest attacks on the conduct of the council were

launched by the Junto, since the tories held back from indicting a
body presided over by the queen's husband and effectively led by one
of their own number, Marlborough's tory brother George Churchill.
Walpole was thus placed in the firing line between the Junto and the
Court. His former colleagues were exasperated at this defence of his
employers, but as he himself put it, 'I never can be so mean to sit at a
board, when I cannot utter a word in its defence.'[3] His actions
produced a strain in his relations with the Junto which lasted for at
least a year. In June 1708 this friction roused comment even in the
Kit-Cat Club, that brilliant gathering of whigs and wits presided
over by Jacob Tonson, which was usually noted for its conviviality.
At one meeting held that month, however, Tonson, admittedly 'in his
cups', accused 'the laughing Admiral', as Walpole was called, of
being 'the greatest villain in the world . . . for forsaking his patrons
and benefactors the Junto, for which poor Jacob was severely
bastinadoed'.[4] It was not in fact until late October or even early
November 1708 that Walpole, along with the dukes of Devonshire
and Newcastle, made his peace with the Junto lords. Even after they
were reconciled Walpole remained on closer terms with the lord
treasurer than with the Junto, being so close that when Godolphin
was on his death bed he recommended him to the duchess of
Marlborough.

This reconciliation came about because the scheme of moderation
had collapsed since the previous parliamentary session. Although it
was doomed anyway, what dealt it a fatal blow was the resignation of
Robert Harley and his associates from the ministry in February 1708.
Among the men whom Harley took out of office with him was Henry
St John, who had been secretary at war since 1704. It seems that the
duke of Marlborough wanted his own secretary Adam Cardonnel to
take over this post, but as he was at that time abroad Walpole was
appointed secretary at war until his return. In fact Walpole
remained secretary until January 1710, when Cardonnel replaced
him upon his own promotion to the post of treasurer of the navy.
Even then Cardonnel was only nominal secretary, for Walpole
continued to perform the duties of the office until George Granville
formally took over in September 1710. Walpole himself remained
treasurer of the navy until early 1711.

He therefore survived the ministerial revolution of 1710, if only for
a few months. Why he remained in office so long after Harley had
ousted Godolphin and many of his whig colleagues had resigned, is
something of a mystery. That Harley wanted to retain his services is
not at all strange, for he was anxious to keep in office as many whigs as
would serve under him and therefore made 'very flattering advances'
to Walpole, telling him that 'he was worth half his party, and pressed

him to continue in administration'.[5] But why Walpole agreed to stay is more problematical. There could be a quite simple explanation: the impecunious and extravagant Walpole desperately needed the emoluments of office. More likely, though, he had come to love power even more than money. Why in that event he lost it in 1711 is also mysterious. It seems likely, however, that he was sacrificed by Harley as a sop to those tory backbenchers who were complaining bitterly that he had kept too many whigs in office. At the same time Walpole must have found his own position acutely uncomfortable as a member of a tory ministry embarking, for all Harley's protestations to the contrary, on negotiations which eventually led to a peace with France and which Walpole more than anybody was to denounce as iniquitous.

When Walpole ceased to be treasurer of the navy in January 1711 he had been in office for over five years, during which he had built up an enviable reputation as an administrator and a politician. His administrative reputation rested mainly on two attributes: one was his capacity for sheer hard work—he thought nothing of getting to his office at six o'clock in the morning to clear correspondence; the other was his unrivalled financial ability, for an admiring colleague admitted that he was 'the best master of figures of any man of his time'.[6] It was this which enabled him to get a grip on the tangled muddle of army accounts while he was secretary at war. And it was doubtless this which recommended him to the demanding post of treasurer of the navy, since as the session 1710–11 was to prove, naval finances were very complicated indeed. Yet though his enemies were to accuse him of corruption, few alleged that he was incompetent.

Walpole's political ability was finally to emerge when he left office and, untrammelled by ties with the government, could lead the whigs without compromise. Here Harley's alleged claim that he was worth half his party was to be vindicated. The major attack on the previous whig administration launched in the first session of the new parliament was on its management of the country's finances. By the spring of 1711 accusations were being made by the tories that the staggering sum of £35,000,000 was unaccounted for. Walpole revealed his mastery of figures and demonstrated that the allegations were entirely specious in two pamphlets, *The Debts of the Nation considered* and *A state of the five and thirty millions*.

Despite his protestations that no financial scandals could be laid at the door of the previous ministry, Walpole was himself vulnerable on this score. In the following session of parliament accusations that he had corruptly profited from a forage contract while secretary at war were raked up against him and used as a pretext to have him expelled the house; he even spent some time in the Tower. The real reason for his expulsion was that he had led the opposition to the preliminary terms of peace with France, which the whigs represented as an outright betrayal of England's allies. Unable to take part in parliamentary debates Walpole took to his pen, defending the whigs against charges of corruption and attacking the tories for negotiating the Treaty of Utrecht in such pamphlets as *The Present state of fairyland* and *A Short History of the Parliament*.

Once the peace was signed, however, the next big issue to occupy the political world was the succession. Whatever basis their fears had in fact, there can be little doubt that the whigs were genuinely worried that the ministry was plotting to betray the protestant succession and to bring in the Pretender on Anne's death. Walpole, back in the house for Anne's last parliament, orchestrated whig debates on this issue. His eloquence was partly responsible for the fact that the government had a majority of less than fifty when a motion was put that the succession was not in danger under her majesty's administration. Since on paper they should have been able to muster over two hundred this was a moral defeat, brought about by the defection of many Hanoverian tories who were concerned at the prospects ahead. Walpole pressed home his advantage, and in the closing weeks of the session the opposition was on the offensive and the government very much on the defensive in parliament. The ministry was relieved when Anne prorogued parliament in July 1714. She never called it again, since she died on 1 August.

With the death of Anne the whigs came into the promised land. Walpole's political apprenticeship was over. Yet although he had served his time he could not yet set himself up in business. He had to serve as a journeyman under Stanhope and Sunderland, and it was not until 1720 that he became a master or before 1722 that the firm of Townshend and Walpole, as the prime minister himself called it, was firmly established.

Walpole's political apprenticeship served him in good stead when he came to take over the administration. It was, of course, a whig apprenticeship. His whiggery took the form of defending the Revolution Settlement through thick and thin and he never compromised on that issue. He emerged as the leading champion of the protestant succession in the last four years of Anne's reign. Yet it was at the same time a Court whig apprenticeship, and this was perhaps even more important. Walpole served two masters, Godolphin and Harley, who attempted between 1705 and 1711 to build up a Court party which could outweigh the tory and whig parties in parliament. They failed for many reasons, among the more crucial of which was the smallness of the Court party and the intensity of party strife. After Anne's death, however, the Court party grew, while party conflict declined. Walpole was uniquely placed to exploit this new situation. He succeeded where Godolphin and Harley had failed.

He was partly successful because he exploited the patronage of the crown more systematically than any previous minister in his determination to sustain a Court party. In dealing with the House of Lords Walpole never tried anything as drastic as the creation of twelve peers at a stroke, as Queen Anne had done in 1712 or a peerage bill such as Stanhope had introduced in 1719. The highest number of peers ennobled at one time was four, a step taken in 1734 to bolster a Court majority which had slumped during the Excise Crisis. About the same time eight peers who had shown disloyalty to Walpole were stripped of their posts, two of them losing their commissions in the army. This was a sharp reminder to the other lords in places under the crown that their jobs depended upon their faithful support of the government. Hopes of preferment also played their part in sustaining loyalty. Walpole deliberately enhanced these by reviving the Order of the Bath, a merit reserved primarily for peers, which enlarged his opportunities for rewarding those who generally supported the government in the House of Lords. Together with these, and the votes of most of the twenty-six bishops and sixteen Scottish peers, Walpole reckoned that he could generally sustain a majority in the upper house. At the accession of George I a majority of the bishops were already whig, and by the time of Walpole's achievement of supreme power almost all were. In alliance with Bishop Gibson of London who, until they quarrelled in 1736, was known as 'Walpole's pope', he carefully vetted preferments to bishoprics to keep the episcopal bench in safe whig hands. He was lucky at the outset of his ministry, since in 1723 six bishoprics became vacant, and by judicious translations he and Gibson advanced nine whig churchmen up the ladder of episcopal preferment. Before long almost all the bishops owed their sees to Walpole, while only one avowed tory, Thomas Sherlock, slipped through the net which he and Gibson had woven, thanks to the assistance of Queen Caroline.

The defection of the bishops in 1736 proved to be a temporary blow to Walpole's control of the upper house. It was due to the first serious upsurge of religious agitation since the repeal of the Occasional Conformity and Schism Acts. As Lord Hervey remarked of parliamentary business in that year, 'all the considerable debates ... were upon church matters.' Country whigs even pushed a measure to repeal the Test and Corporation Acts, though this was defeated by 251 votes to 123. A bill to change the way of collecting tithes from recalcitrant payers, however, fared much better in the Commons. This measure was advocated by quakers who wanted to transfer compulsory collections from the common law courts at

Westminster, a method they claimed was expensive and vexatious, to the justices of the peace in the localities. The bill passed the Commons by 164 to 48, primarily because it received the unexpected support of Walpole himself. The bishops, however, led by Gibson, took offence at what they regarded as a breach of faith, and opposed it in the Lords, where it was defeated by 54 votes to 35, fifteen bishops voting with the majority and none with the minority. This marked the parting of the ways for Gibson and Walpole, who ended their long alliance in ecclesiastical affairs. Thereafter the duke of Newcastle was the minister responsible for church patronage. He managed to ensure that most bishops were back in the ministerial fold before the next session of parliament.[7]

The support of the representative Scottish peers was also assiduously courted. These only grew restive when matters directly affecting Scotland cropped up in parliament, and debates on north Britain were almost as rare as disputes on the Church of England during Walpole's ministry. Several Scots defected at the time of the Excise Crisis, however, and the opposition hoped to exploit their discontent to carry the elections of the Scottish lords against the Court in 1734. Walpole and his Scottish manager Lord Islay pulled out all the stops, and the sixteen recommended by the Court carried the day in Edinburgh. Their loyalty was shaken by the government's response to the Porteous Riots, which caused a number of them, including Islay's brother, the duke of Argyll, to go into opposition, a move which materially weakened Walpole in parliament and assisted in his fall.

Cultivating a Court party in the Commons was a more difficult task given the greater size of the lower house. Nevertheless, systematic patronage was deployed to create, if not a majority, a larger group of dependent members on the Court and treasury benches than had ever been known before. The range of posts available to members of parliament was prodigious. In 1739 an opposition pamphlet listing the voters on each side of a division indicated the positions which they held, beginning with James Abercromby, the deputy governor of Stirling Castle, and ending with Sir William Yonge, the secretary at war.[8] It listed nearly two hundred placemen with posts in the army and navy, the household and departments of state, the law, the colonies and the diplomatic service. There were still many offices in the administration to which the ministry could promote members despite earlier restrictions aimed at cutting down the number of placemen in the Commons, of which the most important had been the disqualification of customs and excise officers, administrators of army accounts, prizes, sick and wounded, transports and wine licences, and governors of plantations.

Indeed insofar as these restrictions had been intended to reduce the proportion of placemen in the house they had signally failed. Under Anne the number in the Commons was about 125. Between 1714 and 1720 it rose to between 155 and 170. During Walpole's premiership it reached around 185. Thus during the first four decades of the eighteenth century the proportion of placemen went up from less than a quarter to about a third of the house. Moreover their reliability in divisions also improved. In Anne's reign it was estimated that only about sixty members were so dependent upon the Court that their votes could be relied on by the ministry under any circumstances. Certainly the number prepared to defect in key divisions could be quite high. In 1705 in a crucial vote on the choice of a Speaker, out of 115 placemen present in the house seventeen voted with the opposition. Placemen became more reliable under Stanhope, though he had to face a massive defection at the time of the peerage bill when, of 152 present and voting, 38 opposed the Court. This contrasts sharply with the behaviour of placemen under Walpole, when the lowest number voting for the ministry in a key division was 132, and the highest number of defectors was 24 in a division when all told 168 were present. The votes of placemen can be ascertained, but nobody knows how many members were bought off with pensions, for the secret service books have not survived. However, there is every reason to believe that the number of pensioners and of others casually bribed with government funds, went up proportionately with the increase of placemen between the era of Godolphin and that of Walpole.

Walpole thus had at his disposal a more solid and reliable phalanx of Court supporters in the Commons than any of his immediate predecessors. This lends substance to the views of his opponents that parliament was in danger of becoming a rubber stamp of the executive. It seemed to them that the terrifying vision of the author of *The Danger of Mercenary Parliaments*, which was significantly re-published in 1722, was becoming real. The *Craftsman* likened the Commons to a monster called Polyglott 'who had above five hundred mouths and as many tongues and fed on gold and silver'; its master 'could make more than three hundred of his tongues at once lick his foot or any other part about him'.[9] The picture of Walpole as a prime minister completely controlling parliament with patronage was perhaps most vividly painted by Sir William Wyndham in a speech to the Commons in March 1734:[10]

> Let us suppose a gentleman at the head of the administration whose only safety depends upon corrupting the members of this house ... suppose him next possessed of great wealth, the plunder of the nation, with a parliament of his own choosing, most of their seats purchased, and their votes bought at the expense of

the public treasure. In such a parliament let us suppose attempts made to enquire into his conduct, or to relieve the nation from the distress he has brought upon it ... suppose ... these reasonable requests rejected by a corrupt majority of his creatures, whom he retains in daily pay, or engages in his particular interest, by granting them those posts and places which ought never to be given to any but for the good of the public: upon this scandalous victory, let us suppose this chief minister pluming himself in defiances, because he finds he has got a parliament like a packed jury, ready to acquit him of all adventures.

Wyndham made this speech in the aftermath of the Excise Crisis, which at first sight seems to contradict his vision of Walpole entrenched in a fortress impregnable to attacks by the opposition. Indeed his withdrawal of the excise scheme apparently reveals him as very vulnerable when his opponents could rouse public opinion to join in the siege. A closer look at this crisis, however, the most serious which he had to face before the very end of his ministry, shows that there was rather more substance in the opposition's case than appeared on the surface.[11]

The excise scheme was not new but an extension of a system started in Anne's reign. Colonial produce imported into England had to pay customs duties even if it was later re-exported, though upon being shipped out again the merchants who handled it had the customs rebated. In order to simplify the procedure and reduce smuggling, bonded warehouses were set up in which colonial produce could be stored without paying customs. If it was not re-exported but sold in Britain, it would pay an excise as equivalent for the customs duty when it came out of bond. In 1709 an experiment had been made with such a system in the case of pepper. It was so successful that in 1723 Walpole extended it to include tea, coffee and cocoa, which increased revenue by about £120,000 a year. In 1733 he put forward a scheme to bring wine and tobacco into the system, which he thought would save between £200,000 and £300,000 per annum.

To prepare the ground for this scheme, Walpole set up a committee to inspect frauds and abuses committed in the customs, which reported in June 1732. It discovered that, since Christmas 1723, 250 customs men had been assaulted, and six murdered, while 251,320 pounds of tea, and 652,924 gallons of brandy had been seized. Walpole presented the scheme primarily as a means to stop several frauds. Thus in connection with the importation of tobacco he detailed five fraudulent practices—declaring for re-export a greater quantity than had been declared upon import, which cost the exchequer an estimated £100,000 a year in the Port of London alone; relanding re-exported tobacco after receiving the drawback; re-exporting stalks mixed with dust to get the drawback; pilfering from ships in the Thames, a practice known as socking; and taking undue advantage of the time allowed for paying customs duties. To obviate all these the current customs duty of $6\frac{1}{3}d$ per pound of tobacco was to be reduced to $\frac{3}{4}d$, which would be refunded on re-export; otherwise an excise of $4d$ per pound would be payable on the release of tobacco from bond. According to Walpole this would benefit the fair trader, cheapen tobacco for the consumer and above all appeal to the landed interest by making it possible to abolish the land tax because of the improved yield from indirect taxes.

So far from proving popular, however, the scheme produced an uproar. The opposition had prepared their case thoroughly, having exercised their arguments the previous year when Walpole reintroduced the excise on salt after a lapse of two years. They had then argued that ultimately all taxes fell on land, which had somewhat taken the edge off Walpole's claim that an increase of indirect taxation eased the burden of direct taxes on the landed interest. To this argument was now added the claim that under the guise of eliminating frauds in the customs Walpole was in fact bent on introducing a general excise, which would be a threat to the liberties and properties of all Englishmen. In the first place it would bring into existence a vast army of new excise officers, which would increase patronage and thereby the executive's power to corrupt. Secondly, this force of officials would have powers to pry into every store, and even search private houses for contraband goods.

In vain did Walpole deny that he had any intention of introducing a general excise, or that the full number of excisemen needed by the scheme was not an army but a mere one hundred and fifty; it was useless to claim that only the fraudulent need fear. His majority in the votes on the scheme slumped from sixty-one on the division on 14 March 1733 to seventeen on 10 April. Walpole then decided that 'this dance it will no further go' and moved that further consideration of the scheme should be postponed until 12 June. Since parliament was not expected to be in session on that date this was in effect dropping the measure altogether. It was the biggest admission of defeat that Walpole made until his fall in 1742.

The erosion of the government's majority between 14 March and 10 April can be attributed to the pressure of public opinion. Certainly the opposition mounted a massive publicity campaign against excise. Pamphlets poured from the press, public demonstrations were held, instructions were presented from fifty constituencies threatening their members with the loss of their seats in the next election if they supported the scheme. Finally a petition against it from the City of London was presented the very day before Walpole announced that he would withdraw it. His announcement was greeted with wild rejoicing in Bristol, Liverpool, London, Oxford and other bastions of opposition across the kingdom.

It appears from an analysis of the voting on the scheme, however, that outside influence caused members to withdraw their support from the government only in the earlier divisions. The crucial collapse from sixty-one to seventeen occurred because of desertions by placemen whose seats were impervious to changes in public opinion. Their behaviour was a response not to the opposition's propaganda campaign but to momentary doubts about the King's backing for Walpole in this crisis.

The support of the crown was absolutely vital for a Hanoverian prime minister, since ministers were still very much the king's servants, and though the first two Georges sometimes gave high office to men they disliked, these did not last long unless they won royal approval. One of the reasons which prompted Walpole to 'screen' the Sunderland ministry from too close an inquisition at the time of the Bubble was that a witch hunt would be disapproved of by George I, whose favour he had obtained only a few months before and was anxious to retain. Although he had partially secured royal approval by helping to effect a reconciliation between George I and his son, the enmity between the two Hanoverians ran too deep for it to be enduring, and there was so little love lost between them that when the Prince heard that his father had died in 1727, his initial reaction was one of joy. His detestation of his father had rubbed off on to his first minister, so that the death of George I was a real crisis in Walpole's relations with the crown. When Walpole broke the news to the new king that his father had dropped dead on the way to Hanover, George II immediately responded 'Go to Chiswick and take your directions from Sir Spencer Compton.' It seemed to all the world that Compton, Speaker of the House of Commons, treasurer of the Prince's household and paymaster to the army, was now to crown his career by becoming prime minister. Walpole felt his power waning as courtiers turned to this rising star. Fortunately for Walpole the favourite turned out to be a nonentity: he could not even draw up a Commons' address to the new monarch and foolishly asked his rival to pen one for him. Sir Robert was able to out-manoeuvre Sir Spencer in the struggle for the King's favour, partly by ingratiating himself with the Queen and partly by demonstrating his superior parliamentary skill. He was on good terms with Queen Caroline, and shrewdly decided to cash in on this rather than to follow advice to cultivate the favour of one of the King's mistresses. He realized that George kept mistresses more for ostentation than for use, and was at heart extremely uxorious. As he later put it, with characteristic coarseness, 'he seized the right sow by the ear.' Caroline's support was so crucial in 1727 that some historians considered her death ten years later a blow to Walpole's influence with the King. By then, however, he was so firmly in George II's favour that the Queen's influence was no longer necessary. Even in 1727 his ability stood him in better stead than Caroline's favour, especially when he demonstrated it by procuring an unprecedentedly large sum for the civil list at the outset of the new reign.

Although he survived the crisis at George II's accession, it was symptomatic of how far his power depended upon the unstinted support of the crown. Indeed George possibly acted as he did then to show Walpole how much he depended upon the King. When during the Excise Crisis it appeared that 'the King grew, every division, more and more uneasy', a group of courtiers, led by the earl of Chesterfield, the earl of Stair, the duke of Bolton and Lord Clinton, attempted a palace revolution. This was the crucial development during the Excise Crisis which led Walpole to drop the scheme. It also led him to seek a renewal of George's commitment to his ministry, which he obtained on 13 April when the king dismissed the earl of Chesterfield, his lord steward, and Lord Clinton, a lord of the bedchamber. By demonstrating clearly that he enjoyed the support of the crown, Walpole dramatically transformed the situation in the Commons, where on 24 April a ballot for commisioners to investigate the frauds in the customs was carried for the Court by eighty-five votes. Before the end of the session proposals to bring in a place bill and to repeal the Septennial Act were both defeated by comfortable majorities. Little wonder then that the opposition regarded parliament as a mere rubber stamp for the Court, and saw Walpole presiding over an empire based on patronage which was impervious to public opinion. The outcome of the general election in 1734 seemed to confirm these views. The opposition tried to drive home the attack but, although it scored some successes in large constituencies where the unpopularity of the excise scheme could be expressed in votes, Walpole survived the polls with a majority still prepared to support him, albeit a smaller one than he had enjoyed after the previous election.

In fact the opposition's view of Walpole was illusory. Although we do not know exactly who made up the 214 members who voted for the excise scheme in the last division on 10 April, there can be no doubt that they did not consist entirely of placemen or dependants of ministers. In any vote the ministry had to rely for a majority on the support of some of the independent members of the house, who amounted to over two hundred. They included most of the ninety-two knights of the shire returned from English and Welsh counties, constituencies too large to be manipulated by the influence of the Court or of a magnate. The rest consisted principally of members whose electoral interests in the boroughs which they represented was strong enough for them virtually to return themselves. If these independents had united into a bloc against the Court then the Commons would have been unmanageable. Fortunately for the ministry they were divided.

Some of them were in more or less permanent opposition. These were perpetual Country members, suspicious of administration and of anybody who was in office or even aspired to it. The hundred to one hundred and fifty tories present in the Commons throughout Walpole's ministry formed the backbone of this element, though there were Country whigs in their ranks and these tended to increase under George II. The rest of the independents were inclined to support the Court on the grounds that it was the duty of parliament to do the king's business and that opposition still smacked of disloyalty. This type was the prize for which ministerial and opposition politicians fought, the first to retain their allegiance, the second to detach them from the Court.

Walpole tried to retain their allegiance by offering them both stability and prosperity. He understood the backbench mentality as well as anybody, and he knew that the squires were weary of the political upheavals of the past fifty years and wanted nothing more than stable government without any excitement. They therefore welcomed a politician who openly boasted that his motto was *quieta non movere*, who offered no threat to the protestant succession, but who left the church well alone and above all kept the country at peace. This contrasted agreeably with the days of Anne, when whigs had raised alarms that the succession was in danger, tories had been even more shrill in their insistence that the church was in danger and a major war had drained the lifeblood from their estates with a swingeing land tax.

It was primarily to appease the country gentlemen that Walpole kept the land tax low. Where during the War of the Spanish Succession it had been assessed at four shillings in the pound, he levied a rate of only two shillings between 1722 and 1726, and although it rose to four shillings in 1727 with a scare over Gibraltar necessitating preparations for war with Spain, it was down to three shillings by 1728 and back to two in 1730. From 1731 to 1732 it was fixed at only one shilling, the lowest rate of the century, and it was the possibility of abolishing the land tax altogether which partly inspired the ill fated excise scheme. After its failure Walpole raised the rate to two shillings in the pound until the outbreak of war compelled him to increase it to four shillings in 1740.

Lowering the level of direct taxation was to some extent facilitated by the reduction of government expenditure in peacetime, particularly on the armed forces; but it was also helped by easing the burden of the national debt and by relying more on indirect taxes. The establishment of the sinking fund in 1717 was Walpole's idea, though Stanhope implemented it, and during his own ministry it redeemed £6 millions of debt. This and the reduction of the rate of interest from five to four per cent in 1727 made the burden more manageable. It is clear, however, that this was as much a political as an economic policy, for he was not averse to raiding the sinking fund when it suited his ends, and made no real attempt to redeem the national debt completely. In 1727 he obtained an extra £100,000 for the civil list from the fund, thereby saving his own political skin, and when Sir John Barnard proposed a further reduction of the rate of interest to three per cent in 1737, Walpole opposed the suggestion because it would offend fundholders in the City, especially those in the East India and South Sea Companies. However, if he did not reduce the debt as much as he might, he did eliminate many of the fears which it had aroused among country gentlemen. He also increased the revenue from indirect taxation to avoid placing too great a strain on landed incomes, raising the duties on candles, leather, malt, salt and sugar. Although he experimented with the abolition of the salt duties between 1731 and 1732 he reimposed them in order to avoid increasing the land tax and thereby run the risk of alienating the country gentlemen.

Not that Walpole's attempts to retain their allegiance should be dismissed as a cynical appeal to their pockets. His offer of political stability was as appealing, if not more so. It is significant that, on the only occasion before the very end of his ministry when he was in serious danger of alienating them, during the Excise Crisis of 1733, the opposition made inroads into their ranks by playing up the alleged dangers to English liberties even while Walpole himself was beguiling them with the prospect of eliminating the land tax altogether. The independents on the backbenches had ideals as well as rent rolls, and Walpole disregarded these at his peril, for an ever vigilant opposition was ready to exploit them against him.

# 10 The Opposition to Walpole

To the opposition Walpole seemed to be in an impregnable fortress, threatened only by a mutiny within. Although there was some substance in this view, which the Excise Crisis, as we have seen, apparently confirmed, in fact Walpole was not in a totally unassailable position. Indeed the opposition themselves must have realized that they grotesquely exaggerated his power, or they would have given up the unequal struggle as futile. Instead they clearly thought that, given favourable circumstances, they could topple him. All it required was to persuade enough of the independent members of the House of Commons, who normally supported the ministry, that it was their duty to oppose him.

In previous reigns these backbenchers had been marshalled by party leaders into tory and whig parties, and they were still recognizable as tories and whigs, even though the passions which had divided them previously had to a large extent cooled. Walpole deliberately tried to heat them up again in order to prevent the opposition from uniting the independents against him. His favourite ploy for this purpose was to exploit any manifestation of Jacobitism as far as he could to identify the tories as Jacobites, thereby making it difficult if not impossible for Country whigs to associate with them.

At the very outset of his ministry he was handed just such an opportunity when his agents unravelled a Jacobite plot associated with Francis Atterbury, the bishop of Rochester. The very existence of a plot was denied by Atterbury's friends, who insisted that the bishop had been framed. Swift satirized the methods employed by Walpole to convict Atterbury in his account of the techniques used by the academicians of Lagado to detect plots: 'If I should say in a letter to a friend, *Our brother Tom has just got the piles*, a man of skill in this art would discover how the same letters which compose that sentence, may be analysed into the following words, *Resist; a plot is brought home, the tour*. And this is the anagrammatic method.' That Atterbury had been in treasonable correspondence with the Pre-

tender cannot now be disputed, though neither can the charge that
Walpole squeezed every ounce of propaganda value out of it. He
conflated at least two plots into one, an abortive one abandoned by
Atterbury in the summer of 1722, and an imaginary one in the mind
of Christopher Layer, 'a simple-minded and busy romantic'.[1] As a
result, when Layer was found guilty and sentenced to death by the
Court of King's Bench, Walpole persuaded parliament of
Atterbury's complicity. Consequently the bishop was sent into
perpetual banishment by hostile majorities in both houses, Habeas
Corpus was suspended for a year and catholics and nonjurors were
subjected to a penal tax of five shillings in the pound. Thus concluded
'Walpole's exploitation of the most successful political scare in the
eighteenth century'.[2] Thereafter, though he never tired of turning up
stones in search of Jacobite schemes, he never found anything so
concrete. Indeed his obsession with Jacobitism became so strong that
some historians have seen in it not a search for a stick with which to
beat the opposition so much as paranoia—not that one can dismiss
his fears as being purely imaginary in view of the outbreak of the
'Forty-Five' three years after his fall.

In reply to Walpole's constant harping on the association between
toryism and Jacobitism, opposition propagandists protested that the
old party distinctions were meaningless. John Trenchard addressed
the electors during the general election of 1722 to 'forget ... the
foolish and knavish distinction of high church and low church, whig
and tory'. He 'wished the old names of distinction and faction buried
deep in the centre; and nothing heard in their room but Court and
Country, protestant and papist, freemen and slaves'.[3] In their
manifesto the authors of the *Craftsman* proclaimed that they had 'used
our utmost endeavours, through the whole course of these papers, to
banish those senseless and fatal animosities, to reconcile all parties to
one another; to unite them in the common interest, the interest and
cause of their country; and to persuade men who are equally zealous
in the pursuit of the same end, though perhaps by different means,
not to defeat it by unreasonable jealousies and reproachful impu-
tations'.[4]

Early in Walpole's ministry, especially in the immediate aftermath
of the Atterbury Plot, such a programme could achieve little, and the
opposition made no headway before 1725. However, the dismissal of
William Pulteney in that year, and the removal of all disabilities,
save the right to sit in the House of Lords, from Bolingbroke who had
returned to England in 1723, provided the opposition with two
leaders who, in their own persons, embodied the kind of coalition
which they called for in the *Craftsman*.

William Pulteney had an impeccable whig pedigree, having voted with the whigs ever since he first entered parliament in 1705. On the accession of George I he had been rewarded for his loyalty to the whig cause with the post of secretary at war. During the whig schism, however, he was even more loyal to Walpole, leaving office with him in 1717. Thereafter they disagreed over tactics, Pulteney, ironically in view of his later activities, objecting to Walpole's association with tories in opposition to the government. The ensuing coolness between them led Walpole to overlook his former colleague in the negotiations leading to his own return to office in 1720. Pulteney was chagrined, but allowed himself to be appeased with the minor post of cofferer of the household in 1723. When the duke of Newcastle replaced Carteret as secretary of state in the following year, however, Pulteney was mortified that he was not offered the position himself. Persuaded by his cousin Daniel Pulteney, a former ally of Sunderland, to go into opposition, he accused Walpole of corruption and was dismissed in 1725. He and Daniel then became the leaders of those whigs who were disaffected to the Court, William owing his supremacy to his superb rhetoric in the Commons, where he was held to be 'a most complete orator and debater'.[5]

Henry St John, Viscount Bolingbroke, on the other hand, had identified himself with the tories from his own arrival in the Commons in 1701. He made his mark there quickly as a leading spokesman for the high-church tory cause, featuring prominently in the moves to outlaw occasional conformity in the opening sessions of Anne's first parliament. Between 1704 and 1708 he had gravitated towards Harley's moderation and had taken office as secretary at war. When Harley resigned in 1708 St John left office with him, but afterwards, in a curious parallel to the relationship between Pulteney and Walpole after 1717, his sympathy with his former 'master', as he called Harley, did not last long. Soon after they both returned to office in 1710 they were at loggerheads politically. Harley wished to maintain moderate counsels and even to keep some whigs in place, while St John associated more and more with the extreme tories who wanted a precipitate peace with France, safeguards for the church and a complete purge of whigs from the administration. Their differences contributed much towards the disintegration of the tory party in the last four years of Anne's reign.

When St John was elevated to the peerage as Lord Bolingbroke in 1712 he resented the fact that he obtained only a viscountcy and not an earldom, blaming Harley, who had himself become earl of Oxford, for his disappointment. In fact it was the Queen who had refused higher promotion for him, the straitlaced Anne objecting to the loose-living St John. For Bolingbroke had a deserved reputation as a rake, which jarred with his role as high-church zealot. This libertine, *bon viveur*, sparkling bottle companion and impatiently ambitious politician was different in almost every way from his puritanical, patient and devious mentor, Oxford. Oxford's approach to parliamentary management, for instance, employed expert wire-pulling for which Bolingbroke could take neither the time nor the trouble. Instead he relied on his oratory, and made rousing and highly charged speeches with fine rhetorical flourishes. Deprived by Walpole of an opportunity to speak in the Lords he put his thoughts on paper and became a principal contributor to the *Craftsman*. Some of his essays there obtained a reputation as philosophical writings and were published separately; but they lack any real profundity, being propaganda masquerading as history and political science. As a propagandist, however, Bolingbroke could be highly persuasive and his essays were the most substantial contemporary critiques of the Robinocracy.

In the *Craftsman* Daniel and William Pulteney and Bolingbroke protested their loyalty to Hanover, in answer to Walpole's charge that the tories in the opposition were in fact Jacobites. This seems to have reflected the reality as well as the wishful thinking of Bolingbroke and Pulteney. Bolingbroke, himself a sufferer in the Pretender's service, returned from France determined to wean the tories from the lost cause of Jacobitism. Moreover, although some recent historians have argued that the bulk of the tories remained obstinately loyal to James Edward, their arguments are based on the suspect evidence of the Pretender's agents which was mostly wishful thinking. It seems that the majority of tory backbenchers, while they might be prepared to drink the Pretender's health in their cups, were in fact resigned to the political facts of life. They were like those Jacobites of whom Horace Walpole wrote, 'that if the Pretender had succeeded, they could have produced many witnesses to testify their zeal for him; [yet] so cautious that no witnesses of actual treason could be produced by the government against them: the very sort of Jacobitism that has kept its cause alive, and kept it from succeeding'.[6] Their attitude of permanent opposition was formed far more by an ingrained 'Country' mentality than by a desire to replace the Hanoverian dynasty. It was on this mentality that the opposition hoped to capitalize by forming the independents, both tories and whigs, into a united Country party. It was not for nothing that the *Craftsman* was subtitled the *Country Journal*.

To achieve their end, the opposition played on themes which had informed Country attitudes since the seventeenth century, calling for shorter parliaments, the elimination of placemen from the House of Commons, and the diminution if not the disbandment of the standing army. The replacement of the Triennial by the Septennial Act in

1716 had been viewed with grave misgivings by backbenchers of both parties, and gave the opposition an opportunity to insist that longer parliaments inevitably produced greater dependence upon the crown. As we have seen, this case was strengthened by an insistence that the patronage of the crown was being deployed systematically to build up a slavish Court party in parliament. Attacks upon the army had served to unite Country whigs and tories at least since William's reign. Country tories viewed it with suspicion, remembering how Cromwell had used armed force to usurp legitimate authority. Country whigs argued that standing armies inevitably acted as agents of absolutism and would be used to subvert the Revolution Settlement, some of their arguments being substantiated by developing views expressed in Harrington's *Oceana*. These 'neo-Harringtonian' views were revived by Bolingbroke in order to unite independents against the Court. Doubtless he was hoping to repeat the success of his political mentor Robert Harley, who in the 1690s had used similar policies to defeat the Junto.

These Country attacks upon the Robinocracy provided opposition leaders not merely with a programme but also with a coherent political philosophy. They claimed that Walpole's system was a gigantic machinery of corruption which threatened to undermine the constitution and to destroy the very fabric of society. In common with the majority of contemporary commentators, they argued that after the Revolution the constitutional settlement had established the finest system which could be devised. Thus they accepted that it had settled limited monarchy in England, the prerogative of the crown being restricted by the representatives of the people assembled in parliament. They took a gloomy view, however, of the prospects of preserving the fine balance of king, lords and commons established in 1689.[7] Their fears that the crown would reduce and ultimately remove the sanction of parliament were based on philosophical convictions, historical observations and trends in the contemporary world.

Many of the themes developed by the opposition had been expounded between 1720 and 1722 by Thomas Gordon and John Trenchard in *Cato's Letters*.[8] These drew on a canon of political philosophy which included the writings of Machiavelli, Hobbes, Harrington and, more recently, Algernon Sydney, Walter Moyle and the third earl of Shaftesbury, as well as Locke, to sustain their critique of Walpole. They got from Machiavelli the notion that kings inevitably exploited every opportunity to increase their power and sought to be absolute. Only the vigilance of the people to preserve their liberties could prevent this from happening. They agreed with Hobbes that unfortunately human nature was base and that a skilful prince could easily prey on man's depravity to corrupt him. Algernon Sydney was quoted for the view that 'Liberty cannot be preserved, if the manners of the people are corrupted', since corrupt politicians would sell liberty to an absolute monarch. The tendency for monarchs to aim at absolutism and for corrupt human nature to aid and abet them, was exemplified in the fall of Rome, which 'fell a victim to ambition and faction, to base and unworthy men, to parricides and traitors; and every other nation must run the same fortune, expect the same fatal catastrophe, who suffer themselves to be debauched with the same vices, and are actuated by the same principles and passions.' Developments in contemporary France, Denmark and Sweden were cited to show that the trend on the continent was towards absolutism. In their pessimism the Country opposition saw themselves engaged in a losing battle against the forces of arbitrary power and corruption, since 'the whole ter-raqueous globe cannot shew five free nations.'

Finally they saw the same tendencies in English society. The establishment of a standing army since the Revolution was regarded as the most ominous development, for such forces had been the main instrument of absolutism on the continent, and in their view liberty could not survive the upkeep of a permanent armed force. Almost as sinister was the rise of the monied interest in the financial revolution which had created an engine for corruption on an unprecedented scale. 'I would gladly know', asked Gordon and Trenchard, 'what advantage ever has, or even can, accrue to the publick by raising stocks to an imaginary value, beyond what they are really worth.'

It turns most of the current coin of England out of the channels of trade, and the heads of all its merchants and traders off their proper business. It enriches the worst men, and ruins the innocent; it taints mens morals and defaces all the principles of virtue and fair dealing, and introduces combinations and frauds in all sorts of traffic. It has changed honest commerce into bubbling; our traders into projectors, industry into tricking, and applause is earned, when the pillory is deserved. It has created all the dissatisfaction complained of, and all the mischief attending it, which daily threaten us, and which furnish reasons for standing or occasional troops: It has caused all the confusion in our public finances: It has set up monstrous members and societies in the body politic which are grown, I had almost said, too big for the whole kingdom. It has multiplied offices and dependancies in the power of the Court, which in time may fill the legislature and alter the balance of the government. It has overwhelmed the nation with debts and burthens under which it is almost ready to sink; and has hindered those debts from being paid off.

Country propaganda developed these themes during Walpole's ministry. The philosophical notion that men's proneness to depravity could be exploited by unscrupulous politicians to enslave them, historical examples of this actually happening and illustrations of the process at work in contemporary Europe and especially England, were inexhaustible topics for the *Craftsman*. They also informed more enduring works of literature produced during Walpole's ministry. Swift demonstrated in *Gulliver's Travels* how Lilliput had sunk from a relatively pure state to a corrupt condition 'by the degenerate nature of man'. Dr Johnson argued in *London* that Alfred's reign had been a golden age when incorrupt statesmen had ruled a virtuous society, and that since then England had degenerated until under Walpole corrupt politicians presided over a vicious capital. Although the actual date of the golden age tended to be rather less precise than this in other Country writings, opposition writers were prone to argue similarly that England had declined from an earlier state of grace to its contemporary corrupt state. They placed the pristine era in a time when the country had been ruled by a natural aristocracy composed of peers and gentry, whose power was based on land. These had governed in the national interest, and under them government was a simple and practical art. They had been usurped by upstart monied men who, led by Walpole himself, had ousted the traditional rulers and governed entirely for their own self-interest, to further which they invented statecraft, whereby government became a complicated, jargon-ridden science. Swift satirized this tendency directly in the third voyage of Gulliver, especially in the contrast between the practical and virtuous landowner Lord Munodi and the impractical and tyrannical governors of Laputa. He also criticized it by implication in his depiction of Brobdingnag, where politics had not been reduced to a science, and where government was confined 'within very narrow bounds, to common sense and reason, to justice and lenity, to the speedy determination of civil and criminal causes'. Brobdingnag was in many ways the embodiment of Country ideals. It had no standing army, the king being amazed to learn from Gulliver that one was kept afoot in England 'in the midst of peace, and among a free people'. Instead it had an unpaid militia commanded by the nobility and gentry, an alternative to a professional force which was frequently urged by the opposition. Although Swift also attacked the monied interest, it was Pope who demonstrated most strikingly Country convictions that a credit economy was inherently more corrupt than more primitive economies:

> Blest paper-credit! Last and best supply!
> That lends corruption lighter wings to fly!
> Gold imp'd by thee, can compass hardest things,
> Can pocket States, can fetch or carry Kings,
> A single leaf shall waft an Army o'er,
> Or ship off Senates to a distant Shore.

Corruption not only eroded the constitutional safeguards against unlimited power, it also rotted the social fabric, since there was a deliberate conspiracy to debauch the people in order to make them surrender their freedom and become slaves. Corrupt standards were therefore not merely creating a mercenary state but were debasing all ranks. Honesty was at a discount among professional men and merchants, who were aping the corruption of the Court, while vice was rampant among the lower orders. Corruption, according to the *Craftsman*[9]

> has vitiated the country in the same manner that it has poisoned the City, and worked itself into every part of our constitution, from the highest offices of life, down to the lowest occupations in a regular and gradual descent ... from this grand foundation of corruption flow all those little streams and rivulets, which have spread themselves through every part of this kingdom, and debauched all ranks and orders of men.

This notion was a commonplace of Country propaganda. According to Johnson,

> A single Jail, in Alfred's golden Reign,
> Could half the Nation's Criminals contain

while under Walpole,

> Scarce can our Fields, such Crowds at *Tyburn* die,
> With Hemp the Gallows and the Fleet supply.

The reason was that wickedness in high places generated evil below, until it was not safe to walk the streets of London under the Robinocracy. A more direct link between the government and crime in the capital was made by John Gay in *The Beggar's Opera* and Henry Fielding in *Jonathan Wild the Great*. Both works compared the cabinet to a gang of criminals and argued that Walpole was a more successful crook than Macheath and Wild. The corrosive social effects of corruption at Court were nowhere more darkly forecast than by Pope in his final version of *The Dunciad*, in which he compared Walpole to 'A Wizard old' who made 'one mighty Dunciad of the Realm'. Under his regime the lights of civilization, culture, art, science, religion and philosophy are extinguished one by one until

> Thy hand, Great Anarch! lets the curtain fall,
> And Universal Darkness buries All.

Walpole was not inactive in the face of this barrage of hostile propaganda. On the contrary, he tried both to stifle and to answer it. In 1737 he actually resorted to censorship to suppress attacks upon his administration upon the stage, by rushing a playhouse act through parliament which required plays for the future to be approved by the lord chamberlain. There was no similar machinery for the press since the lapsing of the Licensing Act in 1695, but Walpole used the still formidable powers of the government to prosecute for libel as weapons against his opponents. Thus no fewer than eight writs were issued against the *Craftsman*, while its publisher was fined and imprisoned after being tried in 1731. More indirect measures to stifle his critics included a heavy stamp duty imposed in 1725 and periodic interference with the mails to hinder the postal distribution of adverse literature. An ingenious scheme suggested to him by an anonymous projector, whereby the opposition press would be deprived of advertising revenue by the free distribution of advertisements under government auspices, was never tried out. Instead Walpole arranged for the distribution of favourable publications written by his supporters. These did not include men as eminent as Gay, Fielding, Pope and Swift, who wrote on the other side; but neither were they nonentities. Thomas Gordon, whom he bought off from opposition, Lord Hervey and Bishop Hoadly wrote pamphlets in his defence, while such newspapers as the *Free Briton* and the *Daily Courant* did more systematic battle with the opposition periodical press.

Walpole, of course, was quite capable of defending himself against opposition attacks, both in print and in parliament. He once wrote of his chief opponent: 'I believe I could produce as strong instances not only of want of capacity, but of every virtue which can qualify man for a public employment, as the weakest and most wicked administration was ever accused of.'[10] He delivered a particularly deadly blow to Bolingbroke in a Commons debate on an opposition motion to repeal the Septennial Act in March 1734. This was in reply to Wyndham's entertaining supposition of 'a gentleman at the head of the administration whose only safety depends upon corrupting the members of this house'.[11]

When gentlemen talk of ministers abandoned to all sense of virtue or honour, other gentlemen may, I am sure, with equal justice, and, I think, more justly, speak of anti-ministers and mock patriots, who never had either virtue or honour, but in the whole course of their opposition are actuated only by motives of envy, and of resentment against those who may have disappointed them in their views, or may not perhaps have complied with all their desires.

But now Sir, let me too suppose ... let us suppose in this, or in some other unfortunate country, an anti-minister, who thinks himself a person of so great and extensive parts, and of so many eminent qualifications, that he looks upon himself as the only person in the kingdom capable to conduct the public affairs of the nation, and therefore christening every other gentleman who has the honour to be employed in the administration by the name of blunderer: suppose this fine gentleman lucky enough to have gained over to his party, some persons really of fine parts, of ancient families and of great fortunes, and others of desperate views, arising from disappointed and malicious hearts; all these gentlemen, with respect

to their political behaviour, moved by him, and by him solely; all they say either
in private or public, being only a repetition of the words he has put into their
mouths, and a spitting out of that venom which he has infused into them; and yet
we may suppose this leader not really liked by any, even of those who so blindly
follow him, and hated by all the rest of mankind: we will suppose this anti-minister
to be in a country where he really ought not to be, and where he could not have
been but by an effect of too much goodness and mercy, yet endeavouring with all
his might, and with all his art, to destroy the fountain from whence that mercy
flowed.

This was a superb speech, a brilliant reminder that not the least
important prop of Walpole's power was his own ability, as a
parliamentary orator, to appeal to the backbench mentality. Such
rhetoric sufficed to keep country gentlemen quiet for much of his
ministry. In a time of crisis, however, as in the months when
opposition to the excise scheme had him fighting with his back to the
wall, he could pull off this magnificent exercise in character
assassination, which helped not only to defeat the attack on the
Septennial Act but also to send Bolingbroke back into exile. He was
so discredited by 1735 that he packed his bags and returned to
France, never to trouble Walpole again.

Although Walpole's supporters protested that the government was
not corrupt and that patronage was employed to reward rather than
to bribe men for their loyalty, their protestations were offset by a
series of notorious cases which demonstrated that the Court was not a
model of political purity. The lord chancellor was found guilty in
1725 of embezzlement and corruption, and fined £30,000. In 1727 a
government supporter was expelled from the Commons after having
been detected in a fraud concerning estates forfeited from former
South Sea Company directors. In 1732 the Charitable Corporation,
which was supposed to use its capital to lend small sums of money to
the poor, was discovered to have employed it for the financial benefit
of its projectors. Next year another scandal was exposed involving the
York Building Company. Yet although supporters of Walpole were
involved in all these cases he emerged relatively unscathed. A
generation which could stomach the South Sea Bubble could swallow
the lesser scandals with little effect. Walpole himself was quite cynical
about the allegations of corruption made by the opposition. As he put
it 'I am no saint, no spartan, no reformer'. His association with men
like William Yonge, whose 'name was proverbially used to express
everything pitiful, corrupt and contemptible' and whom even
George II called 'stinking Yonge' did little to improve his image.[12] It
is significant that where his own immediate predecessors, Godolphin,
Harley and Stanhope, had all left office poorer than they had entered
it, Walpole himself amassed a fortune during his twenty year
premiership. The period of his administration was undoubtedly

coarser, more materialistic and indeed more corrupt than the previous era. Its materialism and corruption bred cynical indifference.

Another reason besides cynicism and indifference which rendered opposition accusations of corruption ineffectual was that they were self-defeating. After all, what did the opposition offer to put in its place? The answer was, of course, themselves, and they were singularly vague about just how this would purge the political system of impurities. When the *Craftsman* was dealing with wickedness in high places it could be devastatingly pointed. Thus history was ransacked from Sejanus to Wolsey to drive home parallels of corruption rivalling Walpole's. But when it came to what would occur if Walpole fell, trenchant details were replaced by vapid generalizations. On one occasion, it ran a story of how Samos had been rescued from a corrupt administration by a good patriot, such as itself, who had opened the king's eyes to the iniquities of his ministers. What happened next? 'Immediately after their disgrace, plenty was restored, credit revived, traffic began again to flourish, the people were happy; and the king's throne was established in peace and in glory for many generations.'[13] The message seems to have been that, once Walpole had been ousted, everybody would live happily ever after. Even the *Idea of a Patriot King* was not much less generalized and vague. The opposition to Walpole lived in a day-dream when they argued that corruption would vanish with his fall. The knowledge that many of the opposition leaders who wished to replace him had no better records, and in Bolingbroke's case much worse, cannot have persuaded many independents to espouse their cause.

Walpole was able to fight off every attack upon the citadel of which he was the governor. The greatest threats to his position came, not from the besieging opposition, but from mutinies within the garrison. Between 1722 and 1729, apart from the crisis on George II's accession, the main danger was posed by those allies of his rival Sunderland who survived in the ministry after the death of their leader, of whom the most formidable were Lord Carteret, secretary of state for the southern department, the duke of Roxburgh, secretary for Scotland, and the earl of Macclesfield, who was lord chancellor. From 1730 onwards Walpole's ascendancy was challenged by discontented elements among his own following, beginning with his old friend Townshend and eventually involving lord chancellor Hardwicke and the duke of Newcastle.

Carteret was Walpole's chief rival after Sunderland's death. A man of considerable charm, wit and intelligence, his ability to speak German made him very influential with the king. Walpole suspected that he was employing this influence to design a more ambitious foreign policy than he, as first lord of the treasury, could contemplate financing. His suspicions were confirmed in 1723 when Carteret used the opportunity of being abroad with George I in Hanover to urge upon the King a more aggressive attitude towards Russian expansion in the Baltic. Walpole planned to remove him from the secretaryship to a less influential post as soon as possible. His chance came when Carteret bungled an attempt to obtain a dukedom for the prospective French husband of the niece of the Countess von Platen, the king's mistress. His influence at the French regent's court, cultivated by Luke Schaub, the British ambassador, proved insufficient to obtain this favour. George I was insulted, and one of the first signs of Carteret's disgrace was the replacement of Schaub in Paris by Horace Walpole, the prime minister's brother.

It was Carteret's intrigues in Dublin rather than in Paris which enabled Walpole to get rid of a troublesome colleague. Ireland was in uproar at this time because of the grant in 1722 of a patent by the treasury to the duchess of Kendal to issue copper coins to meet the chronic shortage of small change. Since the duchess had sold the patent to William Wood for £10,000, the coins were known in Ireland as 'Wood's halfpence'. As far as the Irish were concerned it was a scheme whereby Wood would make money *from* rather than *for* Ireland. All sections of Irish society, from the Anglo-Irish establishment to the catholic peasantry, were up in arms against the scheme, their indignation brilliantly captured in Swift's caustic *Drapier's Letters*. Carteret expressed sympathy with the objections to the patent, which enabled Walpole to suggest his removal to Ireland as lord lieutenant in order to deal with the crisis. It was an inspired stroke, although it did not prevent the recall of Wood's patent in 1725.

Alleged connivance at resistance to English measures, this time in Scotland, also enabled Walpole to get rid of Roxburgh. The prime minister proposed to levy an additional duty on Scottish malt, a proposal which provoked rioting in Glasgow. Roxburgh did little to suppress these riots and was even suspected of inciting them. Walpole persuaded the King that his Scottish secretary had been culpably lenient in dealing with the rioters, and George obliged in 1725 not only by dismissing Roxburgh but also by abolishing the office of secretary of state for Scotland. Thereafter Walpole managed the affairs of the northern kingdom through the agency of the duke of Argyll and his brother the earl of Islay.

Macclesfield presented Walpole with another opportunity for removing a ministerial rival when he was discovered to have embezzled £100,000 by selling masterships in chancery. He was impeached in 1725, found guilty, and was forced to resign. Thus by

George I's death Walpole had sent his main rival, Carteret, into virtual exile in Ireland and had succeeded in removing Roxburgh and Macclesfield. His former colleagues doubtless relished the prospect of his fall on George II's accession, but Walpole so outmanoeuvred Sir Spencer Compton on that occasion that there was no further threat from that quarter. Instead in 1728 Compton went to the upper house as earl of Wilmington, to be replaced as Speaker of the Commons by Arthur Onslow, a reliable supporter of the prime minister. By 1729 Walpole was so firmly in the new king's favour that he persuaded him to dismiss Carteret from the post of lord lieutenant of Ireland. The dangers of a coup engineered by former associates of Sunderland were at last removed.

In 1730, however, Walpole faced the first serious opposition from his own supporters, which was to become increasingly significant throughout the next decade, until he fell as much through dissension in his cabinet as from the superior strength of his parliamentary opponents. The cause of this internal friction was his conduct of foreign policy. Under George I Walpole played a minor role in the formulation of foreign policy, leaving it to the King and the secretaries of state. Unfortunately the secretaries did not always produce policies which he found acceptable, and he had to intervene. On the first occasion this led to Carteret's removal in 1724 and his replacement as senior secretary by Lord Townshend, the duke of Newcastle being promoted to the vacant secretaryship. In 1725 the diplomatic pattern of western Europe, which had been established since the Treaty of Utrecht, was seriously disturbed when Spain and the Empire were reconciled in the Treaty of Vienna. Previously the main threat to European peace had been the probability of friction between these two powers. Now peace seemed to be threatened from the possibility that these new allies would combine against the other major powers in Europe. They seemed above all to threaten Britain, since Philip V granted trading concessions to the Ostend East India Company, making it appear a serious rival to the British East India Company, while Charles VI agreed to help Spain retake Gibraltar and Minorca. Armed with this reassurance Philip laid siege to the rock in 1727. Walpole was particularly afraid of Austro-Spanish support for the Pretender, and wrote to Townshend in October 1725, 'if we are to be engaged in a war, which I most heartily deprecate, 'tis to be wished that this nation may think an invasion by a sovereign power, or an evident design of such an invasion, the support of the Pretender, and the cause of the protestant succession, are the chief and principal motives that obliged us to part with that peace and tranquillity and the happy consequences thereof which we now enjoy.'[14] It has been well said that 'it is the fear of the Pretender

which seems more than anything else to have haunted Walpole in foreign politics.'[15]

Townshend's response to the Treaty of Vienna was to isolate the Emperor by constructing a system of alliances, starting with the Treaty of Hanover in 1725, between Britain, Hanover, France and Prussia, and eventually involving Holland, Sweden and Denmark. The Treaty of Hanover, however, shocked Walpole because of the costly undertakings which Townshend agreed to with the allies. Among them was an agreement that Britain should take 12,000 Hessian troops into her pay, thereby bringing her armed strength up to 26,000 men. This in itself was ammunition which the opposition used to rouse the independents on the backbenches against the government. War with Spain also forced Walpole to raise the rate of the land tax to four shillings in the pound for the first time since becoming prime minister. Townshend's reaction to the Treaty of Vienna, therefore, caused serious friction between the two ministers. As Lord Hervey put it, 'Till the making of this treaty [of Hanover] Sir Robert Walpole never meddled at all with foreign affairs; they were left entirely to Lord Townshend, whilst Sir Robert's province was confined solely to parliamentary and domestic concerns.'[16] He now decided to take the initiative in foreign policy.

Walpole's solution to the Austro-Spanish threat to peace was not to isolate Austria but to buy off Spain. In 1729, therefore, he negotiated the Treaty of Seville with Spain behind Townshend's back. He was so pleased with the success of this initial venture into diplomacy that he celebrated it in a pamphlet, *Observations upon the Treaty between the Crowns of Great Britain, France and Spain*. However, this independent initiative in foreign policy brought to a head a growing antagonism between the two ministers. There were many minor irritants. Townshend disliked the way his own power and prestige, both nationally and locally in East Anglia, were being eclipsed by the rising star of Walpole. Sir Robert himself explained the disagreement when he said 'as long as the firm of the house was Townshend and Walpole the utmost harmony prevailed; but it no sooner became Walpole and Townshend than things went wrong.'[17] After some months waiting for events to justify him, Townshend resigned in May 1730. The duke of Newcastle took over as senior secretary, while the southern secretaryship was given to William Stanhope, the man who had negotiated the Treaty of Seville and who had been rewarded with a peerage, becoming Lord Harrington. In Newcastle and Harrington, Walpole had two subservient colleagues and for the next few years he controlled foreign policy.

Once in charge of foreign policy Walpole reversed Townshend's strategy of isolating the Emperor, regarding a breach with the

Imperial court as an unfortunate break with the traditional whig policy of maintaining good Anglo-Austrian relations. He therefore negotiated the second Treaty of Vienna in 1731: Charles VI agreed to rescind the Ostend East India Company's charter in return for England's guarantee of the claim of his daughter, Maria Theresa, to the hereditary Habsburg lands on his death.

Walpole not only revived the former whig system of rapprochement with the Emperor, he also continued Stanhope's policy of friendship with France in order to maintain peace in Europe. This was bound to run into trouble. The alliance with France had originally been a pure marriage of convenience, based on the insecurity of the two regimes at a time of Jacobite rebellion in Britain and the advent of a regency in France. Once both dynasties were secure their mutually conflicting interests were bound to reassert themselves sooner or later. The coming of age of Louis XV and the birth of a dauphin in 1729 meant that France could afford to play her proper role in European affairs. In 1730 the French began to fortify Dunkirk, contrary to the Treaty of Utrecht and despite protests from Walpole. The opposition profited from this in the Commons. Then in 1731 twenty-two English labourers were kidnapped by French marauders and taken to France. One of them wrote to his wife begging her to apply 'to the duke of Argyle and the quality and to the parish' for their release.[18] These were pinpricks. More seriously, the French reacted adversely to Walpole's rapprochement with the emperor, seeing in it an encouragement of Habsburg ambitions.

The peace of Europe was finally shattered by a revival of the age-old Bourbon-Habsburg rivalry. In 1733 the Bourbons of France and Spain came to agreement in the so-called First Family Compact, and combined in a war against Austria to back the claims of Louis XV's father-in-law to the throne of Poland in opposition to a candidate supported by the Emperor. In the War of the Polish succession, which lasted from 1733 to 1735, French and Spanish troops attacked Austrian possessions in Lorraine and northern Italy. Yet Walpole never moved a finger to help the Emperor despite the Treaty of Vienna. Even George II and Queen Caroline wanted him to go to war, but Walpole managed to persuade them and a number of critical cabinet colleagues that the outbreak of war on the eve of the general election of 1734 would be very damaging to the government, especially since it had just been badly shaken in the Excise Crisis. He later boasted of his inactivity to the Queen, pointing out that 50,000 men had been 'slain this year in Europe, and not one Englishman'. Walpole was probably right to argue that a war in 1733 would have been unacceptable to the English ruling class, but when he continued to argue that any war would be unacceptable to it then he was seriously out of touch. He had lived through the War of the Spanish Succession, and had been conscious of the tremendous strain that this had placed on the country and particularly on the landowners. This had persuaded him that peace was essential to keep them loyal to the regime. He failed to appreciate that by the mid-1730s another generation had risen which had not known the strains of a major war, and which regarded warfare as glorious and even beneficial.

The main clamour arose for reprisals against Spain's interference with British trade in Spanish colonies. Legitimate trading concessions to British merchants in the Treaty of Utrecht had been disappointingly small, being confined to the Asiento, or contract to supply slaves to the colonies, and the right to send one ship a year directly to them. Since 1713, however, a thriving illicit traffic had grown up. The Spanish authorities interfered with this by means of a growing number of coastguards who interrupted the commerce. Between 1713 and 1731 they appropriated 180 British ships, one of them captained by the immortal Jenkins, who claimed that his ear was cut off by a Spanish coastguard in 1731. During the early 1730s there was in fact a lull in the activities of the coastguards, but upon their renewal in 1737 the opposition raised an outcry which became an uproar in March 1738, when Captain Jenkins appeared before the House of Commons with his ear pickled in a bottle.

Walpole was not moved to defend illicit trade with the Spanish colonies; but he did become embroiled with Spain over the legitimate trade of the South Sea Company. He negotiated the Convention of Pardo in 1739, which settled terms of compensation for the innocent British traders hurt by Spanish activities, on condition that the South Sea Company paid £68,000 claimed by Spain. Although Walpole persuaded the Commons to agree to this settlement, albeit by small majorities, the South Sea Company protested against it, and withheld payment of the sum demanded. In retaliation Spain suspended the Asiento in May 1739. This was regarded as a pretext for war, and in October Walpole wearily gave in to the clamours for hostilities, now coming from some of his own colleagues as well as from the opposition, and declared war on Spain. 'It is your war', he candidly told the duke of Newcastle, 'and I wish you well of it.'

At first the war did go well, for in December 1739 Admiral Vernon successfully attacked Porto Bello, a victory much hailed in England. Thereafter, however, the outlook became more gloomy. An attack on Carthagena was a dismal failure, and Britain looked like being committed to a disastrous naval war when a land war broke out in Europe over the Austrian succession. Walpole had pledged Britain by treaty to support the claim of the late Emperor's daughter to the

Habsburg inheritance, but again he was reluctant to join in the fighting. Eventually, bullied by both George II and by colleagues in the cabinet, led by Newcastle and Hardwicke, he persuaded the Commons to vote a large sum of money for Maria Theresa just before parliament was dissolved in 1741.

The general election of 1741 was the beginning of the end for Walpole. Ironically, in contrast to 1734, there were signs of a swing to his government in open constituencies where public opinion counted. But this could not offset defeats in two areas where the ministry was usually strong, Cornwall and Scotland, which between them returned eighty-nine members to parliament. In both Walpole had found it expedient to dispense with the services of the managers he had 'inherited' on his accession to power, and to hand the management over to new men.

In 1725 Scottish patronage was taken out of the hands of the duke of Roxburgh and placed in those of the duke of Argyll and his brother the earl of Islay. Islay undertook the management of the Court's interest in Scottish elections and, although between them the Campbell brothers could return only about seven members on their own interest, their alliances with many of the men who controlled the very small Scottish constituencies, the hereditary sheriffs in the counties and the leading families in the boroughs, usually ensured a comfortable majority for the administration among the forty-five Scottish MPs. Unfortunately for Walpole, relations with Scotland were anything but usual in 1741, thanks to the Porteous Riots. In January 1736 three smugglers tried to rob an excise officer in Fife, failed and were arrested. One of them was sentenced to transportation, the other two to death. Of those condemned to death one escaped because of the help of sympathizers, who were so numerous that a detachment of the city guard under Captain Porteous was ordered to ensure that no attempt was made to help the other escape his execution. In fact there was no hostile demonstration until after he had been hanged, but then the crowd harassed the troops until they were provoked into opening fire, killing six people. Porteous was subsequently brought to trial on a charge of murder, found guilty and condemned to death. The Queen, acting on behalf of her husband who was away in Hanover, ordered a stay of execution. On the eve of the day when Porteous should have been hanged, however, a well-disciplined crowd of some 4,000 people broke into the prison and, taking the law into their own hands, lynched him.[19]

This breakdown of law and order in Edinburgh was seized on by the opposition as an opportunity to embarrass the ministry in April 1737. They brought in a bill to imprison the provost, disband the city guard and to demolish an obstacle to troop movements in order to facilitate crowd control. Although his Scottish supporters, including Argyll and Islay, protested that this would punish the innocent rather than the guilty, Walpole went along with the measure. Realizing that the punitive aspects of the bill were costing Walpole support, the opposition changed their tactics, denouncing it as a threat to liberty. Walpole thereupon compromised, and the bill was restricted to the dismissal of the provost of Edinburgh, and a fine of £2,000 on the citizens, which was to be given to Captain Porteous' widow. Although they welcomed the amendments, the ministry's Scottish supporters still resented the measure. Argyll went into open opposition, and while Islay remained loyal he was unable to prevent a defeat for the government in the Scottish elections of 1741.

Walpole also fared badly in the Cornish elections in that year. His main agent there was Richard Edgecombe, who in 1733 had been made 'the disposer of the government's money for buying the Cornish elections for members in parliament', when he had ousted Lord Falmouth, the previous manager for the Court in Cornwall.[20] Although Edgecombe was a Devon man, with no territorial interest in Cornwall, government money went a long way to bribing the tiny electorates of many Cornish boroughs, and after the 1734 election most of the county's forty-four members were supporters of the administration, despite the opposition to their returns of the disgruntled Falmouth.

By 1741, however, Falmouth had found a potent ally in the Prince of Wales, who had extensive electoral interests in Cornwall. Previously this had been at the disposal of the government, but in 1737 Frederick quarrelled with George II, and went into opposition, taking eight dependent members with him. The significance of Frederick's breach with the Court went much further than the alienation of his own immediate supporters. It meant that for the first time since Walpole became prime minister the opposition had a legitimate focus for their activities. Just as Walpole had himself used Leicester House to legitimize his opposition to George I during the whig schism, so his opponents found it a convenient cloak for their own designs. The tories could ostentatiously identify with an heir apparent other than the Pretender, while whigs could look forward to the death of George II to realize their own ambitions when the reversionary interest came into its own.

Just how effective the cause of the Prince of Wales could be in uniting Walpole's enemies and undermining his parliamentary support first became apparent in February 1737 when the opposition moved that Frederick should be voted £100,000 a year instead of the £50,000 recommended by the Court. The motion was defeated by only thirty votes in a crowded house, and would have been carried if forty tories had not decided to abstain on the grounds that to carry the proposal would derogate from the royal prerogative. In July 1737 the Prince exacerbated the quarrel with his parents by withdrawing his pregnant wife from Hampton Court to ensure that she would not give birth in a palace where the King and Queen were resident. This insult goaded his parents into ordering him to vacate St James's, an order which Walpole, to his discomfiture, had to pass on, thus ensuring that the prince continued in opposition to him. Frederick opposed Walpole wherever he could in the general election of 1741, and was particularly successful in Cornwall where, in alliance with Falmouth, the opposition made inroads into the government's majority of 1734, despite the efforts of Edgecombe.

Even so, the ministry survived the polls with a slight majority; but it was a government divided against itself. Newcastle and Hardwicke, formerly firm friends of the prime minister, were dissatisfied with his conduct of the war. Wilmington and Dorset were jockeying to be in good positions when the leader fell. Even placemen became unreliable in divisions. Meanwhile the opposition managed to persuade independent members that the war would go disastrously if Walpole remained in charge. These developments lost him the control of the house. In December a division for the chairmanship of the committee of privileges and elections was carried against the government by 242 votes to 238. In January the consequence of this was another defeat in a division on an election petition from Chippenham by 236 votes to 235.

These are sometimes dismissed as trivial divisions, the occasion rather than the cause of Walpole's fall. Yet they were in fact quite crucial. The committee of privileges and elections heard petitions from defeated candidates at the polls against sitting members returned to parliament, on the grounds that their returns were invalid due to electoral malpractices and that the petitioners should be seated in their stead. Although the committee went through the motion of hearing evidence as if it were a court of justice, in fact it was not an impartial judicial process but a political mechanism to increase the prevalent majority in the Commons. In every other parliament under the first two Georges the ministry controlled it, and used it to hear petitions from Court supporters against Country members in order to oust their opponents and seat men who would vote for the government. Petitions from Country candidates against Court members, by contrast, were deliberately delayed until they were withdrawn or never heard.

Usually these somewhat unscrupulous methods increased the Court majority enormously. In 1715, for instance, eighty-two petitions had been presented, but only twenty-five were heard. As a result of these determinations, twenty-five tories were ousted and the same number of whigs were seated. Of the remaining sixty-one petitions, thirty-two were withdrawn and twenty-nine were never heard. Those withdrawn came from thirty-five tories and only eleven whigs, while those not heard emanated from twenty-five tories and a mere nine whigs. The hearing of election petitions, therefore, confirmed the whig triumph of 1715, and within one session a whig majority of sixty-five at the polls was by this device turned into a lead of 115 on petitions, not counting the Scottish results.

Now for the first time in the eighteenth century the opposition controlled this crucial machinery, and used it to turn down a petition from defeated Court candidates at Chippenham in favour of Country sitting members. Walpole realized that the outcome of this must be the inexorable erosion of government support in the Commons and that he simply could not carry on. He therefore took the decision to resign on 1 February. His resignation after twenty years as prime minister proved too much for the King, who tried to prevent it. When the final vote on the Chippenham election petition was carried for the opposition by 241 votes to 225, however, he was also reluctantly persuaded that there was no alternative, and so he promoted Walpole to the Lords as earl of Orford.

# 11 The Rule of the Pelhams

Walpole's fall was an event of constitutional as well as political importance. It did not occur because he lost the confidence of the crown, for George II was anxious to retain his services: Walpole fell because he lost the support of the Commons. The fact that for the best part of twenty years Walpole had enjoyed both the favour of the crown and the support of a parliamentary majority had concealed the dilemma which could develop when these two vital sources of power were not available to the same minister. Future events, from the rise of the Pelhams to the fall of Lord Bute, were to show that, while the position of a minister was intolerable if he could not command the support of the Commons, it could also be extremely uncomfortable, if not impossible, if he did not at the same time have the full confidence of the crown. Only when Henry Pelham, the duke of Newcastle's brother, was backed by both king and Commons between 1746 and his death in 1754 was there a comparable period of political stability to that which had characterized Walpole's long ministry.

Political developments in the aftermath of Walpole's fall took the form of an immediate reconstruction of the ministry to obtain the essential control of the Commons, and of a longer search to obtain the equally desirable confidence of the crown.[1] At the time of Walpole's resignation the government's supporters in the lower house numbered at most 286. This number was made up of 152 men who composed the Court and treasury party, of whom 124 were employed by the crown; and 134 independents. Together they formed what were known as the 'Old Corps', those Court whigs who had maintained Walpole in power. Had they held together like a well drilled army, as their nickname implied they did, then they would have been an invincible majority in a house which all told numbered only 558 and very rarely had more than 450 members in attendance. However, the votes even of the placemen could not be completely taken for granted, and the narrow divisions which revealed that Walpole had lost control of the Commons were due to the abstentions and even desertions to the enemy of several members of the Old Corps. It was therefore not enough for the leaders of the Old Corps who survived Walpole's fall, principally Hardwicke and Newcastle in the Lords, and Henry Pelham, the leading minister in the Commons, to try to soldier on with them alone. Some reinforcements had to be detached from the opposition groups to ensure them a majority.

The opposition at that time could roughly be divided into two almost equal groups of tories and Country whigs. The tories formed the most homogeneous bloc, although they were split between Jacobites and those who grudgingly accepted the Hanoverian dynasty, but they remained intensely suspicious of the motives and actions of those who advised George II as ministers. The whigs consisted of about eighty independents, mostly country gentlemen who entertained no great political ambitions, and some fifty whose opposition was calculated to exploit their nuisance value in order that the Court might eventually be forced to buy them off with places. These fifty now became the subject of intense overtures, negotiations and deals with the Court. They fell into two groups: those who looked to Carteret and Pulteney for a lead in parliament; and those who were associated with the duke of Argyll and the Prince of Wales. As George II himself observed, 'I saw that I had two shops to deal with.' He in fact chose to deal with the firm of Carteret and Pulteney. In the ensuing distribution of spoils Carteret replaced Harrington as secretary of state, though Pulteney, having in an unfortunate moment issued a self denial repudiating all claims to office, obtained no post but was compensated with a place in the cabinet and a peerage, becoming earl of Bath. The key position of first lord of the treasury, left vacant by Walpole's resignation, went to the earl of Wilmington who, as Sir Spencer Compton, had tried to wrest it from him fifteen years before on the accession of George II. Samuel Sandys, nicknamed 'the motion maker' for his leading role as a Country spokesman under Walpole, became chancellor of the exchequer.

George chose the Carteret connection, who became known as 'the new whigs' more for negative than for positive reasons. He had, after all, dispensed with Carteret's services as lord lieutenant of Ireland in 1729. Yet as he informed Pulteney, 'I rather chose to come to you, because I knew your aim was only directed against my minister, but I did not know but the duke of Argyll wanted to be king himself.' Carteret soon gave him more positive cause to congratulate himself on his choice, however, by indulging the King's concern for Hanover, an indulgence which created friction with the duke of Newcastle and Henry Pelham.

The Pelhams objected to Carteret's pro-Hanoverian policy because they had the task of raising the parliamentary supplies to
finance it. Carteret, a peer since the age of five, had never sat in the
lower house and had little beyond contempt for the routine of
parliamentary management or for those who had to undertake it. As
Wilmington said, 'had he studied parliament more and Demosthenes
less he would have been a more successful minister.' Carteret once
referred to Henry Pelham as having been 'only a chief clerk to Sir
Robert Walpole', adding 'and why he should expect to be more
under me I can't imagine: he did his drudgery and he shall do mine.'
His one maxim was 'give any man the crown on his side and he can
defy anything.' To Henry Pelham, who had witnessed the fall of
Walpole and who had to get the king's business through the House of
Commons, this was not self-evidently true. Pelham, indeed, was more
dependent upon parliament than even Walpole had been. For where
between 1714 and 1739 annual expenditure on the army, the navy
and the ordnance fluctuated between one and a half and three
million pounds, it came to over five and a half millions in 1742 and
reached a peak of eight millions in 1747. Simply to raise these sums
restricted the government's freedom of choice more during a war
than in peacetime. For as Lord Hardwicke pointed out to George II
in 1745, 'in times of peace, sometimes a session of parliament may be
played with, and events waited for; but in time of war, and of such a
war as this is, the case is quite different; and the ill success of it will not
be the ill success of the ministry but of the crown. It may be the loss of
the whole.'

To persuade a parliamentary majority to back the war effort
meant, again in Hardwick's words, 'taking some methods to
reconcile the minds of men to the management of the war, and
making it in some degree popular'. The difficulties in which George
II and Carteret found themselves after Walpole's fall stemmed
largely from the fact that their conduct of the war was no more
popular than his. They were accused of waging it in a way which
would protect the interests of the Electorate of Hanover rather than
those of Britain.

There was some justification in the view that George, at least, was
primarily concerned with Hanoverian rather than with British
objectives in the War of the Austrian succession. At the outset, Maria
Theresa's claim to the hereditary Habsburg lands of Austria,
Bohemia and Hungary was challenged, first by the king of Prussia
who invaded Silesia in December 1740, and then by the Elector of
Bavaria who with French assistance entered the war in 1741; but
George, anxious not to get embroiled as Elector of Hanover, declared
the neutrality of the Electorate. Again in January 1742, when

Charles Albert, the Elector of Bavaria, was chosen emperor as
Charles VII, George voted for him as Elector of Hanover. Maria
Theresa came to terms with Frederick II of Prussia at Breslau in June
1742; George felt that this decreased the immediate threat to
Hanover enough for him to reduce the number of troops supported
by the Electorate, and shifted the burden of financing 16,000 of them
on to the British treasury. Even so he felt reluctant about hazarding
them in Germany in case this jeopardized the neutrality of Hanover.
Thus when an army of Austrian, British and Hanoverian troops, led
by George himself in the colours of the Electorate, inflicted an
unexpected defeat upon the French at Dettingen in June 1743, he
hesitated to follow the victory up with vigorous action against France
and so lost the advantage. Instead of military action he preferred to
treat with the Emperor at Hanau in an attempt to persuade him to
leave the side of France in return for a subsidy which could only be
paid for by Britain. It seemed as though he was using British resources
to defend purely Hanoverian interests, and that the proposed treaty
was 'entirely an Allemanick scheme' designed to secure Hanover in
Germany even though a separate treaty might jeopardize the
common cause.

   In 1744 the shadow boxing which had marked the military
engagements and diplomatic moves between the various forces
aligned in the War of the Austrian Succession ended, and real
fighting began when France declared war on Britain and Hanover in
March, and Austria in May, following up the declaration with an
invasion of the Austrian Netherlands. Although French pressure on
the Netherlands was partly relieved by an Austrian invasion of
Alsace, this had to be called off when Frederick II attacked Bohemia.
These disasters for Maria Theresa and her allies caused them to look
for Dutch assistance, but this was not forthcoming largely because
George II would not commit Hanover to the war as a principal. He
was particularly anxious that the re-entry of Prussia into the war
should not jeopardize the Electorate, and hailed the removal of
Austrian troops from Alsace to Bohemia to fight Frederick as 'a great
thing for Germany and for the Empire'. Asked, 'but what is it, Sir, for
Flanders?', he made no reply.

   If the year 1744 had been disastrous for the cause of Austria and
her allies, 1745 was even more calamitous. In May the allied army
was defeated at Fontenoy, which left Flanders entirely at the mercy
of the French, who overran it as far as Ostend. In July the young
Pretender's rebellion began in Scotland. Throughout the year
Frederick II continued to inflict defeats on Maria Theresa and her
ally Saxony, which culminated in the capture of Dresden in
December. The only way to ease the pressure on the allies seemed to

be to get Prussia and Austria to disengage; yet George, backed by his Hanoverian ministers, was reluctant to negotiate between Maria Theresa and Frederick and only did so under duress. His intervention helped to conclude the Austro-Prussian Treaty of Dresden, which brought hostilities between the two to an end in December. Peace between Prussia and Austria again eased George's fears for the safety of Hanover, and anyway after 1745 his concern for the electorate became no longer a bone of contention. This was mainly due to the fact that its political repercussions in England provoked a crisis in February 1746 which forced the King to take the advice of the Pelhams, who asserted the priority of British interests on the continent.

George's concern for Hanover in the war produced tension both in the cabinet and in parliament. Among ministers it was a constant complaint. As the duke of Newcastle put it as early as 1740, 'the King's unjustifiable partiality for Hanover, to which he makes all other views and considerations subservient, has manifested itself so much ... that no man can continue in the active part of the administration with honour.'[2] Of the inactivity after the battle of Dettingen Newcastle complained, 'had the providential advantages we got at Dettingen been in any measure pursued, in all human probability France must and would have submitted before this time to reasonable and proper terms of peace.' It was after meeting with disapproval from a majority of the cabinet that the Treaty of Hanau was dropped.

If ministers could express such views in private it is not surprising that members of the opposition were even more vehement in their public denunciations. The taking of 16,000 Hanoverian troops into British pay proved to be particularly controversial when it was debated in parliament in December 1742. William Pitt made his mark as the most outspoken critic of this move, claiming in a notorious speech that England had been reduced to the status of 'a province to a despicable electorate'. One opposition member enthusiastically reported that 'Whig and tory has been laid aside a good while and the distinction of Court and Country is now sunk into that of Englishmen and Hanoverians.'[3] Although the payment of the troops was upheld by a majority of sixty-seven, the ministers were plainly rattled and some even contemplated ending the subsidy until the intervention of Walpole, now Lord Orford, persuaded them otherwise. In December 1743 parliament was again treated to a debate on the propriety of keeping Hanoverian troops in British pay, during which 'there were some who said they would never rest till the Hanoverian dominions were separated from the crown.' In this debate the opposition exploited the friction which had been generated between British and Hanoverian troops on the continent, some going so far as to call the forces from the electorate 'poltroons and runaways'.

Both the Pelhams and the opposition laid the blame for the undue influence of Hanover on Carteret. Newcastle confided to his brother that Carteret's 'chief view in all that he does or proposes to do, is the making court to the King by preferring Hanoverian considerations to all others'.[4] Pitt openly attacked him in the Commons as 'an execrable, sole minister, who had renounced the British nation and seemed to have drunk of the potion described in poetic fictions, which make men forget their country', a charge with added venom in view of Carteret's well known partiality for copious potations of burgundy.[5]

These attacks were somewhat unfair, for Carteret in fact had a much greater vision of Britain's role in Europe than that of mere handmaiden to Hanover. He was anxious to restore British prestige and power on the continent to a position which it had not enjoyed since the days of his mentor Stanhope, and he considered that Walpole had demeaned Britain's reputation by his pacific foreign policy. Like Stanhope he fancied himself in the role of arbiter of Europe and sought to build up a system of alliances which would guarantee Maria Theresa in her inheritances against the forces which threatened to deprive her of them, above all France. So far from isolating Hanover from this system he persuaded George II to renounce the Electorate's neutrality in 1742, which even Newcastle admitted was 'the best thing he ever did'. He envisaged a grand alliance of Austria, Britain, the Dutch Republic, Hanover and Savoy, such as had contained French expansion under Queen Anne. He never succeeded in realizing this ambition, but he took a step towards it in 1743 when he negotiated the Treaty of Worms between Britain, Maria Theresa and the king of Sardinia, Charles Emmanuel of Savoy.

While Maria Theresa had been occupied in continental Europe, Spanish forces had landed in her north Italian possessions. The assistance of Savoy, coupled with the British fleet, was considered vital to regain these territories. In the Treaty of Worms these powers allied, though at some cost in both land and money to Maria Theresa, who had to offer Charles Emmanuel Finale and other possessions and a subsidy of £200,000 from the £500,000 granted to her by Britain. To add insult to injury, where Savoy's £200,000 was to be paid for the duration of the war or as long as it was considered to be necessary, her remaining £300,000 was subject to no such guarantee. She therefore obtained from Carteret a supplement to the treaty assuring her subsidy on the same terms as that of Charles Emmanuel.

The Treaty of Worms and especially the supplement irritated the Pelhams for many reasons. In the first place, Carteret was abroad with the King at Hanover at the time and he took full advantage of being away from his colleagues to negotiate the treaty virtually on his own, hardly bothering to inform them what he was doing. His 'insufferable silences', as Newcastle called them, can be explained by the fact that he was affected by the death of his wife or by his lack of an adequate clerical staff. However, they could not be explained away to the Pelhams, who held them to be examples of the arrogance and contempt which Carteret habitually showed for them. Newcastle was particularly galled by the conclusion of a treaty with Savoy, which fell inside his sphere of interest as secretary of state for the southern department, with scarcely a reference to him.

The supplement, committing Britain to open-ended expenditure, was even less welcome to his brother. For in the summer of 1743 Henry Pelham became first lord of the treasury on the death of Wilmington, and was thus in charge of the nation's finances. Carteret had foreseen the difficulties which might be placed in the path of his foreign policy if a rival succeeded to the treasury, and had endeavoured to procure it for the earl of Bath. His plan was forestalled, however, by the earl of Orford, who still remained a potent force with the King even though he had ceased to be prime minister. Orford used his influence with George II to persuade him that Pelham was the best qualified to succeed Wilmington because of his financial ability and his leadership of the commons. In December he also succeeded Sandys as chancellor of the exchequer. Pelham's promotion gave him and Newcastle a majority in the cabinet, which they used at the end of the year to get it to reject the supplement in the Treaty of Worms by nine votes to four.

Brilliant though Carteret's diplomacy was, it did not achieve the results he desired. On the contrary, the Treaties of Hanau and Worms helped to bring Frederick II back into the war, while the projected coalition against the French was thwarted by the reluctance of the Dutch to come into the war as principals. The Pelhams became more and more convinced that this reluctance was due to Carteret's concern for Hanover, and that, in order to bring the Dutch in and consequently bring the war to a conclusion, he must go. Newcastle delivered an ultimatum to the King on 1 November 1744, in the names of himself and three cabinet colleagues and with the backing of seven other ministers. Its gist was that either the earl of Granville, as Carteret had become in October, should be dismissed or they would resign. George's first reaction was to send the memorial back without comment but, realizing that he could not simply ignore it, he tried to divide the Pelhamites. When this failed he turned to 'the other shop' he had passed over in 1742, the leaders of the main opposition groups, but these too replied 'that they could not serve with Lord Granville, or under him'. It seems, ironically, that the Pelhams had Bolingbroke to thank for blocking this line of retreat for the King.[6] The now superannuated tory politician had become a friend of Hardwicke's on his second return from France and was regarded, or at least regarded himself, as an elder statesman. George II was therefore obliged to capitulate, and Granville left the ministry. It was the second time in less than three years that the King had been forced to drop a minister who enjoyed his confidence and he petulantly let his displeasure be known.

The reconstruction following Granville's departure from the ministry brought about what was known as the Broad Bottom Administration, so-called because it included a wide cross-section of politicians. For the first time under the Hanoverians posts were offered to country tories, again thanks to Bolingbroke's intercession. Office was given to Sir John Hynde Cotton and John Philipps, who became respectively treasurer of the chamber and a commissioner of trade, while in the localities tory gentlemen who had not been justices of the peace for decades were at last allowed to sit on the commissions. The ministerial aspect of the reconstruction, however, was relatively short-lived. Within six months Philipps had resigned, while Cotton was dismissed in 1746. The main feature of the Broad Bottom was an alliance between the Old Corps and a number of politicians who were collectively called the 'new allies', to distinguish them from the now discredited 'new whigs'. The earl of Harrington replaced Granville, a move that was acceptable to the King. But when the Pelhams proposed the appointments of the earl of Chesterfield and William Pitt to the posts of lord lieutenant of Ireland and secretary at war, George refused to give office to two inveterate Hanover-baiters. To Chesterfield's claim, he riposted, 'he should have nothing: a peremptory command not to trouble him with any more of such nonsense; that he had been forced to part with those he liked; but would not be prevailed on to take into his service those that were so disagreeable to him'. The Pelhams, however, insisted until Chesterfield was grudgingly taken in, though they prudently dropped Pitt's pretensions.

Broad Bottom had the support of the Commons, the session of parliament which followed the changes being one of the quietest for some years. But it had not the backing of the King. As one supporter of it noted, 'the common vogue is that the outs are much caressed at

Court and the ins as remarkedly disregarded and that the broad bottom will soon be no bottom.'[7] George's resentment of the Pelhamite coup lasted a long time. He insisted that his hand had been forced, and that Granville had been removed from his service without his consent. For over a year he gave the Pelhams a hard time, insulting them in private and continuing to seek Granville's advice behind their back. Nor did the ministerial changes produce the kind of policy changes which the Pelhams had desired. The Dutch still refused to declare war on France, while it was found necessary to continue to pay the Hanoverian troops. To add to the difficulties of the Pelhams the outbreak of the 'Forty-Five' necessitated recalling the King from Hanover, and on his arrival he treated them more cavalierly than ever, openly showing his preference for Granville. A showdown was threatened in September but was averted until the danger of the rebellion receded. Then in February 1746, the final act in the drama was played.

The Pelhams took the initiative by again insisting that Pitt should be made secretary at war. George, determined not to give in to their demands, turned to Granville and Bath to rescue him from their clutches by forming a ministry. There ensued the mass resignation of the Pelhamites on 10 and 11 February. An astute observer commented:[8]

> The generality of mankind, who see only the outside of things, ascribe all this to the refusal of Mr Pitt to be secretary at war, but that point has been given up these ten days. The true source is the countenance given to Granville and Bath, who have generally opposed whatever had been proposed by the other party and obstructed all their measures. But the affair which immediately contributed towards this revolution was a proposition in council to carry on the war with the utmost vigour on the continent even though the Dutch should not declare war, which was opposed with one voice by all the Pelhamites, who finding the interest in the closet to increase against them resolved at last, though I fear too late, to make this stand for their country. If they could have been prevailed on to do it two years since some good might have accrued from it; but now I have no opinion of it, though many people say it will be impossible for these new men to go on but that they shall all be in again in a month or less.

Lord Chesterfield wrote to Newcastle that this would make it 'impossible that the two earls can carry on the business, unless they have a strength in parliament, which I am not aware of; for I take it for granted that by much the greatest part of your Old Corps will stick to you, and I cannot think that many of the old opposition will join them, so that, in my mind, your situation is better than it has been this great while, your way is clearer; you must be called for again; and that upon your own terms.'

Chesterfield's prophecy proved correct. Although Bath took over the treasury and Granville both secretaryships, their ministry scarcely lasted forty-eight hours. A satirical *History of the Long Administration* claimed that it lasted 'forty-eight hours, three quarters, seven minutes, and eleven seconds; which may truly be called the most wise, and most honest of all administrations, the minister having, to the astonishment of all wise men, never transacted one rash thing, and what is more marvellous, left as much money in the treasury as he found in it'. Many politicians refused to join it and one wit joked, 'it was not safe to walk the streets at night for fear of being pressed for a cabinet counsellor.' Granville and Bath had no alternative but to resign, though after the fiasco it was observed that 'Lord Granville is as jolly as ever, laughs and drinks; owns it was mad, and that he would do it again tomorrow.'

The Pelhams were reinstated, this time on their own terms. As far as they were concerned the most important condition was that George should give them his entire confidence. They were less concerned about the ministerial adjustments dependent upon their return. Most of Granville's remaining supporters in the ministry were rooted out, though some remained. Moreover, Pitt was not given the post of secretary at war, though the demand for it had ostensibly precipitated the crisis. Instead he had to settle for the lucrative but lesser posts of vice treasurer of Ireland and paymaster general. As J. B. Owen observed, 'These changes established the administration on the dual basis of the Old Corps and the new allies which was to endure, with minor alterations, until Pelham's death in 1754.'[9]

It was in the midst of the ministerial crisis that Charles Edward Stuart, the twenty-four year old 'Young Pretender', landed in the west of Scotland to raise a rebellion on behalf of his father James Edward. His first landing was on the island of Eriskay on 23 July 1745, with about a dozen companions and hardly any resources. A year before a much better equipped expedition, with French assistance, had set sail from France, but had been beaten back by a superior British fleet and bad weather. Now Charles arrived with such little help that even his supporters, dismayed at his chances, urged him to return. Yet within weeks he had an army of 1,500 men to confront the government forces under Sir John Cope, which numbered less than 4,000. Cope assembled his army at Stirling and marched north to intercept the Young Pretender, then thought better of it and diverted to Inverness instead. This move allowed the Jacobite army to proceed to Perth, gathering reinforcements all the time, including the so-called duke of Perth and Lord George Murray, whom the Prince made lieutenant generals. Under these leaders the Jacobites, now about 2,400 strong, crossed the Forth and took Falkirk. Government troops in Edinburgh, apart from the garrison of the castle, withdrew from the city to Prestonpans on their approach, leaving the Scottish capital open to the Prince. Charles entered Edinburgh early on 17 September. By 19 September the royal army, reinforced by Cope who joined it by sea from Inverness, advanced to try to retake the city. The Prince marched out to meet them, and the two armies, both of which numbered about 2,500, engaged in battle on 21 September at Prestonpans, where Cope's forces were routed. Cope himself fled to Berwick-upon-Tweed. Scotland was in the hands of the Young Pretender, while panic reigned in England.

Although Charles had triumphed in Scotland, it would be over-romantic to describe the subsequent invasion of England as a conflict between the Scots and the English. Scotland was far too divided by the rebellion for such a notion to hold. The royal army which inflicted the final defeat on the Prince's forces contained no fewer than three Scottish regiments, while in addition the government could count on the active support of such Scots as the duke of Argyll and Lord Loudoun. The division of loyalties in Scotland is often attributed to geography, the suggestion being that the lowlands were loyal and the highlands Jacobite; but even this is too simple. The most northerly clans, for instance, the Mackays, Monroes and Sutherlands, were strongly opposed to the Young Pretender, while many clans, such as the Gordons, Grants, Mackenzies and Mackin-toshes, were divided among themselves. The duke of Atholl was a Hanoverian, while his brother, Lord Tullibardine, fought for the Prince. No single generalization can do justice to the complexity of motives which led men to assemble in Edinburgh to support the rebellion during the six weeks which Charles spent there before moving south. Most Catholics and some episcopalians went there for religious reasons. Those who wanted to end the union, because it had subjugated Scotland to England or because they simply hated 'English' taxes, especially customs and excises on Scottish products, paradoxically joined forces with those who wished to subjugate England to Scotland. And doubtless there were those who went along for sheer adventure and the hopes of booty.

On 3 November the Jacobite army, now about 5,500 strong, left Edinburgh. It marched down to Carlisle, thus avoiding General Wade who was stationed in Newcastle upon Tyne with forces which included 6,000 Dutch troops brought over under the terms of a treaty whereby the United Provinces had promised to help defend the protestant succession. Although Wade tried to intercept the Prince he was unable to get further west than Hexham because the road was impassable after a snow storm. Proceeding via Preston, Manchester and Macclesfield the Jacobite army arrived at Derby on 4 December. There was then no army between the Prince and London for the duke of Cumberland, who had gone to meet him, was at Lichfield.

Fear gripped the capital. Initially the Jacobite landing had been dismissed as a trivial diversion, out of harm's way. After Prestonpans, however, it had to be taken seriously. A run on the Bank started as early as September, and demands for *specie* had to be stalled by payments in sixpences. As Charles marched south the value of stocks fell. Londoners improvised a variety of schemes to augment the trained bands in preparation for their own defence, mobilizing motley troops whose disarray and unpreparedness were satirized by Hogarth in *The March to Finchley*. In fact, and perhaps fortunately, they never heard a shot fired in anger, for on 6 December the Prince reluctantly sounded the order to retreat.

Charles had attracted very few converts to his cause in England. About three hundred had been organized into a regiment at Manchester under Francis Townley, but these were not enough to make up for those Scots who had deserted him between Edinburgh and Carlisle. Now his army of less than 5,000 was faced with troops under the duke of Cumberland numbering over 10,000 who were less than a day's march away, while Wade was hurrying down from the north with as many more. Together with the defenders of London the government had no less than 30,000 men to pit against Charles. The military prospects of taking England as well as Scotland were, to say the least, bleak. North of the border Jacobite chances seemed better, and so they began to march back the way they had come. Charles was hotly pursued up the west of England, his rearguard being engaged by the advancing forces under Cumberland near Penrith. The Jacobites managed to beat off their pursuers and crossed the border on 20 December. There Cumberland called off the pursuit and went south to resist an anticipated French invasion.

Since the departure of the rebels from Scotland most of the country had been retaken by government forces. Lieutenant General Handysyde, who had replaced Cope, had reoccupied Edinburgh, while Lord Loudoun held Inverness. Early in January 1746 the Prince marched east from Glasgow and took Stirling. On 17 January he engaged government troops under Lieutenant General Hawley at Falkirk. The battle was confused. As Hawley wrote soon after it, 'I can't say we are quite beat today, but our left is beat, and their left is beat.' Nevertheless he failed to stop the advance of the Jacobite army and retreated to Edinburgh. On 30 January he was replaced as commander by the duke of Cumberland, sent to Scotland when the threatened invasion failed to materialize. Next day Cumberland advanced to Linlithgow, forcing the Prince to call off his futile siege of Stirling Castle and to retreat towards Inverness. After hard going through thick snow over the pass of Killiecrankie the Jacobite army arrived at Inverness on 20 February. Cumberland advanced slowly after them by the more sheltered coastal route through Perth and Aberdeen. Finally, in April, at the head of 9,000 men he caught up with the half-starved rebels, who numbered about 5,000, at Culloden. There on 16 April the remnants of the Prince's army were cut to pieces by withering artillery. At the end of the day about a thousand had been slain. Charles fled, leaving the message, 'Let every man seek his own safety the best way he can.' After an epic journey he made his way back to France.

Jacobitism was now a completely spent force. Cumberland pursued the refugees from the Young Pretender's army to the remotest fastnesses, earning his nickname of 'the butcher' en route. Many were slaughtered in the retreat, and nearly 3,500 were captured. This fulfilled a prophecy made by one English MP, on hearing of alleged atrocities committed by the highland host in Carlisle, that 'when they come to be dispersed . . . they must expect to be massacred wherever they are found.'[10] About 120 rebels were executed. To make sure that the highlands would no longer be capable of rebellion the government passed a series of measures in 1747, the most significant of which were the Disarming Act and the act abolishing hereditary jurisdictions in Scotland. The first made the bearing of arms and even the wearing of kilts and tartans illegal. The second struck a blow at the power of the clans by taking away the right of chiefs to exercise jurisdiction separate from the king's courts and even the right to claim military service from their dependants. These acts eradicated, as far as legislation could, a complete culture and way of life.

The only serious threat the Pelhams had to face after 1746 came from Frederick, the Prince of Wales, who wanted 'to have the influence due to his rank'.[11] He clothed this not unnatural desire in the high language of rescuing his father from the toils of the Pelhams, which became more and more unconvincing as George II transferred to them the confidence he had previously placed in Walpole and Granville. Frederick attached to him, in Horace Walpole's words, 'the refuse of every party'—old Leicester House cronies, disappointed followers of Bath and Granville, the tories, again led by the now decrepit Bolingbroke, and a handful of renegades from the government, of whom the most conspicuous was George Bubb Dodington.[12] They never numbered enough to give the Pelhams great difficulties in parliament, nor did they have the talent to form a viable alternative to the Old Corps and its new allies. As Hardwicke had commented to the King in 1745, 'if your majesty looks around the House of Commons, you will find no man of business or even of weight left, capable of heading or conducting an opposition.' Their one hope lay in the general election which was expected to take place in 1748 when the septennial span of parliament ran out. The Pelhams nipped these hopes in the bud persuading George to break with the convention whereby seven years were allowed to elapse between dissolutions, and to dissolve parliament in 1747. As Dudley Ryder recorded on 4 June, 'The King has just taken resolution to dissolve the parliament at end of this sessions. The view is to disappoint the Prince, who is beginning to intermeddle in most of the boroughs against the next parliament in order to set up a violent opposition. But this measure will deprive him of a year's preparation and the flame intended to be raised next sessions by popular bills.'[13] The election of 1747 was one of the quietest of the century, with only sixty-two constituencies in England and Wales actually going to the polls. It resulted in the return of 338 ministerial supporters, 97 opposition whigs and 117 tories. This majority of over 120 ensured that Henry Pelham could now count on the support of both king and parliament as no politician had been able to do since the fall of Walpole.

Once Pelham's position was secure he wished to extricate Britain as soon as possible from the War of the Austrian Succession, primarily on account of the heavy financial burden which it placed upon the country. The national debt, which had stood at nearly £47 millions in 1739, rose to over £76 millions by 1748. As Pelham informed his brother in August 1748, 'I was in hopes, by a peace being soon made, and by a proper economy in the administration of the government afterwards, to have been the author of such a plan as might, in time to come, have relieved this nation from the vast load of debt it now labours under.'[14] Newcastle, however, was less impressed by the financial arguments and held out for a reversal of military fortunes which would bring the war out of stalemate into an advantageous position for the allies. This waiting upon events exhausted the patience of two fellow secretaries, Harrington and Chesterfield, who both resigned, the first in 1746, the second in 1748, before the duke agreed to accept terms of peace.

Negotiations were begun at Breda in 1746 and resumed at Aix-la-Chapelle the following year. The basis of a treaty lay in offsetting the gains of France and her allies on the continent against Austrian successes in Italy and British naval victories. In 1746 the French under Marshal Saxe had conquered the whole of the Austrian Netherlands and the next year had invaded Zealand, inflicting defeat on Britain and her allies at Lauffield. At the same time, on the death of Philip V of Spain in 1746 his successor Ferdinand had withdrawn Spanish forces from northern Italy, most of which fell to Austrian and Sardinian troops, who even made an abortive attempt to invade Provence in 1747. Meanwhile the British captured Louisburg in 1745, thereby acquiring Cape Breton, and inflicted defeats on the

French off Cape Finisterre and Belleisle in 1747. Peace was consequently signed in October 1748 on the broad basis of a restoration of conquests. Britain ceded Cape Breton while France abandoned the Austrian Netherlands. Maria Theresa, however, was obliged to recognize the cession of Silesia to Prussia and parts of her inheritance in northern Italy to Sardinia and Spain. Although Britain did not gain territorially, she obtained from France renewed recognition of the Hanoverian succession, symbolized by the expulsion of the Young Pretender by the French, and from Spain a renewal of the Asiento agreement until 1750.

Once peace was attained, Pelham could turn to the task of reducing the financial burden imposed by the war. It was a job for which he was well equipped, being in George II's opinion a better financier than Walpole. Within two years of the end of the war the number of troops had been reduced from 50,000 to under 19,000 and the number of seamen from over 51,000 to 10,000, while government expenditure was lowered from nearly £12,000,000 per annum to £7,000,000. By 1752 Pelham was able to reduce the land tax from four shillings in the pound to two shillings. In 1749 he introduced a measure to consolidate the national debt and to reduce the rate of interest from four to three per cent by 1757. His methods of managing the debt made the state less reliant on the three great financial corporations, the Bank, East India Company and South Sea Company, and also made recourse to the sinking fund less necessary.

Retrenchment implied a more pacific foreign policy, and this in turn involved Pelham in curbing the diplomatic ambitions of his brother. Even after the Peace of Aix-la-Chapelle, Newcastle pursued an active foreign policy: he intervened in Imperial politics in an attempt to ensure that the Archduke Joseph, son of Maria Theresa and the Emperor Francis II, would succeed to both his mother's hereditary lands and his father's title, thereby avoiding another war for the Austrian succession. Joseph's claim to the Habsburg territories was undisputed, but his succession to the Imperial throne could only be achieved with the support of the electoral college. A preliminary sounding of his chances of being elected emperor, however, could be obtained by the traditional method of having him first chosen as king of the Romans by the nine imperial electors. Four of them, including the Elector of Hanover, could be depended upon; but to gain a majority involved intrigues, bargains and ultimately money in the form of subsidies which only the British treasury could supply. Newcastle in fact approached Bavaria and Cologne in 1750 with offers of subsidy treaties, and temporarily succeeded. One opposition spokesman, in a pointed reference to the duke's electoral interests, observed 'with a sneer . . . that he approved *bribing electors*, as he saw *by other instances* how it had contributed to quash opposition'.[15] Pelham, as first lord of the treasury, objected to these subsidies, and was not sorry when his brother's attempts to create a majority for Joseph came to nought in 1752.

During these years the Pelhams faced remarkably little opposition from parliament. The Prince of Wales, realizing that he was reduced to political insignificance for the rest of his father's reign, could only make elaborate plans for his own. He was still working out the details of the changes which he planned to make on his own accession when he unexpectedly died in 1751. As under Walpole, the major threat to governmental stability came not from parliamentary opponents but from disputes in the ministry. The Pelhams themselves quarrelled and at one stage were reduced to communicating through an intermediary. More serious was the rivalry between Newcastle and the duke of Bedford, who had replaced Chesterfield as secretary of state in 1748. Newcastle despised Bedford for his hopeless inefficiency in office, and distrusted him on account of his intrigue with Lord Sandwich, first lord of the admiralty, against whom the duke bore a grudge for his independent initiatives during the peace negotiations. This rivalry strained relations in the cabinet until 1751, when Newcastle succeeded in replacing Sandwich at the admiralty with Lord Anson, whereupon Bedford promptly resigned, to be replaced as secretary by the earl of Holderness, a perfectly compliant colleague for the Pelhams. Bedford and Sandwich thereafter attached themselves to the duke of Cumberland, who picked up some of the shattered remnants of his brother's reversionary interest— enough at least to embarrass the ministry in its attempts to make the princess dowager rather than himself regent in the event of the death of George II while his grandson, the future George III, was still a minor.

During the last four parliamentary sessions of the Pelham administration a number of controversial bills were introduced which taken together show that the brothers were not prepared, like Walpole, to let sleeping dogs lie. For example, in 1751 the calendar was reformed and an effective gin act passed, while in 1753 a major change was made in the marriage laws and a bill enacted to facilitate the naturalization of Jews.

Lord Chesterfield was primarily responsible for the measure whereby England's calendar was brought into line with that used extensively in Europe. Until the sixteenth century western Europe had employed the Julian calendar, so-called because it was devised under Julius Caesar. By the time Gregory XIII became pope this was ten days out of phase with the solar year, largely because each centennial year had been regarded as a leap year. To compensate for this accumulation the Gregorian calendar, named after the pope, was devised, which added ten days to the Julian calendar and thereafter sought to keep pace with the solar year by making only every fourth centennial year a leap year. Since this was held to be a popish measure, much of protestant Europe including England declined to adopt it and stayed on the Julian calendar. The year 1600 was a leap year in both calendars, so that England remained only ten days behind the continent throughout the seventeenth century. In 1700, however, the Julian calendar added a leap day, while the Gregorian did not, so that thereafter England was eleven days behind the continent. Thus when it was 12 June in Paris it was 1 June in London, a situation which made life awkward for diplomats like Chesterfield as well as for historians of eighteenth-century diplomacy. To make matters even more complicated, the Julian calendar began the year on 25 March while the Gregorian started it on 1 January, so that 12 January 1751 in Paris was 1 January 1750 in London. To rectify this situation an act was passed in May 1751 which provided for the suppression of the eleven days between 2 and 14 September 1752, the second being followed by the fourteenth, while the new year was to commence on 1 January. The resultant outcry 'give us back our eleven days' is often dismissed as the blind reaction of an ignorant mob; but in fact the change gave reasonable grounds for concern at all levels of society, necessitating nice calculations about rents, leases, debts and wages, as well as superstitions about saint's days and holy days which were exploited by almanac makers, who devised calendars showing the 'old' as well as the new days for some years ahead.

The Gin Act of 1751 was the most effective of several laws passed in the early eighteenth century to regulate the consumption of spirits. Where previous measures had attempted to control the trade by adding swingeing duties to the price and restricting the issue of licences to retailers, with little or no effect, this concentrated on the distillers, stiffening the penalties for supplying gin to unlicensed retailers. Being much more readily enforceable it appears to have had the desired effect, for the orgy of gin-drinking abated shortly after its passage.

The concern for reform of the marriage laws which gave rise to Hardwicke's Marriage Act, so styled because it was framed by the lord chancellor, stemmed from aristocratic and gentry families who wished to control the choice of wives and husbands for their sons and daughters more effectively than existing provisions allowed. Although the proclamation of banns or the issue of a licence from the archbishop or diocesan were necessary steps towards matrimony, they did not prevent minors from marrying without the wishes or even the knowledge of their parents, particularly in London where, it was claimed, there was a regular trade in clandestine marriages especially in the neighbourhood of the Fleet Prison. Horror stories were told of how young gentlemen were inveigled into wedlock by prostitutes, and young ladies by confidence tricksters, with the connivance of unscrupulous clergymen, the notorious Fleet parsons. To stamp out this alleged practice Hardwicke proposed that the consent of guardians should be made explicit in the case of minors, that residence should be established and that marriage registers should be kept. The bill met with some opposition in parliament, especially from Henry Fox, who had himself clandestinely married the eldest daughter of the duke of Richmond. Fox argued that it delivered children up to the tyranny of their parents or guardians, whose choice of marriage partners was based more on material than on emotional considerations, and that it would consolidate the grip of a narrow oligarchy upon the landed property of England whose members would never marry outside their own circle. He also claimed that it would prove a great inconvenience to the poor, placing an unnecessary obstacle in their path to wedlock, and thereby discourage marriage and encourage vice. Despite these objections the bill was carried and became law in June 1753.

Opposition to the Jewish Naturalization Act was more successful. In itself this was a mild measure, merely making it easier to become naturalized by private acts of parliament, for instance by dropping the words 'on the true faith of a Christian' from the oaths of supremacy and allegiance. It was in part an acknowledgement of the help which City Jews like Sampson Gideon had given to Pelham's financial schemes, especially in the reduction of interest. The bill originally passed through the Lords without arousing much interest, let alone opposition, and although it ran into criticism in the Commons it received the royal assent in May 1753. Before the next session, however, its opponents gathered strength. A petition from the City of London had been presented to parliament protesting against the bill while it was still before the Commons, but after it became law it was attacked throughout the country as a betrayal of the Christian religion. 'The great clamour of 1753', as one historian has called it, was orchestrated by the opposition press, which wildly exaggerated the scope of the measure.[16] It was referred to as though it had actually naturalized Jews, when in fact it merely made it easier for them to apply for naturalization. In the more lurid literature, visions of England inundated with Jews seeking to become British subjects were turned into nightmares of the country being completely subjugated by them. When parliament reassembled the outcry was so vociferous that the ministry reluctantly agreed to repeal the act. It was the more readily persuaded to adopt this course since a general election was due in 1754, and the unpopularity of the act threatened its supporters with retribution at the polls. Just as Walpole had found with his excise scheme so Pelham realized with the Jewish Naturalization Act that it was imprudent to raise a popular clamour on the eve of an election. Like Walpole, Pelham withdrew.

He himself did not live to stand again for Sussex, which he had represented since 1722, for he died in March 1754. Although he seems a pallid prime minister between the robust Walpole and the manic Pitt, his more subdued manner concealed a shrewd and calculating politician. He was reserved and cautious, but behind the reserve there was steel. His low-key approach to politics was itself an asset which enabled him to reconcile very diverse politicians in the Broad Bottom Administration. All could agree on his integrity, which was remarkable in a venal age; unlike Walpole, he died poor. His sober and candid common sense, and above all his financial ability, overcame George II's initial dislike of him. So complete was their reconciliation that on hearing of Pelham's death the King exclaimed, 'now I shall have no more peace.'

# 12 Newcastle and Pitt

The duke of Newcastle succeeded his brother as first lord of the treasury. Newcastle's personal foibles, his extreme timidity, his compulsive chattering, his absurd anxieties about such matters as unaired beds, made him a prime object for the attentions of those eminent eighteenth-century gossips, Lord Hervey and Horace Walpole. Their anecdotes and reminiscences depicted a ridiculous and mediocre buffoon who has strutted through the ages masquerading as him. Yet they need to be balanced with an appraisal of the fact that he held high office for nearly fifty years, since nobody who did so could be totally incompetent, even in the eighteenth century. Some contemporaries were prepared to concede this much, even Lord Waldegrave grudgingly admitting that 'upon the whole, he seems tolerably well qualified to act a second part, but wants both spirit and capacity to be first in command.'[1] Newcastle acted a second part from 1717 to 1754, first as lord chamberlain and then, after 1724, as secretary of state.

This long continuance in office is itself a measure of the political stability which the early Hanoverians managed to establish in England, and the duke epitomizes those aristocratic whigs who underpinned that stability by their complete commitment to the protestant succession, and their readiness to spend money and effort on maintaining it. Indeed he probably expended more of both than anybody else. Although he did not bankrupt himself by electoral activities so much as by keeping up a ducal style of living, itself a necessary ingredient of his political success, he did maintain an extensive interest in a number of scattered constituencies. It is sometimes suggested that he owed his favour in high places to his electoral patronage and his willingness to make it available to the Court, but this undervalues his usefulness to the government in other spheres. The very fact that he left behind him the largest collection of papers for any politician of his age in itself documents the astonishing degree to which he was prepared to do the essential donkey work of a system which depended upon patronage. There was scarcely a sphere of activity left untouched by this noble drudge.

When he became prime minister in 1754, however, his promotion bore out Waldegrave's remark. Newcastle failed to keep his brother's system going. He inherited the backing of George II; but he lost the confidence of the Commons to William Pitt. It was not until the establishment of the Pitt-Newcastle ministry in 1757 that the two essential prerequisites of power, which had upheld the Pelhams for eight years, the favour of the crown and the support of the Commons, were again to be combined behind the same ministers.

Newcastle did not lose the confidence of the Commons because he lost a general election. On the contrary, the results of the 1754 election were more favourable to the ministry than those of 1747, producing a government majority of over two hundred, the largest in the century. The duke himself had much to do with bringing about this result, presiding for the first time over the government's electoral management as well as his own constituencies and spending £27,000 in the process, which helped to return some seventy members. He was delighted at this outcome, claiming 'the parliament is good beyond my expectations, and I believe there are more whigs in it, and generally well disposed whigs than in any parliament since the Revolution.'[2]

The trouble was that by taking over as prime minister from his brother, Newcastle was reverting to the system which had obtained before Walpole. Since the death of Sunderland in 1722 the prime minister had sat in the Commons. As Newcastle's closest adviser, Lord Hardwicke, admitted, 'the precedents of my Lord Godolphin's and my Lord Sunderland's time have been overruled by the long habits of seeing Sir Robert Walpole and Mr Pelham there [in the Commons] which go as far back as the memory of most people sitting there . . . reaches.'[3] Certainly it was necessary, as Pitt told Newcastle, for there to be 'a minister *with the king* in the House of Commons', by which he meant a cabinet minister.[4]

A central issue in the political conflict of the years following the death of Henry Pelham was that the duke of Newcastle's inheritance of the full powers exercised by his brother was contested by those who argued that he could not lead the Commons effectively from the Lords. They did not insist that the prime minister should be a commoner, merely that he should yield the direction of the Commons to a colleague of cabinet rank, one who enjoyed access to and the confidence of the king. Otherwise, they argued, the leader of the house would not command sufficient respect from its members. The credit of the crown not merely enhanced the dignity of a minister but was absolutely vital to enable the leader of the lower house to function effectively.

Despite the fact that George II is sometimes seen as a figure-head king, obliged to surrender effective power to ministers such as Walpole and the Pelhams, he was in fact still the source of all authority.[5] Ministers were very much the king's ministers and were even regarded as his servants. The king's willingness to grant access to the closet, signified by his promotion of a minister to cabinet rank, was a practical as well as a symbolic gesture: his refusal could cramp the style of any politician who aspired to the leadership of the Commons. These constitutional and political facts of life made Newcastle's position as prime minister doubly difficult, since his search for a man to lead the Commons was restricted to those whom George was prepared to tolerate. At the best of times the King had not been easy to get along with and, ever since his accession, politicians from Walpole onwards had suffered from his impatience and irascibility. Age had not mellowed him, for even Lord Waldegrave, a sympathetic if not sycophantic observer, admitted in 1758 that George at the age of seventy-four did not disguise his feelings 'when anything disagreeable passes in the closet, when any of his ministers happen to displease him'.[6] Newcastle's problem, therefore, was to recommend to the King a politician acceptable to them both who was prepared to lead the Commons.

There were two men ready to perform this task: Henry Fox, who was secretary at war, and William Pitt, who was paymaster. Neither of them was in the cabinet. Fox, a notorious libertine, 'had been bred a tory . . . but being reconciled to the principles of the Court, by the friendship of his brother with Lord Hervey . . . was made surveyor of the works, and on Mr Pelham succeeding to the head of the treasury . . . was made a commissioner'. When Pelham died Fox made a bid for the premiership, but was outmanoeuvred by Newcastle and Hardwicke. He was then in the duke of Devonshire's connection, which in 1754 was in league with the duke of Cumberland, while Pitt was associated with Lord Cobham's nephews, George Lyttleton and the Grenvilles, 'the cousinhood' as Lord Waldegrave called them, who were currently associating with the dowager princess of Wales. Thus both were connected with the 'reversionary interest', Fox to the man who would assume formidable executive power in a regency should George II die while his grandson was still a minor, Pitt to the young Prince himself. Like his father Frederick before him, the future George III, although only sixteen in 1754, was at odds with the reigning king. As Horace Walpole observed, 'it ran a little in the blood of the family to hate the eldest son.'[7] As the 1750s progressed Leicester House once again became a focus for opposition politicians who attached themselves to the fortunes of young George, his mother and his tutor Lord Bute. Ironically in view of their animosity towards him when George eventually became king, Pitt was one of the first to court their favours.

Yet their connections with the duke of Cumberland and Leicester House gave neither Fox nor Pitt a power base. Both had achieved political prominence in the Commons more for their appeal to the independent country gentlemen than from any significant parliamentary interest. It is true that Fox was 'a most disagreeable speaker . . . inelegant in his language, hesitating and ungraceful in his elocution', yet he was 'skilful in discerning the temper of the house, and in knowing when and how to press, or to yield'.[8] Pitt by contrast was a most fluent orator, capable of spellbinding the Commons with scathing denunciations of ministers, even when they were his own colleagues, and with impassioned appeals to patriotism. He was also a master of the popular theatrical gesture, such as his ostentatious refusal to take the substantial perquisites of the pay office, which endeared him to the backbenchers.

Neither of them was completely acceptable to Newcastle as leader of the lower house. Fox's savage attacks on Hardwicke's Marriage Act the previous year, in which he had not spared the lord chancellor some personal abuse, were not forgotten. At the same time Pitt's sarcastic opposition to the Hanoverian connection was still remembered by George II, who personally preferred Fox; and so Newcastle offered him the post of secretary of state. Fox initially accepted, but soon resigned when he realized that he was not to have much say in policy or patronage, which was effectively to inhibit his management of the lower house. As he himself complained, 'he should not know how to talk to members of Parliament, when some might have received *gratifications*, others not.' He therefore returned to his former post. Sir Thomas Robinson, an able diplomat but in parliamentary terms a nonentity, was accordingly made secretary. There was still effectively no 'minister with the king in the House of Commons'.

Frustrated by their failure to achieve positions of real authority, Fox and Pitt tried to force their claims to higher office by thwarting the measures of their fellow ministers in the Commons. Thus the situation arose whereby the main opposition to the cabinet's proposals came not from those out of office but from their junior colleagues on the treasury bench. Being ministers they could scarcely attack policy, but as Waldegrave commented 'they might attack persons, though not things.' They poured scorn on Robinson, smeared the attorney general, William Murray, with the taint of Jacobitism, and even criticized Newcastle himself as a 'too powerful subject'. The duke, harassed by these exasperating tactics, decided to buy one of them off, and in December 1754 gave Fox a place in the cabinet without ministerial responsibility. Pitt, chagrined at being overlooked, then broke with Fox and exploited his own nuisance value even more determinedly in parliament.

What Pitt needed was a cause to use to discredit the government. One was presented to him with the deteriorating situation overseas, which could be blamed on Newcastle. In 1754 relations between the British and the French in North America, seldom friendly, became positively hostile when a skirmish occurred on the Ohio in which the French commander was killed but the colonial forces, led by George Washington, were obliged to surrender. Early in 1755, therefore, Newcastle sent troops under General Braddock to America and ordered Admiral Boscawen to prevent French supplies reaching Quebec, by way of reprisals. News of both expeditions leaked; Braddock's troops were defeated near Fort Duquesne and their leader killed, while Boscawen managed to prevent only two French vessels from entering the St Lawrence. Newcastle's reaction to these developments was to order reprisals against French merchants, which even Granville condemned as 'vexing your neighbours for a little muck'.

By 1755 it was becoming increasingly clear that the clash of British and French interests overseas would eventually provoke strife in Europe, and probably sooner rather than later. To safeguard Hanover during the forthcoming conflict became a paramount objective of Newcastle's diplomacy. He sought to achieve the security of the Electorate by subsidizing such German princes as he felt were capable of being bribed not to side with the French when war broke out.

Pitt's reaction was characteristically opportunistic. He criticized this policy as 'a mean and subsidiary system' and took the lead in denouncing it in the house. 'Are these English measures?' he asked. 'They will hang like a millstone about the neck of any minister and sink him along with the nation.' One of his associates, Henry Legge, the chancellor of the exchequer, actually refused to sign the warrants for the Hessian subsidy until it had been approved by parliament. Such actions persuaded the ministers to seek an accommodation with Pitt, but at the same time further alienated the King who insisted that they should look to Fox instead; in November 1755 Fox became secretary of state again and this time he was made leader of the Commons. When parliament met, Pitt was scathing about the alliance of Fox with Newcastle, comparing it in a notorious speech to the confluence of the Rhône and Saone, 'this a gentle, feeble, languid stream, and though languid, of no depth—the other, a boisterous and impetuous torrent'. Newcastle, goaded beyond endurance, dismissed

Pitt and his associates Legge, George Grenville and Charles Town-shend.

If the preliminaries to the Seven Years' War had given Pitt opportunities to denounce Newcastle's policies from within the government, the opening of hostilities in 1756 was to provide him with far more ammunition which he was able to use to better effect now that he was no longer a minister. Newcastle's search for Hanover's security initiated the 'diplomatic revolution', which committed Britain more firmly than ever to continental conflict of the kind criticized by Pitt. When the revolution was complete the British, who had allied with Austria against France and Prussia in the previous war, fought the ensuing conflict in alliance with Prussia against Austria and France. The breach with Austria was a break with the old whig system of alliances which had been based on a combination of Britain, the United Provinces and the Austrian Habsburgs in opposition to France. This had made sense during the War of the Spanish Succession, but the subsequent decline of the Dutch, the acquisition of Hanoverian interests by Britain, and above all the rise of Prussia removed much of the common ground between the old allies. The Dutch became intent on avoiding war at any cost, British ministers sought as much to defend Hanover as to contain France, while the Austrians were more concerned to protect themselves against Frederick the Great than against Louis XV; this last point was made clear to Newcastle in 1755 when proposals to renew the Anglo-Austrian treaty against France foundered on Vienna's insistence that defence against Prussia should also be included in the treaty. In order to protect Hanover, therefore, the duke turned initially to Russia, with whom the Convention of St Petersburg was signed in 1755. The king of Prussia, who was alleged to fear Russia more than God, took alarm at this Anglo-Russian rapprochement, and sought to neutralize its effect by coming to terms with Britain himself, which he did in January 1756 when he negotiated the Convention of Westminster. The diplomatic revolution was completed when Austria and France allied in response to this convention. Newcastle's alliance with Prussia to protect Hanover was grist to Pitt's mill that British interests were being sacrificed for the defence of the Electorate. Pitt argued that he was prepared to allow Hanover to be overrun while Britain concentrated on obtaining French territory outside Europe. Then when war ended extra-European gains could be traded for the recovery of the Electorate.

Events elsewhere also strengthened Pitt's case against Newcastle. In May 1756 the French took Minorca, a victory which was generally attributed to Admiral Byng's calling off an engagement with the French fleet and withdrawing to Gibraltar. Newcastle's reaction to the news was, typically, panic: 'this war is hopeless and may be ruinous.' He determined to find a scapegoat in the unfortunate Byng, assuring a City deputation that 'he shall be tried immediately, he shall be hanged directly.' News from America was no more reassuring, for in May an attack on Fort Niagara failed, while in August Oswego, a fort on Lake Ontario, fell to the French.

These disasters, especially the loss of Minorca, raised a popular clamour. 'This loss', wrote Waldegrave, 'was the principal cause of that popular discontent and clamour which overturned the administration; or rather occasioned the panic, which obliged our ministers to abdicate.' One ballad of the day contained the words 'to the block with Newcastle and the yardarm with Byng'. Nine counties and several towns addressed the King demanding an inquiry. A novel form of political satire, the caricature, often attributed to George Townshend, first made its appearance in England during the outcry over Minorca. The furore influenced the independent country gentlemen and threatened the government's control of the Commons. Newcastle, isolated in the Lords, needed able lieutenants in the lower house to stave off the expected attack from Pitt. His best spokesmen there were William Murray, the attorney general, and Henry Fox. Then suddenly, to Newcastle's great consternation, he lost their good offices. Murray insisted on becoming lord chief justice of the king's bench when the post fell vacant, and was promoted to the Lords as Baron Mansfield. Even more devastating was Fox's resignation from the secretaryship in October. Although Newcastle had borne the brunt of the outcry against the loss of Minorca in the summer, Fox was apprehensive that when parliament met, since he was 'the only figure of a minister' in the Commons, he would then draw 'all the odium' upon himself.

Deserted by Murray and Fox, Newcastle threw in the towel and resigned on 11 November. His resignation might be seen as his typical reaction to a crisis. Certainly his latest biographer is of the opinion that there was nothing in the circumstances which necessitated so drastic a step; the government had not experienced a defeat in the Commons, nor was likely to do; 'the duke simply lost his nerve.'[9] But there was more to it than that. Although the ministry had a parliamentary majority on paper, in practice this was insufficient. Pitt appreciated this when he warned the duke not to rely on a paper majority: 'Indeed, my Lord, the inside of the house must be considered in other respects besides merely numbers, or the reins of government will soon slip or be wrested out of any minister's hands.' He complained that Newcastle's style of government had reduced the Commons to 'an assembly of atoms; the great wheels of the machine are stopped.' Without a policy which won the approval of the independent country gentlemen, and lacking a firm direction which would keep the 'Old Corps' in line, Newcastle lost the confidence of the Commons. In part this was the result of his attempt to govern from the upper house. In part it stemmed from his style of leadership, which imposed so little sense of direction and uniformity upon the ministry that it is hard to see in what sense he was a prime minister. As Pitt complained:[10]

> I don't call this an administration, it is so unsteady. One is at the head of the treasury; one, chancellor; one, head of the navy; one great person, of the army— yet is that an administration? They shift and shuffle the charge from one to another; says one, I am not general; the treasury says, I am not admiral; the admiralty says, I am not minister. From such an unaccording assemblage of separate and distinct powers with no system, a nullity results.

And no doubt in part Newcastle's resignation stemmed from his peculiar psychology, his inveterate timidity and liability to worry over trifles and to panic in an emergency. But in the end Newcastle resigned because he dare not face the consequences of Pitt's wrath being directed against him in the Commons without an able leader there to protect him.

After his resignation George II tried desperately to avoid the unpalatable task of putting Pitt at the head of the ministry, but this proved impossible and the Great Commoner took office virtually on his own terms. The first of these was a refusal to serve with Newcastle, and instead the duke of Devonshire became first lord of the treasury. This made Devonshire nominal prime minister and saved George the technical embarrassment of actually asking Pitt to form a ministry. But though Pitt remained secretary of state, he was in practice head of the administration. Thus he insisted that Henry Legge should be chancellor of the exchequer, when Devonshire himself would have preferred Fox, and replaced Anson at the admiralty with Lord Temple. He also dictated the policies which the ministry pursued. One of its first acts was to send home foreign troops in England brought over by Newcastle to secure the country against a possible French invasion. Pitt hoped to make England independent of such humiliating assistance by settling the militia on an effective defence footing. When the measure he pushed to effect this was eventually implemented in 1757, however, it caused riots. Another controversial military move was his raising of two regiments from highland Scots who had taken part in the 'Forty-Five'. Pitt was particularly proud of the way in which he employed their martial valour *for* rather than *against* the state.

The Pitt–Devonshire ministry was short-lived. It was on shaky foundations in both the Commons and the closet. In parliament the

Old Corps still regarded Newcastle as its leader, and had the timid duke had the courage to form an opposition the new ministry could scarcely have survived. Instead he held back from opposing Pitt in the Commons, though the Great Commoner was aware of his weakness there, and tried to offset the Old Corps by reliance on the independent country gentlemen. He was realistic enough to acknowledge that his supporters would prove a broken reed in an emergency, and accepted that without some realignment of parliamentary forces he would probably only survive one session.

The only hope of consolidating his position lay with the King, but it became increasingly manifest that George was utterly opposed to him. He particularly disliked having Temple foisted upon him as first lord of the admiralty, finding him personally objectionable. 'As to Temple', George protested to Waldegrave, 'he was so disagreeable a fellow, there was no bearing him, that when he attempted to argue, he was pert, and sometimes insolent; that when he meant to be civil he was exceedingly troublesome, and that in the business of his office he was totally ignorant.'[11] He appealed to Waldegrave and other leading politicians to rescue him from the obnoxious ministers, even asking them to save him the trouble of dismissing them by outvoting them in parliament. Waldegrave, however, warned him that 'ministers being routed by parliament might be a bad precedent.'[12] The only way out of George's difficulties was to form an alternative administration.

It is true that Pitt attempted to mollify the King by excessive obsequiousness when in the royal presence. He also tried to reassure George that he was not antagonistic to the Electorate of Hanover by asking the Commons to vote supplies 'for the just and necessary defence and preservation of the Electoral dominions'. He even went out of his way to applaud the Prussian treaty, which he had vehemently denounced when in opposition. But all this was to no avail. It merely shocked the independents in the Commons who had hoped for a 'Country' foreign policy when Pitt took office, and yet did nothing to reassure the King. Pitt also lost some of his popularity when he came out against Byng's execution. At a time when the whole country seemed to be clamouring for the admiral's blood, with addresses coming in from nine counties and the City of London demanding his execution, Pitt urged a reprieve both on the King and parliament. This was not only unpopular but unavailing, and on 14 March 1757 Byng was executed, as Voltaire sardonically commented, 'pour encourager les autres'. Pitt's temporary unpopularity gave the King the nerve to dismiss him. George's fear that Pitt's policy would jeopardize Hanover was shared by his son the duke of Cumberland, who refused to go to the continent as commander-in-chief unless his father dismissed the prime minister. In April 1757 the King obliged by summarily removing Pitt from office.

Pitt was aware that his activities in office had somewhat tarnished his image as the Country patriot, and carefully retrieved it by getting eighteen cities in the control of tories and Country whigs sympathetic to him to confer upon him the honour of freeman.[13] In Horace Walpole's celebrated phrase, 'for some weeks it rained gold boxes.' During these weeks Britain was without a government, and it was not until Newcastle and Pitt were reconciled and agreed to take office together in June that political stability was restored. Newcastle again took the treasury and thus was nominally prime minister, while Pitt became secretary though he was effectively the premier, for he would not join with the duke 'unless sure of power'. This gave the ministry the combined support of the Commons and the King, and produced equilibrium for the first time since the death of Henry Pelham. It was to last until the death of George II. Meanwhile it was on such broad foundations in parliament that opposition almost disappeared. Newcastle commanded the allegiance of the Old Corps, those Court whigs who had upheld the government since the days of Walpole, while Pitt appealed to the independent country gentlemen, both tory and whig. Court and Country were thus united and together enjoyed an unbeatable majority.

While tranquillity reigned at home, abroad these were among the most dynamic years in British history. Britain was engaged in a global struggle against France; in Europe, in North America, in the Caribbean, in Africa, even in India.

The war between Britain and France which broke out in May 1756 following the French attack upon Minorca broadened out to include Prussia and Austria when Frederick the Great invaded Saxony at the end of August. Although Prussia had taken the initiative, Austria survived the assault and in June 1757 inflicted a heavy defeat on Frederick at Kolin. The Hanoverian army under the duke of Cumberland was likewise defeated at Hastenbeck in July by the French, who thereby virtually conquered Hanover. Cumberland, blaming 'the tory doctrine of a sea war' for his difficulties, negotiated with them a convention at Klosterseven in September which was in effect a capitulation. A naval expedition sent from England to Rochefort in an attempt to distract the French from harassing Hanover and Prussia was a dismal failure. By the end of October 1757 the French were in control of Ostend in the Austrian Netherlands while the Russians occupied Berlin. Just when it seemed as though all British interests on the continent were lost, however, Frederick retrieved the situation by defeating the combined forces of Austria and France first at Rossbach in November and then at

Leuthen in December. These successes enabled Pitt to persuade the King to repudiate the humiliating Convention of Klosterseven and even to dismiss Cumberland from the command of the army, which was an ironic reversal of their roles in April. The duke was replaced at home by Pitt's friend Ligonier, and abroad by the much more competent Prince Ferdinand of Brunswick, who drove the French out of Hanover, pushing them across the Rhine in April 1758 and defeating them in the battles of Rheinberg and Crefeld in June. Frederick of Prussia, fortified with an annual subsidy of £670,000 voted by the British parliament in April, defeated the Russians at Zorndorf in August. Pitt continued his policy of strategic naval expeditions to assist the continental campaign, successfully sending Commodore Holmes with a squadron to capture Emden in February, and despatching rather less impressive combined forces to raid St Malo and Cherbourg. The cost of these expeditions to France was so out of proportion to the damage they inflicted that the French joked about the English going to break their windows with guineas. After another futile attempt on St Malo, with heavy losses, they were abandoned.

The continental war went badly for the allies in 1759, despite the victory of Ferdinand of Brunswick over the French at Minden on 1 August. Even this success was blighted for Britain by Lord George Sackville's refusal to obey an order to advance, for which he was cashiered by a court martial. A few days later Frederick the Great's army was pulverized by Austro-Russian forces at Kunersdorf in Saxony. A new spirit had entered French councils with the appointment of Choiseul in 1758, and it became manifest in the following year with elaborate plans for an invasion of England. Fortunately for the British government these plans were intercepted by the secret service, and in July Admiral Rodney attacked the boats lying in Le Havre in wait for the invasion. Indeed British naval operations in this year more than offset the gloomy military situation on the continent. In August the French Mediterranean fleet was defeated off Lagos, in Portugal; while in November their Brest fleet was destroyed by Admiral Hawke in Quiberon Bay. The year 1759 was in fact the 'wonderful year' proudly celebrated in the sea-shanty 'Hearts of Oak'. Not only did it witness defeats for the French along the Mediterranean and Atlantic coasts of France itself; it was also celebrated for bringing victory to British arms in North America, the West Indies and Africa.

At the outset of the Seven Years' War the colonial interests of Britain and France were causing friction at the vague edges of their territorial influence in North America. The thirteen British colonies which were to become the United States of America, together with

Newfoundland and Nova Scotia, impinged along their western frontiers upon huge French territories which stretched from the mouth of the St Lawrence across to the Great Lakes and down the Mississippi to New Orleans. There was a state of undeclared war between the colonists of the two nations throughout the early eighteenth century, which was merely exacerbated when formal hostilities were declared in Europe. The westward expansion of British settlers met with a determined French effort to contain them, a determination which had led to the construction of a chain of forts from New Orleans to Quebec in the years before 1756. The French indeed were on a much better military footing at the outset of the war for, as Waldegrave admitted, 'though our colonies were superior to those of the enemy in wealth and the number of inhabitants, the French were as much our superiors in military discipline: almost every man amongst them was a soldier, most of the Indians were attached to their interest.' They took the initiative under Montcalm by capturing Fort William Henry on Lake George in August 1757, at a time when a British attack on Louisburg was called off by Lord Loudoun. However, Loudoun was replaced by Amherst in 1758 and a more spirited attack made on Louisburg in July, this time with success. Meanwhile forces under Abercromby advanced against Montcalm as far as Ticonderoga, where they met with formidable resistance and were forced back. Another expedition under Colonel Forbes took Fort Duquesne in November, renaming it Fort Pitt, which later became Pittsburgh.

The opening shots in the North America campaign scarcely presaged the complete collapse of French power on the continent which occurred in 1759 and 1760. During the summer of 1759 Amherst gained the French forts of Niagara, Ticonderoga and Crown Point. In Canada, after a long combined operation involving seamen and soldiers, Saunders and Wolfe succeeded in taking Quebec from the French on 13 September, Wolfe dying in the moment of victory. The capture of Quebec signalled the end of French power in Canada. Amherst followed up Wolfe's success in 1760, taking Montreal in September. In October he wrote to Pitt, 'I can assure you, Sir, this country is as quiet and secure as any other province of his majesty's dominions.'

During the seventeenth century the British had acquired scattered possessions among the West Indian islands, but the French had taken the lion's share of the pickings left after earlier Spanish colonization. Thus among the Leeward and Windward Islands Britain claimed a string from the Virgin Islands in the north to Barbados in the south, but the French held the two richest, Guadeloupe and Martinique. An expedition was sent out under Admiral Hopson to gain one of these prizes to use as barter for the return of Minorca, and initially attempted to take Martinique in January 1759. Repulsed from that island it went on to capture Guadeloupe in May, adding Marie Galante in June.

At this time the British and the French had only a foothold in Africa, France owned factories on the west coast including Senegal and the island of Goree. An expedition under Captain Marsh and Major Mason, again superbly coordinating naval and military tactics, took Fort Louis, Senegal, in April 1758. Another under the command of Commodore Keppel captured Goree later in the year, and although technically this victory did not belong to the *annus mirabilis* of 1759, it can be included among its successes since news of the capture did not reach England until then.

Both the French and English East India Companies had factories in India: the main French possessions were Pondicherry, Surat and Calicut, while Bombay, Calcutta and Madras were in British hands. As in North America there was a permanent state of friction between the rival powers which formal declarations of war in Europe only heightened. During the war of the Austrian Succession the French had taken the initiative under Dupleix, commander at Pondicherry, and had actually captured Madras, although this was returned to Britain at the Treaty of Aix-la-Chapelle. This treaty did not, however, end hostilities in India, which took the form primarily of a diplomatic war between Dupleix and the British governor at Madras, Thomas Saunders, for the allegiance of rival native rulers. One of the agents employed by the East India Company to foment these rivalries was Robert Clive, formerly a clerk in their employment. When the Seven Years' War broke out the strategic manoeuvrings were intensified. The first major development was the capture of Calcutta by the subahdar of Bengal, an ally of the French, and the imprisonment in the notorious Black Hole of those who did not escape. George Pigot, who had replaced Saunders as governor in 1755, sent Clive to retake Calcutta, which he did in January 1757, and defeated the subahdar in the battle of Plassey in June, replacing him with an English puppet ruler.

Although Clive ousted the French from Bengal they were still formidable rivals to the British in the south, where they again beseiged Madras in 1758. This time the garrison held out, and the appearance of an English fleet in February 1759 raised the siege. After that British forces under Eyre Coote took the offensive, and completely overcame French military power in India with the capture of Pondicherry itself in January 1761.

British arms were thus engaged in a global conflict during the Seven Years' War, fighting on all four known continents. To what extent this was seen as a world war in England at the time depends to some extent on the interpretation of Pitt's strategic policies. To his admirers the Great Commoner had a global conception of strategy, and sought to coordinate activities in all theatres of war, including even India. Thus he expressed his concern to protect British interests in the east and to support expansion in India against the French in various ways—sending a new regiment out to help Coote, which arrived in 1759; getting an annual subsidy of £20,000 voted for the East India Company while hostilities lasted; and considering the acquisition of Mauritius to hamper the French supply route. Pitt had a family interest in Indian affairs for his grandfather Thomas had been governor at Madras in Anne's reign; but it is hard to see how he could have integrated military campaigns there in a total plan of strategy, given the immense difficulties of communication. It could take two years for news of events in India to reach England and for instructions to get back.

It is possible that he conceived of the Atlantic as a single strategic area, and employed the navy to coordinate the war effort in theatres in Europe, Africa and America. He certainly used raids on the French coast as diversions to the military campaigns in Germany, although it is doubtful whether the results were worth the cost and effort which had to be put into them. He also grasped the importance of North America and the East Indies and realized that gains there could be used to offset territories lost in Europe.

Yet there were so many contradictions in his approach to strategy that it is hard to see how he reconciled them even in his own mind. In opposing Newcastle's subsidy system he argued that Britain should not engage in a costly continental war but should make her main effort at sea. This was in essence the old tory 'blue water' policy, traditionally dear to the hearts of the country gentlemen on the backbenches who disliked huge standing armies and the heavy financial burdens they imposed, not least on their own estates, yet were prepared to pay for an active navy. When in office, however, he supported the king of Prussia up to the hilt, to the tune of £670,000 a year, and in 1761 was paradoxically to claim that he had conquered Canada in Germany.

In reaction to the tendency to give Pitt all the credit for the successes of the war and to applaud the brilliance and originality of his strategic thinking, there has been of late a movement in the opposite direction which rather belittles the man and his achievement. Certainly he was unpleasant, devious, inconsistent, impossible to work with, subject to alternate bouts of frenzy and despair, a megalomaniac even, at one time telling Devonshire, 'I am sure I can save this country and nobody else can.' Yet at the same time his demonic energy inspired awe, fascination and enthusiasm for the war in his ministerial colleagues and in the admirals and generals who fought the campaigns.

Of course it was not just a one-man show. The government which led Britain to its greatest triumphs in the eighteenth century also deserves praise. Newcastle's efforts in raising the prodigious sums involved, £15,500,000 being voted for the year 1760 alone, tend to be underestimated, and certainly were by Pitt. Anson, the hero of the circumnavigation of 1740 to 1744, was a superb first lord of the admiralty who should be given much of the credit for the magnificent way in which the navy was deployed in so many theatres during the hostilities.[14] So should the admirals Boscawen, Hawke, Rodney and Vernon. The generals who carved out new empires from French control in America and India, Amherst, Wolfe and Coote, actually fought and won the battles. Pitt is often praised for choosing such excellent officers, but he was lucky, for his choice tended to be hit and miss and some of his appointments, for example, Hopson who failed to take Martinique, were uninspired.

It is sometimes asserted that Pitt welded the different parts of the administration into an efficient war machine, supervising and even superseding the activities not only of his cabinet colleagues but also of junior ministers and humble clerks. An analysis of his administrative measures, however, fully bears out Horace Walpole's judgment that he 'kept aloof from all details, drew magnificent plans, and left others to find the magnificent means'.

When all due allowance is made for Pitt's shortcomings, however, and credit given to others where it is due, the fact remains that he was a great war minister. His theatrical posturings and belligerent rhetoric were exactly what the country needed, a vision of itself greater than that projected by his predecessors as prime minister, the pacific Walpole, the able but self-effacing Pelham, the timid and neurotic Newcastle. Perhaps only Granville had the potential to see a world role for Britain, but he was long past his prime, and rarely sober. In the last analysis Pitt's greatness can only be measured against the rival alternatives, and here he was a giant among pygmies. None realized this more than John Brown, who published a celebrated *Estimate of the manners and principles of the times* in 1757, the gist of which was that the country was being weakened by effeminacy. The following year he brought out *An Explanatory Defence of the Estimate*, praising Pitt for restoring national vigour.

Unfortunately Pitt's obsession with the war blinded him to the growing desire for peace, even or perhaps especially among the country gentlemen who applauded his greatest feats. By 1760 they were beginning to look askance at the rocketing war budgets, and to wonder if Britain had gained enough overseas to enable her to withdraw with profit from a continental war which looked like being prolonged indefinitely, as the armies of Frederick and Ferdinand seemed to be deadlocked in the struggle against Austria, France and Russia. Frederick suffered the humiliation of a Russian occupation of Berlin between 9 and 12 October, but rallied sufficiently to defeat the Russians at the battle of Torgau on 3 November. Ferdinand spent most of the summer sparring with the duke de Broglie in the region between Kassel, Korbach and Warburg. Although he defeated the French at Warburg on 31 July, that same day Broglie took Kassel, which filled the allied commander with despair. To compensate for the loss of Kassel, and to divert Broglie from Hanover, Ferdinand attempted to take Wesel on the Rhine, but a surprise attack on the French at Kloster Kamp, near Wesel, on 16 October failed, and the allied army withdrew having lost 1,615 men, most of them British.

The growing unease among English taxpayers was brilliantly exploited by Israel Mauduit in his *Considerations on the present German War*, which appeared in 1760. Julian Corbett, who compared its effect with that of Swift's *The Conduct of the Allies*, and who speculated that its real author might have been Lord Hardwicke, expressed its gist: 'with merciless cogency he points out the political folly of a country with a weak army and a powerful navy engaging in a war between continental states ... and all for the integrity of a small German province in which England had no real interest.'[15] 'And what is this Germany to Britain?' the pamphlet demanded:

> Could we but be true to ourselves, and pursue the advantage which providence has put into our hands, and by seizing our enemies islands, make ourselves masters of that trade.... Let then the French rage as they please; let them bribe and threaten the several German courts, till they learn to unite; let the Empire suffer French armies to march from the Rhine to the utmost Danube; and pillage every city in their passage, from Manheim to Belgrade; all these cannot build a single frigate to annoy our coast with.

While George II lived, Pitt could afford to ignore the growing war weariness and pacific sentiments which his erstwhile supporters were now expressing, but with the death of the old king on 25 October 1760 there came to the throne a monarch who shared such views himself. In his first address to the privy council the young George III referred to 'this bloody and expensive war', and although Pitt managed to moderate the criticism by changing the expression to 'expensive, but just and necessary war' when the speech was published, it was obvious that the policies of the prime minister and the attitude of the new monarch were fundamentally at variance. It was an ironic fate for Pitt, who had risen to prominence as a patriot who attacked the Hanoverian connection on most occasions, to be committed to a major war in defence of Hanover at the accession of a patriot king who boasted that he gloried in the name of Briton, and despised 'that horrid Electorate'. Pitt might have been as Dr Johnson put it, 'a minister given by the people to the king' in 1757; but in 1760 he no longer caught the popular mood. Those who paid the piper began to call the tune of peace, which Pitt would not, and perhaps could not, play. George III demonstrated on his accession that he intended to be the piper himself, and that peace would indeed be his theme. In doing so he initiated a sequence of events which was to transform the political scene in the next three years.

# Notes

## 1 Constitution

1 W. A. Speck, *Tory and Whig: the Struggle in the Constituencies, 1701–1715* (London, 1970), p. 16. Compare Geoffrey Holmes, *The Electorate and the National Will in the First Age of Party* (Lancaster, 1976), p. 23.

2 John Dennis, *Vice and Luxury Publick Mischiefs: or Remarks on . . . The Fable of the Bees* (London, 1725) p. xvi.

3 Browne Willis, *Notitia Parliamentaria* (3 volumes, London, 1715–50), II p. 172.

4 T. H. B. Oldfield, *An Entire and Complete History . . . of the Boroughs of Great Britain* (6 volumes, London, 1792) II, p. 155.

5 D. Defoe, *A Tour through the Whole Island of Great Britain*, edited by P. Rogers (London, 1971), p. 252. Defoe observed that 'several inmates, or lodgers, will, sometime before the election, bring out their pots, and make fires in the street, and boil their victuals in the sight of their neighbours, that their votes may not be called in question.'

6 See table below, pp. 297–8.

7 Betty Kemp, *King and Commons* (London, 1959) appendix B, p. 149, provides a table of the numbers of MPs vacating seats on appointment to office. Of the 509 who did so between 1715 and 1761, 115 were not subsequently returned to the house. Most of these, however, were appointed to offices which disqualified them from sitting in the Commons while others did not stand for re-election. See R. Sedgwick, editor, *History of Parliament: the Commons, 1715–1754* (2 volumes, London, 1970) and Sir Lewis Namier and J. Brook, editors, *History of Parliament: the House of Commons, 1754–1790* (3 volumes, London, 1964).

8 Defoe, *op. cit.* p. 128.

9 J. Macky, *A Journey through England* (5th edition, 2 volumes, London, 1732) II, p. 41. On pages 278–90 Macky published a contemptuous list of decayed Cornish boroughs.

10 N. Curnock, editor, *The Journal of the Rev. John Wesley (standard edition,* London, n.d.) IV, p. 100.

11 *The Old Whig* no. 1, 19 March 1719. Addison was defending the peerage bill, which the opposition attacked as being a threat to the balanced constitution. Both sides agreed that the balance was desirable and that the constitution reflected and preserved it. Differences of emphasis arose over

the nature of the relationship between the three powers. Some writers asserted that they should be independent of each other, others that they should be interdependent. Usually the opposition argued the desirability of independence and insisted that the dependence of the Commons upon the crown was constitutionally undesirable, while the Court maintained the necessity for interdependence. Paradoxically, in the debates on the peerage bill, Court supporters urged the importance of making the House of Lords independent of the crown, while the opposition insisted that the royal prerogative of making peers was essential for the well being of the constitution. Steele, for instance, who took issue with his old collaborator Addison on the peerage bill, argued that it could not make the Lords so independent that England would become an aristocracy. *The Plebian* no. 1, 14 March 1719.

12   *The Third Charge of Sir Daniel Dolins to the Grand Jury and other Juries of the County of Middlesex; at the general quarter sessions of the peace held the sixth day of October, 1726* (London, 1726) pp. 2–3. See also his first *Charge*, of 7 October 1725 and his second *Charge*, of 8 April 1726, which was a paean to the 'immense and inexhaustible treasures of happiness, which we are blest withal', p. 33. Compare the *Charges* of Whitelocke Bulstrode to the Grand Jury and other Juries of Middlesex . . ., 21 April and 9 October 1718 and 4 October 1722; Sir Richard Cocks, *A Charge given to the Grand Jury of the County of Gloucester at the Midsummer Sessions 1723*; and the *Charges* of Sir John Gonson . . . to the Grand Jury of the City and Liberty of Westminster, 24 April and 11 July 1728 and 3 July 1729.

13   R. Wallace, *Characteristics of the Present Political State of Great Britain* (London, 1758), quoted in H. T. Dickinson, editor, *Politics and Literature in the Eighteenth Century* (London, 1974) p. 121.

14   T. Gordon and J. Trenchard, *Cato's Letters* (4 volumes, London, 1755) I, pp. 91–2: no. 14, 28 January 1721.

15   Dickinson, *op. cit.* p. 82.

16   J. Locke, *Two Treatises of Government*, edited by P. Laslett (Cambridge, 1960) p. 395.

17   S. and B. Webb, editors, *English Local Government from the Revolution to the Municipal Corporations Act* (9 volumes, London, 1906–29) I, p. vi.


## 2   Social Structure

1   D. Defoe, *A Review of the State of the British Nation*, 22 January 1709.

2   Joan Thirsk and J. P. Cooper, *Seventeenth-century Economic Documents* (Oxford, 1972), p. 795.

3   David Hume, *Essays Moral, Political and Literary* (Oxford, 1963), p. 579.

4   Defoe *op. cit.*

5   See table in appendix, pp. 297–8, which should be consulted to clarify the discussion in this chapter.

6   G. Holmes, 'Gregory King and the Social Structure of Pre-industrial England', *Transactions of the Royal Historical Society* XXVII (1977).

7   Defoe *op. cit.* J. Jean Hecht, *The Domestic Servant Class in Eighteenth-century England* (London, 1956).

8   *Craftsman* no. 43, 5 May 1727.

9   *Remarks on the Laws relating to the Game* (1753), pp. 5–6.

10   J. Warburton, *London and Middlesex illustrated by a true and explicit account of the names, residence, genealogy and coat armour of the nobility, principal merchants and other eminent families trading within the precincts of this most opulent city and county (the eye of the universe) all emblazoned in their proper colours, with references thereunto; shewing in what manuscript books, or other original records of the herald's office, the right of each person respectively may be found: in justification of the subscribers, and others, who have been encouragers of the new map of London and Middlesex, whose arms are engraved therein: and at the same time to obviate that symbolical or heraldic mystery (so industriously inculcated by some heralds) that trade and gentility are incompatible until rectified in blood by the sovereign touch of Garter King of Arm's scepter* (London, 1749).

11   G. Miège, *The Present State of Great Britain* (1715), p. 169.

12   See J. Ray, *A Compleat Collection of English Proverbs*, (3rd edition, 1737), p. 245, where the explanation is given that Cales or Calais knights 'were made . . . by Robert earl of Essex to the number of sixty, whereof (though many of great birth) some were of low fortunes: and therefore Queen Elizabeth was half offended with the earl, for making knighthood so common. Of the numerousness of Welch gentlemen, nothing need be said, the Welch generally pretending to gentility. Northern lairds are such who in Scotland hold lands in chief of the king, whereof some have no great revenue. So that a Kentish yeoman (by the help of hyperbole) may countervail etc.'

13   J. C. Beckett, *Landownership in Cumbria, 1680–1750* (unpublished PhD thesis, University of Lancaster, 1976); Miège, *op. cit.* p. 170.

14   *The Travels through England of Dr Richard Pococke*, edited by J. J. Cartwright, (2 volumes, London, 1888–9) I, p. 12.

15   *Lord Macaulay's Essays and Lays of Ancient Rome* (London, 1893), p. 735. 'Towards the close of the year 1715, while the rebellion was still raging in Scotland, Addison published the first number of a paper called the Freeholder. Among his political works the Freeholder is entitled to the first place. Even in the Spectator there are few serious papers nobler than the character of Lord Somers, and certainly no satirical paper superior to those in which the Tory foxhunter is introduced. This character is the original of Squire Western, and is drawn with all Fielding's force, and with a delicacy of which Fielding was altogether destitute.'

16   J. Macky, *A Journey through England*, p. 30. 'I thought myself here in Holland', he continued, 'the houses having all rows of trees before their doors, with benches to sit on, as there, and little gardens behind.'

17   Defoe, *A Tour through the Whole Island of Great Britain*, p. 171.

18   Macky, *op. cit.* p. 148.

19   R. G. Wilson, *Gentlemen Merchants* (London, 1971), p. 214.

20   R. Robson, *The Attorney in Eighteenth-century England* (London, 1959), p. 86.

21   E. Hughes, 'The Eighteenth-century Estate Agent', in H. A. Cronne,

T. W. Moody and D. B. Quinn, editors, *Essays in British and Irish History* (London, 1949), especially p. 193; G. E. Mingay, editor, *Land Labour and Population in the Industrial Revolution* (London, 1967), especially p. 10.

22   Quoted in N. Sykes, *Church and State in England in the Eighteenth Century* (Cambridge, 1934), p. 157.

23   Macaulay, *History of England*, edited by T. F. Henderson, (London, 1907), pp. 86–7.

24   G. E. Mingay, *English Landed Society in the Eighteenth Century* (London, 1956), pp. 86–7; R. A. C. Parker, *Coke of Norfolk* (Oxford, 1975), p. 33.

25   W. G. Hoskins, *The Midland Peasant* (London, 1957), pp. 226, 244; Mingay, *op. cit.* p. 86.

26   Sir George Clark, *A History of the Royal College of Physicians* (London, 1966) II, p. 540.

27   Quoted in B. Hamilton, 'The Medical Professions in the Eighteenth Century', *Economic History Review* IV (1951), p. 148.

28   Defoe, *The Compleat English Tradesman* (3rd edition, 2 volumes, 1732) I, pp. 1–2, 329.

29   Robson, *op. cit.* p. 54.

30   *The Present Taxes compared to the Payments made to the Publick within the Memory of Man* (1749), p. 51.

31   R. Williams, *Keywords* (London, 1975), p. 53.

32   *A Short Essay on the Corn Trade* (1758) p. 5. Compare W. J. Shelton, *English Hunger and Industrial Disorders* (London, 1973).

33   *The Vices of the Cities of London and Westminster traced from their Original* (n.d.), p. 49.

34   D. Gadd, *Georgian Summer: Bath in the Eighteenth Century* (London, 1971), p. 56; *A Journey from London to Scarborough* (1734), p. 44.

35   Defoe, *Compleat English tradesman, op. cit.* I, p. 2.

36   J. Breus, *The Fortune Hunters* (1754), p. 15.

37   Defoe, *Review, op. cit.*

38   C. W. Chalklin, *The Provincial Towns of Georgian England* (London, 1974), p. 5.

39   *Luxury Pride and Vanity the Bane of the British nation* (1747), p. 10.

40   *Queries relating to the Poor of England* (1720).

41   9 George II, c. 22, quoted in E. P. Thompson, *Whigs and Hunters* (London, 1975), p. 270.

42   G. Howson, *Thief-Taker General: the Rise and Fall of Jonathan Wild* (London, 1970), p. 238.

43   *Ibid.* pp. 312–14.

44   Thompson, *op. cit.* pp. 94, 156, 163.

45   *Bulletin of the Society for the Study of Labour History* (1972), p. 14.

46   P. Linebaugh, 'The Tyburn Riot against the Surgeons', in D. Hay, P. Linebaugh and E. P. Thompson, editors, *Albion's Fatal Tree* (London, 1975), p. 88.

47   T. Alcock, *Observations on the Defects of the Poor Laws and on the Causes and Consequences of the Great Increase and Burden of the Poor* (1752), p. 15.

48   J. Smith, *Memoirs of Wool* (2 volumes, 1756) I, p. 83.

49   Quoted in E. P. Thompson, 'Time, Work-discipline and Industrial

Capitalism', in M. W. Flinn and T. C. Smout, editors, *Essays in Social History* (Oxford, 1974), p. 56.
50 *Observations on the Office of Constable* (1754), p. 27.

## 3 Social Change

1 For the shortcomings of the evidence for estimating the population between 1700 and 1801 and the difficulties involved in interpreting it, see M. W. Flinn, *British Population Growth, 1700–1850* (London, 1970), pp. 16–24. The pattern suggested here is taken from J. D. Chambers, *Population, Economy and Society in Pre-industrial England* (Oxford, 1972), p. 19.

2 O. Levine, 'The Demographical Implications of Rural Industrialization: a Family Reconstituted Study of Shepshed, Leicestershire, 1600–1851', *Social History* II (1976). In Shepshed the mean age of marriage dropped between 1750 and 1824 from 28·5 to 24 for men and from 27·4 to 24·1 for women.

3 Compare Levine, *op. cit.* p. 189 for the argument that the falling mean age of marriage in Shepshed could have led to a significant increase in population, so much so that whereas the rate of reproduction between 1700 and 1749 would have doubled the population in just over two hundred years, that obtaining between 1750 and 1824 would have achieved the same result in forty years.

4 Though serious dissent is expressed in J. D. Post, 'Famine, Mortality and Epidemic Disease in the process of Modernization', *Economic History Review*, XXIX (1976), p. 37.

5 *An Answer to Dr William Brackenbridge's Letter*, p. 37.

6 *Four Topographical Letters written in July 1755* (1757), p. 55. 'It stands on the side of a hill, forming nearly a half moon; the lower part is filled with the workshops and warehouses of the manufacturers, and consists chiefly of old buildings; the upper part of the town, like St James's, contains a number of new, regular streets, and a handsome square, all well built and well inhabited.'

7 D. Defoe, *A Review of the State of the British Nation*, 22 January 1709.

8 J. Beresford, editor, *Memoirs of an Eighteenth-century Footman* (London, 1927). Macdonald served twenty-eight masters in thirty years.

9 Adam Smith, *The Wealth of Nations*, edited by A. Skinner, (London, 1974), p. 245.

10 H. Fielding, *A Proposal for making an Effectual Provision for the Poor* (1753), pp. 24–5, 73–4. There was in fact an act of William III's reign which protected people against removal within forty days of arriving in a parish if they could produce a certificate from the officers of a parish where they had a settlement.

11 R. A. C. Parker, *Coke of Norfolk*, p. 17.

12 E. Hughes, *North-country Life in the Eighteenth Century* (2 volumes, Oxford, 1952, 1965) I, p. 3.

13 J. C. Beckett, *Landownership in Cumbria, 1680–1750*.

14 *Observations on the Past Growth and Present State of the City of London* (1751), p. 19.

15  R. G. Wilson, *Gentlemen Merchants*, p. 136.
16  G. Jackson, *Hull in the Eighteenth Century* (London, 1972), pp. 110–14.
17  *ibid.* p. 106.
18  *Letters from a Moor at London to his Friend at Tunis* (1736), p. 42.
19  D. Defoe, *The Compleat English Tradesman* I, p. ix.
20  *An Account of Several Workhouses for Employing and Maintaining the Poor* (1725).
21  *ibid.* p. 34.
22  *Rules and Orders to be observed by the Officers and Servants in St Giles's Workhouse, and by the Poor therein* (1726).
23  *An Account of several Workhouses, op. cit.* pp. 53–4.
24  F. M. Eden, *The State of the Poor: or, an History of the Labouring Classes in England* (3 volumes, London, 1797) I, p. 283.
25  Alured Clarke, *A Collection of Papers relating to the Country Hospital for Sick and Lame etc. at Winchester* (1737), p. iv.
26  *A Short View of the Frauds, Abuses and Impositions of Parish Officers with some Considerations on the Laws relating to the Poor* (1742).
27  T. Alcock, *Observations on the Defects of the Poor Laws* (1752), p. 37.
28  *Letters from a Moor at London, op. cit.* p. 27. In fact the 'Moor' was almost certainly an anonymous Englishman.
29  Burridge, *An Answer to Dr William Brackenbridge's Letter, op. cit.* p. 36.
30  *Luxury, Pride and Vanity the Bane of the British nation* (1747), pp. 4, 17.
31  James Burgh, *Britain's Remembrancer* (3rd edition, 1747), p. 15.
32  R. M. Wiles, *Serial Publication in England before 1750* (Cambridge, 1957), p. ix.
33  Burgh, *op. cit.* p. 18.
34  Defoe, *A Tour through the Whole Island of Great Britain*, p. 520.
35  D. Hay, P. Linebaugh and E. P. Thompson, editors, *Albion's Fatal Tree*, p. 20.
36  *An Account of the Endeavours that have been used to Suppress Gaming Houses* (1722), p. 26. In 1757 gaming could still be said to be 'the capital pleasure, as well as trade, of most men of fashion'. John Brown, *An Estimate of the Manners and Principles of the Times* (7th edition, 1758), p. 41.
37  *Cato's Letters*, nos. 31 and 33, 27 May and 17 June 1721.
38  Defoe, *Compleat English tradesman, op. cit.* I, p. ix.

## 4  The Established Church and its Rivals

1  Spencer Cowper, editor, *The Diary of Mary Countess Cowper* (London, 1864), p. 4, corrected from the MS. in Hertfordshire Record Office.
2  Quoted in D. B. Horn and Mary Ransome, editors, *English Historical Documents, 1714–1783* (London, 1957), p. 197.
3  N. Sykes, *Church and State in England in the Eighteenth Century* (Cambridge, 1934), p. 36.
4  B. Williams, *The Whig Supremacy* (2nd edition, Oxford, 1962), p. 81.
5  Sykes, *op. cit.* p. 120.
6  *ibid.* p. 187.
7  E. Cobden, *An Essay tending to Promote Religion* (1755), pp. 39, 43.

8   M. Murault, *Letters describing the Character and Customs of the English and French Nations* (1726), pp. 6–7.

9   J. Brown, *An Estimate of the Manners and Principles of the Times*, (7th edition, 1758), p. 85.

10   T. Stackhouse, *The Miseries and Great Hardships of the Inferior Clergy in and about London* (1722), p. 83.

11   Quoted in Sykes, *op. cit.* p. 228.

12   *A General View of our Present Discontents* (1710), p. 25.

13   *The Anatomy of the Heretical Synod of Dissenters at Salter's Hall* (1719), pp. 7, 20.

14   H. Broxap, *The Later Nonjurors* (London, 1924), p. 214. *The Causes and Reasons of the present Declension among the Congregational Churches in London and the Country* (1766), p. 2 agreed that methodism 'has been very injurious to the dissenting interest'.

15   British Library Lansdowne MS. 1024 f. 492.

16   Horn and Ransome, *op. cit.* pp. 408–9.

17   *ibid.* p. 408.

18   *The Works of . . . William Warburton* (7 volumes, London, 1788–94) I, p. 264; *A Short Way with Prophaneness and Impiety*.

19   S. Chandler, *The Scripture Account of the Cause and Intention of Earthquakes* (1750), p. 32.

20   G. Burnet, *History of My Own Time* (6 volumes, Oxford, 1833) III, p. 242.

21   C. R. Cragg, *From Puritanism to the Age of Reason* (Cambridge, 1966), p. 82.

22   A. Boyer, *The Political State of Great Britain* (London, 1715) IX, p. 64.

23   N. Curnock, editor, *The Journal of the Rev. John Wesley* II, p. 377.

24   J. Beecham, editor, *The Works of the Rev. John Wesley* (11th edition, 14 volumes, London, 185 V, pp. 14–21; VIII, pp. 327–8, 333.

25   *A short history of Methodism* (1765), p. 5.

26   British Library Additional MS. 33029 f 73.

27   *The works of . . . William Warburton, op. cit.* IV, p. 626.

28   H. Rimius, *A candid narrative of the rise and progress of the Herrnhutters, commonly called Moravians* (1753).

29   J. S. Simon argued that 'there can be no doubt that the relationship between the "religious societies" and the "united societies of the people called methodists" was so close that the latter cannot be understood without an intimate knowledge of the former.' J. S. Simon, *John Wesley and the Religious Societies* (London, 1921), p. 5; but its exact nature is extremely difficult to establish. There seems to have been little in the way of continuity. On the contrary, members converted to methodism were apparently expelled from the societies, which led Whitefield to protest that the methodists had far more in common with the original aims of the religious societies than had their descendants: 'the first religious societies answered as to their spirit, experience and ends of meeting to the methodists's societies, as face answers to face in the water.' *A Letter to the Right Reverend the Bishop of London* (London, 1744), p. 22. For the societies for reformation of manners see T. C. Curtis and W. A. Speck, 'The Societies for Reformation of

Manners: a Case Study in the Theory and Practice of Moral Reform',
*Literature and History*, no. 3 (1976).
30   J. Breus, *The Fortune Hunters* (1754), p. 103.
31   Rowland Hill, *Imposture Detected*.
32   T. Barnard, *An Historical Character relating to the Holy and Examplary Life of the Right Honourable Lady Elizabeth Hastings* (1742).
33   T. Jollie, *A Sermon preached to the Societies for Reformation of Manners at Salter's Hall on Monday October 1st, 1739* (1739), p. 19.
34   J. Walsh, 'Elie Halevy and the Birth of Methodism', *Transactions of the Royal Historical Society* xxv (1975), p. 19.
35   *The Bristol Riot* (1714), p. 6. 'Those high church colliers hardly ever heard of religion, till Cheverel [sic] was the word.'
36   Walsh, *op. cit.* p. 17.
37   W. J. Warner, *The Wesleyan Movement in the Industrial Revolution* (London, 1936), pp. 230–31.

## 5   The Economy of Early Hanoverian Britain

1   Daniel Defoe, *A Tour through the Whole Island of Great Britain*, p. 54. The same theme also informs Defoe's *The Compleat English Tradesman*. In the first volume he illustrated his notion of a national economy with examples of how ordinary domestic consumption stimulated demand for goods made throughout England. For example, the wardrobe of a country grocer's wife would contain clothes made in twelve different parts of the country. i, p. 332. In the second volume he stressed how demand from the capital stimulated home industries by concluding 'it is not the kingdom makes London rich, but the City of London makes all the kingdom rich.' ii, p. 140.
2   London poll book, 1722, preface.
3   Sarah Fielding, *The Adventures of David Simple* (Cambridge, 1973), p. 76.
4   G. Rudé, *Hanoverian London* (London, 1971), p. 146.
5   *ibid.* p. 20.
6   *A Proper Reply to the Scandalous Libel . . . the Trial of the Spirits*, quoted in Dorothy George, *London Life in the Eighteenth Century* (London, 1931), p. 331.
7   J. Wimpey, *Rural Improvements* (1775), quoted in G. E. Mingay, 'The Agricultural Depression, 1730–1750', *Economic History Review* viii (1956), p. 336.
8   J. E. Handley, *Scottish Farming in the Eighteenth Century* (London, 1953); T. C. Smout, *A History of the Scottish People, 1560–1830* (London, 1972), pp. 111–25, 271–81; W. Ferguson, *Scotland, 1689 to the Present* (Edinburgh, 1968), p. 170. It is interesting that corn prices in Scotland did not fall between 1730 and 1750 as they did in England. R. Mitchison, 'Scottish Corn Prices in the Seventeenth and Eighteenth Centuries', *Economic History Review* xvii (1965), p. 288.
9   *Ways and Means to Raise the Value of Land* (1736), p. 7.
10   P. Fritz, *The English Ministers and Jacobitism* (Toronto, 1975), pp. 148–49; W. A. Speck, *Tory and Whig: the Struggle in the Constituencies, 1701–1715*, p. 120.
11   *Four Topographical Letters written in July 1755* (1757), pp. 62–3.

12 'Several hundred hands are employed in it, insomuch that £20,000 a year is paid in wages.' A. Young, *A Six Months Tour through the North of England* (4 volumes, 1770) III, p. 13. See also M. W. Flinn, editor, *The Lawbook of the Crowley Ironworks* (Durham, 1957).

13 P. Deane and W. A. Cole, *British Economic Growth, 1688–1959* (Cambridge, 1962), p. 58.

14 Defoe, *Tour, op. cit.* p. 429.

15 Arthur Young, *A six weeks tour* (London, 1768), p. 251; *A six months tour, op. cit.* IV, pp. 580–5.

16 Defoe, *Tour, op. cit.* pp. 436, 439–40.

17 Quoted in W. Albert, *The Turnpike System in England* (Cambridge, 1972), p. 180.

18 J. Woodward, *An Account of the Rise and Progress of the Religious Societies* (1701), preface.

19 A. Smith, *The Wealth of Nations*, p. 517.

20 *An Enquiry into the Melancholy Circumstances of Great Britain* (?1743), p. 36.


# 6  The Making of the English Ruling Class

1 E. Burke, 'Reflections on the Revolution in France', in B. W. Hill, editor, *Edmund Burke on Government, Politics and Society* (London, 1975), p. 309.

2 *ibid.* p. 317.

3 Cornwall Record Office, Carew Pole MS. BO/29/63.

4 G. Burnet, *History of My Own Time* VI, p. 224.

5 A. Foord, *His Majesty's Opposition* (Oxford, 1964), p. 296.

6 J. Macky, *A Journey through England* II, p. 235.

7 J. Brooke, *The House of Commons, 1754–1790: Introductory Survey* (Oxford, 1964), p. 167.

8 R. Patten, *The History of the late Rebellion* (London, 1717) pp. 93–4.

9 Christ Church, Oxford, Wake MS. 17, i, f. 242: W. A. Speck, *Tory and Whig*, pp. 121–2.

10 Bodleian MS. Carte 117, f. 177.

11 Bodleian MS. Eng. Misc. e, 180. f. 4. quoted in G. S. Holmes and W. A. Speck, editors, *The Divided Society: Party Conflict in England, 1694–1716* (London, 1967), p. 135.

12 *The Freeholder* no. 22, 5 March 1716.

13 *The End and Design of God's Judgments* (1722), p. 25.

14 R. A. C. Parker, *Coke of Norfolk*, pp. 15, 19, 20.

15 G. C. A. Clay, *Two Families and their Estates: the Grimstons and the Cowpers from c. 1660–c. 1815* (unpublished PhD thesis, Cambridge, 1966), p. 215.

16 P. G. M. Dickson, *The Financial Revolution* (Oxford, 1967), p. 295.

17 J. H. Plumb, *Sir Robert Walpole* (2 volumes, London, 1956, 1960) I, p. 367.

18 *Craftsman* nos. 134, 331, 332.

19 'English advice to the freeholders of England', in Sir Walter Scott, editor, *Somers' Tracts* (London, 1815), XIII, p. 523.

20 *Craftsman* no. 346.

21  A. Boyer, *The Political State of Great Britain for 1711* (London, 1718), p. 275.

22  Bolingbroke, *A Letter to Sir William Windham* (1753), p. 22.

23  G. V. Bennett, *The Tory Crisis in Church and State* (Oxford, 1975), p. 294.

24  J. H. Plumb, *The Growth of Political Stability in England, 1675–1725* (London, 1967), p. 168.

25  *Craftsman* no. 151.

26  H. M. Atherton, *Political Prints in the Age of Hogarth* (Oxford, 1974), p. 100.

## 7  The Establishment of the Hanoverian Dynasty

1  H. T. Dickinson, *Bolingbroke* (London, 1970), p. 130.

2  A. Boyer, *The Political State of Great Britain* (London, 1715), IX, pp. 16–17.

3  For George I's relations with Schulenberg and Kielmansegge see Ragnild Hatton, 'George I as an English and a European Figure' in P. Fritz and D. Williams, editors, *The Triumph of Culture* (Toronto, 1972), pp. 192–8.

4  British Library Additional MS. 47028 f. 7.

5  G. deForest Lord, editor, *Poems on Affairs of State* (7 volumes, New Haven, 1962–75) VII, edited by F. Ellis, pp. 617–25.

6  G. Burnet, *History of My Own Time* VI, p. 13.

7  Lord Campbell, *Lives of the Lord Chancellors* (London, 1846) IV, pp. 428–9.

8  G. C. Parke, editor, *Letters and Correspondence of . . . Henry St John, Lord Viscount Bolingbroke* (London, 1798) I, p. 11.

9  W. Cobbett, *Parliamentary History* (London, 1811) VII, pp. 21–4.

10  Dickinson, *op. cit.* p. 162.

11  Boyer, *op. cit.* X, p. 168.

12  W. Michael, *The Beginnings of the Hanoverian Dynasty* (London, 1936), p. 28.

13  Bolingbroke, *Works* (London, 1844) I, p. 140.

14  N. Tindal, *The Continuation of Mr Rapin's History of England* (London, 1753) XVIII, p. 314.

15  Boyer, *op. cit.* X, p. 121.

16  Sir Charles Petrie, *The Jacobite Movement* (London, 1959), p. 232.

17  *ibid.* p. 249.

18  Bolingbroke, *op. cit.* p. 148.

19  Michael, *op. cit.* p. 39.

20  J. H. Plumb, *Sir Robert Walpole* I, p. 221.

21  J. Oldmixon, *The History of England* (London, 1735), p. 635.

22  Boyer, *op. cit.* IX, p. 25.

23  Michael, *op. cit.* p. 281.

## 8  Stanhope's Ministry

1  *An Excellent New Ballad: being the Second Part of the Glorious Warrior* (London, 1710).

2  F. Ellis, editor, *Poems on Affairs on State* (New Haven, 1975) v, p. 401.
3  A. Boyer, *The Political State of Great Britain* (London, 1715) ix, pp. 394–6.
4  British Library Additional MS. 47028, f. 257: Sir John Perceval to Charles Dering, December 1718.
5  *ibid.* f. 223: same to same, 6 February 1718.
6  P. G. M. Dickson. *The Financial Revolution*, p. 101. This account of the Bubble is largely derived from Dickson's.
7  British Library Additional MS. 47029, f. 40: Perceval to Byrd, 15 October 1720.
8  Dickson, *op. cit.* p. 158.
9  *ibid.*
10  N. A. Brisco, *The Economic Policy of Robert Walpole* (New York, 1907), p. 24.
11  J. H. Plumb, *Sir Robert Walpole* i, p. 316.
12  *ibid.* p. 339.
13  Dickson, *op. cit.* p. 176.
14  *ibid.* p. 198.
15  Historical Manuscripts Commission 14th report, appendix ix, Onslow MSS, p. 504, quoted in Dickson, *op. cit.* p. 160. Compare Sir John Perceval's comment in June 1720: 'The top tories have now condescended to put themselves in the Court list for subscriptions to South Sea, and all the papists who had money are deep in the stock, so that were the Pretender to attempt a new invasion he would be surprised to find what numbers of his old friends would wish him at the bottom of the sea.' British Library Additional MS. 47029, f. 34.
16  See the contests in Bedford, Bodmin, Colchester, Queenborough, Liverpool, Lincoln, Woodstock, Ilchester, Dunwich, Southwark, Calne, Evesham, Hull and Carmarthenshire in R. Sedgwick, editor, *The House of Commons, 1715–1754* (2 volumes, London, 1970).

## 9  The Robinocracy

1  Historical Manuscripts Commission, Portland MSS, v, p. 333. The speech was published as *The Speech of R—— W—p—le Esq, at his Election at Lyme Regis*, 31 August 1713.
2  J. H. Plumb, *Sir Robert Walpole* i, p. 97.
3  W. Coxe, *Memoirs of the Life and Administration of Sir Robert Walpole Earl of Orford* (4 volumes, London, 1816) i, p. 37.
4  Historical Manuscripts Commission, Portland MSS, iv, p. 493.
5  Coxe, *op. cit.* pp. 57–8.
6  *ibid.* p. 64. Oldmixon admired Walpole's 'exquisite skill in the knowledge of the finances, which made that great critic, Arthur Manwaring Esq. say he was the best figureman in the kingdom'. *History of England* (London, 1735), p. 615.
7  T. F. J. Kendrick, 'Sir Robert Walpole, the Old Whigs and the Bishops, 1733–1736', *English Historical Review* (1968) LXXXIII.
8  *Gentlemen's Magazine*, June 1739.
9  *Craftsman* no. 55, 22 July 1727.

10 W. Cobbett, *Parliamentary History of England* (London, 1811), IX, pp. 459–65.
11 This account of the Excise Crisis is heavily reliant upon P. Langford, *The Excise Crisis* (Oxford, 1975).

## 10 The Opposition to Walpole

1 G. V. Bennett, 'Jacobitism and the Rise of Walpole', in N. McKendrick, editor, *Historical Perspectives: Studies in English Thought and Society in Honour of J. H. Plumb* (London, 1974), p. 87.
2 *ibid.* p. 71. See also G. V. Bennett, *The Tory Crisis in Church and State, 1688–1730: the Career of Francis Atterbury, Bishop of Rochester* (Oxford, 1975), pp. 223–75; P. S. Fritz, *The English Ministers and Jacobitism between the Rebellions of 1715 and 1745* (Toronto, 1975), pp. 67–108.
3 *Cato's Letters* no. 69, 10 March 1722.
4 *The Craftsman* (7 volumes, 1731) I, pp. vi–vii.
5 R. Sedgwick, editor, *The House of Commons, 1715–1754* II, p. 375.
6 Horace Walpole, *Memoirs of the Last Ten Years of the Reign of George the Second*, edited by Lord Holland (two volumes, London, 1822) I, p. 15.
7 For the constitutional debate see above pp. 20–23.
8 *Cato's Letters* nos. 18, 26, 31, 107.
9 *Craftsman* no. 1, 5 December 1726.
10 *Observations upon the Treaty between the Crowns of Great Britain, France and Spain* (London, 1729), pp. 28–9.
11 W. Corbett, *Parliamentary History of England* IX, pp. 471–2.
12 Sedgwick, *op. cit.* p. 567.
13 *Craftsman* no. 129, 21 December 1728.
14 B. Williams, 'The Foreign Policy of England under Walpole', *English Historical Review* (1900) XV, p. 670.
15 *ibid.* p. 268.
16 Lord Hervey, *Memoirs of the Reign of George the Second*, edited by J. Wilson Croker (3 volumes, London, 1884) I, p. 111.
17 W. Coxe, *Memoirs of the Life and Administration of Sir Robert Walpole* II, p. 390.
18 Williams, *op. cit.* XVI, p. 450.
19 A. T. Dickinson and K. Logue, 'The Porteous Riot: a Study of the Breakdown of Law and Order in Edinburgh, 1736–1737', *Journal of the Scottish Labour History Society* no. 10 (1976).
20 Sedgwick, *op. cit.* p. 3.

## 11 The Rule of the Pelhams

1 This account of events between 1742 and 1746 is heavily indebted to J. B. Owen, *The Rise of the Pelhams* (London, 1956).
2 W. Coxe, *Memoirs of the Administration of . . . Henry Pelham* (2 volumes, London, 1829) I, p. 21.
3 Bodleian Library MS. Don. c. 105. f. 197: John to Richard Tucker, 14 December 1742.

4  B. Williams, *Carteret and Newcastle* (Cambridge, 1943), p. 165.
5  *ibid.* p. 151.
6  A. Foord, *His Majesty's Opposition* (Oxford, 1964), pp. 250–51.
7  Bodleian MS. Don. c. 107. f. 69: John to Richard Tucker, 12 January 1746.
8  *ibid.* f. 226: same to same, 11 February 1746.
9  Owen, *op. cit.* p. 301.
10  Bodleian MS. Don. c. 107. f. 174: John to Richard Tucker, 23 November 1745.
11  Foord, *op. cit.* p. 261.
12  *ibid.* pp. 262–5.
13  R. Sedgwick, editor *The House of Commons, 1715–1754* I, p. 57.
14  Coxe, *op. cit.* II, p. 15.
15  Horace Walpole, *Memoirs of the Last Ten Years of the Reign of George the Second* I, p. 222.
16  T. W. Perry, *Public Opinion, Propaganda and Politics in Eighteenth-century England: a Study of the Jew Bill of 1753* (Harvard, 1962); see also G. A. Cranfield, 'The London *Evening Post* and the Jew Bill of 1753', *Historical Journal* (1965) VIII.

## 12  Newcastle and Pitt

1  Lord Waldegrave, *Memoirs from 1754 to 1758* (London, 1821), p. 14.
2  Sir Lewis Namier and J. Brooke, *The History of Parliament: the House of Commons* (3 volumes, London, 1964) I, p. 62.
3  R. Browning, *The Duke of Newcastle* (New Haven, 1975), p. 246.
4  R. Sedgwick, editor *The House of Commons, 1715–1754* I, p. 61.
5  J. B. Owen, 'George II Reconsidered', in Anne Whiteman, J. S. Bromley, and P. G. M. Dickson, eds. *Statesmen, Scholars and Merchants: Essays in Eighteenth-century History presented to Dame Lucy Sutherland* (Oxford, 1973).
6  Waldegrave, *op. cit.* p. 20.
7  Horace Walpole, *Memoirs of the Last Ten Years of the Reign of George the Second* I, pp. 80–81.
8  Lord Chesterfield, *Characters of Eminent Personages* (London, 1777), pp. 38–40.
9  Browning, *op. cit.* p. 252.
10  Walpole, *op. cit.* II, p. 34.
11  Waldegrave, *op. cit.* p. 14.
12  Lord Ilchester, *Henry Fox, First Lord Holland* (2 volumes, London, 1920) II, p. 39.
13  P. Langford, 'William Pitt and Public Opinion', *English Historical Review* (1973) LXXXVIII.
14  R. Middleton, 'Pitt, Anson and the Admiralty, 1756–1761', *History* (1970) LV.
15  Julian S. Corbett, *England in the Seven Years War* (2 volumes London, 1907) II, pp. 144–5.

# Bibliography

## Bibliographies

The most useful general compilation is still S. Pargellis and D. J. Medley, editors, *Bibliography of British History: the Eighteenth Century 1714–1789* (Oxford, 1951), although it badly needs bringing up to date. A more recent bibliography was contributed, anonymously, to B. Williams, *The Whig Supremacy, 1714–1760*, edited by C. H. Stuart (2nd edition, Oxford, 1962), pp. 434–68. Since 1970 the annual 'Current Bibliography of the Eighteenth Century' published in the *Philological Quarterly* has provided a comprehensive survey of current literature. The *Economic History Review* also publishes annually a list of books on the social and economic history of Britain published in the previous year, together with a review of periodical literature. The *Urban History Yearbook*, published annually by Leicester University Press since 1974, contains a current bibliography of urban history and a survey of research in progress.

## Sources

For printed sources there is no short title catalogue for the eighteenth century, though one is actively being considered. However, social and economic history is well served by L. W. Hanson, editor, *Contemporary Printed Sources for British and Irish Economic History, 1701–1750* (Cambridge, 1963). The works of some leading authors have been ably catalogued, for example J. R. Moore, *A Checklist of the Writings of Daniel Defoe* (Bloomington, Indiana, 1960), which despite being too inclusive is very helpful. There is as yet little to guide the student through the great mass of anonymous pamphlets, poems and printed ephemera, though mention must be made of D. Foxon, *English Verse, 1701–1750* (2 volumes, Cambridge, 1975). The enormous mass of public and private papers which document the politics of the period remain for the most part in manuscript in the Public Record Office, the British Library, county record offices, libraries and country houses. A tiny fragment has, however, been either catalogued or even edited. Some public records have been listed by the List and Index Society, for example Sheila Lambert, *List of House of Commons Sessional Papers, 1701–1750* (London, 1968). Some private papers have been calendared by the Historical Manuscripts Commission, its report on the Egmont papers being particularly relevant. Among the most important editions of political materials, which any student of the period should consult, are Lord Hervey, *Some Materials towards Memoirs of the Reign of George II*, edited by R. Sedgwick (3 volumes, London, 1931); Horace Walpole, *Memoirs of the Reign of George II*, edited by Lord Holland (3 volumes, London, 1847) and W. S. Lewis, editor, *Horace Walpole's Correspondence* (39 volumes, New Haven, 1937–74). Many contemporary documents of a generally useful nature are also provided in D. B. Horn and Mary Ransome, editors, *English Historical Documents, 1714–1783* (London, 1957), which contains excellent general and specific bibliographies.

## The Constitution

There are several useful collections of documents illustrating the working of the constitutional machinery, of which E. N. Williams, *The Eighteenth-century Constitution* (Cambridge, 1960) is among the more comprehensive. For interpretative commentaries the student should consult Mark Thomson, *A Constitutional History of England, 1642–1801* (London, 1938) and Sir William Holdsworth, *A History of English Law* x (London, 1938). A more up-to-date complete treatment is lacking, owing perhaps to the declining interest in constitutional history.

For the ways in which constitutional monarchy developed after 1689 see Jennifer Carter, 'The Revolution and the Constitution' in G. Holmes, editor, *Britain after the Glorious Revolution* (London, 1969). Relations between the crown and parliament are the theme of Betty Kemp, *King and Commons, 1660–1832* (London, 1959). The crucial role of the electorate, often overlooked by earlier writers, is discussed in J. H. Plumb, *The Growth of Political Stability in England, 1675–1725* (London, 1967). What little contemporary debate there was about reforming the system of representation is clarified in J. Cannon, *Parliamentary Reform, 1640–1832* (Cambridge, 1973). The debate on the constitution has been the subject of several studies by H. T. Dickinson: *Politics and Literature in the Eighteenth Century* (London, 1974); 'The Eighteenth-century Debate on the "Glorious Revolution"', *History* LXI (1976); 'The Eighteenth-century Debate on the Sovereignty of Parliament', *Transactions of the Royal Historical Society* XXVI (1976). It also informs J. G. Pocock, 'Machiavelli, Harrington and English Political Ideologies in the Eighteenth Century', *Politics, Language and Time* (London, 1972); Caroline Robbins, *The Eighteenth-century Commonwealthman* (London, 1959) and I. Kramnick, *Bolingbroke and his Circle* (Cambridge, Mass., 1968).

The cabinet can only be studied properly in a number of articles in learned journals. E. Trevor Williams, 'The Cabinet in the Eighteenth Century', *History* XXII (1937) summed up the literature to date in a bibliographical note. Since then the only substantial contribution has been J. H. Plumb, 'The Organization of the Cabinet in the Reign of Queen Anne', *Transactions of the Royal Historical Society* VII (1957). On the origins and development of the office of prime minister see the biographies in H. Van Thal, editor, *The Prime Ministers* I (London, 1974). The duties of the two secretaries are demonstrated in Mark Thomson, *The Secretaries of State, 1681–1782* (Oxford, 1932).

Local government in general is still best served by the pioneering studies of S. and B. Webb, *English Local Government* (9 volumes, London, 1906–29). Certain aspects of their work have, however, been superseded by J. R. Western, *The English Militia in the Eighteenth Century* (London, 1965) and G. E. Oxley, *Poor Relief in England and Wales, 1601–1834* (Newton Abbot, 1974).

## Social Structure

The best overall view of society is Dorothy Marshall, *English People in the*

*Eighteenth Century* (London, 1956), though for an introduction to recent quantitative approaches the student should consult P. Laslett, *The World we Have Lost* (London, 2nd edition, 1971). For the aristocracy and gentry in general see G. E. Mingay, *English Landed Society in the Eighteenth Century* (London, 1956) and H. J. Habakkuk, 'England', in A. Goodwin, editor, *The European Nobility in the Eighteenth Century* (London, 1967). Particular families can be studied in G. Scott Thompson, *The Russells in Bloomsbury* (London, 1940), Elizabeth Hamilton, *The Mordaunts* (London, 1965) and R. A. C. Parker, *Coke of Norfolk* (Oxford, 1975). There are any number of biographies of individual peers and gentlemen, but few bring out their style of living as well as C. H. C. and M. I. Baker, *The Life and Circumstances of James Brydges, First Duke of Chandos* (Oxford, 1951) and R. Kelch, *Newcastle: a Duke without Money* (London, 1974).

Attempts to provide a broad view of the commercial middle classes were made in R. B. Westerfield, *Middlemen in English Business, 1660–1760* (New Haven, 1915) and W. E. Minchinton, 'The Merchants in England in the Eighteenth Century', *Explorations in Entrepreneurial History* x (Cambridge, Mass., 1957). Their generalizations must be modified in the light of more recent local studies, especially R. G. Wilson, *Gentlemen Merchants* (Manchester, 1971) which looks at the businessmen in Leeds, G. Jackson, *Hull in the Eighteenth Century* (London, 1972) and T. M. Devine, *The Tobacco Lords: a Study of the Tobacco Merchants of Glasgow and their Trading Activities c. 1740–90* (Edinburgh, 1975).

There is no comprehensive survey of the professional middle classes in this period. For the professions as a whole see E. Hughes, 'The Professions in the Eighteenth Century', *Durham University Journal* XIII (1951). Physicians, surgeons and apothecaries are discussed in B. Hamilton, 'The Medical Professions in the Eighteenth Century', *Economic History Review* IV (1951). The attractions of a military career are touched on in I. F. Burton and A. Newman, 'Promotion in the Eighteenth-century Army', *English Historical Review* LXXVIII (1963). The legal profession should be studied in R. Robson, *The Attorney in Eighteenth-century England* (London, 1959). For the clergy see below, pp. 291–2. Embryo bureaucrats appear in W. R. Ward, 'Some Eighteenth-century Civil Servants', *English Historical Review* LXX (1955). Another incipient profession, that of the land steward, or estate agent, was investigated in two articles, E. Hughes, 'The Eighteenth-century Estate Agent' in H. A. Cronne, T. W. Moody and D. B. Quinn, editors, *Essays in British and Irish History in Honour of James Eadie Todd* (London, 1949); and G. E. Mingay, 'The Eighteenth-century Land Steward' in E. L. Jones and G. E. Mingay, editors, *Land, Labour and Population in the Industrial Revolution* (London, 1967). The land steward can also be considered to have occupied the upper reaches of the hierarchy of domestic servants, which is described in J. Jean Hecht, *The Domestic Servant Class in Eighteenth-century England* (London, 1956). For the mass of people below the middle classes see Dorothy Marshall, *The English Poor in the Eighteenth Century* (London, 1926) and Dorothy George, *London Life in the Eighteenth Century* (London, 1925). Social conditions in the capital city are also dealt with in George Rudé, *Hanoverian London* (London, 1971). Three recent studies have superseded all previous accounts of crime and criminals: J. M. Beattie, 'The Pattern of Crime in England, 1660–1800', *Past and Present* no. 62 (1974); J. M. Beattie, 'The Criminality of Women in Eighteenth-century England', *Journal of Social History* IX (1975); D. Hay, P. Linebaugh and E. P. Thompson, editors, *Albion's Fatal Tree* (London, 1975).

## Social Change

Demographic history is currently a growth industry and its principal products are learned articles, for which there is a house magazine, *Population Studies*. For editions of the more valuable contributions see D. V. Glass and D. E. C. Eversley, editors, *Population in History* (1965); 'Historical Population Studies', *Daedalus* xcvii (Cambridge, Mass., 1968); M. Drake, editor, *Population in Industrialization* (London, 1969); and P. Laslett, editor, *Household and Family in Past Time* (Cambridge, 1972). For one scholar's authoritative attempt at a synthesis see J. D. Chambers, *Population, Economy and Society in Pre-industrial England* (Oxford, 1972).

Urban history is also attracting increasing attention. The best introduction to urbanization in this period is C. W. Chalklin, *The Provincial Towns of Georgian England* (London, 1974). C. W. Chalklin and M. A. Havinden, editors, *Rural Change and Urban Growth, 1500–1800* (London, 1974) contains some useful 'Essays in English Regional History in Honour of W. G. Hoskins'.

For different views of mobility among the landed classes see H. J. Habakkuk, 'English Landownership, 1680–1740', *Economic History Review* x (1940); C. Clay, 'Marriage, Inheritance and the Rise of Large Estates in England, 1660–1815', *Economic History Review*, second series xxiii (1968); B. A. Holdernesse, 'The English Land Market in the Eighteenth Century', *Economic History Review* xxvii (1974).

The incidence of riots after 1740 is recorded in R. F. Wearmouth, *Methodism and the Common People of the Eighteenth Century* (London, 1945), chapter 1. Crowd behaviour is studied in detail in G. Rudé, *Paris and London in the Eighteenth Century* (London, 1952) and E. P. Thompson, 'The Moral Economy of the English Crowd in the Eighteenth Century', *Past and Present* no. 50 (1971).

Cultural changes are less well charted, but J. H. Plumb has pioneered various areas in 'The Public, Literature and the Arts', in P. Fritz and D. Williams, editors, *The Triumph of Culture: Eighteenth-century Perspectives* (Toronto, 1972); *The Commercialization of Leisure in the Eighteenth Century* (Reading, 1973); and 'The New World of Children in the Eighteenth Century', *Past and Present* no. 54 (1975). Popular literacy has been explored in L. Stone, 'Literacy and Education in England, 1640–1900', *Past and Present* no. 42 (1969), popular education in V. Neuberg, *Popular Education in the Eighteenth Century* (London, 1971), and popular literature in I. Watt, *The Rise of the Novel,* (London, 1971), R. M. Wiles, *Serial Publication in England before 1750* (Cambridge, 1957) and R. M. Wiles, *Freshest Advices: Early Provincial Newspapers in England* (Ohio, 1965).

## The Established Church and its Rivals

Among earlier works C. J. Abbey and J. H. Overton, *The English Church in the Eighteenth Century* (2 volumes, London, 1878) can still be read with profit. The leading authority on the anglican church is Norman Sykes, among whose many contributions *Church and State in England in the Eighteenth Century* (Cambridge, 1934) is indispensable. For more recent studies see G. V. Bennett and J. D. Walsh, editors, *Essays in Modern Church History in Memory of Norman Sykes* (London, 1966). For dissent, E. D. Bebb, *Nonconformity and Social Economic Life, 1660–1800* (London, 1935) offered a pioneering statistical study. Tudor Jones, *Congregationalism in England* (London, 1962) is a largely narrative history of one of the sects, while R. T. Vann, *The Social Development of English Quakerism, 1655–1755* (Harvard, 1969) is a quantified analysis of another. N. Crowther Hunt, *Two Early Political Associations: the Quakers and the Dissenting Deputies in the Age of Sir Robert Walpole* (Oxford, 1961) shows how dissenters organized pressure groups to campaign for civil liberties. Most previous work on the catholics has been superseded by J. Bossy, *The English Catholic Community* (Cambridge, 1975). The rise of deism is dealt with in G. R. Cragg, *From Puritanism to the Age of Reason* (Cambridge, 1966), and its impact in R. N. Stromberg, *Religious Liberalism in Eighteenth-century England* (Oxford, 1954), and J. Redwood, *Reason, Ridicule and Religion: the Age of Enlightenment in England, 1660–1750* (London, 1976).

There is an enormous literature on the evangelical revival, to which R. Davies and E. G. Rupp, editors, *A History of the Methodist Church of Great Britain* (London, 1965) i is a good introduction. Among recent works on Wesley, F. Baker, *John Wesley and the Church of England* (London, 1970) is outstanding. On the social aspects of the revival see A. Armstrong, *The Church in England, the Methodists and Society, 1700–1850* (London, 1973) and A. D. Gilbert, *Religion and Society in Industrial England: Church, Chapel and Social Change, 1740–1914* (London, 1976). John Walsh has established himself as the leading authority on the early years of the revival. See his essay 'Origins of the Evangelical Revival' in *Essays in Modern Church History* edited by G. V. Bennett and J. D. Walsh, and 'Elie Halévy and the Birth of Methodism', *Transactions of the Royal Historical Society* xxv (1975).

## The Economy

Two textbooks provide excellent introductions to the economic history of the period: L. A. Clarkson, *The Pre-industrial Economy in England, 1500–1750* (London, 1971) and C. Wilson, *England's Apprenticeship, 1603–1763* (London, 1965). The major statistics are conveniently summarized in T. S. Ashton, *Economic Fluctuations in England, 1700–1800* (Oxford, 1959), and analysed in P. Deane and W. A. Cole, *British Economic Growth, 1688–1959* (2nd edition, Cambridge, 1965). Secondary works are synthesized into a provocative thesis in A. J. Little, *Deceleration in the Eighteenth-century British Economy* (London, 1976), the argument of which is diametrically opposed to that advanced here. Little provides a useful bibliography of recent writings, though he omits E. A. Wrigley, 'A Simple Model of London's Importance in Changing English Society and Economy, 1650–1750', *Past and Present* no. 37 (1966), a modern endorsement of Defoe's views in *The Compleat English Tradesman* (London, 1735) and *A Tour through the Whole Island of Great Britain*, edited by P. Rogers (London, 1971).

Economic historians have used the concepts of four 'revolutions' in their analyses of the period's main trends: financial, commercial, agricultural and industrial. The first is dealt with definitively in P. G. M. Dickson, *The Financial Revolution* (Oxford, 1967), the second stimulatingly in R. Davis, *A Commercial Revolution: English Overseas Trade in the Seventeenth and Eighteenth Centuries* (Historical Association pamphlet, 1967). The best collection of statistics relating to commerce, on which many generalizations are based despite warnings about the methodological difficulties which they pose, is in E. B. Schumpeter, *English Overseas Trade Statistics, 1697–1808* (Oxford, 1960). There are a number of important articles on commercial developments, some of which appear in W. E. Minchinton, editor, *The Growth of English Overseas Trade in the Seventeenth and Eighteenth centuries* (London, 1969) while many others are listed in its full bibliographical essay. Two conflicting views of trends in agriculture are presented in J. D. Chambers and G. E. Mingay, *The Agricultural Revolution, 1750–1880* (London, 1966) and E. Kerridge, *The Agricultural Revolution* (London, 1967). The articles by A. H. John in L. S. Pressnell, editor, *Studies in the Industrial Revolution presented to T. S. Ashton* (London, 1960) and E. L. Jones, editor, *Agriculture and Economic Growth in England, 1650–1815* (London, 1967) should also be consulted.

There are probably more studies of the early stages of industrialization than of all other economic trends put together. P. Mantoux, *The Industrial Revolution in the Eighteenth Century* (12th edition, London, 1961) with an introduction by T. S. Ashton, still provides a good framework in which to place more recent studies. For a more up-to-date treatment, with a full bibliography, see Phyllis Deane, *The First Industrial Revolution* (Cambridge, 1965).

Communications by water have been exhaustively studied in T. S. Willan, *The English Coasting Trade* (London, 1936), and the same author's *River Navigation in England* (London, 1964). The bad state of the roads indicated in S. and B. Webb, *English Local Government; the King's Highway* (London, 1913) should be modified in the light of W. Albert, *The Turnpike System in England, 1663–1840* (London, 1972).

The debate on the social effects of economic expansion is discussed in two articles by A. W. Coats: 'Changing Attitudes to Labour in the Mid-eighteenth Century', *Economic History Review* XI (1958); and 'Economic Thought and Poor Law Policy in the Eighteenth Century', *Economic History Review* XIII (1960). The case that warfare stimulated rather than stagnated economic activity is forcibly argued in A. H. John, 'War and the English Economy, 1700–1763', *Economic History Review* VII (1955). The impact of the state on economic activity can also be studied in E. Hughes, *Studies in Administration and Finance* (Manchester, 1934) and E. E. Hoon, *The Organization of the English Customs System, 1696–1786* (Newton Abbott, 1968).

## The Making of the English Ruling Class

The polarization of the governing elite into rival parties under the later Stuarts has been superbly analysed in G. Holmes, *British Politics in the Age of Anne* (London, 1967) and J. H. Plumb, *The Growth of Political Stability in England, 1675–1725* (London, 1967). See also W. A. Speck, 'Conflict in Society' in G. Holmes, editor, *Britain after the Glorious Revolution* (London, 1969). The personnel of the ruling class which emerged under the early Hanoverians is best studied in R. Sedgwick, editor, *The History of Parliament: The Commons, 1715–1754* (2 volumes, London, 1970) and L. Namier and J. Brooke, editors, *The House of Commons, 1754–1790* (3 volumes, London, 1964). The most intricate analysis of how the ruling class exerted control of the machinery of government is in L. Namier, *The Structure of Politics at the Accession of George III* (2nd edition, London 1957), a work of fundamental importance for the politics of the whole period. G. E. Mingay argues that the gentry were replaced as the governing class in the eighteenth century by the aristocracy in alliance with an emergent bourgeoisie in *The Gentry: the Rise and Fall of a Ruling Class* (London, 1976). For relations between the government and the City of London see A. J. Henderson, *London and the National Government, 1721–1742* (Durham, North Carolina, 1945) and Lucy Sutherland, 'The City of London in Eighteenth-century Politics' in R. Pares and A. J. P. Taylor, editors, *Essays presented to Sir Lewis Namier* (London,

1956). The view that a ruling-class ideology found expression in laws to protect property is most tendentiously expressed in E. P. Thompson, *Whigs and Hunters: the Origin of the Black Act* (London, 1975).

## The Establishment of the Hanoverian Dynasty

W. Michael, *The Beginnings of the Hanoverian Dynasty* (London, 1936–7) and *The Quadruple Alliance* (London, 1939); translated by A. and G. E. MacGregor from German volumes published much earlier, provide the best narrative introduction to the period following Anne's death. For the legacy left by the turbulent politics of her reign, see G. Holmes, editor, *Britain after the Glorious Revolution* (London, 1969), especially the last essay where Professor Holmes himself analyses the struggle between Harley and St John, laying down the lines of an interpretation subsequently substantiated by Sheila Biddle, *Bolingbroke and Harley* (London, 1975). The defeat of the tories at the polls is dealt with in W. A. Speck, 'The General Election of 1715', *English Historical Review* xc (1975). Much light on the politics of the period is shed in J. M. Beattie, *The English Court in the Reign of George I* (Cambridge, 1967). Ragnhild Hatton is at work on a biography of George I, and some interesting sparks from her anvil illuminate the pages of her article 'George I as an English and a European Figure' in P. Fritz and D. Williams, editors, *The Triumph of Culture* (Toronto, 1972). Jacobitism has been treated romantically in several studies, of which Sir Charles Petrie, *The Jacobite Movement* (London, 1959) can be recommended, though the more sober analysis of G. H. Jones, *The Mainstream of Jacobitism* (Harvard, 1954) should also be consulted.

## Stanhope's Ministry

Stanhope's political career is given adequate treatment in B. Williams, *Stanhope* (Oxford, 1932), though there is a more up-to-date sketch in A. Newman, *The Stanhopes of Chevening* (London, 1969). There is no biography of Sunderland. The foreign policy of the period can be studied in the laborious narratives of J. F. Chance, *George I and the Northern War* (London, 1909) and *The Alliance of Hanover* (London, 1923), though for the period up to 1717 there is the more readable J. Murray, *George I, the Baltic and the Whig Split of 1717* (London, 1969). Further repercussions should be studied in G. C. Gibbs, 'Parliament and Foreign Policy in the Age of Stanhope and Walpole', *English Historical Review* lxxvii (1962) and D. McKay, 'The Struggle for Control of George I's Northern Policy', *Journal of Modern History* xlv (1973). Anglo-Dutch relations are dealt with authoritatively in R. Hatton, *Diplomatic Relations between Great Britain and the Dutch Republic, 1714–1721* (London, 1950). There is a useful collection of documents in J. F. Naylor, editor, *The British Aristocracy and the Peerage Bill of 1719* (Oxford, 1968). J. Carswell, *The South Sea Bubble* (London, 1960), is a popular account of the debacle, while P. G. M. Dickson, *The Financial Revolution* (Oxford, 1967) provides a more scholarly analysis of its financial mechanics. It should also be used to modify the otherwise definitive account of Walpole's role in J. H. Plumb, *Sir Robert Walpole* i (London, 1956).

## The Robinocracy

Among modern biographies of Walpole that by J. H. Plumb, *Sir Robert Walpole* (2 volumes, London, 1956 and 1960) is paramount. A third volume dealing with the years after 1734, is eagerly awaited. Meanwhile H. T. Dickinson, *Walpole and the Whig Supremacy* (London, 1973) deals convincingly with the major questions most students ask about the Robinocracy, while G. Holmes, 'Sir Robert Walpole' in H. Van Thal, editor, *The Prime Ministers* I (London, 1974) and Betty Kemp, *Sir Robert Walpole* (London, 1976) concentrate on the constitutional significance of his premiership. There is an acute analysis of one of the major events of Walpole's ministry in P. Langford, *The Excise Crisis* (Oxford, 1975). The same author's *Great Britain, 1688–1815* (London, 1976) provides a clear introduction to the complex diplomacy of the period, which should be followed up in D. B. Horn, *Great Britain and Europe in the Eighteenth Century* (Oxford, 1967).

## The Opposition to Walpole

Walpole's exploitation of the Jacobite threat is examined in P. Fritz, *The English Ministers and Jacobitism, 1715–1745* (Toronto, 1975), while the plot of 1722 is most skilfully analysed in G. V. Bennett, *The Tory Crisis in Church and State* (Oxford, 1975), a biography of Francis Atterbury, bishop of Rochester. C. B. Realey, *The Early Opposition to Sir Robert Walpole* (Philadelphia, 1931) is still useful for an account of how Walpole's opponents gradually built up between 1722 and 1727 from demoralized fragments to a working alliance. For a more recent treatment see A. Foord, *His Majesty's Opposition, 1714–1830* (Oxford, 1964). There have been a number of studies of Walpole's chief rival, of which the best is H. T. Dickinson, *Bolingbroke* (London, 1970). For the ideology of the opposition see this in conjunction with I. Kramnick, *Bolingbroke and his Circle: the Politics of Nostalgia in the Age of Walpole* (Cambridge, Mass., 1968). Both have been criticized for not paying enough attention to the history of political ideas by Q. Skinner, 'The Principles and Practice of Opposition: the Case of Bolingbroke versus Walpole' in N. McKendrick, editor, *Historical Perspectives: Studies in English Thought and Society in honour of J. H. Plumb* (London, 1974).

## The Rule of the Pelhams

J. B. Owen, *The Rise of the Pelhams* (London, 1956) is indispensable. There is no satisfactory biography of Henry Pelham, the most recent, J. Wilks, *A Whig in Power* (Evanston, 1964) being disappointing. The sketch by A. Newman, 'Henry Pelham' in H. Van Thal, editor, *The Prime Ministers* I (London, 1974) should be consulted. Pelham's brother has at last been the subject of a full biography, R. Browning, *The Duke of Newcastle* (London, 1975). The struggle between the Pelhams and Carteret is best studied in B. Williams, *Carteret and Newcastle* (Cambridge, 1943). Invaluable contemporary documents were published in P. Yorke, *The Life and Correspondence of Philip Yorke, Earl of Hardwicke* (3 volumes, Cambridge, 1913). The political repercussions of the quarrel between George II and the Prince of Wales are discussed in A. Newman, 'Leicester House Politics, 1748–1761', *English Historical Review* LXXI (1961), and documented in A. Newman, editor, 'Leicester House Politics, 1750–1760, from the papers of John, Second Earl of Egmont', *Camden Miscellany* XXIII (London, 1969). There is a full, albeit controversial, account of the passing and repeal of the Jewish Naturalization Act in T. W. Perry, *Public Opinion, Propaganda and Politics in Eighteenth-century England* (Cambridge, Mass., 1962). For the 'Forty-Five' see Katherine Tomasson and F. Buist, *Battles of the '45* (London, 1967) and D. Daiches, *Charles Edward Stuart* (London, 1973).

## Newcastle and Pitt

For Newcastle's spell as prime minister H. T. Dickinson, 'The Duke of Newcastle' in H. Van Thal, editor, *The Prime Ministers* 1 (London, 1974) should be consulted in addition to the studies of the duke mentioned above. The standard biography of Pitt is B. Williams, *The Life of William Pitt, Earl of Chatham* (2 volumes, London, 1913). Of many biographies written since, J. H. Plumb, *Chatham* (London, 1953) is a stimulating brief life and S. Ayling, *The Elder Pitt, Earl of Chatham* (London, 1976) is a full treatment. There has been no similar study of Henry Fox since Lord Ilchester, *Henry Fox, First Lord Holland* (2 volumes, London, 1920). The struggle between the two men and their sons was the subject of E. Eyck, *Pitt versus Fox* (London, 1950). Britain's role in the Seven Years' War provided the focus of J. Corbett, *England in the Seven Years War* (2 volumes, London, 1907) and Sir Reginald Savory, *His Britannic Majesty's Army in Germany during the Seven Years War* (Oxford, 1966).

# Appendix: English Social Structure, 1690–1760

Gregory King's 'Scheme of the income and expense of the several families of England ... for 1688' compared with Joseph Massie's 'Estimate of the social structure and income, 1759–1760'.

| KING | | | | MASSIE | |
|---|---|---|---|---|---|
| Number of families | Heads per family | Number of persons | Classification | Number of families | Annual income or expenses (£) |
| 160 | 40 | 6,400 | Temporal lords | | |
| 26 | 20 | 520 | Spiritual lords | | |
| 800 | 16 | 12,800 | Baronets | | |
| 600 | 13 | 7,800 | Knights | | |
| 3,000 | 10 | 30,000 | Esquires | | |
| 12,000 | 8 | 96,000 | Gentlemen | | |
| | | | (Massie does not distin- | 10 | 20,000 |
| | | | guish the top ranks by | 20 | 10,000 |
| | | | status, but by financial | 40 | 8,000 |
| | | | turnover per family per | 80 | 6,000 |
| | | | annum) | 160 | 4,000 |
| | | | | 320 | 2,000 |
| | | | | 640 | 1,000 |
| | | | | 800 | 800 |
| | | | | 1,600 | 600 |
| | | | | 3,200 | 400 |
| | | | | 4,800 | 300 |
| | | | | 6,400 | 200 |
| 5,000 | 8 | 40,000 | Persons in greater offices and places | | |
| 5,000 | 6 | 30,000 | Persons in lesser offices and places | | |
| | | | Civil officers | 16,000 | 60 |
| 2,000 | 8 | 16,000 | Eminent merchants | | |
| 8,000 | 6 | 48,000 | Lesser merchants | | |
| | | | Merchants | 1,000 | 600 |
| | | | ,, | 2,000 | 400 |
| | | | ,, | 10,000 | 200 |
| | | | Master manufacturers | 2,500 | 200 |
| | | | ,, ,, | 5,000 | 100 |
| | | | ,, ,, | 10,000 | 70 |
| | | | ,, | 62,500 | 40 |
| 10,000 | 7 | 70,000 | Persons in the law | 12,000 | 100 |
| 2,000 | 6 | 12,000 | Eminent clergymen | 2,000 | 100 |
| 8,000 | 5 | 40,000 | Lesser clergymen | 9,000 | 50 |
| 40,000 | 7 | 280,000 | Freeholders, better sort | | |
| 120,000 | 5½ | 660,000 | ,, lesser sort | | |
| | | | ,, | 30,000 | 100 |
| | | | ,, | 60,000 | 50 |
| | | | ,, | 120,000 | 25 |

| KING | | | Classification | MASSIE | |
|---|---|---|---|---|---|
| Number of families | Heads per family | Number of persons | | Number of families | Annual income or expenses (£) |
| 150,000 | 5 | 750,000 | Farmers | 5,000 | 150 |
| | | | ,, | 10,000 | 100 |
| | | | ,, | 20,000 | 70 |
| | | | ,, | 120,000 | 40 |
| 15,000 | 5 | 75,000 | Persons in liberal arts and sciences | 18,000 | 60 |
| 50,000 | 4½ | 225,000 | Shopkeepers and trades-men | | |
| | | | Tradesmen | 2,500 | 400 |
| | | | ,, | 5,000 | 200 |
| | | | ,, | 10,000 | 100 |
| | | | ,, | 20,000 | 70 |
| | | | ,, | 125,000 | 40 |
| 60,000 | 4 | 240,000 | Artisans and handicrafts Manufacturers of wood, iron etc. | | |
| | | | Country 9s per week | 100,000 | 22·5 |
| | | | London 12s | 14,000 | 30 |
| | | | Manufacturers of wool, silk etc. | | |
| | | | Country 7s 6d | 100,000 | 18·75 |
| | | | London 10s 6d | 14,000 | 26·25 |
| 5,000 | 4 | 20,000 | Naval officers | 6,000 | 80 |
| 4,000 | 4 | 16,000 | Military officers | 2,000 | 100 |
| 50,000 | 3 | 150,000 | Common seamen | | |
| | | | Seamen and fishermen | 60,000 | 20 |
| 364,000 | 3½ | 1,275,000 | Labouring people and outservants | | |
| | | | Husbandmen (6s per week) | 200,000 | 15 |
| | | | Labourers, country 5s | 200,000 | 12·5 |
| | | | Labourers, London 9s | 20,000 | 22·5 |
| | | | Innkeepers, alesellers | 2,000 | 100 |
| | | | Alesellers, cottagers | 20,000 | 40 |
| | | | ,,       ,, | 20,000 | 20 |
| 400,000 | 3¼ | 1,300,000 | Cottagers and paupers | | |
| 35,000 | 2 | 70,000 | Common soldiers | 18,000 | 14 |
| | | 30,000 | Vagrants, as gypsies, thieves, beggars, etc. | | |
| TOTAL | | 5,500,520 | | | |

NOTE: King's table has often been reproduced. See G. Holmes, op. cit. above p. 276 *n*.6. Massie's was published by Professor P. Mathias in 'The social structure in the eighteenth century: a calculation by Joseph Massie', *Economic History Review*, second series x (1957–8), pp. 42–3. The information from Massie has here been recast to correspond to King's twenty-six 'ranks, degrees, titles and qualifications', save that categories used in the later estimate which were not employed by King have been introduced where they seemed to be most appropriate. The juxtaposition of figures and classifications indicates which of the latter are common to both compilations, and which unique to one or the other. For reasons given above, p. 33, King's estimates of income and expenditure are not supplied.

# Index

Abercromby, James (1706–81), 269

Acherley, Roger (?1665–1740), 20

Acts of parliament:
Abolition of hereditary jurisdictions in Scotland, 251
Affirmation, 102
Bill of Rights, 12, 87
Bubble, 198
Calendar reform, 254–5
Churches, new (1711), 112
City elections, 159
Combinations of workmen, legislation against, 81, 164
Corporation, 11, 91, 92, 102, 103, 151, 194, 195, 210
Disarming, 251
Gin, (1736) 60, 80; (1751) 65, 255
Jewish naturalization, 151, 256–7
Licensing (press), 91, 92, 104, 227
Licensing (stage), 226–7
Marriage, 83, 255–6
Militia, 28, 80, 265
Mutiny, 13
Occasional conformity, 12, 94, 102, 149, 151, 192, 194, 210
Property qualifications (JP's), 146
Property qualifications (MP's), 37, 143
Regency, 15, 19, 170–71, 186, 204
Riot, 80, 164, 181, 183
Schism, 93, 94, 102, 149, 151, 192, 194, 210
Septennial, 4, 21, 147, 162, 164, 183, 185, 195, 216, 222, 227
Settlement (1662), 69
Settlement (1701), 11, 12, 13, 15, 23, 91, 169, 187, 204
Test, 11, 91, 92, 102, 103, 151, 194, 195, 210
Toleration, 92, 101, 119
Toleration (Scotland), 179
Triennial, 12, 21, 183, 222
Uniformity, 91
Vagrancy, 59
Waltham Black, 59, 164
Workhouses, 77, 78, 164

Addison, Joseph (1672–1719), 20, 21, 40, 145, 155, 192, 275–6 n 11, 277 n 15

Africa, 124, 270

Agriculture, 127–32

Aislabie, John (1670–1742), 162, 198, 201

Aix-la-Chapelle, treaty of, 252–3

Amherst, Jeffrey (1717–97), 269

Anne (1665–1714), queen of England (1702–7), of Great

Anne—*contd*
    Britain (1707–14), 14, 15, 21, 23, 26, 92, 169, 170, 178, 209, 221
Anson, George, lord, (1697–1762), 254, 265, 272
Apothecaries, *see* Medicine
Apprenticeship, 74–5
Argyll, John Campbell 2nd duke of (1678–1743), 189, 211, 235, 240, 249
Aristocracy, 35, 36
Army, 5, 22, 52, 58, 144–5, 223, 225
Assiento, 125, 234
Atterbury, Francis, bishop of Rochester (1662–1732), 91, 92, 152, 158, 160, 172, 183, 219–20
Attorneys, *see* Lawyers
Austria, 188, 241, 243, 252, 263, 267, 273

Bakewell, Robert (1725–95), 130
Bangorian controversy 94–5, 151, 195
Bank of England, 33, 124, 155, 159, 196, 197
Banks, Joseph, 45
Baptists, *see* Dissenters
Barnard, Sir John (1685–1764), 156–7, 218
Barrell, Francis (1663–1724), 88
Bath, earl of, *see* Pulteney, William
Battles:
    Cape Passaro (1718), 193
    Crefield (1758), 368
    Culloden (1746), 251
    Dettingen (1743), 242
    Falkirk (1746), 250
    Fontenoy (1745), 242
    Glenshiel (1719), 193
    Hastenbeck (1757), 267

    Kolin (1757), 267
    Kunersdorf (1759), 268
    Lagos (1759), 268
    Lauffield (1747), 252
    Leuthen (1757), 268
    Minden (1759), 268
    Minorca (1756), 263, 264
    Montreal (1760), 269
    Ohio (1755), 262
    Plassey (1757), 270
    Preston (1715), 181
    Prestonpans (1745), 249
    Quebec (1759), 269
    Quiberon Bay (1759), 268
    Rheinberg (1758), 268
    Rochefort (1757), 267
    Rossbach (1757), 267
    Sherriffmuir (1715), 182
    Ticonderoga (1758), 269
    Torgau (1760), 273
    Warburg (1760), 273
    Zorndorf (1758), 268
Bedford, John 4th duke of (1710–71), 38, 254
Berington, Joseph (1746–1827), 103
Bernstorff, Andreas Gottlieb von (1649–1726), 173, 189, 194
Berwick, James Fitzjames duke of (1670–1734), 181–2
Birmingham, 67, 133, 279 *n* 6
Birth rate, 63–4
Bishops, 36, 96–7, 210–11
Blackburne, Lancelot (1658–1743), 96
Blackstone, Sir William (1723–80), 20
Böhler, Peter, 109
Bolingbroke, Henry St John viscount (1678–1751): early career, 158, 160, 169, 170, 178, 179, 206–7, 221–2; political ideas, 20, 22, 155,

Bolingbroke—*contd*
157, 177, 222, 229; followers, 171; later career, 228, 246, 251
Boscawen, Sir Edward (1711–61), 262
Boscawen, Hugh, *see* Falmouth
Bothmer, Johann G. Graf von (1656–1732), 173
Bourne, Reverend Henry (1696–1733), 116
Bowes, George (1701–60), 37, 43
Boyer, Abel (1667–1729), 159, 183
Braddock, Edward (1695–1755), 362
Bradshaigh, Sir Roger (?1675–1747), 37
Brady, Robert (d. 1700), 22
Bremen and Verden, 187, 194
Bridgewater, Francis Egerton 3rd duke of, (1763–1803), 136
Brindley, James (1716–72), 135–6
Brisco, N. A., 199
Bristol, 17, 36, 77, 111, 112, 116
Bromley, William (1664–1732), 148, 171, 172
Brooke, John, 151
Brown, John (1715–66), 98, 272
Brydges, James, *see* Chandos, duke of
Burke, Edmund (1729–97), 143, 145
Burlington, Richard Boyle 3rd earl of (1695–1753), 38, 49
Burn, Reverend Richard (1709–85), 28
Burnet, Gilbert, bishop of Salisbury (1643–1715), 40, 105, 146
Burrington, George, 66, 82
Bury St Edmunds, 162

Bute, James Stuart 3rd earl of (1713–92), 260
Butler, Joseph, bishop of Durham (1692–1752), 102, 104
Byng, John (1704–57), 263, 264, 266

Cabinet, 23, 24, 174
Calamy, Edmund (1671–1732), 102
Calendar, reform of, 254–5
Camden, Sir Charles Pratt earl of (1714–94), 22
Campbell, *see* Argyll, Islay, Loudoun
Canning, Elizabeth (1743–73), 59
Cape Passaro, 193
Cardington, 67
Cardonnel, Adam (d. 1719), 207
Caroline, queen (1683–1737), 24, 93, 215, 216
Carteret, John lord, earl Granville (1690–1763), 26, 194, 229–30, 231, 240, 241, 244–8, 262
Carthagena, 234
Catholicism, 3, 11, 28, 102–3
*Cato's Letters*, 201, 220, 223–4
Chandos, James Brydges 1st duke of (1673–1744), 35, 38, 39, 46, 198
Charitable corporation, 79, 228
Charles II (1630–85), king of England (1660–85), 13, 22, 27, 36, 91, 123, 149
Charles VI (1685–1740), emperor (1711–40), 192, 231, 233
Charles XII (1682–1718), king of Sweden (1697–1718), 187, 194

Charles Albert, elector of Bavaria (1697–1745), emperor Charles VII (1742–5), 242

Charles Edward, the Young Pretender, *see* Stuart

Charles Emmanuel III, duke of Savoy (1701–73), king of Sardinia (1730–73), 244, 245

Chatham, earl of, *see* Pitt, William

Chesterfield, Philip Dormer Stanhope 4th earl of (1694–1773), 26, 216, 246, 247, 254–5

Chippenham, 237–8

Choiseul, Etienne F. duc de (1719–85), 268

Chubb, Thomas (1679–1747), 76

Civil list, 14, 216

Clarke, Reverend Samuel (1675–1729), 100

Clarke, Sir Thomas (1703–64), 76

Class, 31, 40, 51, 61, 69–70, 165–6

Clergy, 46, 91–6, 98–9, 152, 153

Clive, baron Robert (1725–74), 270

Cobden, archdeacon Edward (1684–1764), 98

Cocks, Sir Richard, 2nd bart (d. 1726), 6

Coke, Thomas (1697–1759), 37, 156

Collier, Jeremy (1650–1726), 5

Collins, Anthony (1676–1729), 104

Commissions of the peace, 28–9

Commons, House of, *see* Parliament

Compton, Sir Spencer, earl of Wilmington (?1673–1743), 27, 215, 231, 240, 245

Constitution, 2–3

Convocation, 93, 94, 95

Coote, Sir Eyre (1726–83), 270, 271

Cope, Sir John (d. 1760), 248, 249

Cornwall, 19, 117, 236–7

Cotesworth, William (?1668–1726), 75

Cotton, Sir John Hynde (?1689–1752), 246

'Country', 4, 5, 6, 7, 165, 191, 217, 220, 222–6, 243

County, *see* Local government

'Court' 4, 5, 7, 165, 191, 209, 210, 220, 228–9, 243

Cowper, Mary countess (1685–1724), 91

Cowper, William earl (d. 1723), 93, 156, 174, 175, 176

*Craftsman, The*, 36, 52, 158, 161, 212, 220, 222, 226, 227, 229

Craftsmen, 54–5

Cragg, G. R., 105

Craggs, James the elder (1657–1721), 198, 201

Crime, 59–60, 86, 89–90

Crowley's ironworks, 133, 283 *n* 12

Culloden, 251

Cumberland, William Augustus duke of (1721–65), 250–51, 254, 266–7

Customs, 28, 41

Darby, Abraham (1677–1717), 134

Darling, Robert, 75

Darlington, countess of, *see* Kielmansegge

Death rate, 64–6

Defoe, Daniel (?1661–1731), 5, 31, 32, 41, 49, 50, 54, 75, 90, 282*n* 1;

Defoe—*contd*
  *Tour through . . . Great Britain* 3,
    17, 19, 42, 120, 135, 136,
    137, 275 *n* 5
Deism, 104–5
Delavals, the, 73
Delmé, Sir Peter (d.1728), 42,
    157
Dennis, John (1657–1734), 16
Derwentwater, Sir James Rad-
    cliffe 3rd earl of (1689–
    1716), 181
Devonshire, William Cavendish
    4th duke of (1720–64), 265
Dickson, P. G. M., 199–200
Dissenters, protestant, 11–12, 47,
    100–102
Doddington, George Bubb
    (1691–1762), 256
Dolins, Sir Daniel (d.1728), 20
Domestic service, *see* Servants
Dubois, cardinal Guillaume
    (1656–1723), 188
Duck, Stephen (1705–56), 76
Dutch, the, 188, 193, 232, 247,
    263
Dyer, John (*c.* 1700–58), 67

East India Company, 33, 124,
    125, 155, 159, 196, 197, 218,
    270
Eaton, Daniel (1698–1742), 45
Eden, F. M. (1766–1809), 78
Edgecombe, Richard (1680–
    1758), 236
Edinburgh, 235–6, 248–9
Education, 39, 82–3
Egmont, earl of, *see* Perceval, Sir
    John
Elections, 21, 146–7, 153, 161,
    163, 177; (1715), 147, 176–
    8; (1722), 202; (1734), 216;
    (1741), 21, 235, 237;
    (1747), 252; (1754), 259

Electorate, 16, 17, 19, 164
Enclosures, 68, 80, 130–31
Enthusiasm, 105–6, 116
Esquires, 36
Evangelicals, 119
Excise, 28, 41, 141, 213
Excise crisis, 158, 213–15, 216,
    218, 219

Falmouth, Hugh Boscawen 1st
    viscount (d. 1734), 163,
    236–7
Family, the, 63
Farmers, 48, 53
Farquhar, George (1678–1707),
    52
Ferdinand of Brunswick, prince
    (1721–92), 268, 273
Ferdinand VI (1713–59), king of
    Spain (1746–59), 252
Fielding, Henry (1707–54), 40,
    51, 52, 53, 59, 69, 89, 99,
    226, 277 *n* 15
Fielding, Sarah (1710–68), 123
Financial revolution, 123–4
Foreign policy, 24, 187–9, 192–
    3, 230, 231–4, 241–5, 252–3,
    262–4, 267–71, 273
Forster, Thomas (?1675–1738),
    181, 183
Fort Duquesne, 262, 269
Fox, Henry, 1st Lord Holland
    (1705–74), 256, 260, 261,
    262, 264, 265
France, 188, 192, 193, 233, 242,
    252, 253, 263, 267, 268, 270,
    273
Frederick II (1712–86), king of
    Prussia (1740–86), 242, 243,
    245, 263, 267, 268, 273
Frederick, prince of Wales
    (1707–51), 23, 26, 236–7,
    240, 243, 251–2, 254
Freeholders, 47–8

Garrick, David (1717–79), 147

Garth, Sir Samuel (1661–1719), 33

Gay, John (1685–1732), 39, 52, 59, 226, 227

Gentlemen, 36–41, 54

George I (1660–1727), king of Great Britain (1714–27): accession, 169, 170; and cabinet, 24, 174; character of, 172; and Church of England, 91, 93; and civil list, 14; and Hanover, 25, 173, 187, 188, 189; and Prince of Wales, 189, 196, 215; and privy council, 174–5; restrictions on power of, 12–13, 15; and South Sea Bubble, 201, 215; title of, 11; and tories, 172–4; and whigs, 174–5

George II (1683–1760), king of Great Britain (1727–60): accession of, 215; and cabinet, 24; and civil list, 14; death of, 273; and Hanover, 241–3; and ministerial appointments, 26, 27, 215, 216, 238, 240, 246–8, 257, 259–60, 265, 266; as Prince of Wales, 189, 195, 196; and 'Septennial Convention', 21, 251–2

George III (1738–1820), king of Great Britain (1760–1820): as minor, 254, 260; accession of, 1, 273–4; and ministerial appointments, 26

Georgia, 107–8, 110

Germain, lord George, *see* Sackville

Gibraltar, 193, 231

Gibson, Edmund, bishop of London (1669–1748), 93, 94, 210, 211

Gideon, Sampson (1699–1762), 42, 157, 256

Glasgow, 43, 74, 140

Godolphin, Sidney earl of (1645–1712), 185, 200, 206, 209, 210

Goldsmith, Oliver (1728–74), 68, 147

Gordon, Thomas (d. 1750), 22, 89, 201, 227

Gough, Strickland (d. 1752), 102

Grand tour, 39

Granville, *see* Cartaret

Granville, George, baron Lansdowne (1667–1735), 145, 163

Gregory XIII, pope (1502–85), 254–5

Grimshaw, Reverend William (1708–63), 112, 119

Grub Street, 34, 85

Guadeloupe, 269, 270

Gyllenborg, count Karl (1679–1746), 190

Habeas Corpus, 13, 164, 181, 183, 220

Halifax, Charles Montagu earl of (1661–1715), 174, 185

Hanau, treaty of, 242, 245

Hanmer, Sir Thomas (1677–1746), 148, 171, 172

Hanover, electorate of, 12, 25, 172, 187, 188–9, 190, 194, 232, 241–4, 263, 266

Hanover, treaty of, 232

Hanway, Jonas (1712–86), 90

Harcourt, Simon 1st viscount (1661–1727), 175

Hardwicke, Philip Yorke earl of (1690–1764), 53, 83, 229,

Hardwicke—*contd*
237, 240, 241, 246, 251, 255, 256, 259

Hare, Francis, bishop of Chichester (1671–1740), 98

Harley, Robert, *see* Oxford, earl of

Harrington, James (1611–77), 22, 223

Harrington, William Stanhope 1st earl of (?1690–1756), 232, 246, 252

Harris, Howel (1714–73), 112

Hastings, lady Elizabeth (1682–1739), 114

Hastings, lady Margaret (d. 1768), 114

Hawkins, William (1722–1801), 86

Hawley, Henry (*c*. 1679–1759), 250

Heathcote, Sir Gilbert (?1651–1733), 33, 42

Hervey, John lord (1696–1743), 210, 227, 258

Hoadly, Benjamin bishop (1676–1761), 21, 94–6, 227

Hobbes, Thomas (1588–1679), 22, 89, 223, 224

Hogarth, William (1697–1764), 49, 61, 81, 90, 250

Hospitals, 64–5

Hughes, Edward, 72

Hull, 43, 74, 75

Hume, David (1711–76), 31, 85, 104

Huntingdon, Selina countess of (1767–91), 114

Independents, *see* Dissenters

Industry, 43, 132, 133–4

Interest, rate of, 153, 154, 156, 218, 253

Islay, Archibald Campbell earl of (1682–1761), 211, 235–6

Jacobitism, 6, 7, 28, 79–80, 103, 107, 115, 150, 152, 166, 169, 170, 190, 193, 219–20, 222, 240; 1715 rebellion, 103, 179–183; 1745 rebellion, 30, 103, 248–51

James II (1633–1701), king of England (1685–8), 3, 11, 13, 22, 27, 123, 169, 170

James Francis Edward, the old Pretender, *see* Stuart

Janssen, Sir Theodore (?1658–1748), 42

Jenkins, Robert (fl. 1731–8), 234

Jewish naturalization, 256–7

Johnson, Dr Samuel (1709–84), 105, 225, 226, 274

Joseph II, emperor (1765–90), 253, 254

Judiciary, 12–13

Junto, the, 26, 148, 175, 185, 186, 187, 204, 205, 206, 207, 223

Justices of the peace, 28–9

Kay, John (fl. 1733–64), 134

Kent, William (1684–1748), 38

Kielmansegge, baroness Sophia Charlotte von Platen, (?1673–1725), 173

King, Gregory (1648–1712), 31, 32, 33

King, Peter lord (1669–1734), 33

Klosterseven, Convention of, 268

Kyrle, John (1637–1724), 139

Labourers, 56–7, 61, 68

Lackington, James (1746–1815), 118

Landowners, 33–4, 39–41, 70–73, 144, 145, 152–6, 158

Land tax, 72, 141, 154, 155–6, 217, 232, 253

Latitudinarianism, 99–100, 105
Law, William (1686–1761), 5, 106, 107, 108
Lawrence, Edward (d. 1740?), 45
Lawyers, 45–6, 51, 144, 153
Layer, Christopher (1683–1723), 220
Leeds, 41, 43, 73, 74
Legge, Honourable Henry Bilson (1708–64), 262, 265
Leicester House, 121, 196
Ligonier, John 1st earl (1680–1770), 268
Lillo, George (1693–1739), 41, 53
Lincolnshire, 12
Linebaugh, Peter, 60
Literacy, 83–4
Liverpool, 17
Local government, 27–30, 146
Locke, John (1632–1704), 14, 21, 22, 89, 95, 104, 165
London: crime in, 60; death rate in, 65, 66; earthquakes in (1750), 88; growth of, 6, 66, 121; industry, 123; literacy in, 84; markets in, 44, 120, 127, 137; merchants in, 42, 73, 75, 123, 125; religion in, 112–13; riots in, 160; servants in, 57; wages in, 69; West End of, 121; vice in, 138
Lords, House of, *see* Parliament
Loudoun, John Campbell 4th earl of (1705–82), 269
Louis XIV (1638–1715), king of France (1643–1715), 13, 123, 151, 155, 179, 188
Louis XV (1710–74), king of France (1715–74), 179
Louisburg, Cape Breton, 252, 269

Macaulay, Thomas Babington (1800–59), 3, 40, 46, 277 *n* 15
Macclesfield, Thomas Parker 1st earl of (1666–1732), 230–31
Macdonald, John (1745–79), 68
Machiavelli, Niccolo (1469–1527), 22, 223
Macky, John (d. 1726), 19, 42, 43
Magdalen hospital for penitent prostitutes, 90
Marlborough, John Churchill 1st duke of (1650–1722), 33, 35, 162, 174, 185, 189, 207
Manchester, 112
Mandeville, Bernard (?1670–1733), 84, 85, 89, 90, 138, 139
Mansfield, Honourable William Murray 1st earl of (1705–93), 261, 264
Mar, John Erskine earl of, (1675–1732), 179, 180
Maria Theresa (1717–80), 233, 234–5, 241, 242, 243, 244, 253
Marine Society, 90
Marriage, 62–3, 71–2, 83
Marryot, Matthew, 77
Mary of Modena (1658–1718), 169
Mary II (1662–94), queen of England (1689–94), 14
Massie, Joseph (d. 1784), 37
Mauduit, Israel, 273
Medicine, 49–50, 51, 53, 118
Merchants, 42, 43, 53, 54, 74–6, 144, 153, 154
Methodism, 47, 106–19
Middlesex, 28
Miège, Guy (1644–1718?), 37, 38

Militia, 28, 146, 225
Mining, 43–4
Minorca, 186, 263–4, 267
Monied interest, 156–7, 224, 225
Montcalm, Louis Joseph marquis de (1712–59), 269
Montesquieu, Charles de Secondat baron de (1689–1755), 14
Moravians, 108–9
Murray, William, *see* Mansfield, earl of

Namier, Sir Lewis, 1, 26
Navy, 52
Newcastle, Thomas Pelham-Holles 1st duke of (1693–1768): character of, 258; electoral interest of, 161; ecclesiastical patronage of, 211; finances of, 35, 38, 71; first lord of treasury, 267, 272; lord chamberlain, 195–6; prime minister, 26, 258, 259, 262, 263, 264, 265; secretary of state, 221, 231, 232, 234, 237, 243, 244, 245, 247, 248, 252, 253–4
Newcastle upon Tyne, 81, 112, 116
Newspapers, 82
Nicolson, William, bishop of Carlisle (1655–1727), 96, 97
Nonconformists, *see* Dissenters
Nonjurors, 28, 94
Norris, Sir John (?1660–1749), 188
Nottingham, Daniel Finch 2nd earl of (1647–1730), 36, 39, 171, 174, 183

Oglethorpe, James Edward (1696–1785), 107

Old Sarum, 19
Onslow, Arthur (1691–1768), 200, 231
Orford, Edward Russell earl of (1653–1727), 148, 175, 185, 188, 190, 205
Ormonde, James Butler 2nd duke of (1665–1745), 178, 181
Oswego, 264
Owen, J. B., 248
Oxford, Robert Harley 1st earl of (1661–1724): and Bolingbroke, 221–2; impeachment of, 178–9, 192; and patronage, 160; as prime minister, 169, 174, 207–8; as secretary of state, 25, 206, 207; and South Sea Company, 153, 196
Oxford, 17, 39, 107, 108

Pakington, Sir John (1671–1727), 148, 172
Pardo, Convention of, 234
Parish, the, 29–30
Parliament: House of Commons, 15, 25, 143, 144, 148, 160, 211–18, 239, 259, 261
House of Lords, 14–15, 25, 35, 143, 148, 160, 210–11
Parnell, Thomas (1679–1718), 31–2
Peasants, 48
Peerage bill, 15, 70, 195–6
Peirce, James (?1674–1726), 102
Pelham, Honourable Henry (1696–1754): and the city, 159; death of, 257; financial policy of, 241, 252, 253; and landed interest, 156; MP for Sussex, 19; prime minister, 26, 239, 245; and tories, 152

Perceval, Sir John 1st earl of Egmont (1683–1748), 198, 285 *n* 15
Petrie, Sir Charles, 182
Philip V (1683–1746), king of Spain (1700–46), 149, 188, 192, 193, 231, 252
Philipps, John (1700–64), 246
Physicians, *see* Medicine
Pitt, George (?1663–1735), 37
Pitt, William 1st earl of Catham (1708–78): associates of, 263; and Cartaret, 244; and the City, 125, 159; and George II, 26, 246, 247, 273; and George III, 274; and Hanover, 243, 262, 263; Macaulay on, 3; paymaster, 248, 259, 260, 261, 264; prime minister, 265–7, 271–2
Placemen, 15–16, 22, 212, 239
Plumb, J. H. 160, 199, 200, 205
Poland, 233
Poor relief, 28, 29, 34–9
Pope, Alexander (1688–1744), 39, 49, 84, 139, 225, 226
Population, 2, 62–6
Post office, 41, 42
Porteous, lieutenant (d. 1737), 235
Porto Bello, 234
Portugal, 125
Pretender, *see* Stuart
Presbyterians, *see* Dissenters
Preston, 17, 39–40, 181
Prestonpans, 249
Prime minister, 25–7
Privy council, 23, 170, 174–5
Professions, 51–3, 76, 153
Providence, 87–9
Prussia, 242, 243, 263, 267
Pulteney, Daniel (d. 1731), 221, 222

Pulteney, William earl of Bath (1684–1764), 148, 190, 220, 221, 222, 240, 245, 247, 248

Quadruple Alliance, 193
Quakers, 210–11; *see also* Dissenters
Quebec, 269
Queen Anne's Bounty, 46, 47
Queen's College, Oxford, 39, 114
Quiberon Bay, 263

Radcliffe, John (1650–1714), 76
Ranelagh gardens, 85
Religious societies, 110, 114
Richardson, Samuel (1689–1761), 49, 84
Riots, 79–81, 117, 235–6
Roads, *see* Transport
Robethon, Jean de (d. 1722), 173
Rochester, Lawrence Hyde 1st earl of (1641–1711), 158
Roxburgh, John Ker 1st duke of (d. 1741), 230
Royal College of Physicians, 50, 53
Rumford workhouse, 78
Russia, 187, 189, 194, 263, 267, 268, 273
Ryder, Dudley (1691–1756), 76, 252

Sacheverell, Henry (1674–1724), 91, 93, 150, 186, 203
Sackville, lord George Germain (1716–85), 268
St James's 4, 121
St John, *see* Bolingbroke
St Malo, 182
Salisbury, Sally (?1691–1724), 76
Salisbury, 166

Salters Hall, 102

Sandwich, John Montagu 4th earl of (1718–92), 254

Sandys, Samuel (?1695–1770), 240, 245

Sardinia and Savoy, *see* Charles Emmanuel

Saxe, Maurice de (1696–1750), 250

Schaub, Sir Luke (1690–1758), 230

Schools, 82–5

Schulenberg, Ehrengard Melusina baroness von (1667–1743), 172–3

Schutz, baron Ludwig Justus von, 179

Scotland, 15, 131, 140, 179, 180, 181–2, 193, 211, 230, 235–6

Secretaries of state, 24–5

Secker, archbishop Thomas (1693–1768), 102

Servants, 34, 38, 39, 40, 44, 57–8, 68, 121

Seville, treaty of, 232

Shaftesbury, Anthony Ashley Cooper 3rd earl of (1671–1713), 22, 89, 105

Sheriffmuir, 182

Sherlock, Thomas, bishop of London (1678–1761), 88, 93, 210

Shippen, William (1673–1743), 172

Shopkeepers, *see* Tradesmen

Shovel, Sir Cloudesley (1650–1707), 76

Shrewsbury, Charles Talbot duke of (1660–1718), 171

Smith, Adam (1723–90), 51, 69, 86, 87, 133, 139, 140

Smollett, Tobias George, author of *Roderick Random* (1721–71), 75

Smuggling, 126–7; *see also* Customs, Excise

Societies for reformation of manners, 5–6, 86–7, 110, 114, 115

Somers, baron John (1651–1716), 148, 171, 174, 185

Somerset, Charles Seymour 6th duke of (1662–1748), 206

South Sea Bubble, 72, 73, 75, 80, 156, 196–201, 228

South Sea Company, 34, 97, 124, 153, 155, 159, 196, 197, 198, 200, 218, 228, 234

Southwark, 41

Spain, 124, 193, 233, 234

Stanhope, Charles (1673–1760), 198, 201

Stanhope, James 1st earl of (1673–1721): and Bolingbroke, 170; death of, 201, 202; early career of, 186; foreign policy of, 192, 193, 194, 244; Occasional Conformity and Schism Acts, 94, 194–5; peerage bill, 15, 195, 196; prime minister, 184, 191, 192, 193, 194; secretary of state, 174, 188; South Sea scheme, 196–9; and whig schism, 190

Stanhope, William, *see* Harrington, earl of

Steele, Sir Richard (1672–1729), 40, 52, 54, 148, 276 *n* 11

Strafford, Thomas Wentworth 3rd earl of (1672–1739), 178

Stuart, Charles Edward, the Young Pretender (1720–88), 248–51

Stuart, James Francis Edward, the Old Pretender (1688–1766), 7, 11, 150, 169, 178, 179, 188, 193, 200, 231–2

Succession, 150, 152, 169

Sunderland, Charles Spencer 3rd earl of (1674–1722), 148, 171, 174, 185, 189, 190, 192, 198, 201, 202

Superstition, 115–16

Sweden, 187, 190, 194

Swift, Jonathan (1667–1745), 20, 49, 60, 84, 88, 89, 104, 139, 149, 219, 225, 230

Sydney, Algernon (1622–83), 224

Sykes, Norman, 93, 97


Tawney, R. H., 96

Taxes, 123–4, 154; *see also* Customs, Excise, Land tax

Temple, Richard Grenville earl (1711–1779), 265, 266

Thompson, E. P., 60

Tillotson, archbishop John (1630–94), 105, 106

Tindal, Matthew (?1653–1733), 104

Tindal, Nicholas (1688–1744), 180

Toland, John (1670–1722), 104

Tories, 1, 6, 13, 30, 92, 147–52, 170–72, 173–4, 175, 176, 196, 219, 222, 240, 267

Townley, James (1714–78), 60

Towns, growth of, 66–7

Townshend, Charles 2nd viscount (1674–1738), 174, 185, 186, 189, 190, 196, 231, 232

Townshend, George 1st marquis (1724–1807), 264

Trade, 2, 124–7, 156, 157–8

Tradesmen, 32, 50–51, 54, 55, 115, 123

Transport: water, 135–6; road, 73, 80, 136–7

Trenchard, John (1662–1722), 20, 22, 89, 220

Tucker, Josiah (1712–99), 61

Tull, Jethro (1674–1741), 130

Turnpikes, *see* Transport

Tyburn, 60


Utrecht, treaty of, 149, 150, 151, 170, 171, 188, 192, 209, 231, 234


Vagrants, 58–9, 69

Vanbrugh, Sir John (1664–1726), 35, 38, 40, 49, 52

Vauxhall, 85

Verden, *see* Bremen

Vernon, Edward (1684–1757), 234

Vice, 86–7

Victor Armadeus II, duke of Savoy (1666–1732), 193

Vienna, 1st treaty of, 231–2

Vienna, 2nd treaty of, 233


Wake, William (1657–1737), 96

Waldegrave, James 2nd earl (1715–63), 258, 259, 260, 264, 266, 269

Wallace, Robert (1697–1771), 20

Walpole, Horace (1678–1797), 189

Walpole, Horace, 4th earl of Orford (1717–57), 222, 251, 258, 260, 267

Walpole, Sir Robert, earl of Orford (1676–1745); and cabinet, 24; and Carteret, 229–30; and church, 93, 151; and City, 125, 159; and the constitution, 20, 22, 23; and Cornwall, 236–7; and corruption, 7, 228–9; and the crown, 27, 215–16; early

Walpole—*contd*
career, 175, 186–7, 203–10; and excise scheme, 213–15; fall of, 237–9; financial policies, 217–18; foreign policy, 151, 231–4; and House of Commons, 211–13, 227–8; and House of Lords, 210–11; and Jacobitism, 152, 183, 219–20; later influence of, 245; paymaster, 175; and peerage bill, 195–6; prime minister, 25–6, 71; and propaganda, 226–7; and Scotland, 235–6; and South Sea Bubble, 198–202; and trade, 157–8; and whigs, 148; and whig schism, 190–91

Waltham Blacks, 59, 60
Warburton, William, bishop of Gloucester (1698–1779) 46, 95, 103
Ware, Isaac (d. 1766), 44
Washington, George (1732–99), 262
Webbs, Beatrice and Sidney, 27
Wedgwood, Josiah (1730–95), 75
Welch, Saunders, 61, 90
Wesley, Charles (1707–88), 106, 108, 109, 110, 119
Wesley, John (1703–91), 19, 102, 106, 107, 109, 110, 111–19
West Indies, 126, 269, 270
Westminster, 1, 4, 13, 17, 19, 30, 57, 121, 161
Westminster, Convention of, 263

Wharton, Thomas 1st marquis of, (1648–1715), 148, 163, 171, 175, 185, 189
Whigs, 1, 6, 7, 30, 93, 147–52, 170, 174–6, 185, 191, 204–5, 219, 238, 240, 267
Whitbread, Samuel (1758–1815), 74
Whitefield, George (1714–70), 106, 109, 110, 111, 113, 117, 281 *n* 29
Wigston Magna, 48
Wild, Jonathan (?1682–1725), 59, 226
William III (1650–1702), king of England (1689–1702), 5, 6, 13–14, 15, 16, 21, 24, 41, 92, 123
Williams, Basil, 96
Wilmington, earl of, *see* Compton, Sir Spencer
Wolfe, James (1727–59), 269
Wood, William (1671–1730), 230–31
Woodward, Josiah, 138
Workhouses, 77–8
Worms, treaty of, 244–5
Wyndham, Sir William (1687–1740), 172, 181, 212, 213

Yeomen, 47–8
Yonge, William (d. 1755), 211, 228
Yorke, Philip, *see* Hardwicke, earl of
Young, Arthur (1741–1820), 136

Zinzendorf, Nikolaus Ludwig Graf von (1700–1760), 108